RELIGION AND PUBLIC LIFE

The Legacy of Monsignor John A. Ryan

Edited by

Robert G. Kennedy
Mary Christine Athans, B.V.M.
Bernard V. Brady
William C. McDonough
Michael J. Naughton

University Press of America,® Inc.
Lanham · New York · Oxford

University Press of America,® Inc.
4720 Boston Way
Lanham, Maryland 20706
UPA Acquisitions Department (301) 459-3366

12 Hid's Copse Rd.
Cumnor Hill, Oxford OX2 9JJ

Printed in the United States of America
British Library Cataloging in Publication Information Available

Library of Congress Cataloging-in-Publication Data

Religion and public life : the legacy of Monsignor John A. Ryan /
edited by Robert G. Kennedy … [et al.].
p. cm
Includes bibliographical references.
1. Ryan, John Augustine, 1869-1945. 2. Catholic Church—Clergy.
3. Economics—Religious aspects—Catholicism.
I. Kennedy, Robert G.

BX4705.R83 R45 2001 282'.092—dc21 2001041570 CIP

ISBN 0-7618-2091-4 (cloth : alk. paper)
ISBN 0-7618-2092-2 (pbk. : alk. paper)

™ The paper used in this publication meets the minimum requirements of American National Standard for Information Sciences—Permanence of Paper for Printed Library Materials, ANSI Z39.48—1984

CONTENTS

INTRODUCTION

On the weekend of 14-17 September 1995, scholars from India, Europe, and around the United States gathered at the University of St. Thomas in St. Paul, Minnesota to commemorate the fiftieth anniversary of the death of Msgr. John Augustine Ryan. The theme of the conference was not merely a retrospective of Ryan's work, but also an exploration of the vitality of the tradition he helped to initiate. This volume is a collection of many of the papers presented at the conference.

Msgr. Ryan was born in Vermillion, Minnesota, just south of the Twin Cities, in 1869. He was educated at the St. Thomas Aquinas Seminary (now the University of St. Thomas) and in 1894 was a member of the first group to enter the new theologate, the St. Paul Seminary (now the School of Divinity of the University of St. Thomas). Shortly after Ryan's ordination in 1898, Archbishop Ireland assigned him to the Catholic University of America in Washington to do graduate studies. Ryan became interested in economics and wrote his doctoral thesis on the idea of the living wage. From 1902 to 1915 he was professor of moral theology at the St. Paul Seminary, leaving to take a position on the faculty of the Catholic University. He remained in Washington until his retirement, becoming one of the most influential churchmen in the country. Shortly before his death on 16 September 1945, he returned to St. Paul.

His interest in public affairs was rooted in his conviction that the church must engage itself in the life of the secular community, or in other words, that faith had a proper role to play in shaping social life. In this he was inspired by the 1891 encyclical of Pope Leo XIII, *Rerum novarum*, which described a role for the church in responding to the new crisis created by the rise of industrialism.

This theme, that moral theology failed in its task if it could not generate practical applications, was a constant throughout Ryan's professional life. In 1911, for example, he drafted a controversial bill that was introduced into the Minnesota state legislature requiring a minimum wage, one of the first in the country. A few years later, shortly after the end of the First World War, he wrote a document addressing the issue of "reconstructing" American society that argued for such (now common) policies as unemployment insurance, social security, public housing, restrictions on child labor, and the rights of women in the workplace. Ryan's proposals were adopted by the bishops of the United States in 1919 and became a foundation of their efforts in the public policy arena for decades after. In 1920, the bishops established the National Catholic Welfare Conference (which evolved into the United States Catholic Conference) and named Ryan to be the director of the Social Action Department, a position he held until his retirement.

The next two decades were increasingly busy for Ryan, who became the principal Catholic spokesman for social reform in America. In 1932 he was asked to become an informal advisor for Franklin D. Roosevelt, then running for his first term as president. Many of the elements of the Bishops' Program of 1919 found a place in Roosevelt's plans and Ryan became an outspoken advocate for the president. In fact, journalists gave him the title "The Right Reverend New Dealer." In 1937 he became the first Catholic priest to deliver the benediction at a presidential inauguration.

In his day, Ryan was considered something of a socialist, and fiercely criticized for his positions. Critics insisted that his views were contrary to the teaching of the church. However, when Pope Pius XI published the social encyclical *Quadragesimo anno* in 1931, Ryan found his views vindicated at the highest level. Indeed, the pope himself named Ryan a monsignor two years later. And while he is best known for his work for social reform, it is worth remembering that his attention was not simply focused on issues of political economy.

The essays collected here were written with Ryan in mind, though they range further than his work did. The authors are conscious of being heirs to a tradition (to which Ryan was a conspicuous American contributor) of applying Christian social thought to practical problems. Attention is paid not only to questions of public policy and economics, but also to many emerging issues in the management of business. Within the past fifty years business organizations have grown dramatically in influence and importance and we are certain that Ryan himself would have marked and commented upon that growth.

In yet another way the papers of the conference reflect the influence of Msgr. Ryan and others like him. He was a pioneer in developing an interdisciplinary competence, in his case in theology and economics. His ability to bring together two different fields, and the fruit he was able to harvest from doing so, continue to serve as an inspiration to those who hope to bring Christian social thought to bear on contemporary problems. Indeed, the conference itself, which brought together scholars from such diverse fields as engineering, philosophy, theology, economics, and business administration, was a product of his example. Our purpose in publishing these essays is to celebrate Msgr. Ryan's legacy and to contribute to an exploration of its relevance for the future.

Monsignor John A. Ryan. From the Department of Archives and Manuscripts, The Catholic University of America.

Reflections on the Life of Monsignor John A. Ryan

HARLAN BECKLEY

I must say that it's a rather daunting experience for a young Protestant from Illinois, a farm boy, to come into the archway at the University of St. Thomas, with Albertus Magnus Hall on one side and Aquinas Hall on the other side. Let me begin by saying that I am humbled, honored, and very sorry to be here making these remarks. The reason is that Monsignor George Higgins, who was originally scheduled for this talk, is unable to be here.

Monsignor Higgins is far more qualified than I am to convey something of John Ryan's personality and character. I phoned him and asked for some of his reflections. Monsignor Higgins recalls Ryan as uncommonly blunt in conversation, a trait that he attributes to Ryan's farm background in Minnesota. Accompanying this bluntness is what Monsignor Higgins describes as an "earthy sense of humor" also indicative of Ryan's upbringing and taste for the mildly unconventional. Higgins knew John Ryan personally from 1940 until Ryan's death in September of 1945.

Among his most fascinating remembrances was when, as a young priest, in June 1945, he was assigned the task of escorting the dying John Ryan back to St. Paul to be near his childhood home in death. Tickets for the flight were arranged very late—ironically, Higgins added, by a public relations person from the Ford Motor Company.

Ryan presumably didn't know he was being brough back to St. Paul to die, though he must have suspected something when he went to the airport and all his old-time priest friends were there tearfully and permanently bidding him good-bye. When they stopped at the Detroit airport early that morning, Higgins asked Ryan what he would like for breakfast. Ryan asked for a piece of pie which he quickly devoured. Father Higgins asked him what else he would like. "Another piece of pie," was the response. Higgins accommodated but not without thinking this event sufficiently peculiar to remember it more than fifty years later. Ryan's two-pie breakfast may have been the uninhibited impulse of a dying man. On the other hand, perhaps, it was simply a candid man who was willing to buck convention without being too rebellious.

Monsignor Higgins retains a vivid recollection of the flight from Detroit to St. Paul. Ryan spent that entire flight reading a very difficult tome and underlining it. Higgins no longer remembers the name of the book, but was much taken by Ryan's devotion to learning. After he returned to St. Paul, Ryan did publish a tribute to Franklin Roosevelt for the *Review of Politics*. In that essay, he observed that "Roosevelt did more for those who stood most in need of social justice than any other man who occupied the White House." It was Ryan's commitment to the life of the mind as applied to social justice that I wish to highlight in this reflection.

John Ryan's vocation was to teach moral theology, especially economic justice, to the U.S. electorate, especially to Catholic voters and to the politicians. Unlike social reformers and politicians directly concerned with immediate policies, Ryan kept a critical distance from the political arena. He was too much the academic and the moral theologian to become immersed in the fray of politics. Unlike prophetic critics of the ethos, Ryan addressed rational arguments directly to political leaders in the hope of persuading them to change policies. His confidence in the rational and moral capacities of politicians and the electorate was incompatible with the role of a prophet denouncing the cultural ethos.

Ryan's interest in critical moral reflection began at a very young age, not in reading moral theology but characteristically in reading moral thinking about the economy. He tells the story of reading Henry George's *Progress and Poverty* at the age of thirteen or fourteen. His family had borrowed the book from a neighbor in the early 1880s, several years before Henry George's campaign for mayor of New York. Ryan confessed that he did not understand it at the time, but recollected in his autobiography that it promoted his interest in social questions and stimulated his empathy for the poor. That a person of seventy-two should remember that as a lad not yet in high school he was stimulated by reading *Progress and Poverty* discloses something significant about his vocation. For Ryan this seemingly trivial event presaged the life of serious reading in economics and moral reflections on economic issues.

When he came here to St. Thomas Aquinas Seminary, and advanced to the St. Paul Seminary for his higher education and seminary studies, his reading turned toward a more disciplined study of moral theology, though his reading of economics continued throughout his life.

Those familiar with Ryan's life know that his devotion to intellectual pursuit in economic ethics was balanced by an active application of his thinking about justice in the political arena. His fellow students at St. Thomas dubbed Ryan the "Senator" for his activity down the street in the Capitol building.

After teaching moral theology at the St. Paul Seminary from 1902-1915, Ryan went to Washington to become a Professor at the Catholic University, and later head of the Social Action Department of the National Catholic Welfare Conference. These moves served Ryan's vocation as a moral theologian to the politicians. He thought that a synergistic relation among scholarship, moral teaching, and political activism was important. After the publication of *Distributive Justice* in 1916 he moved away from creative scholarship to moral teaching directed at the electorate and the politicians. He stayed close to politics through his position at the Social Action Department. His influence in the Roosevelt administration and with labor leaders has been over-estimated by apocryphal stories and the lore that naturally accompanies his greatest accomplishment in introducing Catholic moral theology into the center of political discussions in this country.

Monsignor Higgins volunteered to me that Ryan's connections with the New Deal have been exaggerated. Ryan's student, Francis J. Haas, was far more involved with politics and labor leaders than Ryan. Neither did Ryan give much attention to the day-to-day matters at the Social Action Department. It was, Higgins emphasized, administered by Father Raymond McGowan, the assistant director. Higgins did not diminish Ryan's achievements but stressed that they were as a professor and not as a political operator in the church, the labor movement, or government.

Ryan's deepest foray in the political arena was his highly controversial national radio speech endorsing Franklin D. Roosevelt for president in 1936. The speech was given at the urging of the National Democratic Committee and, for a period of time, cost him the confidence of Archbishop Michael J. Curley of Baltimore. Ryan's opening paragraph tells us much about his self-perception of his own vocation. "I am making tonight," he acknowledged, "what is liable to be called a political speech. It is not that. It is mainly a discussion of certain political events in the light of the moral law." It was this political act that earned Ryan Father Charles E. Coughlin's sarcastic sobriquet "The Right Reverend New Dealer," which subsequently became the title of Francis L. Broderick's biography of Ryan. Oddly, Ryan made only passing reference to the speech, and made no reference to his controversy with Coughlin, in his autobiography *Social Doctrine in Action*. He does mention with pride that he was, in 1936, the first Catholic priest to participate in the inaugural ceremonies of a president of the United States, an honor that was most likely bestowed on him due to his endorsement speech. Ryan was appropriately wary of what the bishops would think about his open political confrontation with a fellow priest. Ryan himself seemed to have been leery of becoming too political and too little the moral theologian. But in retrospect this speech, not particularly well executed, in Broderick's judgment, probably counts among the many contributions that Ryan made persuading U.S. citizens and politicians to take Catholic social teachings seriously.

Among my most favorite stories of John Ryan is his own telling of events at his seventieth birthday party in 1939. In a comment approaching self-adulation Ryan called the party "one of the most distinguished banquets ever held in Washington." He mentioned by name many of the ecclesiastical officials, politicians, and even business executives among the six hundred guests in attendance at the Willard Hotel. There were also, Ryan noticed in passing, a large number of labor leaders, none of whom he recalled by name. Ryan was not called to grass-roots political or labor involvement. His connections were with church officials, leaders in the electorate and the politicians. But even on this special occasion, proud as he was at receiving the acknowledgment of leading citizens and New Deal politicians, Ryan tempered his praise for the New Deal with criticism. "More should be done," he contended, "to promote a better distribution of purchasing power and to revise the historical capitalism via cooperation of the guild system."

The moral theologian maintained sufficient critical distance from politics to mitigate his allegiance to the New Deal politicians. Even Roosevelt could not avoid a mild rebuke from this plain-spoken moral theologian from a Minnesota farm. Unfortunately, Protestant ethicists and non-Catholic students of U.S. history have paid little attention to John A. Ryan. James Gustafson has written on Ryan, and David Kruger, another Protestant, has written extensively on Ryan. Protestant scholars have, for the most part, ignored Ryan while lavishing attention on Rauschenbusch, the Niebuhr brothers, and others.

My hope is that Ryan's work will be taken more seriously by Protestant ethicists and other intellectuals of our day. Perhaps in this one small respect it is appropriate that I am making these remarks instead of Monsignor Higgins. I, along with a few others, represent an interest in Ryan's theological and economic ethics among Protestant ethicists. Apart from this symbolic significance I am honored to participate in a conference that grants some recognition to a man who has helped to introduce me, as he did many others in his own day, to the riches of Catholic social teachings. He would consider this achievement part of his vocation as a moral theologian.

John A. Ryan, John Courtney Murray, George Higgins, and the Catholic Social Tradition

J. BRYAN HEHIR

In proposing that we look at John A. Ryan, John Courtney Murray, and George Higgins, what I plan to do is to look at them as mediating figures. All three employed what we call in the Catholic tradition "mediating discourse." That is to say, they were convinced that it was necessary to translate the wisdom of the Biblical tradition into categories, principles, rules, and discussions that made it possible to relate the wisdom of the Biblical tradition to the empirical complexity of the world. I will not concentrate on their discourse. I seek to look at a functional view of their lives. That is to say, how they functioned as mediating figures in two senses. First, in the relationship of the universal church to the local church in the United States and secondly, in the relationship of the local church to the culture it is called to serve here in the United States of America.

What I propose to do first is to establish a framework for this functional analysis of the mediating roles of Ryan, Murray, and Higgins. Then I will examine the three figures briefly in those mediating roles and finally say a word about the legacy that this triumvirate offers us as we look at a new century ahead and the task of relating Catholic teachings to that century in this place on the globe.

First, a framework for establishing the mediating function of Ryan, Murray, and Higgins. I think it is possible to think about the Catholic social tradition that all three served as having three dimensions. That is to say, if one looks at the last hundred years of Catholic social teaching it is best, I think, to think about it in three categories. First, the church's relationship to society. This includes, but is not restricted to, the economy. Second, the body of teaching on the church's relationship to the political order. And third, the church's relationship to the world, understood in this sense as the international arena.

Now, when you look at Catholic social teaching in this way there are different figures who make major contributions and there are different issues that arise. For example, one finds the papal encyclicals from *Rerum novarum* through *Centesimus annus* as the major source of Catholic commentary on church/society issues. But if one equated the whole Catholic social tradition with just the social encyclicals, one would miss most of the teaching on church and state, most of the teaching for which Leo XIII and Pius XII and now John Paul II have been responsible. So there is a body of teaching apart from the encyclicals that is really part of the social tradition and yet is focused only on the political order. And finally, if one failed to notice the extraordinary increase in attention to international affairs that begins with the pontificate of Pius XII, I think we would fail to appreciate how the Catholic social tradition has the capacity to grow.

So it is indeed in three areas, church/society, church/state and church/world, that I wish to examine the contribution of Ryan, Murray, and Higgins, noting that all three of them did not contribute to all three areas.

When I talk about them as mediating figures let me simply repeat what I mean. I am trying to look at the way in which they functioned within a context that was set by the universal church. However, their distinctive contribution was the way in which they not only applied the universal tradition to a local situation, but perhaps even more importantly, the way there were able to intrepret the local situation that it enriched the universal teaching of the church. As they did that, as they mediated between the universal and the local, they simultaneously were mediating figures between the life of the church in this country and the political, social, and economic culture in which the church lives.

Let me begin with looking at the three of them in terms of these different dimensions of Catholic teaching. John Ryan's genius lay in his contribution to church/society teaching. Ryan lived during a stage in the development of Catholic social teaching in which a major problem concerned what the church would say about the consequences of the industrial revolution. His contribution was to adapt the universal teaching to the experience of the industrial revolution in the rising economy of the twentieth century.

On the other hand, while Ryan did write in the area of church and state, I would submit that what he did in that area was simply to reflect existing teaching, neither advancing it nor refining it. Finally, while he had interest in international affairs, I don't think one would count Ryan as a major contributor to the church's work in international affairs.

Murray, on the other hand, contributed to the church/society debate in terms of his definition and analysis of what we today call "civil society." This part of Murray's work was highlighted by his comment in *We Hold These Truths* that the great challenge facing any society is to keep society properly civil. For Murray that meant the cultivation of reasonable discourse. It meant a sense of public philosophy that must be shared in society if it is to remain properly civil. In the same way, Murray's statement that freedom is the political method par excellence is rooted in the conception that a society that would be free must be a society where the state is contained by the wider fabric of civil society.

So Murray contributed to the church/society discourse even though that is not what he was primarily known for. His unique contribution, of course, is in the area of church/state teaching and here the notion of a mediator is of particular significance. For by the end of his life Murray had not only served as a bridge between the universal teaching and the American local situation, he had, in fact, creatively drawn from the American experience in such a way that he had produced authentic development and recasting of Catholic teaching on church and state. Of the three figures I'm examining, Murray was the most distinctive in his ability to reshape the wider tradition in light of the local experience of this local church.

Murray had an interest—I think even a greater interest than John Ryan—in the church/world, or church/international relations field, and he in fact made distinctive analytical contributions, although they were much narrower than his church/state work. His 1959 article on the ethics of war and peace remains a standard point of reference in the analysis of the Catholic tradition, and Murray's work in the period right after World War II on the church's conception of a developing international order held a promise that I think was cut short by the dynamics of the Cold War. In other words, and without being able to explore this at length, I think that if one were to look at Murray's writing on international relations in the period right after World War II, one would find there an emphasis on international institutions and the development of international society that to some degree became short-circuited as the Cold War grew more intense and Murray's analysis of foreign policy focused more and more in terms of a Cold War assessment of the world.

George Higgins's contribution to the three areas of church teaching is quite different from either Murray or Ryan. If one were to try to classify Higgins's career I think a term we use today, "public intellectual," would fit. He was a social actor, and has become a senior statesman in American public life. By his own admission he is not and never intended to be primarily a scholar. So Higgins's life and record does not carry the same kind of academic documentation that Ryan's or Murray's does. At the same time, Higgins's unique role moving across different sectors of American society probably involved a wider range of contact than either of the other two. In fact, Higgins's interest cut across all three areas of Catholic social teaching, but with varying degrees of intensity. Like Ryan, his primary focus was on the church/society question. His contribution was not so much in terms of an overall framework of ethical analysis by which the economy can be judged, but much more focused on viewing the church/society issues through the prism of labor, the unions, and the rights and duties of working people. On church/state issues Higgins, who was a very close friend of John Courtney Murray and an intimate companion as Murray developed his own theory, could only be described as an interested observer and commentator. He was not a source of original thought on this question but was a wise source of guidance for the church about who ought to be read on the question.

Finally, on the church and international relations, Higgins demonstrated a personal characteristic that continues to this day. That is an enormous capability to grow and develop. Age does not seem to interfere with this at all. Higgins, in the last fifteen years, has demonstrated a particular interest in the way in which the question of labor-management relations today must be cast in terms of the conception of a global economy, as a notion of a self-contained national economy is harder and harder to sustain, intellectually or practically. Higgins's concern with international affairs does in fact date back to the end of World War II, when he spent some time in Germany right after the end of the war, seeking to share with German culture the knowledge the Americans had gained about labor-management relations. But even more intensively in recent years, particularly as he watched the spread of a global economy, George has become more and more interested in a transnational union movement and his participation in the role of Solidarity in Poland is a whole story in itself.

Now in order to assess their role as mediators in these different areas it is necessary to say a word about the wider context—intellectually, theologically, and socially—in light of which each person worked. For Ryan, the dominant force setting the context of his life, I think, at the universal level, was Leo XIII. Although he lived during the lives of all the popes of the twentieth century up to Pius XII, I think the dominant figure was Leo XIII because he instituted at the end of the nineteenth century what I would call the "Leonine Project." The Leonine Project had three dimensions to it: intellectual, diplomatic or political, and social. Intellectually, as we know, Leo XIII was dismayed at the state of Catholic theology, and Catholic intellectual life generally, at the end of the nineteenth century and therefore instituted the drive for a renewal in Catholic philosophical and theological thought under the auspices of Thomas Aquinas. So the first piece of the framework within which Ryan worked was the neo-Scholastic and neo-Thomistic movement, which was rooted in Leo XIII's *Aeterni patris* and which had an impact on Catholic social thought that extended up through the middle of the twentieth century.

Secondly, Leo XIII was determined to redesign and reconstitute the relationship of the church and the political order. That meant two different things. First, he produced an extensive corpus of church/state teachings, and second, he initiated an aggressive diplomatic effort to reestablish relationships between the church and the major states of Europe (at least). Finally, he was concerned in the social arena that the church respond to the industrial revolution and particularly to the moral consequences of the industrial revolution that led to *Rerum novarum* and then the initiation of the papal social tradition.

Now, what was the relationship of the Leonine Project to Ryan's scholarship and service? I submit that Ryan stayed within the framework of the Leonine Project, intellectually and socially. That is to say, he stayed within the framework of a natural law social ethic, articulated in terms of the neo-Thomistic movement. He stayed within the Leonine Project in terms of the categories it provided as an intellectual frame of reference.

Furthermore, he stayed within the Leonine framework in terms of the social teaching and the teaching on church and state. Now, as we have already discussed, Ryan's major contribution was in the social area. Leo XIII provided a mandate for social reformers in the church on church/society issues, and Ryan took advantage of that space provided by papal leadership to address issues aggressively within the context of the United States.

If one were to look at Ryan's distinctive contribution on church/society issues, I think it would be correct to say that he stayed within the Leonine framework, and provided a kind of creative application and adaptation of the teaching that was his special genius. This was a result of the enormous confidence he had to cut across the areas of both economics and ethics. It was his ability to move back and forth across that line that gave him the capability for the creative adapatation of the universal teaching to the local scene. But it was also his commitment to an inductive approach to moral teaching through an assertion that one had to know the specifics of the concrete situation to which the teaching was applied that gave him the capability to relate the teaching creatively to the local scene. He advanced Catholic social teaching by applying it and deepening our understanding of its concepts.

At the same time he stayed within the Leonine framework on church and state and therefore really added nothing new to the teaching. He did not really add to the debate on church and state. He did not use the inductive approach to democracy that he had used on the American economy, and I think on the whole he was less skillful in terms of politics and ethics than he was in terms of economics and ethics. Indeed, let me make a rather broad statement that I cannot defend within the context of this paper.

I think with both Ryan and Murray one finds examples of the comparative advantage of knowing an area of secular discipline very well. You see the genius of what can happen when somebody really commands the secular discipline to which he or she is applying church teaching. But I think it is also interesting that in both Ryan's and Murray's case, when they moved beyond the area where they had this unique confidence in their command of empirical evidence, they became more conservative in their conclusions. Ryan, the social liberal in the economic area, was actually quite conservative in his conclusions on church and state, and the little bit of commentary that Murray offered on the economic order was remarkably lacking in the kind of dynamic, intellectual critical assessment that he made of the political order. In a sense, he accepted the American economy as a given in the few comments he made in *We Hold These Truths*. I think in both cases it illustrates the value that comes from really knowing an area in depth and at the same time, and the curious, interesting note that they both become more conservative where they are less sure of the empirical area they were analyzing.

Let us turn to Murray for just a moment. Murray's scholarly career began under Pius XI and he died during the pontificate of Paul VI. But I would say that the dominant tone of his intellectual and scholarly life was set by Pius XII, and then by the onset of Vatican II.

Pius XII continued the Leonine Project and brought it to a new level of both sophistication and insight. In the intellectual area, he stayed generally within the framework of the neo-Thomistic movement begun by Leo XIII, but within that framework he gave a much more developed edge to Catholic teaching on human rights and a much more positive conception of democratic governess as a field for cooperation with the church. In the diplomatic area, his activity was more expansive than that of Leo XIII. It was Pius XII who took the church into the postwar world and indeed into the midst of the Cold War diplomacy. However, I think that in the social area he simply extended linearly what Leo had begun. Of the three areas, I think it is the least developed in terms of Pius XII's own work. He was more innovative in both church/state questions and the church's relationship in international relations.

Now if Ryan contributed to the Catholic social tradition from within the framework by creative application, Murray thought, in fact, to revise the very framework that was being used on church/state questions. So there is a distinctively different role here. One accepted the framework and applied it with genuis. The second, in fact, found the framework on church and state inadequate and set out to restructure it as a whole.

As I have said, Murray made some contributions in the area of social teaching and international affairs, but it was his teaching on church and state that was his distinctive contribution. He restructured the discourse of Catholic thought on church and state. He inherited a situation where the dominant teaching was the thesis/hypothesis argument of the late nineteenth century, which argued that the church deserved a treatment of favoritism whenever there was a majority of Catholics in the political community. Second, in addition to the thesis/hypothesis framework, Murray inherited a teaching in which there had not been made a principled statement of religious liberty. There was no principled statement of the church's conviction that each person had a right to religious freedom.

And finally, while there was real support for democracy in the teaching of Pius XII, it was also stated with a certain kind of reservation. Murray set out both to consolidate the work that Pius XII had done on human rights and democracy and to push the edge of the envelope of the teaching on church and state even more aggressively. Like Ryan, Murray used the inductive approach. Ryan probed the American economy in detail. Murray probed the fabric and meaning of democracy in terms of what he called his Anglo-American heritage. And to some degree Murray set out to say to Rome that their understanding of democracy, which made them hesitant about religious freedom, was, in fact, a constricted understanding of what the possibilities of democratic governance offered to the Catholic church. It was a long and torturous journey but by the time the Second Vatican Council met in the 1960s, the church was ready to hear an argument about democracy and human rights with the right of religious liberty central to the fabric of human rights. Murray built on the teachings of Pius XII, but moved beyond where Pius XII never had moved in terms of the principled affirmation of the right to religious liberty and a much richer expression of the significance of democratic equality.

In concluding comments on Murray, let me simply say that while Ryan's life had a kind of completeness about it, so that looking at the end of his life, we might genuinely feel that he had done all that he really had to do, I think Murray was taken from us in an early death. The really interesting question is what more Murray would have said with that astute knowledge of politics and theology that he possessed, and with the new foundation of the document on religious liberty beneath him, about the internal life of Catholicism and the value of freedom. That was where he said the next stage of the debate should go, and at least in my view, we have never had anyone else able to move us through that debate, as tortured as it always is in Catholicism, in the way he might have done.

Finally, some thoughts on Higgins as a mediator. His career moved from the pontificate of Pius XII through the present pope. There are two broad comments to make about Higgins. The first concerns the range of issues that have absorbed his life. While he is rightfully known as one of the labor priests, one cannot forget the critical role that George Higgins played for the Catholic church in the civil rights struggle in the 60s, nor the role that he played in terms of the church's work regarding immigration legislation in the 1970s. Like Ryan, his primary field of attention was the church/society question.

The second comment about Higgins is that I think there is a real dividing line in his career, and it is a dividing line I would call pre- and post-Vatican II. Here it seems to me that one of the really interesting things is the way in which Higgins, who was trained in the theological framework of the manuals of the pre-Vatican II period, has been affected by the theology of Vatican II. Although he is not a theologian, simply by reading on his own the best theologians of the post-Conciliar period, he incorporated their thoughts in his own work. So, while his principal area of contribution was church and society, and while his principal area of professional work was the building up of civil society by the support he personally gave to the union movement and his work on civil rights, there is a way in which Higgins's later life, after Vatican II, was also a life spent looking at the internal life of the church, the area precisely where I think we so miss Murray.

But Higgins was not primarily a scholar. Higgins has been a man who stood at the fault line where the church met the world, whether it was civil society or the state or even the international arena. Higgins has lived a Washington life, and that meant that he lived a life in which he used the multiplicity of personal relationships and the personal respect in which he was held by many people, in the service of people who were less fortunate, struggling for justice, and who turned to the church for help. The great moment, of course, was the way in which Higgins mediated between the AFL-CIO and Cesar Chavez, and helped to connect those two parties at a critical moment in time.

Finally, Higgins has used his reading of theology in recent years to comment on the internal life of the church. He lived in a different time from either Murray or Ryan. Ryan's biographer calls him a papalist as if there was never a thought that there would be any criticism of internal church life or teaching. Charles Curran, in his comment on Ryan, says that to some degree that is an unfair characterization, for everybody was a papalist in John Ryan's time. For his part, Murray turned a critical eye toward church teaching and practice and paid a high price for it. Higgins lived to see a time when there was more freedom for internal commentary, and with that kind of fair moral vision that has always marked his life, he was quite willing to turn the categories by which he assessed civil society to an assessment of the church, whether it be unions within the church or freedom in the church.

I will conclude by suggesting what these three people offer. I think I have said enough to say theirs were really different lives and, in some sense, one would not want to try to put them in the same corner. Their lives were rich, distinctive modes of service for the life of the church. The fact that all three were priests probably marked the period we are talking about, for I think the future of the church's social ministry, even in terms of its positions of leadership, will increasingly lie with lay initiative. This conference, from what I can see from the scholars who have made contributions, is a testimony to that. But these three priests do offer a certain legacy for laity, clergy, or religious who seek to carry on the ministry of Catholic social teachings and Catholic social service in the world.

What do they offer? First of all, they each testify to a characteristic of Catholic moral thought: that it has always had the capacity to be systematic in structure and yet specific in its judgments. That is to say, Catholic moral thought must be thought cultivated in terms of principles that seek universal applications. But we do not remain at the level of a kind of ethereal theory. John Ryan's reduction of the call for a minimum wage to a specification in dollars of what it would mean in the United States is a great teaching example of the Catholic tradition at work. You establish the principle first, but the principle must cut into the debate in a specific way. Murray struggled with the language of democracy, to lay out the basic principles and the meaning of democracy in concrete terms. This, I think, is one of the legacies of these three people. They knew the systematic structure of principle but they were not afraid to take the risk to make specific judgments and to illustrate where the principles led.

Second, all three were convinced, probably more explicitly in the lives of Murray and Higgins than Ryan, that they had a vocation to intrepret the local to the universal. There was no question that we are grateful inheritors of a teaching that comes from a church that is wider than our culture and older than our nation, and we need to be grateful for that. But there is also a need for the local church to speak to the universal church, and that's what Murray did about church and state, and that's what Higgins has done in terms of issues that are as diverse as the union movement and the internal life of the church.

Third, the genius of all three still does not yield specific answers to the questions that we confront in this new century. We are now in a postindustrial society, no longer the industrial society that Leo XIII thought about or even that Vatican II thought about. The character of both our economic life and our political life, the complexity of post-industrial society, as Senator Moynihan has indicated, "breeds its own kind of social questions." Often times, as John Paul has said, in a society like ours, the question is not so much about the quantity of resources available, as about the quality of life and how that quality of life will be shaped in a complex, post-industrial democracy. There is a need in this society for the same creative adaptation of Catholic teaching in terms of the role of the state, the relationship of state and civil society, and the relationship of public and private initiative in the service of human dignity, the same need for creative initiative and creative adaptation today that Ryan demonstrated in his day.

Finally, we are not only in a postindustrial society; we are also in a post-Cold War world where the United States does not have all the answers. Nevertheless, as Vaclav Havel said at Harvard last summer, if the United States is not an intelligent, committed participant, the world as a whole is in much worse shape in terms of its future. Catholic teaching, I think, has something to say to that post-Cold War world but it does not have ready-made answers. It may well be that we need to combine Ryan's creative application with Murray's capacity to restructure the framework itself to make sure that Catholic teaching is adequate to the task ahead. We can look back in gratitude to John Ryan, John Courtney Murray, and George Higgins, but all three of them, by the character of their lives, would encourage us to look ahead, to carry out the task of creative adaptation and restructuring, and to keep ourselves on the fault line where the church meets the world as the way to serve the social ministry of the church.

John A. Ryan and the Presidential Election of 1936

PHILIP GRANT

On March 4, 1933 Franklin D. Roosevelt was inaugurated as the thirty-second president of the United States. Roosevelt in early 1933 was faced with the awesome task of mitigating the acute sufferings of the Great Depression. Between the date he took the oath of office and the summer of 1936 Roosevelt devised a program known as the New Deal, the objective of which was to achieve relief, recovery, and reform. Roosevelt was determined to alleviate human misery, stimulate the economy, reduce unemployment, increase farm income, and regulate banking, the securities industry, and the public utilities.

With a minimum of delay Congress responded to Roosevelt's appeals for drastic action. During the three years and three months between March 1933 and June 1936 the House and Senate approved the National Industrial Recovery Act, the Tennessee Valley Act, the Agricultural Adjustment Act, the Federal Emergency Relief Act, the Banking Acts of 1933 and 1935, the Securities Exchange Act, the National Housing Act, the Rural Electrification Act, the Social Security Act, the National Labor Relations Act, and the Public Utilities Holding Company Act.

Among the prominent individuals warmly sympathetic to Roosevelt's efforts to overcome the tragedy of the Depression and effect sweeping economic and social changes was Monsignor John A. Ryan of the Catholic University of America and Director of the Social Action

Department of the National Catholic Welfare Conference. Monsignor Ryan was undeniably the foremost spokesman of American Catholic social thought in the first half of the twentieth century. Long before the outbreak of the Depression in 1929, Ryan had vigorously complained of the substantial number and wide variety of injustices pervading the nation's economic system. When the impact of the Depression reached its peak in 1933, Ryan insisted that the time had come for massive federal intervention.[1]

Several of the country's major newspapers and periodicals recognized Ryan's genuine enthusiasm for Roosevelt's New Deal. Alluding to Ryan as an "influential supporter of President Franklin D. Roosevelt," the *New York Times* noted that he endorsed "with tongue and pen practically all of the New Deal reforms." The *Washington Post* regarded Ryan as a "staunch supporter" of Roosevelt's administration. *Commonweal*, a well-known Catholic weekly, described Ryan as a "strong supporter of the New Deal."[2]

Such distinguished authors as John J. Delaney, Jay P. Dolan, Alan Brinkley, Henry W. Boden, and Sheldon Marcus also referred to Ryan's New Deal orientation. Delaney portrayed Ryan as an "ardent supporter of President Franklin D. Roosevelt and the New Deal." According to Dolan, Ryan was a "cheer leader for Roosevelt and the New Deal." Brinkley, commenting that Ryan was a harsh critic of traditional capitalism" stressed that he "continued strongly to support" the priorities of the Roosevelt administration. Bowden recalled that Ryan was involved in a multitude of activities, "many of which allied with recover aspects of the New Deal and programs of a president who counted him as a friend." Marcus called Ryan the "well-known social reformer and close friend of President Roosevelt's."[3]

Roosevelt having accomplished the feat of carrying forty-two of the forty-eight states in 1932 became a candidate for reelection to a second term in 1936. Nominated as the presidential Republican opponent was Governor Alfred M. Landon of Kansas. Also entering the 1936 presidential contests was the Union Party candidate William Lemke of North Dakota.

Both the Union Party and the Lemke candidacy owed their origin in large measure to the zeal of the Reverend Charles E. Coughlin, Pastor of the Shrine of the Little Flower in Royal Oak, Michigan. Father Coughlin, who for many years had delivered weekly sermons over nationwide radio, had initially been an avid and outspoken apologist for President Roosevelt and the New Deal. By 1936, however Coughlin had become disenchanted with the president's unwillingness to advocate radical changes in the nation's monetary system. Unlike Roosevelt, Coughlin wanted the nationalization of the banking system and the rigid supervision of currency and credit by means of a federal central bank. In August 1936 Coughlin persuaded the newly-established Union Party that Lemke, who had been a long-standing proponent of currency inflation, would be a logical choice to challenge Roosevelt's bid for reelection.[4]

Between Labor Day weekend and the first week of October, Father Coughlin traveled throughout the Northeast and Midwest delivering speeches on behalf of the Union Party. Although Coughlin was ostensibly campaigning for the election of Lemke, he devoted the bulk of his energies to denouncing Roosevelt. Attracting enormous publicity and drawing large crowds, Coughlin was clearly one of the dominant figures in American politics during the first half of the 1936 campaign.[5]

Over the five-week period Coughlin concentrated his efforts in seven states, appearing in Missouri, Iowa, Illinois, Ohio, Pennsylvania, New York, and Connecticut. Most of these states had substantial populations, and except for Pennsylvania, all had favored Roosevelt in 1932.

In Chicago Coughlin insisted that a vote for Roosevelt was in effect an endorsement of "the Communists, the Socialists." Construing the presidential election of 1936 was a "contest between the basic doctrines of Christianity and the old doctrine of paganism," Coughlin in Brooklyn charged that Roosevelt's policies had been shaped by "experts from Harvard, Yale and Princeton—and from Moscow." In New Haven Coughlin demanded a halt to the "flirting of Communist tendencies by the present national administration." Challenging the President to repudiate the support of the Communists, Coughlin in Des Moines alleged that Earl Browder was "publicly urging his Communist party to vote for Roosevelt and Mr. Roosevelt grins and likes it." Coughlin, claiming that Roosevelt was "Communistic, whether he knows it or not," in Saint Louis accused the President of having "one foot in the sins of modern capitalism and the other foot mired in the mud of Communism." [6]

As the 1936 campaign progressed, Coughlin's rhetoric became more strident. At Cincinnati Coughlin argued that Roosevelt, although professing to be the leader of the Democratic Party, lacked the "internal fortitude to tell the Communists that their lousy criminal votes are not acceptable to him." Denouncing the Roosevelt administration's approach to agriculture, Coughlin in Philadelphia condemned New Deal farm policy as "un-Christian" and "anti-God." In Pittsburgh, while denying that he had actually called the President "a Communist," concluded that the evidence established beyond any doubt that Roosevelt had adopted Communistic activities."[7]

On October 8th Monsignor Ryan delivered a nationwide radio address. Ryan not only vigorously defended the record of President Roosevelt, but also bluntly rebuked both the views and the conduct of Father Coughlin. Insisting that Coughlin's "explanation of our economic maladies is at least ninety percent wrong, and that his monetary theories are at least ninety percent wrong," Ryan argued that Coughlin's economic proposals find no support in the encyclicals of Pope Pius XI and Pope Leo XIII. Ryan, alluding to the New Deal laws as "mild installments of too long delayed social justice," warmly praised Roosevelt as a chief executive "who has shown a better and more sympathetic understanding of your needs and who has brought about more fundamental legislation than any other President in American history." Branding Coughlin's allegations that Roosevelt was influenced by Communism as "ugly," "cowardly," and "despicable," Ryan concluded:

> Men who make up and repeat this charge apparently believe that during a political campaign the eighth commandment should be suspended, abolished, thrown out the window.[8]

Coughlin responded to Ryan in Baltimore on October 10. He reiterated his profound dismay over the ideological tilt of the Roosevelt administration. Mocking Ryan as the "right reverend New Dealer" and the "ecclesiastical spokesman of the Democratic National Committee," Coughlin contended that Ryan had offered no specific objections to his positions on the issues confronting the nation in 1936 and had "compromised himself appearing under the auspices of the Democratic National Committee which paid for the costly radio time that he employed to castigate me." According to Coughlin, Ryan's links to the Democratic Party had "so clouded his utterance as to render their validity questionable even at the outset." While Coughlin commented that "no reasonable person in public life has classified Mr. Roosevelt as a Communist," he nevertheless emphasized that he belongs to that group of Americans" who maintain that Mr. Roosevelt and his agents possess Communistic tendencies."[9]

On October 11 Ryan accused Coughlin of misleading Catholic voters by misquoting the encyclicals of Pope Pius XI and substituting his own words. Ryan was upset that Coughlin had cited such encyclicals to bolster his view that economic exploitation was primarily due to private control of credit. Regretting that Coughlin had implied that the Holy Father was "speaking absolutely instead of conditionally," Ryan explained:

> If the Pope said this Father Coughlin might fairly quote him in support of the proposition that the supreme economic question of today is the private control of money and credit.

Unfortunately for Father Coughlin the Pope made no such general statement.

Stressing that the Holy Father was not suggesting that private control of money and credit existed in the United States, Ryan concluded:

> As a matter of fact, it does not obtain in the United States. At no time during the past three years have men been unable to obtain credit if they could show their bank that they had good prospects of paying interest on the loan and repaying the loan when it was due.[10]

Coughlin on October 12 availed himself of the opportunity to reply to Ryan on the encyclical issue. Coughlin again disparaged Ryan as the "right reverend New Dealer." Certain that Ryan "apparently was unfamiliar" with the writings of Pope Pius XI, Coughlin read the text of the pontiff's encyclical on credit.[11]

Commonweal, reminding its readers that Coughlin had accused the President of favoring communistic policies, explained that Ryan had spoken so forcefully "because the condemnation of the New Deal as communistic was false and absurd—almost as false and absurd as the charge that the social teachings of the Catholic church are communistic." Surmising that it was unlikely that Ryan's assertions would cause Coughlin's followers "to use their reason" and thus subject his "oratory to the logical analysis which so strongly reveals its fatal contradictions," *Commonweal* lamented that Coughlin's "methods lead only toward discord—or disaster." *Commonweal*, also expressing the hope that Ryan's appeal to reason would "increasingly be heeded by Catholics who use their heads," declared:

> All Catholics above the mental level of children, or of morons, should take part in the discussion—not by Father Coughlin's methods but rather by that of the rules of reason followed by Monsignor Ryan.[12]

Obviously disagreeing with the sentiments voiced by *Commonweal* was the *Catholic Review*, the weekly newspaper of the Archdiocese of Baltimore. In an editorial entitled "Two Political Priests," the *Catholic Review* commented that if both Ryan and Coughlin "would retire for some time to the Carthusian order where perpetual silence is observed, they would do a great favor to the Church and the country at large." Deploring the fact that Ryan had "jumped into the political swim over the radio a few nights ago," the *Catholic Review* stressed that the American people were "perfectly justified in their condemnation of political priests." Accusing Ryan of diving "head and heels into plain simple politics," the Baltimore publication described him as "hotly for" the President and the New Deal. The *Catholic Review*, sharply critical of both Ryan and Coughlin, concluded: "They do not represent the Catholic priesthood in this country, and certainly do not represent the Catholic Church."[13]

During the final three weeks of the 1936 presidential campaign Coughlin ignored Ryan and continued to assail the President. On October 13 at Boston he claimed that the Roosevelt administration tended "towards Marxism." In Detroit on October 17 Coughlin faulted the President for failing "to remove the causes which beget Communism." Finally, on October 29 in New York Coughlin, insisting that the Roosevelt administration was controlled by "radicals," declared that it was "no wonder that the Comintern in Moscow advised its members here to vote for Roosevelt.[14]

It was apparent early on election night that Roosevelt would be easily reelected to a second term. When all the ballots were tabulated, Roosevelt triumphed in forty-six of the forty-eight states. The final distribution of the popular vote was:

Roosevelt	27,747,636	(60.6%)
Landon	16,679,543	(36.0%)
Lemke	892,492	(2.0%)

Based on the magnitude of Roosevelt's victory it seemed reasonable to assume that Ryan's defense of the President and the New Deal had no statistical impact on the actual outcome of the 1936 election. Ryan did, however, have the satisfaction of witnessing Roosevelt's total vote rise from 22,809,638 in 1932 to 27,747,636 in 1936 and his plurality escalate from 7,050,737 to 11,068,093. Moreover, Ryan undoubtedly perceived that Lemke's minuscule share of the popular vote suggested that Father Coughlin's scathing attacks on Roosevelt commanded virtually no support within the ranks of the electorate. While Coughlin had consistently denounced Roosevelt, Ryan had reminded the American people that the President's New Deal had proved helpful to millions of deprived citizens and that the reforms advocated by the President had definitely and positively changed the character of society in the United States.

Notes

1. A scholarly biographical account of Ryan prior to 1933 may be found in Francis L. Broderick, *Right Reverend New Dealer: John A. Ryan* (New York: Macmillan, 1963), 1-210.

2. *New York Times*, September 17, 1945, p. 19; *Washington Post*, September 1, 1945, pp. 1, 10; *Commonweal* (September 28, 1945): 565.

3. John J. Delaney, *Dictionary of American Catholic Biography* (Garden City: Doubleday, 1984), 501-2; Jay P. Dolan, *The American Catholic Experience* (Garden City: Doubleday, 1985), 402; Alan Brinkley, *Voices of Protest: Huey Long, Father Coughlin and the Great Depression* (New York: Alfred A. Knopf, 1982), 130-31; Henry W. Bowden, *Dictionary of American Religious Biography* (Westport, Connecticut: Greenwood Press, 1977), 388-89; Sheldon Marcus, *Father Coughlin: The Tumultuous Life of the Priest of the Little Flower* (Boston: Little, Brown, 1973), 65.

4. David H. Bennett, *Demagogues in the Depression: American Radicals and the Union Party, 1935-1936* (New Brunswick: Rutgers University Press, 1969), 189-200; Edward C. Blackorby, *Prairie Rebel: The Public Life of William Lemke* (Lincoln: University of Nebraska Press, 1963), 217-24; Arthur N. Schlesinger, Jr., *The Politics of Upheaval* (Boston: Houghton Mifflin, 1960), 555-61; *New York Times*, August 16, 1936, pp. 1, 27; August 17, 1936, pp. 1, 12, 13, 14, 15, 16.

5. Charles J. Tull, *Father Coughlin and the New Deal* (Syracuse: Syracuse University Press, 1965), 1-145; Earl Boyea, "The Reverend Charles Coughlin and the Church: The Gallagher Years," *Catholic Historical Review* (April 1995): 211-25; Forrest Davis, "Father Coughlin," *Atlantic Monthly* (December 1935): 659-68; Francis P. McBride, "Charles Edward Coughlin," *Dictionary of American Biography,* Supplement Ten (New York: Charles Scribner's Sons, 1995), 150-52.

6. *Chicago Daily Tribune*, September 7, 1936, pp. 1, 4; *Brooklyn Eagle*, September 12, 1936, pp. 1, 11; *St. Louis Post Dispatch*, September 23, 1936, V, 1, 4; *New York Times*, September 7, 1936, pp. 1, 7; September 12, 1936, pp. 1, 2; September 17, 1936, pp. 8; September 20, 1936, p. 28; September 27, 1936, p. 17.

7. *Cincinnati Enquirer*, September 26, 1936, pp. 1, 2; *Philadelphia Inquirer*, September 27, 1936, pp. 1, 10; *New York Times*, September 26, 1936, pp. 1, 3; September 27, 1936, pp. 28; October 9, 1936, pp. 18.

8. *Washington Post*, October 9, 1936, pp. 1, 4; *New York Times*, October 9, 1936, pp. 1, 18.

9. *Baltimore Sun*, October 11, 1936, pp. 1, 16; *Washington Evening Star*, October 11, 1936, pp. B-2.

10. *Washington Post*, October 1, 1936, pp. 1; *New YorkTimes*, October 12, 1936, p. 18.

11. *New York Times*, October 13, 1936, pp. 24.

12. *Commonweal* (October 23, 1936): 597-98.

13. *New York Times*, October 16, 1936, p. 21.

14. *Boston Herald*, October 16, 1936, pp. 1, 14; *New York Times*, October 18, 1936, pp. 2; October 30, 1936, pp. 1, 18; *Herald Tribune*, October 15, 1936, pp. 15.

John A. Ryan and Development in Catholic Economic Ethics

Just before his manual of moral theology went forever out of print, Henry Davis introduced his revised 1958 edition with these words: "All of morality has been treated with the greatest of intelligence and scholarship for over three centuries. There is no room for originality here." Manualists like Davis give credibility to the claim that a whole era of Catholic moral writing is now irrelevant. In the words of one commentator, Catholic neoscholastic morality in the century before Vatican II was marked by its "monolithic, physicalist, and a-historical" approach (John Gallagher, *Time Past, Time Future* [1990] 257-58).

The era of which the commentator speaks was, of course, the era of John A. Ryan. And it is not uncommon to hear that however noble Ryan's intentions were, his writing suffers all the drawbacks of the era: Ryan's was "not really theological writing," opined a voice at the latest meeting of the *Society of Christian Ethics.*

The four papers gathered in this section do not support the common wisdom about the era of preconciliar Catholic morality, in general, and about Ryan, in particular. These papers are all arguments about the development of moral doctrine. All four essays can be read, on a general level, as demonstrating both the necessity and occurrence of development in Catholic moral thinking in the years before the Second Vatican Council.

The first paper in this section is Harlan Beckley's "Theology of Prudence in John Ryan's Economic Ethics." Beckley is the strongest advocate here for a theological reading of Ryan's word. Beckley says Ryan's claim that the common good should "be taken distributively as well as collectively" is a theologically based insistence that the unity of creation in God means that individual rights and the common good will not conflict over the long run. Beckley also argues that Ryan moved Catholicism's thinking on a right to private property beyond Leo XIII's firm defense of that right in *Rerum novarum*. Beckley sees in Ryan both an instance of development in Catholic moral thinking and an occasion to look for more development. He says Ryan, like some other Catholic thinkers, is somewhat "naive" on the tasks involved in reaching the common good. Beckley's paper, perhaps more than the others in this section, demonstrates both the general truth of development of Catholic moral thinking in the neoscholastic period and the particular point on Ryan as an example of that development.

Michael Stebbins' paper, "Toward a Developmental Understanding of the Common Good," does not address the particular subject of Ryan at all. Stebbins' focus is Bernard Lonergan's understanding of "the human good" as a good always discovered in the particularities of culture and history. Stebbins sees Lonergan, from his earliest writings, as proposing a theologically based understanding of our moral obligations. What Beckley demonstrates in Ryan, Stebbins demonstrates in Lonergan: any ethic that is theologically-based must display a prudent willingness for change in the particular material norms that express more unchanging principles. For all is ordered to the authentic good or "true value" of human beings, a good we hold in common and formulate historically as contingent creatures of the one God.

John Pawlikowski's paper, "Papal Teaching on Economic Justice: Change and Continuity," like Stebbins', is a more general treatment of development in Catholic social teaching with no specific treatment of John A. Ryan. Pawlikowski shows that the continuity in papal thinking about economic justice stems from a theologically motivated irenicism that rejects all theories of class warfare. Pawlikowski and his sources show a developing understanding of the common good and of distributive justice that focuses increasingly on the rights of the world's most vulnerable people. In a move reminiscent of Beckley's concern about a theological "naiveté" in Ryan's theology, Pawlikowski wonders whether the irenicism in contemporary papal teaching on economic justice is adequate to confront the enormous inequalities of our day.

Daniel Rush Finn's paper, "Catholic Social Thought on Property: An Urgent Need for Extension and Renewal," like Beckley's essay, focuses the discussion of moral development on a particular issue. Finn's concern is both to demonstrate and call for development. He show how Catholic teaching about usury was able to change when the traditional understanding of money as a good created by God for human consumption was deepened to an understanding of money as a usable asset. What remains constant in Catholic thinking is a principle about fairness; what changed was a specific moral rule. Finn says the Catholic tradition has not yet differentiated its understanding of property in a similar way: we still talk about property only as a good created by God. Thus, John Locke's understanding of property as including the creativity behind and emerging from a human being's labor remains an "unanswered challenge" for Catholic moral thinking. What Finn shows is that precisely a deeper theological rethinking about property (one, he says, John Ryan saw a need for) will help sharpen Catholic teaching on property against libertarian defenses of all property as "earned" by the individual's labor.

What all four essays share is a conviction that a theological perspective will help illumine some of the most intractable of current questions in economic ethics. What the first and last of these essays add to that general point is the evidence that John A. Ryan's own thought on questions of economic ethics was driven by his theological concerns—concerns opening him to understand that moral thought must develop—and not by the over-hardened, "monolithic" postures of some system.

Theology and Prudence in John Ryan's Economic Ethics

HARLAN BECKLEY

You may have heard it said, as I have, that John Ryan crafted his economic ethics independently of his theology. Ryan's contribution to moral theology is sometimes unjustly diminished due to this erroneous view. To be sure, Ryan did not write much about theology, and his economic ethics were uninformed by what he termed the "Supernatural" of religion or by biblical revelation. We shall see that this exclusion of grace and revelation from economic ethics differentiates what Ryan calls "expediency" from prudence as envisioned by some other Christian ethicists. These considerations notwithstanding, there can be no gainsaying the deep influence of Ryan's neo-Thomist theology on his ethics.

In his foreword to *The Norm of Morality*, Ryan observed that his argument would appeal to non-Catholics and non-Christians; it will appeal, he continued, "to all persons who believe in God as the Creator and Ruler of the Universe." On the other hand, those "who deny the existence of a spiritual soul and who believe that man is merely a highly organized animal" will, Ryan held, deny the central thesis of my ethics.[1] Ryan was fully aware that his view of human rational nature and the intrinsic worth and dignity of individual humans was inextricably related to his belief in God.

He had no need for biblical revelation nor for divine grace to claim knowledge of economic rights and justice, but as is the case with Ryan's mentor, Thomas Aquinas, the content and application of the natural law is highly dependent on theology as it can be known apart from grace and revelation.[2]

I will, in this lecture, examine the ways in which Ryan's theology shaped the exercise of prudence in his economic ethics.[3] This focus on prudence will illustrate my general point about the impact of theology on Ryan's ethics, but it should also clarify our thinking about the relation between theology and prudence in social ethics more generally. To the extent that we share Ryan's theology or hold differing theological views, how should our practice of prudence be revised or deepened to accord with our theology? Is the theology backing Ryan's view of prudence defensible, or does it need to be altered, thereby altering his practice of prudence as well? To aid in sharpening these questions, I will sketch briefly differences and similarities between Ryan and three contemporary theological thinkers: John Howard Yoder, James M. Gustafson, and Martin Luther King, Jr.

Human Welfare: Moral Values and Prudence

Ryan is cited often for his claim, in a 1913 debate with the socialist Morris Hillquit, that in the long run "moral values and genuine expediency" are identical in the matter of social institutions.[4] In the preceding sentence, he had claimed that the moral quality of socialist policies "can be determined only through an examination of their bearing upon human welfare."[5] This joining of moral values and expediency in the concept of human welfare, which after the publication of *Quadragesimo anno* Ryan absorbed into the concept of social justice, is the key to his understanding of the relation between prudence and justice. Human welfare considers how the development of the individual toward her proximate end in temporal life and her ultimate end in God is related to the social welfare or common good of the economy and society. Ryan distinguished it, on the one hand, from the common good considered independently of each individual's good and, on the other hand, from moral values and norms for individual self-development considered without regard for how the common welfare impinges on the development of individuals. Human welfare determines the morality of acts and institutions on the basis of whether they are expedient in providing for the development of persons toward their God-given telos.

For the purposes of this essay, I will note four features of Ryan's concept of human welfare. First, it is theologically grounded in the belief that the "human personality is a distinct entity, created by God, with rights and duties and destined for an eternal end with God."[6] Second, human welfare warns against determination of right and wrong solely on the basis of moral values and norms deduced from the telos of rational human nature. Social ethics must examine how economic and/or social welfare bears on the opportunities for persons to comply with their moral duty for self-development. This prudential consideration required that Ryan consider economics and the common good in making judgments about the justice of acts and institutions. Third, due in part to his understanding of God's ordering of life so that all humans can achieve their proximate divinely appointed end, Ryan clung firmly to the view that individual rights are, in the long run, in complete harmony with good economics. No human right necessary for the proper self-development of an individual needs to be sacrificed for the sake of the common good or for the equal rights of others. Fourth, human welfare can be known and achieved without relying on God's redemptive work in history or on the unrequited sacrifices of individuals for the sake of progress toward justice. The route to justice is rational persuasion and ordinary democratic politics. Each of these four points requires explication.

Theology for a Teleological Ethic

The first point regarding Ryan's theological backing for human welfare informs his position regarding the last three, more properly ethical, points. Three aspects of this theology are important, and they correlate respectively, albeit loosely, with the last three ethical features of human welfare. However, the correlation is sufficiently loose that we will need to keep all three theological themes in mind as we examine the three more specifically ethical points.

God as Telos

First, the norm of human welfare is grounded in the divinely appointed proximate end for human nature. God is primarily telos and only secondarily lawgiver. In *The Norm of Morality*, Ryan devoted separate chapters to morality based on rational human nature and morality based on the natural law, and he gave pride of place to the former. He further declared that his approach based on rational nature is "superior to that appearing in the majority of manuals."[7] Ryan's ethics is fundamentally teleological. Whatever "conduces" to the proximate end for which humans were created, Ryan contended, "will necessarily agree with the norm" for the moral life. Natural rights, which form the foundation for Ryan's economic ethics, are judged on the basis of empirical inquiry into their consequences for permitting or furthering each person's proximate end. These rights are means by which the possessor is enabled to reach "the end appointed to him by nature."[8]

This emphasis on God as end rather than God as lawgiver augmented the role of prudence in Ryan's economic ethics. The starting point for Ryan's economic ethics was not subject to empirical and consequentialist tests. He believed that every human has equal dignity commensurate with the self-evident end of his rational nature. This a priori affirmation of dignity entails some rights, such as the right to life and the right to a decent livelihood, without empirical inquiry into their particular circumstances and consequences. But most rights depend, in differing degrees, on regard for their economic expediency.

Harmony in God's Order

Second, Ryan's moral reasoning seems to be shaped by the theological belief that God ordered creation so that if injustice were set aside, every person could receive the means for self-perfection. Though he did not state this belief unequivocally, his claim that humans are created by God with rights and duties and destined for their final end strongly implies it. Since God is infinitely wise, good, and truthful, Ryan surmised, "perfect human happiness must somewhere be obtainable."[9] He was, of course, referring to the ultimate end in God. Temporal self-perfection is, nonetheless, closely linked to ultimate happiness. The proximate end is in "harmony with and conducive to the ultimate end" and "equally obligatory" with the conditions for the ultimate end.[10] In his autobiography Ryan reflected that it is noble to battle for "social conditions which will permit an ever-increasing host of persons to live in a manner worthy of adopted children of God."[11] Given this close connection between the ultimate and proximate end appointed by God, Ryan's belief that God has provided for every person's ultimate end almost certainly applies to the rights necessary for each person's proximate end as well.

In any case, Ryan's moral reasoning reflects this belief. In considering the feasibility of the right to a decent livelihood, Ryan wrote that the concrete existence of the right supposes that the total goods available are sufficient to "afford a decent livelihood for all."[12] In commenting on the Bishops' Program of Social Reconstruction, Ryan defended the practicality of the right to a decent livelihood on the grounds that God wishes for every person to have the means to a reasonable life and salvation.[13] Ryan tested other rights more severely on empirical grounds, but his moral reasoning deviated only slightly from the view that whatever is necessary for every human to attain her self-perfection is also expedient. This sanguine view that rights and prudence are united in human welfare was, I contend, formed by his theological belief in God's ordering of creation so that every human could achieve his proximate end in life.

Participation in Divine Reason

My third theological point concerns human participation in God's reason. It is possible for every person without the aid of grace or revelation. Divine reason is the source of the intuitions by which humans distinguish among the values of activities and goods.[14] All rational agents are capable of knowing and achieving the proximate end of human life without the aid of grace or revelation. One finds scattered throughout Ryan's writings the remark that economic justice will not be achieved without a reformation of the human heart or "a revival of genuine religion," but Ryan did not have in mind conversion to the biblical proclamation or a divine regeneration of reason. What we need, he insisted, is a saner conception of welfare, a conception of the right life as a life that accumulates and consumes material goods only to the extent that they are necessary to advance development of the intellectual and spiritual faculties. This, of course, is the moral norm Ryan referred to in *The Norm of Morality* as appealing to all of those who believe in God as creator and ruler of the universe; it is welfare as "taught by Christianity and reason."[15] Thus, Ryan had theological reasons for believing natural reason sufficient to know and advance his program of justice.

Economics Informs Natural Rights

Ethics

In matters of economic ethics, Ryan did not view norms and rights, except for each person's most general right to the essential means to self-perfection, as determinative independent of circumstances and consequences. Economic inquiry is crucial for determining which norms and rights are conducive to self-development and how these rights can be secured in the present economic circumstances.

This emphasis on economic expediency moved Ryan to undertake a serious study of economics during his four years of study at St. Paul's and to devote maximum possible attention to economics in his doctoral studies.[16] Ryan was discriminate in appropriating the economics he read. He understood that no particular school fully grasped the realities of an economy, and he rejected the view that economic laws are so intractable that conditions cannot be adjusted in order to satisfy human rights.[17] Ryan advised Catholic economists to treat economics first as a descriptive science "pointing out the laws or uniformities involved," but also not to stop at description. They must put these laws to use "as a means for promoting the common good and social justice," his later term for human welfare.[18] Ryan negotiated the interaction between economics and ethics as though there was a "porous boundary" between them. This interaction is in two directions. First, it allows economics to shape the content of what rights and what patterns of distribution are the best means to achieve human welfare. Second, it allows theological ethics to demand that economics discover how conditions can be altered to assure that every person has an opportunity to achieve his God-given telos.[19]

The effects of economically informed prudence on Ryan's ethics are demonstrable at three levels: his openness to massive transformations of economic institutions and systems, his delineation of specific rights, and his canons of distributive justice.

Prudence and Economic Systems

Ryan's commitment to reforming capitalism is widely acknowledged; less emphasized are his suggestions that he would abandon capitalism entirely if it could not secure the moral rights of individuals. In considering economic objections to a minimum wage in *Distributive Justice*, Ryan noted that if the competitive economic system cannot provide for the right to a family living wage, then the competitive organization of industry is bankrupt. If the right to a living wage cannot be secured in the competitive system, so much the worse for the system. In his preface to the third edition to *Distributive Justice*, Ryan commented that after the Second World War, the prevailing economic system will probably be very different from capitalism. This economic revolution may, he continued, "render the entire structure of my treatment of distributive justice outmoded and necessitate a radical revision of it."[20] These are the musings of an ethicist prepared to transform his conception of distributive justice on the basis of changing economic realities.

Expediency in his economic ethics did not incline Ryan toward radical change. More often than not, it tempered his backing for revolutionary proposals. Ryan's primary argument against socialism was its inability to provide the economic means for individual self-development.[21] Clearly, Ryan's judgment about the relative justice of economic systems was flexible, depending primarily on their economic consequences for securing individuals the means for self-perfection.

Prudence and Specific Rights

The large role for prudence in Ryan's determination of specific rights is apparent in his argument for the right to a living wage. Its influence was more pronounced in his views on the right to private property and the merely presumptive rights of rent, interest, and profits.

Living wage: In his book *A Living Wage*, Ryan concluded that since the only access to a decent livelihood in the present organization of industry is via a living wage, the right to a living wage will obtain as long as the present economic system exists. This moral affirmation was, however, insufficient for Ryan without a sustained examination of the economic feasibility of a living wage.[22] During the thirties, when unemployment joined low wages as a significant obstacle to the right to a living wage, Ryan used macroeconomic theory, especially John Hobson's theory of underconsumption, to argue for a set of redistributive policies to stimulate demand and employment.[23] He continued to insist on the economic feasibility of the right to a living wage, but new policies were now required to satisfy it. Ryan's persistent examination of the feasibility of a living wage under different economic conditions reflects his commitment to introduce economics into moral reasoning about specific rights.

Private property: Economic studies had a greater impact on the content of rights more indirectly linked to individual welfare. The right to private property is the prime example. Ryan did not consider it an a priori right. The argument for the right to private property, Ryan commented, "is obviously empirical, drawn from consequences." Moreover, he remarked that if private property cannot be shown to be "necessary for human or individual welfare," its "moral justification . . . disappears" and "[t]he institution may then be abolished . . . without any violation of individual rights."[24] These are bold words in light of Pope Leo XIII's contention that the right to private property is deduced from the essential nature of humans as reasoning creatures.[25]

Ryan, of course, believed that private property is "necessary as a *social institution.*"[26] He cited two kinds of consequentialist grounds. First, it is an indispensable incentive for economic efficiency. Second, it fosters "psychic goods which are an integral element of normal life."[27] Private property is not an intrinsic right, but the empirical evidence shows that is has a positive effect on economic welfare and that it fosters individual self-development. On the other hand, this prudential approach led Ryan to place numerous restrictions on the right to use and receive benefits from private property. Moreover, it radically reduced the amount of property that should be included as private. In an essay on the public ownership of industrial property, Ryan suggested that the nationalization of industry could be permitted up to the point that it would "deprive individuals of ample opportunities of investing their money in productive enterprises."[28] He left plenty of latitude for public ownership of property.

Rents, interest, and profits: Unlike the right to private property, the rights to rent, interest, and profits are not natural rights. They are merely presumptive rights. Presumptive rights constitute claims on others as long as these rights contribute to economic well-being as a means to assure each individual access to opportunities for self-development (viz., through a living wage). Rents nor interest can be justified on the grounds of the desert of the recipient. Their justification must be sought in what Ryan refers to as "extrinsic and social considerations."[29] Profits are in part a reward for the efforts of the entrepreneur, but the principal justification for large profits, which Ryan condoned under conditions of competition and fair treatment of labor, lies in the benefits that efficient business practices offer for the social welfare. This justification, Ryan observed, meets the criteria of human welfare as it unites ethical soundness and social expediency.[30] Ryan's economic expediency tended to support standard capitalist practices, but it also led him to propose restrictions on these three means of receiving income.[31] Once prudence enters into moral reasoning, new empirical findings can alter established patterns of moral judgment, whether they be progressive or conservative.

Prudence and Distributive Justice

Ryan's canons of distributive justice are primarily guides to the distribution of income and wealth. We should not be surprised that the six canons culminate with human welfare, which "summarizes all that is ethically sound and socially feasible" in the other five canons.[32] As we should expect, the canon of needs is the foundation of distributive justice, for this canon seeks to treat persons equally "as beings endowed with the dignity and the potencies of personality." It requires that every person receive what she needs to attain the end of her rational nature. This canon is insufficient, however, for it does not account for productive activities. It is especially inadequate for considering how distribution can injure the social welfare required for the long-term provision of needs.[33] Hence, Ryan incorporated the canon of efforts and sacrifice, which measures both meritorious self-development and contributions to economic welfare, and the canons of productivity and scarcity, which "measure economic value rather than ethical worth."[34] When these canons regarding economic production are folded into the canon of human welfare, Ryan's criteria for judging economic distribution places economic expediency in the service of safeguarding the opportunity of every person to reach her divinely appointed end.

Theology

His view of God as the final end and orderer of creation enabling the achievement of the proximate end of human nature clearly shaped Ryan's injection of prudential economic considerations into moral judgments about distributive justice, rights, and economic systems. From his theological perspective, humans are religiously and morally obligated to employ economically informed prudence in determining what rights and economic policies advance each individual's opportunity for self-perfection. We could fruitfully contrast the coherence between Ryan's theology and practice of prudence with many optional views in theological and philosophical ethics, including liberation and political theologies, for which eschatology informs ethics. I will highlight the connection between theology and prudence in Ryan's economic ethics by a brief comparison with the dramatically differing views of John Howard Yoder.

Faithfulness to Christ

I will focus on two major theological differences. First, as every theological ethicist knows, Yoder's ethics is founded on faithfulness to Jesus of Nazareth. Furthermore, the way to which Christ calls us is distinctly incompatible with a natural morality founded solely on God as creating and ordering human life to its ultimate and proximate end. Faithfulness to Jesus rules out constructing social norms and rights on the basis of a telos for humankind or its individual members. Jesus' renunciation of violence is, Yoder tells us, founded on his prior renunciation of "compulsiveness of purpose" and his willingness to renounce "legitimate ends" rather than to violate the dignity of others through coercion or violence.[35]

This faithfulness to Jesus precludes prudent pursuit of a goal. "[D]iscipleship is not guided by the goals it seeks to reach," Yoder writes, "but by the Lord it seeks to reflect."[36] Moreover, we cannot be sure that discipleship will be effective in achieving the most desirable outcome. "We cannot sight down the line of our obedience to the attainment of the ends we seek."[37] The disciple of Christ must willingly "accept the apparently ineffective path of obedience, trusting in God for the results."[38]

God's Providence

Yoder refuses to concede that discipleship is imprudent. He rejects the charge of imprudence because of a second major theological difference with Ryan. For Yoder, God's providence is not parallel to an ordering of life that can be known and that closely follows the cause and effect pattern of events as this pattern is discerned by historians, economists, and others outside the faith. God's providence is hidden in the lordship of the crucified and resurrected Christ.[39] Faith in the resurrected Christ means that Christians should interpret God's rulership of history as a relationship between the cross and resurrection, and not as one of cause and effect.[40] To trust that Christ is lord is then to trust that God will use the obedient suffering of the Christians to bring about the triumph of the divine cause. Thus, the imperative to obey Christ and trust in God for the results is not foolish faithfulness. Discipleship is not, Yoder insists, doing justice though the heavens may fall.[41] The "prudence" of this ethic is founded on an understanding providence that expands the relevant frame of history beyond what economists and ordinary prudence consider.

Though this ethic of discipleship claims prudence of its own kind, it declines to incorporate the social sciences into the determination of fundamental ethical norms. In sharp contrast to Ryan, neither "nature" nor the "sciences" have authority when looked at alone. They must be reinterpreted in light of the confession of the lordship of Christ.[42] Instead of having a porous boundary with the sciences, ethics is nearly impervious to them. If prudence trusts in God's rule through the resurrection, one's moral judgments ought not rely on what is known of the divine order apart from Christ.

A Christ-informed ethic does not necessarily lead to a view of prudence so radically different from Ryan's. Martin Luther King, Jr., elevated the role of Christ in social ethics, but gave a much larger role to prudence and human agents directing history toward its telos than Yoder admits. However, focusing on Yoder's specific view of discipleship demonstrates how dramatic differences in theology lead to markedly different views of prudence and of the place of empirical studies in social ethics. I contend that one cannot fold Yoder's understanding of discipleship and God's providence into a traditional Catholic teleological theology like Ryan's.

The Harmony of Rights and the Common Good

Yoder does not perceive harmony between morality and effective pursuit of morally legitimate ends. Ryan did. Recall Ryan's assertion that moral values and expediency are identical in the long run. Recall his parallel theological belief that a wise and good God orders creation so that every person can have the means to perfect his proximate end in life. This view that rights are in harmony with each other and with the common good deeply influenced Ryan's use of prudential reasoning.

Ethics

Living Wage

Two of Ryan's applications of economics will illustrate this interpretive judgment. First, we have already noted that Ryan's economic analyses persistently determined that a minimum living wage would promote economic welfare without causing appreciable unemployment. In one analysis, he concluded that higher wages would improve the productivity of workers, require intelligent management to develop more efficient methods of production, drive inefficient businesses from the field, and increase consumer demand by putting money at the discretion of wage earners who need to spend if for consumption. Under these conditions, the small amount of unemployment likely to occur from a minimum living wage can be remedied by legislation to deal with the problem of unemployment and to provide for industrial and vocational training.[43] When, in the thirties, Ryan emphasized macroeconomics to deal with the problem of unemployment, he argued that the redistributive effects of a minimum wage were expedient for increasing consumer demand and stimulating employment. He then relished in the observation that this economic fact illustrates how "good ethics is in harmony with good business."[44] Despite lingering doubts about the payment of a living wage in a competitive industrial economy, Ryan was highly sanguine about that possibility. He was apparently certain that economics could find a way to meet the demands of the right to a decent livelihood. It was not the dismal science for Ryan.

Labor Participation in Management

The second example is perhaps more stunning. Ryan's argument against Hillquit for the economic inefficiency of socialism rested on the naiveté of socialist thinking that workers can be expected to elect managers who could organize an efficient workplace.[45] Yet in justifying his own later proposal for workers to participate in business management in order to develop their creative and directive capacities, Ryan claimed that "the employer and community will be benefited through a larger and better product."[46] The apparent incompatibility between these two arguments reveals how Ryan's optimism regarding the economic feasibility of satisfying rights colored his economic analyses.

These illustrations do not demonstrate that Ryan's economic analyses were wrong. In most cases, his analyses were probably superior to those of his opponents, though his repeated assertions about the positive economic effects of a minimum living wage were surely exaggerated. Nor do they suggest that Ryan used economics to support rights arrived at on other grounds. We have already seen how the content of Ryan's right to private property—and even more so the presumptive rights to receive rent, interest, and profits—were profoundly shaped by his empirical studies. Nevertheless, these examples illustrate a pattern of sophisticated economic analyses that doggedly cling to the view that good economics is good ethics as though it were a principle, as it seems to have been for Ryan.

Theory: Rights and the Common Good

This consonance of morality and expediency in practical reasoning is also reflected in Ryan's theoretical comments about the relation between individual rights and the common good. Ryan introduced the terms "human welfare" and "social justice" into moral reasoning so that moral judgments would take account of the common good. He believed that Kant and other moral theorists exaggerated the rights of individuals in a way that allowed the strong to oppress the weak.[47] Prudent judgment, Ryan held, should consider "the welfare of society . . . as something immediately and formally different from the welfare of its members." Yet the ultimate purpose for considering the common good is "the good of all of its component individuals."[48] The common good, Ryan reiterated often, is the "common welfare taken distributively as well as collectively."[49] He resisted the possibility that the common good and rights could conflict over the long run. "[S]ocial and individual welfare are [not only] interdependent, . . .; [they are] fostered by the same means and hindered by the same obstacles."[50]

Theory: Self-sacrifice

Ryan often curtailed individual presumptive rights for the sake of the common good. In that sense, he curbed individual liberties and asked persons to sacrifice for the sake of the whole. He never imagined, however, the need for individuals and groups to sacrifice any of what he called "absolute rights," especially those essential for self-development. This feature of Ryan's moral reasoning is most striking in his reluctance to override even the most implicit contractual obligations for the sake of the common good. Ryan held, for example, that even though human welfare justifies a high tax on capital gains on land sales, the state is obligated to compensate those who lose money as a result of its instituting the tax. He reasoned that the state had violated an implicit promise in introducing a capital gains tax after the landholder purchased her land.[51] If rights constituted by implicit contracts are held to be nearly sacred, rights that are means to self-perfection are fully sacred. Ryan left little room in his social ethics for individual or group sacrifices. "It is not reasonable," he wrote, "to expect men to devote themselves completely to any other end than their own highest good."[52]

Theory: Gustafson on the Common Good and Self-sacrifice

The contrast with the ethics of James Gustafson is conspicuous. Gustafson asserts, "The relationship between the good of individual parts and the common good is reciprocal, but is seldom, if ever, harmonious." Moreover, "the common good of various wholes is an object of proper concern not only for the sake of the parts but also for the sake of those wholes."[53] Gustafson agrees with Ryan that the good of individuals and the common good are interdependent and that attention to the common good is necessary for the sake of individuals, but they clearly disagree about the harmony between the common good and the good of individuals. Gustafson concludes that "[r]estraints and denials of interests, even those that have a considerable justification, are simply part of the ordering of life," and characterizes his ethic as one that warrants instances of self-sacrifice.[54] While Ryan called for sacrifices of interests unrelated to the true welfare of individuals, he never offered a moral justification for sacrificing individual rights for the sake of the common good. Ryan consider the latter collectivism, which he associated with socialism and communism.

God as Telos versus God as Direction

This ethical difference may be traced to theological differences. Those familiar with Gustafson's theology know that he shares Ryan's view of God as ordering creation so that it provides a direction for human life and well-being. However, Gustafson does not share Ryan's view that the direction issues in a knowable telos. What we know about the direction of God's ordering certainly does not assure us that there is a telos, proximate or ultimate, in which humans can attain total perfection and fulfillment.[55] Piety, Gustafson contends, does not trust the powers that bear down on us to fulfill all our perceptions of the human good.[56] Although there is good reason to affirm God's beneficence, it is only from a constricted view of God's purposes that we practice moral reason with the presumption that the end for which God created the world includes the complete good of humans, individually or collectively.

From Gustafson's theocentric perspective, prudence will require at times that we adjudicate among the irreconcilable conflicting moral claims of individuals and of the common good. He shares with Ryan "a stress on the importance of consequences."[57] In this stress they both differ from Yoder. The difference between Ryan and Gustafson occurs regarding the extent to which prudence may reveal conflict among fundamental moral claims.

Given Gustafson's theological perspective, morally prudent judgments may require that what Ryan calls the absolute rights of individuals be sacrificed for the sake of others or for the well-being of the whole.[58] Whereas empirical studies and prudence enter into Ryan's ethical judgments in the determination of what specific rights satisfy the self-evident proximate end of human nature, they enter into Gustafson's ethical judgments about the potential conflict among these rights of individuals and their incongruity with the common good. Ryan's theology backs his confidence that expedient economics can satisfy the absolute rights of every individual, a confidence Gustafson's theology precludes. We are moved once again to recognize the correlation between Ryan's neo-Thomist theology and his economic ethics.

Justice without Redemption

For a variety of theological reasons, among them the corrupted rationality of humans,[59] Gustafson also repudiates the view that rights and the patterns of justice can be known with relative certitude. We could examine how the role of sin as corrupted rationality and redemption figure into differences between Gustafson's and Ryan's ethics for reforming injustice,[60] but a brief comparison and contrast between Ryan and Martin Luther King, Jr., will focus us more specifically on theology and prudence in Ryan's method for reforming economic injustice.

Unlike Gustafson, King shared Ryan's belief that justice for all can be achieved in history. King repeatedly reminded audiences that "God struggles with [alongside of] us, and that the arc of the moral universe, although long, is bending toward justice."[61] King had in mind a social structure that "uplifts the human personality," an ideal entailing the potential for each individual's fulfillment.[62] Neither King nor Ryan embraced Gustafson's pessimism regarding the harmony of individual rights and the common good.

Unlike Yoder, King shared Ryan's emphasis on prudence in social ethics. Although he could, as Yoder does, interpret history in terms of cross and resurrection rather than cause and effect,[63] King's thinking and his actions sight down along the line of obedience to the cross of nonviolence to the political achievement of justice. The role of prudence in King's moral reasoning is nowhere more pronounced than in his defenses of nonviolent direct action. Nonviolence is, he maintained, the only "strategy for change . . . that will bring the Negro into the mainstream of American life as quickly as possible."[64]

Because they shared optimism about the harmony of rights and an emphasis on the role of prudence in social ethics, King's and Ryan's divergence in accounting for sin and redemption in prudential reasoning about the means for achieving justice is all the more instructive. It vividly reveals the effect excluding grace and biblical revelation had on Ryan's social ethics.

Conversion of Ethos and Prudence

The differences between King and Ryan can be expressed in two theological and ethical observations. The first point concerns whether a conversion of cultural ethos is essential for achieving justice. Ryan's did not view ethos criticism as a significant part of reforming activity. He concentrated instead on making the narrower arguments of practical moral reasoning accessible to those who needed to be persuaded in order to change policies.[65] Ryan's confidence in the power of rational persuasion in the political arena is exemplified in his vocational choices. Ryan desired to leave St. Paul Seminary and join the faculty at Catholic University in 1915, Broderick observes, because he wanted to go closer to the centers of reform.[66] Ryan's position at Catholic University and in the Social Action Department of the National Catholic Welfare Conference enabled him to carry out what he considered a prudential strategy for reform: introduce moral reason into the national debates about economic policy.

My favorite illustration of this strategy is Ryan's response to the U.S. Supreme Court ruling in 1923 that a Washington, D.C. minimum-wage law violated the due process clause of the fifth amendment. This judgment occurred during a period when Ryan's views were suffering a series of defeats that might have convinced the most optimistic reformer of the limits of moral argument as an effective means for securing justice. Yet Ryan responded to this decision with a pamphlet delineating the errors in the Court's opinion because its social philosophy was informed by an eighteenth-century individualistic rights theory.[67] He did not accuse the justices of corruption, nor did he denounce the cultural ethos that influenced the court's reasoning and decision. Ryan saw no reason to shift the balance in reforming efforts toward the economic power of the labor movement.[68] He concentrated on a legal and moral counter argument to the Court's opinion. If human participation in divine reason enables all rational persons to have knowledge of the natural right to a living wage, this response was prudent, not because it was cautious but because it was the most probable means for advancing justice.

Ryan's response to the Court's decision in *Adkins v. Children's Hospital* instructively juxtaposes his focus on the judicial and legislative process with King's insistence that significant reform is not possible unless it aims beyond the law.[69] King's judgments about reform were informed by his view that sin renders reason, devoid of purifying faith, self-serving,[70] and by his experience of recalcitrant white racism. Few whites, King believed, can see the injustice of segregation until they are confronted collectively by the nonviolent movement and redeemed from the inertia of past injustices. King's writings reverberate with calls for black Americans to accept their mission to redeem the soul of America so that justice can be done. Nonviolent action is necessary to redeem the collective white conscience by confronting and exposing its contradictory commitments.[71] This commitment to supplementing legal reform with nonviolent resistance, which distinguished King from the NAACP, also distinguishes his strategy for reform from Ryan's.

These practical differences mirror theological differences. Ryan's use of moral and economic arguments without taking action to regenerate the common-sense reason of culture appears quite imprudent—because it is too cautious—from the perspective of King's interpretation of events through the redemptive suffering of Christ.[72] Ryan's approach was backed by his theological affirmation that the participation of rational nature in divine reason is sufficient to enable all humans to know what justice requires.

Self-sacrifice and Progress

King's claim for the efficacy of suffering raises a second point of significant disagreement. From Ryan's perspective, King's repeated call for the victims of injustice to accept suffering willingly appears an unnecessary sacrifice of individual rights for the sake of justice. Without embracing Gustafson's view that the divine ordering of life may require individuals and groups to forfeit rights, King justified the suffering of innocents as the only means to redeem the unjust collective conscience of America. King's most often cited articulation of this justification came at the funeral of four girls killed in the bombing of the 16th Street Baptist Church in Birmingham. King eulogized that "they did not die in vain. . . . History has proven over and over again that unmerited suffering is redemptive. . . . [T]his tragic event may cause the white South to come to terms with its conscience."[73] If suffering can produce redemption and redemption is the necessary means for achieving justice, a willingness to risk suffering for the sake of justice is prudent and a moral imperative.

Ryan never expected such sacrifice from laborers. He urged labor to assert its rights when they were denied. To ask for more is morally questionable as well as imprudent from a theological perspective urging the constitution and end of human rational nature, unqualified by Christ's redemptive suffering, as the source of moral rights and duties. The connections between his view of prudent reform and his theology are palpable.

Conclusions and Issues

I trust that I have demonstrated beyond a reasonable doubt that Ryan's economic ethics is dependent on his theology, but what more has been accomplished?

First, I hope to have shown that a teleological ethics of the kind that Ryan adopted from neo-Thomism backs the use of prudence at an early stage in the process of moral reasoning. Prudence shapes the content of norms and rights, not merely their application. Ryan's theology also warrants use of the social sciences in judging what is right and not merely as instrumental for applying ethics determined on other grounds. On the other hand, Ryan's belief in the divinely appointed end of human nature guards against the determination of the right on the basis of one or another school of economic thought.

Second, I think this study demonstrates that a view of God's ordering as directing creation to the fulfillment of human individuals and groups ultimately places prudence in the service of the ends of individuals. The social sciences and experience are effectively barred from raising doubts about the harmony of individual rights and the long-term common good. Prudence never dictates that individuals sacrifice their means to true self-fulfillment for the sake of the good of the whole.

Third, Ryan's view that humans participate in divine reason without the aid of grace warrants the use of public rational argument as the most practical means for social reform. From this perspective, political confrontation for the sake of redeeming the reason of a corrupted and complacent collective conscience is imprudent and morally dubious to the extent that it requires unnecessary sacrifices.

Fourth, I trust we have seen that to adopt theologies different from Ryan's compels one to reject or revise Ryan's practice of prudence. Theologies that begin with faithfulness to the character of Jesus of Nazareth as a radically distinctive alternative to all other values and norms in the culture, theologies that sharply juxtapose God's providence with interpretations of the course of events emerging from the sciences and social sciences, theologies that deny an ordering of life that assures the means for complete human fulfillment, and theologies that interpret progress in history in light of the redemptive suffering and resurrection of Christ—all of these theologies are incompatible with Ryan's economic ethics.

I have only contrasted Ryan's theology and exercise of prudence with these important alternative views. I have not effectively evaluated Ryan's position or the other options. Perhaps, however, Ryan's theological ethics now appears a suitable beginning point for thinking about the place of prudence in social ethics. Most of us will find Ryan's narrowly rational view of prudence, uninformed as it is by grace or redemption, both theologically and ethically deficient. Some of us will find Ryan's assumption of a complete harmony of moral rights and the common good morally naive and theologically anthropocentric. The recent proliferation of seemingly legitimate rights to include group rights[74] and environmental rights[75] as well as civil and economic rights heightens the sense that Ryan is naively optimistic.

Few persons will adopt Ryan's theology or his view of prudence without emendations, but we should take care before abandoning his position. Yoder's understandings of Christian obedience and God's providence—largely uninformed by experience (other than Christ-shaped experience) and the sciences—risk tremendous human costs based on a highly particularistic account of faithfulness. Gustafson's theocentric theology correctly warns us, in my judgment, that the relations between individual rights and ends and the common good are not harmonious. On the other hand, Gustafson has not demonstrated why we should consider the good of the whole independently of its benefits to the parts, at least in the long run. Ryan may be right that the common good should be considered distributively and not merely for its own sake.

Finally, King's theology and ethics of redemptive suffering have a strong hold on our generation because the movement he led was effective and those who suffered in service of this movement are martyrs whose lives inspire and give meaning to our own. On the other hand, we should not forget that Ryan's moral arguments also contributed to significant advances in economic justice during the New Deal. Further, not all suffering has proved as redemptive or as prudent as the suffering of individuals in the civil rights movement. Ryan's approach to reform may be more prudent and less costly in human suffering than an approach to reform that indiscriminately follows King's pattern of redemptive suffering. King's theology of redemptive suffering corrects Ryan's optimism, but a variation on Ryan's prudential reason might be theologically and ethically defensible.

In sum, John Ryan's economic ethics—understood in its full theological, ethical, and empirical dimensions—remains a rich source for contemporary ethical reflection on prudence, as well as on other topics in ethics.

Notes

1. John A. Ryan, *The Norm of Morality: Defined and Applied to Particular Actions* (Washington, D.C.: National Catholic Welfare Conference, 1944), v.

2. Ryan's separation of the natural ethics from the supernatural virtues was much sharper than Aquinas's, but that is distinct from the point that for both natural morality relies heavily on a divine ordering of creation through which humans move toward their end in God.

3. Although Ryan did not write about prudence as a moral virtue, his reference to expediency and prudence and the role they play in his moral reasoning are compatible with the Thomist understanding of prudence as the disposition to develop means appropriate to the end of moral acts and of human life. Ryan's use of the term "expediency" should not be confused with prudence as appropriate means to advance one's enlightened self-interest.

4. Morris Hillquit and John A. Ryan, *Socialism: Promise or Menace?* (New York, Macmillan, 1914), 58. Charles E. Curran, *American Catholic Social Ethics: Twentieth-Century Approaches* (Notre Dame: Notre Dame University Press, 1982), 38-41, and Patrick W. Gearty, *The Economic Thought of Monsignor John A. Ryan* (Washington, D.C.: The Catholic University Press of America, 1953), 247-49.

5. Hillquit and Ryan, *Socialism*, 58. Ryan was referring specifically to policies regarding "artificial capital," but his point about human welfare as the determinative ethical consideration applies to all economic institutions and policies.

6. John A. Ryan and Francis J. Boland, C.S.C., *Catholic Principles of Politics* (New York: Macmillan, 1950), 1.

7. Ryan, *The Norm of Morality*, v.

8. John A. Ryan, *A Living Wage* (New York: Macmillan, 1906), 44.

9. Ryan, *The Norm of Morality*, 7.

10. Ryan and Boland, *Catholic Principles of Politics*, 11.

11. John A. Ryan, *Social Doctrine in Action: A Personal History* (New York: Harper & Brothers, 1941), 289.

12. Ryan, *A Living Wage*, 79.

13. John A. Ryan, *Social Reconstruction* (New York: Macmillan, 1920), 69.

14. Ryan, *A Living Wage*, 50. David Krueger notes this same point in his Ph.D. dissertation, "The Economic Ethics of John A. Ryan and Gustavo Gutierrez," (University of Chicago, 1988), 17.

15. John A. Ryan, *Distributive Justice*, 1st ed. (New York: Macmillan, 1916), 316-18, 433; idem, *The Norm of Morality*, v.

16. See Francis Broderick, *Right Reverend New Dealer: John A. Ryan* (New York: Macmillan, 1963), 21, 31-34; Ryan, *Social Doctrine in Action*, 45-54, 62-69.

17. Ryan, *A Living Wage*, 6-10.

18. John A. Ryan, "Two Objectives for Catholic Economists," *Review of Economy* 1/1 (December 1942): 4-5.

19. The image of a "porous boundary" between the sciences and ethics so that the sciences can alter the content of ethical norms, not just their application, is taken from James M. Gustafson, "Tracing A Trajectory," *Zygon: Journal of Religion & Science* 30/2 (June 1995): esp. 180. Ryan restricts the influence of science more severely than Gustafson does because Ryan does not permit empirical evidence to enter into his judgments about the proximate end of humans in relation to God or the capacity to provide the means for everyone to achieve that end. We shall note the implications of this theological and ethical difference later.

20. John A. Ryan, *Distributive Justice*, 3rd ed. (New York: Macmillan, 1942), v.

21. Ryan, *Socialism: Promise or Menace*, 58-69.

22. Ryan, *A Living Wage*, 100-101, 151-233.

23. See Gearty, *The Economic Thought of Ryan*, 171-72, 185-95, 199-200, 312. Ryan was acquainted with John Maynard Keynes' *General Theory* soon after it was written in 1936, but he never advocated counter-cyclical fiscal

policy. Ryan saw no need for budget deficits to remedy unemployment and the Depression.

24. Ryan, *Distributive Justice*, 1st ed., 60-61.

25. Pope Leo XIII, *Rerum novarum*, 15 May 1891, par. 6. See Curran, *American Catholic Social Ethics*, 46, for references to Ryan's disagreement with Pope Leo and criticisms from his fellow Catholics.

26. Ryan, *Distributive Justice*, 1st ed., 59.

27. John A. Ryan, *The Church and Socialism and Other Essays* (Washington: The University Press, 1919), 6, 4.

28. John A. Ryan, "Public Ownership vs. Socialism," in *Declining Liberty and Other Papers* (New York: Macmillan, 1927), 263.

29. Ryan, *Distributive Justice*, 1st ed., 186.

30. Ibid., 255-56.

31. In the twenties Ryan began to argue against stockholders receiving profits through dividends because they have no role in the efficiency of a business (John A. Ryan, *The Christian Doctrine of Property*, [New York: The Paulist Press, 1923], 18-30), and in the thirties he argued that the government should restrict the market rate of interest to two percent in order to produce a more equitable distribution and stimulate consumer demand (John A. Ryan, *Seven Troubled Years 1930-1936: A Collection of Papers on the Depression and on the Problems of Recovery and Reform* [Ann Arbor, Mich.: Edwards Brothers, 1937], 252-53).

32. Ryan, *Distributive Justice*, 1st ed., 252.

33. Ibid., 244-46.

34. Ibid., 246-51, esp. 247.

35. John Howard Yoder, *The Politics of Jesus*: Vicit Agnus Noster, 2nd ed. (Grand Rapids, Mich.: William B. Eerdmans, 1994), 237.

36. John Howard Yoder, *The Original Revolution: Essays on Christian Pacifism* (Scottdale, Penn.: Herald Press, 1971), 39. This passage was brought to my attention by Kelly L. Brotzman.

37. Ibid., 154.

38. Ibid., 63.

39. Ibid., 155

40. Yoder, *The Politics of Jesus*, 232.

41. John Howard Yoder, *The Priestly Kingdom: Social Ethics as Gospel* (Notre Dame: University of Notre Dame Press, 1984), 37-38.

42. Ibid., 11.

43. Ryan, *Distributive Justice*, 1st ed., 409-11.

44. Ryan, *Seven Troubled Years*, passim and esp. 260.

45. Ryan, *Socialism: Promise or Menace*? 58-66.

46. Ryan, *Distributive Justice*, 3rd ed., 334-336. These two proposals are distinguished by substance and time. Ryan hypothesized a socialist proposal in which the directors of industries are elected by the workers who have no ownership in industry while his later proposal for an industrial democracy retained stockholder-elected directors yet calls for active participation in management by workers who share in ownership the business. As for timing, Ryan did not begin to advocate labor participation in management for several years after his debate with Hillquit. Nonetheless, these arguments also appear contradictory in tone, especially in their understandings of what motivates laborers and their level of managerial competence.

47. Ryan, *A Living Wage*, 63.

48. Ryan, *The Church and Socialism*, 78.

49. Ryan and Boland, *Catholic Principles of Politics*, 145; idem, Seven Troubled Years, 174-76.

50. Ryan, *The Church and Socialism*, 78.

51. Ryan, *Distributive Justice*, 1st ed., 110-13.

52. Ryan, *A Living Wage*, 58. The statement is made in the context of an example that requires individuals to sacrifice their existence for the sake of social welfare, and we might thus take it to be an exaggeration that applies only to such dramatic examples, but ample evidence indicates that Ryan would have defended this statement as a proposition. Still, he argued for sacrifices that are difficult to reconcile with a singular focus on attaining the highest good in this life. Perhaps the adverbial modifier "completely" permitted moral justification for sacrifices such as Ryan's justification for conscription and indirect killing of noncombatants in the time of war on the grounds of duty to one's country (*A Living Wage*, 45-46). These justifications for sacrificing life appear, however, to be confined to the military sphere. I know of no examples in his economic ethics where Ryan even considered the moral legitimacy of less severe sacrifices for the common good.

53. James M. Gustafson, *Ethics from a Theocentric Perspective*, vol. 2: *Ethics and Theology* (Chicago: University of Chicago Press, 1984), 19. See nearly the same claims in Gustafson's criticism of utilitarian ethics (109-10) and a similar statement again in Gustafson's conclusions on moral reasoning (298).

54. Ibid., 21-22. For Gustafson, this emphasis on self-sacrifice is enabled and required by faithfulness to Christ (22), manifesting the influence of introducing Jesus Christ into social ethics from a theological perspective more like Ryan's than Yoder's.

55. Gustafson argues against Thomas's contention for a knowable telos in which human life is individually and collectively perfected and fulfilled (ibid., 54-55). The argument could easily be applied to Ryan.

56. James M. Gustafson, *Ethics from a Theocentric Perspective*, vol. 1: *Theology and Ethics* (Chicago: University of Chicago Press, 1981), 272.

57. Gustafson, *Ethics from a Theocentric Perspective*, vol. 2, 112. For Ryan, the consequences that count are the consequences for securing each person's rights to the means to self-perfection. For Gustafson, they are the consequences for relating ourselves and all things appropriate to our and their relations to God (ibid., 146), which will not in every instance be positive consequences for Ryan's rights.

58. Ibid., 308.

59. Gustafson, *Ethics from a Theocentric Perspective*, vol 1, 300-302.

60. Gustafson, like Yoder and King and unlike Ryan, retains a significant role for redemption from sin in his ethics (ibid., 307-17) as well as in his theology (ibid., 247-51). Thus, we could examine how these theological beliefs are reflected in his views about the methods and possibilities of ethical reform as they are contrasted with Ryan's views, which are uninformed by God as redeemer. The comparison would be complicated, however, by the way their differences regarding God as telos would also have to be factored into their similarities and differences concerning prudential reform.

61. Martin Luther King, Jr., "Stride Toward Freedom," in *A Testament of Hope: The Essential Writings of Martin Luther King, Jr.*, ed. James W. Washington (San Francisco: Harper & Row, 1986), 460. King's hope is founded on an understanding of God markedly different from Ryan's. Reflecting the influence of his studies with Boston Personalists, King wrote that his hope that history is moving toward justice is founded on a belief that the universe is under the control of a loving purpose so that humans have a cosmic companion in their struggle toward justice. God, as this cosmic companion, is "responsive to the deepest yearnings of the human heart" ("Pilgrimage to Nonviolence," in *A Testament of Hope*, 40). God is a companion in the human struggle for realizing individual personality, not the telos of human rational nature that authorizes a natural law grounded in an established order of the creator. We shall not explore the ethical implications of this theological difference except insofar as it is manifest in King taking solace in a highly personal God in the midst of redemptive suffering.

62. See, for example, King's criteria for just laws in "Letter from a Birmingham City Jail," in *A Testament of Hope*, 293.

63. In "Stride Toward Freedom," the sentence following King's affirmation that the universe is moving toward justice adds: "We have lived under the agony and darkness of Good Friday with the conviction that one day the heightened

glow of Easter would emerge on the horizon" (King, "Stride Toward Freedom," 460).

64. King, "Where Do We Go From Here?" in *A Testament of Hope*, 592.

65. For an account of the distinction between ethics as practical moral reasoning and ethics as ethos criticism, see Gustafson, *Ethics from a Theocentric Perspective*, Vol., 1, 69-72.

66. Ibid., 89.

67. See John A. Ryan, *The Supreme Court and the Minimum Wage* (New York: Paulist Press, 1923).

68. As Broderick points out, Ryan was never very close to the labor movement (*Right Reverend New Dealer*, 131). Part of the reason for this distance was Ryan's confidence in reform through rational arguments for legislation, a confidence labor thought imprudent.

69. King, "Stride Toward Freedom," 484-85.

70. King, "Pilgrimage to Nonviolence," 36. King claimed to have learned his realism about social change from Reinhold Niebuhr. He even cites Niebuhr on the obdurate injustice of groups ("Letter from Birmingham City Jail," 292). King may be correct about where he learned his brand of realism, but he did not share Niebuhr's judgment that the injustice of groups is intractable. King believed that the group conscience, when confronted and exposed by nonviolent direct action, could be redeemed and integrated into a community of justice. Taylor Branch may be right when he asserts that King inverted Niebuhr: the injustices of groups are highly malleable; it is the immorality of individuals that is intractable (*Parting the Waters: America in the King Years 1954-63* (New York: Simon and Schuster, 1988), 702.

71. See King, "Love, Law, and Civil Disobedience," in *A Testament of Hope*, 48, for a very un-Niebuhrian account of the goodness in human nature that can be reclaimed by nonviolent civil disobedience.

72. One example of King's use of this interpretive principle appears as early as January, 1956 when he spoke to a black crowd in Montgomery about a series of terrorist bombings, including an attempted bombing of his own home. "We must now somehow believe that unearned suffering is redemptive," King commented, in exhorting the crowd to trust in the efficacy of nonviolence ("Stride Toward Freedom," 466).

73. Martin Luther King, Jr., "Eulogy for the Martyred Children," in *A Testament of Hope*, 221-22. This use of the eulogy was directed to my attention by James H. Cone, *Martin & Malcolm & America: A Dream or a Nightmare* (Maryknoll, N.Y.: Orbis Books, 1992), 85.

74. For a subtle discussion of the difficulties and possibilities for reconciling apparent conflicts between group rights and individual civil and

economic rights, see Sumner B. Twiss & Bruce Grelle, "Human Rights and Comparative Religious Ethics: A New Venue," *The Annual of the Society of Christian Ethics* (1995): 40-46.

75. Environmental ethicists can be extraordinarily sanguine about reconciling environmental rights or moral claims with individual human rights. In his monograph *Sustainability: Economics, Ecology, and Justice* (Maryknoll, N.Y.: Orbis Books, 1992), John B. Cobb, Jr., calls for a way of life as sacrifice in a life of poverty on the one hand (16-17), but then portrays this way of life as true human fulfillment for all persons (esp. 31-33 on "A Hopeful Future") and remains highly optimistic that a sustainable global economy can exist in harmony with justice and the development of human welfare for poor, third-world societies (45-48). James A. Nash, in an essay on frugality, is more sensitive to the potential conflicts between legitimate individual interests and the demands of the common good (154) and between the economic rights of those in underdeveloped nations and environmentally sustainable economies in the wealthy nations (157-59). See "Toward the Revival and Reform of the Subversive Virtue: Frugality," *The Annual of the Society of Christian Ethics* (1995). Ryan did not factor environmental or group rights into his ethics. The point here is how these legitimate moral claims make it increasing more difficulty to sustain Ryan's view of a divine ordering that sustains a harmony of individual moral rights and claims with each other and with the common good.

Toward a Developmental Understanding of the Common Good

J. MICHAEL STEBBINS

The notion of the common good is a central and enduring feature of Catholic social teaching. In our time it has also become a problematic notion. As our society and culture become more pluralistic, it becomes increasingly difficult to reach agreement about just what the common good consists of. Without going deeply into the issue of pluralism and the search for consensus, I want to try to contribute to the discussion of the common good by drawing attention to some of Bernard Lonergan's ideas about what he calls "the human good." The human good and the common good are not precisely the same thing; nonetheless, I think that using the notion of the human good as a backdrop might clarify our understanding of what the common good is and what is involved in pursuing it effectively. At the end of this essay I also want to suggest some ways in which this approach might affect our ideas about the role of business in promoting the common good.

By "the human good" Lonergan means any good that is brought into being through human intelligence and choice.[1] That is to say, the human good is whatever results when human beings think about the difficulties and opportunities their lives present them with, decide how to respond, and then follow through with appropriate action for change. This means that the human good is not some abstract ideal, a remote goal that we can aim for but never hope to reach. Quite the contrary—the human good exists in every society, in every period of history. It is the concrete set of goods that actually exist in any time and place as a result of human intelligence and choice. So when we're talking about the human good, we're talking about something real, something that is already an aspect of the world we live in, a reality that we can identify if we pay attention to our own experience and the experience of people in other times and places.

It might be worth pausing here briefly just to underscore the concreteness of Lonergan's notion of the human good. Although sketched in theoretical terms, it arises out of experience (as does all good theory); and it's sufficiently penetrating that it can cast light on any specific human situation that one might care to name. It takes people where they are and as they are. Because it is rooted in experience and not the product of airy speculation, it takes note of the fact that the good that human beings produce is flexible: this good develops as human beings and their communities develop, even though certain of its elements are constant. In short, it's a theory that carries a very practical payload.

The next thing to be said about the human good is that it has three aspects.[2] This is an extremely important point and one which, to my knowledge, is unique to Lonergan's analysis. Without an understanding of what these three aspects are and how they are interrelated, our effort to grasp the full reality of the good that humans produce will be partially frustrated.

The three kinds of good that together constitute the human good are interrelated. For the sake of having an image to work with, they can be thought of as occupying three different levels. On the bottom level are particular goods, the kind of goods we are most familiar with. To the extent that any thing or activity meets a human want or need on a particular occasion, that thing or activity is a particular good. Examples could be listed *ad infinitem*: the lunch you just ate, the clean clothes you put on this morning, the conversation you recently had with a family member, listening to a lecture, getting a base hit, hearing a song on the radio, the gas in your car, scratching an itch, reading a psalm, taking a nap, attending a family reunion, having an umbrella in the rain—these are all instances of what Lonergan means by the term "particular goods." This conference is a particular good, and so is the fact that each of us is here.

The next level of the human good, the level above the level of particular goods, is the structural good.[3] The structural good refers to the way a whole social order is set up or organized. In every society, people participate in groups, organizations, and structures whose function is not just to produce a particular good for a particular person on a particular occasion, but rather to ensure ongoing patterns of cooperation so that particular goods of some kind get produced over and over, meeting the needs of many people over time. These patterns are all part of the structural good. A business is a pattern of cooperation functioning within the structural good: Ford Motor, for example, is a complex organization designed to produce motor vehicles to meet the particular transportation needs of a host of people (including other businesses) this year and next year and the year after that. The economy as a whole is an aspect of the structural good on a far vaster scale. Families are a part of the structural good and, Lonergan would argue, one of the most important[4]: they provide a framework of love and support for family members from one generation to the next. The various elements that govern traffic flow—signals, laws, the arrangement of streets, the customary adjustments that drivers make to each others' moves—together function as an element of the structural good.[5] Schools, judicial systems, clubs, parishes and congregations, political parties, air traffic control systems, farms, block-watch groups, labor unions, alumni associations, hospitals, day-care centers, religious orders, libraries, Little League teams—these are all aspects of the structural good. They are all structural in the sense that they represent more-or-less stable patterns of cooperation that produce streams of particular goods for groups of people on a continuing basis. Moreover, this patterned cooperation is the product of human intelligence and human choice; however imperfect, it is the way that a particular society or community is actually dealing with the difficulties and opportunities facing it at any given time.

Of course, the more complex this patterned cooperation, the more numerous the roles that have to be played and the more specific the skills needed by those who play them. Hence the structural good involves not just organizing people but educating them, helping them to develop the talents and virtues and sensibilities that will allow them to make the best use of their intelligence and freedom in responsible service to the community. Clearly, the structural good cannot develop without a corresponding development of the persons who take part in it. Hence the process of equipping people to participate effectively in the structural good—a process that has both formal and informal components and that necessarily differs from person to person—is itself a crucial aspect of the structural good.

So far I have talked about two aspects of the human good: particular goods and the structural good. Why is it so important to distinguish them from one another? Because most of the particular goods that are a part of our lives are in fact the product of a vast web of interconnected patterns of cooperation. A salad at dinner is a particular good. But the way we generally procure salads is by buying the ingredients at a grocery store: a fairly simple transaction from the standpoint of the shopper, but it implicates a host of people and routines: all the employees of the store in their interrelated functions; the corporation that owns the store; the suppliers of the products sold by the store, the bank that handles its money, the outfits that maintain its cooling and heating equipment; and government is involved at every point through various laws, regulations, and policies regarding food quality, taxation, employment, transportation, interstate commerce, pesticide use, land and water management, and so on. I don't mean to belabor this issue. They point is this: particular goods that meet particular needs usually are the product of a set of interlocking routines and institutions that are part of the structural good. Consequently, if we approve of some particular good, then we also at least implicitly approve of the structural good that produces it. By the same token, to call for change on the level of the particular good—say, an increase in certain particular goods for all, or a shift in the distribution of certain goods—requires that we also take responsibility for devising and bringing into being the new elements of the structural good that would produce the desired results in a stable, ongoing fashion. Obviously, then, to exercise responsibility for the human good in an effective way demands not only commitment but also a high degree of intelligence: on the level of the structural good, figuring out what to do and how to do it can be a problem of daunting proportions, since a change in one part of the structure is apt to reverberate throughout the whole.

As an example, you might think about the changes the structural good underwent in the United States during the Second World War. Because there was an urgent need to produce a great number of certain kinds of specific goods—tanks, ships, planes, ammunition, uniforms, and so on—a massive shift had to occur in patterns of cooperation across the board. Resources were diverted to building factories to produce the needed goods in sufficient quantities. Existing factories and businesses were reconfigured to meet the new demands. Materials that once might have been thrown away were collected and recycled; scarce commodities were rationed. Women went to work in great numbers, a change that had not just economic but also social consequences. The point is simply this: particular goods and structural goods mutually imply one another; a significant change in one normally goes hand-in-hand with a significant change in the other.

There's a third level of the human good that needs to be addressed if we want to avoid leaving out an important part of the picture. For this level Lonergan uses the term "value," which refers to a particular or structural good that is truly good, rather than just apparently good.[6] (Note that this definition differs from the usual meaning of the term, which is more abstract.) Particular goods, and the structural good that generates them, meet human needs and wants of various kinds. But not all needs and wants are equally choiceworthy; nor are all structural goods. In other words, some goods are better than others, some goods have greater value than others. We are confronted with this fact whenever we have to choose between competing particular goods: Should I exercise or eat? Should I mow the lawn or spend some time with the kids? It shows up even more starkly when a choice has to be made on the level of the structural good: Should I keep my current job or look for another? Should I vote for the candidate who promises to lower my taxes? Should I send my children to private school or public? Our national debates about welfare reform, education, abortion law, immigration policy, and all the rest are debates about the relative value of different possible arrangements of the structural good. The collapse of communism in the former Soviet Union and the Soviet bloc was the result of a collective judgment that that system of government and economic organization was less valuable, less choiceworthy, than an alternate system, namely, some form of democratic capitalism.

Values, of course, are a very touchy subject. The question about what is truly valuable and who is qualified to say so is a burning issue of our era. And, as you know, there's a pronounced tendency on the part of many people in our culture to presume that the question about values can't be settled objectively. For it seems that what anyone considers valuable is simply a matter of his or her perspective, and perspectives ultimately cannot be fully shared: we are each condemned, finally, to see things not as they are but only as they appear to us from our own personal, unique, and essentially private point of view.

But the notion of the common good that I'm describing for you this afternoon is predicated on an entirely different understanding of value.

Lonergan maintains that there is an intelligible scale of values, that is, a ranking of values that reflects the true goodness of things in relation to one another. Our time this afternoon doesn't permit me to discuss this in detail, but let me outline the basic elements of the scale. Lowest on the scale are vital values, goods associated with the needs and desires of the body. Above them are social values, which comprise the particular goods and structural good of technology, the economy, and the political order. Higher yet are cultural values, which are the norms, symbols, stories, and traditions that give meaning to the goods of the social order. Still higher than these are personal values, by which Lonergan means not the values held by a person but rather persons themselves, individually and communally, especially insofar as they are dedicated to living intelligently and responsibly. At the pinnacle are religious values, which are constituted by religiously converted persons engaged in communal service of the Kingdom of God.[7] This scale, the integral scale of values, isn't arbitrary: it reflects the God-given makeup of the human person, whose needs and desires are structured in this same way.

The upshot of this analysis (about which a lot more could be said) is that particular and structural goods are choiceworthy to the extent that they reflect this authentic scale of value, in which lower values are subordinated to higher. By the same token, goods are not choiceworthy to the extent that they reflect a distorted scale of values, a scale in which the relation between lower and higher values gets partially or wholly reversed. Think, for example, of the countless instances in our lives as individuals and as a society in which vital values have trumped all other concerns.

What I've tried to do so far, then, is to sketch the three basic aspects or levels of the human good. The good that is produced via human intelligence and choice not only meets human wants and needs; it also involves patterns of cooperation that ensure that many people will have various wants and needs met on a regular and continuing basis; and the particular goods and structural good that are actually operative at any time and place reflect a greater or lesser degree of value, of true goodness. The point is, in order to speak accurately about the human good, in order to do justice to it in its full concreteness, we have to take account of all three aspects. Furthermore, these are not arbitrary or a priori categories that Lonergan is forcing onto our experience of reality. Though we may not ever have heard or used the terms before, though we may never have explicitly put this analysis to use, all of us in our daily living actually do have to think and make decisions about particular goods, the structural good, and values. It's unavoidable—it's the way humans actually happen to operate.

I said earlier that my reason for speaking about Lonergan's notion of the human good was to shed some light on what the common good is. The connection is fairly straightforward. A community achieves its common good to the extent that its structural good and the particular goods that flow from it reflect the integral scale of values. The common good, in other words, is the human good as properly oriented to values. Like the human good, the common good is concrete; it is not some far-off, abstract ideal; it is not a state of super-perfection, but a reality that exists on a sort of sliding scale: it occurs precisely to the extent that a given community succeeds in establishing a way of life that is truly good for its members.

Up to this point I've been speaking about the human good, and now the common good, as if it were a static reality. But the title of this essay said something about development. So now I need to say something about the way the human good, the common good, develops. How does any community move forward from its present state, whatever it may be, to an ever fuller realization of the common good?

Here again Lonergan provides what I consider a helpful way of thinking about the problem. Throughout his career he was intensely concerned with identifying the forces that make for social progress and social decline. Some of his writings from the 1930s, when he was still a graduate student, reveal an almost anguished awareness of the social ills of that time, especially the economic catastrophe of the Great Depression and the precarious condition of Western democracy as it found itself confronting Stalinism in the Soviet Union and the rising threat of fascism in Western Europe. He came to the conclusion that the history of the human good, the concrete playing-out of the human situation, could be described in terms of the interaction of three trajectories or vectors: progress, decline, and redemption.[8]

First of all, progress. The human good of a society can change for the better over time. Such change generally begins with someone having a bright idea, an insight into how the present situation might be improved upon. If the idea is worked into a practical plan of action, if it attracts sufficient support, if it is effectively implemented, then it leads to a changed situation. If the idea is comprehensive and powerful enough, it can make its effects felt throughout the whole structural good of a society. The insight that sets this process in motion may be technological: think of the sweeping transformations made possible by the advent of railroads, the automobile, electronics. These inventions led to profound changes not only in the economy but also in the social and cultural order generally. The insight may be primarily political in nature—the Declaration of Independence and the Constitution express the ideas that gave birth to a new nation and a new system of government. It may be primarily religious—think of the influence of Christianity over the past two millennia.

The point is that any significant progress in the human good requires a significant change in the structural good, in the overall setup (and I'm presuming here that the change is in harmony with the authentic scale of values). Furthermore, every instance of progress constitutes a new situation that, in turn, is open to the occurrence of further insights that can extend the development and correct its imperfections. A society that could sustain this self-correcting process indefinitely would experience continual progress in its enjoyment of the common good.

Now Lonergan emphasizes that this kind of progress occurs only insofar as people in a society are authentic. To be authentic, to operate authentically as a human being, means something very specific to Lonergan.[9] First of all, it means being the kind of person who notices what's going on, who asks questions, who wonders whether things could be done in a better way. This is what Lonergan calls "being attentive." It means being the kind of person who pursues the question about improving some concrete situation by creatively envisioning possible alternative ways of doing things. This is "being intelligent." It also means being the kind of person who strives to evaluate these different possibilities objectively, who resists the temptation to leap to conclusions and instead bases his or her view of what actually can be done on the available evidence. This is "being reasonable." And finally, being authentic also means having the willingness to devote oneself to the good, to make decisions and take steps that augment the presence of real value in the world. This is "being responsible." Each of us is authentic in the measure that we are attentive, intelligent, reasonable, and responsible. Anyone who lives this way is cooperating with the dynamism of their nature; they are living as God intended human beings to live. And many people do in fact succeed in living this way to one degree or another.

But to require authentic human living of a whole society over a long period of time is a tall order; and so seamless social progress is a rare phenomenon. In the world as we know it, progress is halting, fragmentary, and liable to suffer reversal. We are continually faced with the discouraging contrast between "the idealism of human aspiration and the sorry facts of human performance."[10] Human affairs are marked not just by progress but by decline.

Lonergan maintains that social decline is due to human unauthenticity, to the lack of sufficient attentiveness, intelligence, reasonableness, and responsibility among the members of a given society. Problems that exist or are in the making get overlooked. There is a dearth of the creativity needed to conceive the new possibilities that lie waiting to be brought forth from the present situation. Popular views of the current situation and what should be done about it are based not on thoughtful judgments but on ill-considered opinions or personal whims. Decisions about social policy are made not because they reflect what is truly good for society as a whole but because they satisfy the desires of the most powerful group.

Lonergan points out that unauthenticity thwarts progress not only because groups and individuals make choices according to a distorted set of values, but also—and just as important—because it represents a breakdown in the functioning of human intelligence. A self-centered person may be extremely insightful about what he or she wants and very clever at working out ways to get it. But unlike the authentic person, who keeps asking and answering questions in pursuit of what is truly good, the egoist cuts off further questioning as soon as his or her own needs are taken care of. The same holds for any group that insists on pursuing what it considers to be its interests in a way that undermines the ability of other groups to pursue their own legitimate interests. The only knowledge that is considered worth acquiring is knowledge that's somehow relevant to the pursuit of the group's narrowly construed advantage. Questions that might challenge the group's biased view of the world are treated as superfluous; programs for change that address the needs of the whole community are dismissed as impractical. The point here is that the unauthenticity of individuals and groups blocks the free functioning of human intelligence; and when human intelligence is frustrated in this way, the creativity needed to work out new approaches to the common good never gets released.

It's easy enough to see why this truncated approach to living produces social decline. When groups seek only their own advantage, they resist social policies that might affect them adversely. The creative energy that might have been put to use in service of the common good gets spent in designing strategies to maintain the group's edge in relation to its competitors. Cooperation is replaced by mutual distrust and a struggle for power. The structural good increasingly reflects the desires of the most powerful groups. Bright ideas about how to achieve real progress languish unless they manage to attract the attention of the wealthy and the powerful. The entire social order becomes distorted; it lacks coherence, because it's largely an accidental accumulation of fragmentary ideas, the result of a series of compromises. In such a situation, doing the intelligent thing becomes increasingly difficult because there is so little support for it. Reasonable argument loses its ability to persuade; and to the extent that people prefer the distorted order to the common good, they subscribe to the ideologies and rationalizations that clothe the present setup with a false air of respectability. Examples of this phenomenon in our own century are all too familiar.

I've been trying to discuss the way in which the human good or the common good develops. What I've said thus far can be summed up very briefly: authenticity in persons and communities leads to progress; unauthenticity leads to decline. Now it goes without saying that there are no pure cases of either progress or decline. It may be that, at certain points in its history, a particular society is primarily in one mode or the other. But it's important to recognize that elements of progress and decline are present in every human social situation. They are in tension with one another, and each exerts its characteristic influence on the human good. This means that anyone who accepts responsibility for promoting the common good always has to take account of the fact that making progress involves undoing the effects of decline. And since decline is the result of unauthenticity, the common good can emerge only to the extent that the members of a society rid themselves of their habits of inattentiveness, unintelligence, unreasonableness, and irresponsibility. But what would make such a change possible? How can biased minds reach good judgments and disordered desires attain rightly ordered goods?

Lonergan's answer is that, in the end, there is only one effective remedy for human unauthenticity: conversion. By conversion he means especially the change that occurs in a person who experiences the gift of falling in love with God, or, in more traditional terms, the gift of grace or of the Spirit.[11] It is God speaking an inner word, an inward communication of God's own life. Lonergan describes this gift in the following terms:

> Being in love with God, as experienced, is being in love in an unrestricted fashion. All love is self-surrender, but being in love with

> God is being in love without limits or qualifications or conditions or reservations. Just as unrestricted questioning is our capacity for self-transcendence, so being in love in an unrestricted fashion is the proper fulfilment of that capacity.
>
> That fulfilment is not the product of our knowledge and choice. On the contrary, it dismantles and abolishes the horizon in which our knowing and choosing went on and it sets up a new horizon in which the love of God will transvalue our values and the eyes of that love will transform our knowing.[12]

Religious conversion involves a radical shift in a person's total orientation. It displaces selfish concern with a love for God that spills over into a love for the universe that God has created, a love that seeks good of other persons and groups, a love that is willing to accept suffering for the sake of undoing the effects of evil and accomplishing the good. It makes the search for truth an extension of the desire to learn as much as possible about the person one has fallen in love with. Conversion restores the human person to a state of authenticity.

Besides speaking to us inwardly through the Spirit, God also has spoken through the outer word of the Son. The Christian church is the human community that has been formed in response to this twofold self-communication of God.[13] By its witness, its fellowship, and its service to the world, the church participates in the redemptive process by which God is overcoming unauthenticity and its corrosive influence on human living. Together with all people who have experienced God's love, the church has the responsibility of promoting progress and undoing decline. It performs this function especially by inviting people to hear the message of Jesus, to listen carefully for the inner word of the Spirit, and to give themselves over to the transforming power of God. Though the church takes various positions on how the structural good of a society ought to be changed or maintained, though it establishes structures for dealing with particular social ills, the most fundamental way in which it promotes the common good is by facilitating the occurrence of conversion and working to ensure that the effects of conversion, once it occurs, continue to radiate and deepen in people's lives. Everything follows from God's replacing the heart of stone with a heart of flesh.

The third vector or trajectory affecting the human good, then, is redemption, the healing presence of God in human minds and hearts. Like progress and decline, it is not a pure state; rather, in every human situation one can expect to find an interplay of progress, decline, and redemption. The concrete shape of things is the resultant of those three forces. Progress is present to the extent that intelligent and responsible choices are being put into effect in the social order; decline is present to the extent that intelligent and responsible choices are blocked by bias and sin; and redemption is present to the extent that grace is overcoming decline and reestablishing the possibility of progress on a new and more secure foundation. Unless we think about the common good in this context, we are not dealing with the world that really exists.

I want to say just a few things about what this analysis might mean for understanding the link between business and the common good. In the first place, businesses constitute part of the structural good of a society. The function of an individual business is to produce needed goods on an ongoing basis, and to produce new goods to meet new needs as they arise. The function of businesses taken together within an economy is to produce a standard of living that meets certain needs of the population on an ongoing basis. Lonergan's notion of the common good implies that the answer to the question "What is business for?" has to take account of this broader social context.

Second, business contributes to social progress in the measure that it operates attentively, intelligently, reasonably, and responsibly. By its very nature, business is an essential and positive good within the social order. But in the measure that it fails to operate according to those standards, it acts (sometimes unwittingly) as a force for social decline. When this occurs, business is being less than what business ought to be.

Third, businesses will operate authentically only to the extent that the people in them live authentically. Hence, the extent to which a business succeeds in contributing to the common good will in large measure be determined by the kind of people who work there, especially those with responsibility for running the company.

Fourth and finally, a good deal of recent writing on the subject of faith and work speaks of work as co-creation: work is religiously meaningful because through it we participate in God's work of creating the world. This is a fruitful avenue for reflection. But it may not go far enough in making us think about the role of business in assisting the emergence and development of the common good. Creation and co-creation, it seems to me, have to do with the elements of the human good that we considered under the heading of progress: God created the world and saw that it was good. But besides creation there was the fall; and in response to human sin the Son and Spirit made the infinite love of God an effective healing force in human history. This means that we can't fully understand business from the perspective of faith until we can explain how business contributes to God's redemptive work in the world. Concretely speaking, where is grace operative in business, and how does the influence of grace make it possible for business to engage in the process of undoing decline? I end with this question not because I have an answer, but because it indicates the scope of the work that still needs to be done if we are to have an adequate Catholic understanding of the role of business in the world God is creating and redeeming.

Notes

1. Bernard J. F. Lonergan, "Topics in Education: The Cincinnati Lectures of 1959 on the Philosophy of Education," *Collected Works of Bernard Lonergan* (hereafter *CWBL*), vol. 10, ed. Robert M. Doran and Frederick E. Crowe (Toronto: University of Toronto Press, 1993), 32.

2. "Topics in Education," pp. 33-43; Lonergan, *Method in Theology*, 2d ed. (Toronto: University of Toronto Press, 1971), 47-52. Cf. *Insight: A Study in Human Understanding*, 5th ed., *CWBL* vol. 3 (Toronto: University of Toronto Press, 1992), 237-39, 619-21.

3. Lonergan calls this "the good of order." Although the term is appropriate enough, the word "order" can have connotations, at least for some people, of rigidity, authoritarianism, the suppression of diversity, and so on. Since those connotations have nothing to do with what Lonergan's trying to express, I refer instead to "the structural good."

4. Lonergan says that the family is "[t]he most efficacious example of the good of order," and goes on to add that "It is in their personal relations with one another that the members of a family concretely perceive their good of order. Through personal relations there is a concrete, immediate apprehension of what the good of order concretely is. It is useful to have a theoretical structure, to be able to speak of the good of order generally, but the simplest and most effective apprehension of the good of order is in the apprehension of personal relations" ("Topics in Education," 41).

5. For an illuminating exploration of this example, see Kenneth R. Melchin, "Moral Knowledge and the Structure of Cooperative Living," *Theological Studies* 52 (1991): 495-523.

6. On the notion of value, see *Method in Theology*, 12, 30-41.

7. It is often the case that a given instance of the good reflects more than one kind of value. A Thanksgiving dinner, for example, could be an instance of all five of the categories on the scale of value: a meal (vital); a family event (social); an event that links the family members to a formative American story

(cultural); an event that provides an opportunity for the family members to reevaluate their understanding of themselves, of each other, of their role as American citizens, and to recommit themselves accordingly (personal); an event that provides an opportunity for expressing gratitude to God for the gifts of family and country (religious).

8. *Insight*, chs. 7, 20; "Topics in Education," 49-70; *Method in Theology*, 52-55, 115-18; "Healing and Creating in History," *A Third Collection: Papers by Bernard J. F. Lonergan, S.J.*, (New York: Paulist Press, 1985), 100-109.

9. See the references to "Authenticity" in the index of *Method in Theology*.

10. "Finality, Love, Marriage," *Collection*, *CWBL* vol. 4 (Toronto: University of Toronto Press, 1988), 26.

11. *Method in Theology*, 105-7.

12. Ibid., 105-6.

13. Ibid., 361.

Papal Teaching on Economic Justice: Change and Continuity

JOHN T. PAWLIKOWSKI

Introduction

In my studies on official modern Catholic teaching on economic justice, particularly the research I undertook in connection with the publication of the United States Catholic Conference (USCC) volume *Justice in the Marketplace*[1] that appeared as a companion piece to the Bishop's *Pastoral Letter on the Economy*, I have been increasingly struck by the basic consistency in outlook that runs through the social encyclicals from Leo XIII to John Paul II. While there certainly have been marked shifts in certain areas of papal teaching (e.g. the papacy of John XXIII clearly represented a transition to a far more egalitarian social vision), five themes have remained central from Leo XIII to John Paul II. They are: (1) no absolute rejection of private property; (2) no support of class struggle; (3) no formal endorsement of capitalism; (4) a preferential option for the rights of workers; and (5) firm support of unionization.

I will examine the major areas of change and consistency in papal teaching on economic justice, focusing especially on the five areas highlighted above. In the final section of this essay I will discuss the controversy, still continuing, over the proper interpretation of *Centesimus annus*. Does this encyclical represent a decided shift toward capitalism in the way Michael Novak and others have claimed? Or is it fundamentally in continuity with previous papal thought?

The Legacy of *Rerum novarum*

The publication of the first papal social encyclical *Rerum novarum* was in many respects a startling event when one considers the previous history of Catholicism and the personal background of Pope Leo XIII. No real precedent existed in the church for such a declaration. Catholic social thought was still largely grounded in a medieval view of society in which there existed little basis for human rights claims, including economic ones.[2] And Leo XIII himself was generally in league with the more conservative, aristocratic forces in Catholicism that were trying everything imaginable to fend off the assault upon their economic hegemony by the newly aroused and organized working classes.

The path that led to the development of *Rerum novarum* was rather complicated. It began with a prophetic address to the upper classes of Paris in 1868 by the future Cardinal Mermillod. In his speech he tried to convey to the ruling elite something of the awful conditions faced by the majority of laborers whom he described as abandoned and exploited. He coupled this with a warning that the newly established workers' movement would escalate into a raging torrent that might engulf all the structures of the established order unless the Catholic church could find ways of responding to their outrage. Other Catholic leaders, including Frederic Ozanam and Augustin Cochin, stepped forth with the same dire message. But their warnings generally went unheeded among the Catholic elite. A few individuals, however, did respond. They began to associate in new groups that eventually laid the foundations for *Rerum novarum*. It is to their efforts that we now briefly turn.

In France the traumatic social events of 1870-1871 led to the formation of a group known as the "Committee for the Formation of Catholic Workers' Clubs in Paris" ("L'Oeuvre des Cercles"). While still exhibiting an evident paternalism in dealing with workers' concerns, they nonetheless managed to begin a certain breakdown in the rigid class barriers that infected French society by incorporating people from all spheres of life in their social discussions.

Another important group emerged in Rome with the personal support of Leo XIII. Cardinal Mermillod, a central member of this papal consultation, was able to bring to it the experience of the already existing workers' clubs in France. Beginning in 1881 this group of papal consultors turned their attention to the application of central themes in Thomistic thought to the new social realities in Western Europe.

Several of the leading members of this original papal consultation, including Mermillod and Count Franz Kuefstein of Austria, went on to become key members of a group known as the Fribourg Union that appeared on the scene a few years later in 1884. The work of this group eventually proved decisive in establishing a viable framework within the classical Catholic tradition for addressing the plight of the working class.

The Fribourg Union was largely comprised of lay members representing virtually every part of Europe. Cardinal Mermillod assumed a kind of spiritual leadership of the Union that met once a year between 1885 and 1891. Though the members exhibited a common commitment to social ideals, their political outlook varied greatly. Some remained entrenched in the aristocratic mind-set while others had become committed partisans of newly emergent democratic trends. All were staunchly committed to Catholic teaching and papal authority. At the outset they set as their goal the study of work, property, and society in the context of Thomistic thought as well as the establishment of international legislation that would reflect their scholarly research and discussions.

In the seven years of its existence, the Fribourg Union continued to focus on several central issues. The first of these was the just wage and the role of state intervention in ensuring it. The union's position was that work must be regarded as more than a commodity. It represented a personal act of the worker. If undertaken faithfully, work entitles a person to a salary sufficient to provide adequate subsistence for the worker and his family. This salary would be the fruit of contractual negotiations between employers and employed—there was no universal criterion for a just wage. Because negotiations were involved, workers had the right to organize themselves so that their representatives could truly speak in their name. The Union generally took a reserved stance towards direct state intervention to secure a just wage, approving it only in those cases where an employer resisted any form of negotiation with the workers. On this point, the Union situated itself midway between the liberals who opposed intervention under any circumstances and the socialists who championed it. For the Union subsidiarity was to be maintained if at all possible. *Rerum novarum*'s stance on this question closely parallels that of the Union.

The Fribourg Union also steered a middle course when it came to private property. The basic right was strongly affirmed, especially for rural areas. This represented a direct challenge to the collectivization schemes being proposed by the socialists. But having established private property as a basic human right, the Union qualified it a bit by emphasizing as well each person's right to subsistence, which was eventually termed a "primordial" right. It is clear when one examines the Union papers that its members remained uncomfortable with the way in which the liberals had elevated private property to the pinnacle of the human rights ladder. In the end the Union remained somewhat ambivalent in this area, something that is true as well for *Rerum novarum*.

Throughout the course of its deliberations the Union directed its attention to a general discussion of capitalism as an overall socio-economic system. In some of its conversations the Union clearly leaned toward a basically negative view of capitalism, seeing it as inseparably entwined with egotism and usury. In general, the Union shared the general European Catholic view of capitalism as integrally linked with secular liberalism and Protestantism.

The principal focus of the Union was the creation of a viable alternative both to capitalism and socialism. The economic model it eventually devised, known as the *regime corporatif*, was described by the Union as rooted in natural human groups that correspond to natural interests and common social functions. This model was to find its way into the first two papal social encyclicals. Both the Union and the popes involved fervently hoped that this new social model, rooted in medieval visions of a just and tranquil social order, would prevail and help overcome the chaos then rampant in Europe, a social situation they attributed to the combined influence of rationalism, capitalism, and above all Protestantism, which in their minds had generated a major decline in political authority and the rapid spread of individualism.

Ultimately the Fribourg Union must be said to have chosen the road of social reform rather than social revolution. The appeal of their work to Leo XIII[3] and his aristocratically inclined advisors lay in the fact that the social reform the Union proposed was tied to a social model firmly grounded in the Scholastic tradition. As Normand Paulhaus has correctly stated, the Union's purpose in proposing the establishment of a corporative system "was simply to reform the contemporary socio-economic order and rid it of its worst defects. The medieval spirit, not its institutions, served as the 'old wine' that they tried to pour into 'new wineskins.'"[4]

Quadragesimo anno: Reaffirmation and New Perspectives

Forty years after the publication of *Rerum novarum* Pius XI released the second major social encyclical. It picked up on many of the themes originally set forth in *Rerum novarum*: the dignity of labor; the rights of workers to organize and even to participate in some measure in ownership, management, and profit; the belief that Communist and even more "moderate" socialist economic theories inherently contradict basic Christian moral principles.

Quadragesimo anno also added some new dimensions to Catholic social teaching. Economic concentration had become far more pronounced in the 1930s than it was in the time of Leo XIII. So Pius XI gave this matter special attention. In a number of addresses prior to the encyclical itself[5] he denounced those who had accumulated invested funds and were using them solely for the sake of personal dominance. The Pope insisted that such activities were destroying the free marketplace and rendering the economic system harsh and cruel. To counter this trend, *Quadragesimo anno* gave special emphasis to a theme that would become central to Catholic social teaching in subsequent years, namely, *subsidiarity*. Though this theme has roots in *Rerum novarum*, it received its classic formulation from Pius XI:

> Just as it is wrong to take away from individuals what by their own ability and effort they can accomplish and commit to the community, so it is an injury and at the same time both a serious evil and a perturbation of the right order to assign to a larger and higher society what can be performed successfully by smaller and lower communities. This is a fixed and unchangeable principle most basic in social philosophy, immovable and unalterable. The reason is that all social activity, of its very power and nature should supply help to the members of the social body, but may never destroy or absorb them.[6]

Commenting on this principle, David Hollenbach insists that it justifies government intervention primarily to undergird persons and smaller communities. But in pursuing such intervention, says Hollenbach, governments must take cognizance of the fact that the family, the neighborhood, religious institutions, and professional and labor groups have an internal dynamic that ought to be respected.[7]

Seen in historical perspective, the principle of subsidiarity appears as a response both to the growing economic concentration in Western capitalist countries that so concerned Pius XI as well as to the challenge of state centralization advocated by various forms of socialism. In recent years the principle's attractiveness has begun to wane somewhat as it has become part of an ideological struggle within Catholicism regarding the social vision demanded by the roots of the Christian faith. The principle has tended to become the backbone of the conservative Catholic attack on the liberal welfare state and on any form of governmental intervention in the economy. This abandonment has elicited a sharp rebuke from Andrew Greeley[8] and John Coleman.[9]

One person who has attempted to reinvigorate the principle of subsidiarity by defusing it as an ideological issue is George Higgins. He has argued that it would be erroneous to assume, in the light of this principle, that voluntary associations always take precedence over state institutions or that "government is best which governs least." Rather, the principle simply demands a far more balanced outlook. On the one hand, state institutions must be required to respect the roles of individuals and voluntary associations in a given society. But equally, governments must be prepared to adopt those programs that are required by the common good and that "are beyond the competence of individual citizens or groups of citizens. The principle of subsidiarity is concerned with the relationship of the state to other societies, not with the nature of the state itself."[10]

The clarifications introduced by Msgr. Higgins are important in bringing some calm into the discussion about the principle of subsidiarity. But they have not solved all the difficulties with the continued use of the principle in my judgment. I remain convinced that the classical interpretation in fact leans somewhat more in the anti-governmental intervention direction than Higgins would admit. While I remain convinced of the principle's value, and even of its spiritual basis, I think it would be best today to cast its substance within the framework of the principle of participation that has become a cornerstone of recent Catholic social teaching. The past several popes, including John Paul II, have placed far greater emphasis on this principle than on subsidiarity itself. The notion of "participation" embodies the most important features of the original principle of subsidiarity while not lending itself quite as much to political manipulation by those forces opposed to any form of governmental intervention in the social sphere.

Pius XII: A New Vision Emerges

The years immediately following the appearance of *Quadragesimo anno*, marked as they were by the scourge of fascism and Nazism, left Catholic leadership little time for any comprehensive analysis of socio-economic issues. Pope Pius XII did deliver a series of radio addresses at Christmas that began to shape a vision of a new world social order that was later to serve as a basic starting point for Pope John XXIII.[11] The horrible realities of World War II had convinced Pius XII of the need for a total overhaul of the international social order.

We must appreciate the profound implication of this call for a new social order in these Christmas messages from the early forties, for there are Catholic social commentators today who have mistakenly claimed that Pius XII contributed little to the advance of the Catholic social vision in the twentieth century. This is simply not the case. While I have critiqued his view of ecclesiology, which contributed to his highly reserved public response to the victimization of Jews, Poles, and others by the Nazis,[12] in the Christmas messages Pius XII boldly withdrew any further Catholic support for efforts to preserve the old social barriers and aristocratic privileges in Europe. He was willing to make a move that the Fribourg Union, Leo XIII, and Pius XI all had resisted. A subtle revolutionary spirit emerges from these Christmas addresses. For Pius XII, nothing short of a fundamental reconstruction of the international economic order would bring about human dignity for all, a dignity that everyone has as a birthright and whose ultimate source is God.

Specific themes that appear in the Christmas sermons include: (1) the economically advantaged nations must assume major responsibility for creating a new economic order devoid of the disequilibrium of past systems; (2) the religious dimensions of human existence cannot be fully grasped apart from an understanding of the profound impact of economic realities on this existence; (3) no analysis of war can bypass an appreciation of its economic dimensions; and (4) subsidiarity ought to remain central in a reconstituted international economic system. Clearly here was the seedbed for many of the principal themes of the social encyclicals that have appeared in the fifty years since the end of World War II.

Building a New World Order: The Vision of John XXIII

The election of John XXIII opened up a whole new era in Catholic social teaching on economic matters. While the first two social encyclicals had basically tried to enhance the rights of the working classes in Europe within the prevailing social system, John XXIII took up the challenge put forth in Pius XII's Christmas sermons.

John XXIII's first social encyclical *Mater et magistra* (1961) begins with an important analysis of the role of private property in Catholic social thought. It speaks of the need for an increased awareness of the social dimensions of property in light of the growing interdependence of the world community. This new "multiplication of social relationships," this "daily more complex inter-dependence of citizens," has become a major feature of contemporary society that the Pope believes can no longer be ignored.[13]

John XXIII felt the need to refine the Catholic approach to private property in order to respond to changed international conditions. In *Mater et magistra* he focuses on "private initiative" more than on private property as such and places great emphasis on the responsibility incumbent upon public authorities to guarantee the effective output of necessary consumer goods and their availability to all citizens.[14] John XXIII appears to regard a government's "overseer" responsibility as highly as he does the principle of private property. And this "overseer" role has a certain permanency about it. It is not something government exercises only occasionally in situations of "last resort." Only in this way can human sustenance be assured on a worldwide basis.

Rerum novaram and *Quadragesimo anno* both placed some limitations on the use of private property. But observance of these limitations was essentially left to individual decision. In *Mater et magistra* a significant shift occurs. The basic decision-making now lies much more with state authorities. Fr. Joseph Gremillion has summarized developments under John XXIII in this way:

> . . . John clearly and definitely carries over the Church's inherited teaching on property into the *aggiornamento* era he is launching. But in so doing he arouses the Church to a reality more basic than the permanence of property: The Church of Vatican II is "inheriting" a society in process of radical transformation, compared with that of past generations, because of socialization, the multiplying complex of relationships, and interdependence among groups and nations . . . In Church teaching, the *common good* is not the glib phrase of a political

> campaign. It forms the bedrock of Catholic social doctrine, more fundamental than property, because its goal and measure is man and his perfection.[15]

Private property is not the only area where we see a marked turn toward an ongoing governmental role under John XXIII. Faced with a doctrinaire form of European socialism Leo XIII was extremely cautious about granting government any significant role in the conduct of economic affairs. Pius XI was a bit more relaxed in this regard, but still fundamentally reserved. For John XXIII economic problems had reached such global proportions that he could see no way out of the present morass without a substantial role for governments. While voluntary groups retained a vital role in their resolution, John XXIII urged a new partnership between such groups and the government and even argued that government was at times obliged to act on its own initiative if economic justice were to be realized.

With the papacy of John XXIII the focus of the Catholic church has shifted from the working classes of Europe and North America to the millions in the Third World living in conditions of intense economic oppression. John XXIII turned Catholic attention toward a restructuring of the economic system on a global level that would provide basic sustenance for the impoverished millions of the world. Nothing in John XXIII's writings suggests that he favored a wholesale abandonment of the prevailing capitalist system in this restructuring process. But he did call for a major overhaul of this system that went beyond the reformist impulses of Leo XIII and Pius XI.

John XXIII's writings clearly recognize the need to adjust economic programs to specific conditions prevailing in a given nation. The church cannot endorse one economic model for all social settings. John XXIII's papacy brought to an end the effort launched by the Fribourg Union and the first two papal social encyclicals to create a distinctively Catholic alternative to existing economic theories. This approach has been continued in the main by his successors, though John Paul II has restored some of the specific condemnations of socialism and capitalism found in the earlier documents.

The Papacy of Paul VI: The Vision Grows More Radical

In his declarations on socioeconomic questions Paul VI borrowed extensively from the writings of John XXIII. At times, however, he pushes a notion of his predecessor beyond prior limits. A case in point is his stance on economic pluralism. Paul VI clearly did not regard Catholicism as wedded to any specific social system rooted in natural law. Nor did he believe it was possible to speak of Catholic social doctrine as such, only of Catholic social teaching or the social teachings found in the scriptures. His letter *Octogesima adveniens*, issued for the eightieth anniversary of *Rerum novarum*, underscores this point:

> It is with all its dynamism that the social teaching of the Church accompanies men in their search. If it does not intervene to authenticate a given structure or to propose a ready-made model, it does not thereby limit itself to recalling general principles. It develops through reflection applied to the changing situations of this world, under the driving force of the Gospel as the source of renewal when its message is accepted in its totality and with all its demands.[16]

Another important feature of Paul VI's approach to economic justice was his emphasis on the centrality of political participation in the process. Economic inequalities were not merely the result of technical flaws in the economic system according to Paul VI. Rather they were the direct result of the lack of meaningful participation and power in the political system. Paul VI thus continued in the footsteps of John XXIII in the focus on *participation* as a vital dimension of the struggle for significant reforms in the international economic order.

There is little doubt that one of the most controversial aspects of Paul VI's teachings on economic justice in *Populorum progressio* and *Octogesima adveniens* had to do with his outlook on private property. He went considerably beyond his predecessors in speaking about legitimate restrictions on private property. In *Populorum progressio* he acknowledges the right of the state to expropriate certain property that is underused, poorly used, whose present use results in hardship for the people or whose use is detrimental for the overall well-being of the nation. He also regards as morally unacceptable the practice of the rich transferring their wealth outside their own country without any regard for the detrimental effect this may have on the national economy.[17]

Paul VI's "socialist" reputation was further enhanced in the eyes of some by his general hostility toward the renewal of liberal ideology in economic affairs in the name of economic efficiency. This was seen by many as the most trenchant critique of the capitalist system ever to appear in a papal document. While many Catholics, especially those in the financial world, took strong exception to what they considered a virtual endorsement of socialism, other Catholics, especially those in the developing countries, saw it as an endorsement for their personal involvement in anticapitalist movements.

The Pontificate of John Paul II: A Theology for Economic Activity

Pope John Paul II has issued three major encyclicals largely devoted to economic questions. They are *Laborem exercens*, *Sollicitudo rei socialis*, and *Centesimus annus*. In addition, his very first encyclical *Redemptor hominis*, though it did not directly focus on economic issues, did establish an overall theological framework that the Pope has employed in arguing his case for greater economic justice in the subsequent papal letters.

In *Redemptor hominis* John Paul argued for the Christological basis of human dignity. Concern for human dignity is a way of manifesting Christological reality in human society. This is an essential ingredient of the church's supernatural mission, not merely a "humanitarian" add-on. Picking up on this basic theme, John Paul posits an integral relationship between faith and economic life in *Laborem exercens* that Richard McCormick has described as an ongoing philosophical meditation on human work in its varied dimension.[18]

Three themes in particular emerge as central in this first of John Paul's economic encyclicals. The first is the centrality of work to the whole social question. Work is examined in two respects. The first is quite traditional—exploitative working conditions are immoral. This immorality stands out even more when one considers the dignity of every human person in the light of Incarnational Christology. Any economic system that reduces work to a mere instrument is to be condemned. This viewpoint also implies the priority of labor over capital. While the way of stating this relationship may be somewhat unique to John Paul II, it is consistent with the tradition that has prevailed since Leo XIII.

While the second major point made by John Paul is the more creative one—work is considered not only for its potential to dehumanize, but as the means whereby the human person assists in the sanctification of creation. Work becomes a vehicle for exercising human co-creatorship. Michael Novak has described this papal theology as "radical," for it argues that "it is in sharing in the creativity of the Creator that the human subject fulfills his vocation."[19]

Thirdly, *Laborem exercens* continues on the path set by John XXIII and Paul VI in emphasizing that a just wage does not exhaust the justice issue relative to workers. More is required. And while a significant part of this encyclical may indeed be termed a theological meditation, as McCormick has so termed it, John Paul does not shun the practical side of such a theology. On the contrary, he becomes quite specific, some would say reflecting the vision of the early Solidarity movement and its program for social reconstruction in Poland. He calls for new forms of profit-sharing, comanagement, and co-ownership of productive property as an inherent part of worker's rights. Companies have not satisfied their justice obligation to their employees merely by paying a just wage. Some appropriate form of worker participation in ownership and decision making is also required in the papal vision.

The theology of *Laborem exercens* has generated considerable controversy in Catholic circles. Michael Novak has interpreted the encyclical as a firm endorsement of some central themes in democratic capitalism. According to Novak, John Paul has so centered economic activity around the graced individual that any notion of legitimate class struggle or any exaggerated contrast between oppression and liberation are ruled out as valid components of an economic ethic. Rather, Novak insists, in *Laborem exercens* the Pope has made the presence or absence of creativity the critical question for such an ethic.[20] Novak likewise holds that John Paul's cocreational theology of work justifies viewing capital as the material embodiment of labor and favors private ownership over any form of nationalization or collectivization.

Higgins, who has also praised the encyclical, regards it as posing a far greater challenge to Western capitalism than people like Novak would admit. The Pope's strong reaffirmation of the union movement together with his call for a direct role for workers in the ownership of the means of production raise serious questions about classical capitalist positions. When John Paul speaks of workers as fully entitled to regard themselves as part owners of the great workbench at which they labor, he seems to be picking up on a theme that historically has been much closer to socialism than capitalism.

John Paul II's more recent social encyclicals *Sollicitudo rei socialis*[21] and *Centesimus annus*,[22] focus far more directly on particular socio-economic questions than the more theological reflections presented in *Laborem exercens*. All of John Paul's social encyclicals must also be placed in relation to the numerous talks the Pope has given during his extensive travels in which he has often spoken to specific conditions of economic justice. I make this point because certain commentators—such as Michael Novak on "human creativity"[23] and George Weigel[24] on "freedom"—tend to isolate a particular emphasis by the Pope in such a way that it ultimately distorts his overall position on socioeconomic justice. Without question John Paul II gives high priority both to human creativity and human freedom in any economic system. He knows quite well from his own experience under Communism how devastating their absence can be for human initiative and productivity. Nevertheless, to say that human creativity or human freedom stand by themselves as the cornerstone of John Paul's teaching on economic matters is to misread seriously his ultimate message.

Throughout his pontificate John Paul II has defended the principle of participation in economic life. Without it an economy ultimately not only stagnates, but also likely results in forms of economic concentration that leaves millions in, or near the edge of, poverty. The right of economic initiative is strongly affirmed in *Sollicitudo rei socialis*. And in *Centesimus annus* John Paul affirms free-market mechanisms more strongly and directly than any of his predecessors. But, though John Paul is certainly a "philosophical" pope, he is by no means merely interested in the intellectual triumph of one ideology over another. His primary focus is the impact of a particular system on the body politic. In this context neither of the two more recent social encyclicals, nor John Paul II's many regional addresses on economic questions, allow for the use of triumphal language relative to capitalism in the manner of Novak or Weigel.

John Paul II explicitly warns Western nations in *Centesimus annus* against any premature euphoria regarding their economic systems. While the market economy initiative lives on, major structural adaptations are required if it is ever to reach its true potential of sustaining a system of global justice. And the Pope is clear about his belief that these adjustments are not apt to occur merely as a result of the market's internal dynamics. There is a role for the state in such readjustment, though on this point he is definitely less specific than Paul VI. Indirectly we might argue that John Paul supports the notion of international debt cancellation for impoverished countries, a position advocated by the Pontifical Council for Justice and Peace.[25]

There is admittedly some ambiguity in *Centesimus annus* regarding capitalism. While the encyclical's affirmation of market mechanisms flows quite well from its stress on participation in economic life, the condemnation of the welfare state we find in paragraph #48 is a bit jarring. It seems to be an intrusion into the text. Fr. Bryan Hehir, with his typical reserve, merely terms it "puzzling."[26] He says, and I agree, that the duties presented as incumbent upon the state in other sections of this encyclical and in John Paul's other writings include many, if not most, of the activities covered by the label "welfare state." My guess is that this view represents the outlook of forces within the church not fully in accord with the principal architects of the encyclical.

The evidence for the centrality of restrained state intervention is so strong in the overall corpus of the present pope's writings that this one paragraph cannot undo the basic thrust of his thinking. *Centesimus annus*,[27] as well as the Pope's earlier address at Yankee Stadium in 1979,[28] are but two examples of this papacy's commitment to a fundamental reform of economic structures through governmental processes. John Paul II seems almost as concerned with the effect of economic concentration on personal initiative in the Western nations as he has been with regard to socialist states. His address on fishing problems in Newfoundland, picking up on themes from *Laborem exercens*, calls on fishermen to unite in cooperatives in a way that restores to them a sense of ownership of their trade.[29]

To say that John Paul II remains profoundly critical of the capitalist system is no exaggeration. His disappointments with it are similar to those voiced by his immediate predecessors in the papacy. His objections are not so much ideological, as they were with Leo XIIII and even with Pius XI, but based on concrete results of the system in operation. So the claims of Michael Novak that papal criticism of "capitalism" pertains to a form of capitalism other than that which we know in North America may hold true for the first two papal social encyclicals, but clearly does not apply to the recent ones, especially those issued by John Paul II.

For John Paul II the basic questions to be asked about capitalism (or any economic system) are what is its basic impact on people throughout the globe and increasingly, particularly in *Sollicitudo rei socialis* and *Centesimus annus*, how has it affected the realm of nature? This is the ultimate papal barometer. And by that standard of measurement capitalism continues to fail the test in large measure despite its acknowledged philosophical superiority. Speaking in Edmonton, Alberta, John Paul was as blunt as possible: "The poor peoples of the South—poor in different ways, not only lacking food but also deprived of freedom and human rights—will sit in judgment of those peoples of the North who take these goods away from them, amassing to themselves the imperialistic monopoly of economic and political supremacy."[30]

In an address on May 15, 1991, shortly after the release of *Centesimus annus*, the Pope told a group of international economic and political experts gathered in Rome to commemorate the one-hundredth anniversary of *Rerum novarum* that growing economic imbalances among the nations of the world brought on by large concentrations of wealth must be ended. He also cited the ravaging effects of pollution in the same speech. Coming as it did so soon after the release of the encyclical, this address may be seen as a Vatican counterbalance to those commentators who inaccurately interpret *Centesimus annus* as endorsing the triumph of capitalism.[31]

The same can be said as well for a major statement on the church's social teaching that John Paul II delivered on September 9, 1993, at the University of Latvia in Riga in which he offers his own explicit interpretation of how to read *Sollicitudo rei socialis* and *Centesimus annus* in terms of capitalism. The Pope emphasized that Catholic social doctrine cannot be viewed as "a surrogate for capitalism." While the church has consistently condemned "socialism," it has likewise "distanced itself from capitalistic ideology, holding it responsible for grave social injustices." John Paul underlined that, even after the collapse of communism, grave doubts have to be raised about the validity of capitalism. While he believes in the "market economy," such an economy acquires legitimacy only if it is circumscribed with a strong juridical framework that truly enables it to promote the freedom of all people. The Pope also stressed that Catholicism is not tied to any specific political or economic system, but primarily offers a social theology that evaluates all concrete systems in the light of human dignity, moral law, and the divine plan for the human community.[32]

Surely these two major statements by John Paul himself, following the publication of *Centesimus annus*, should undercut any legitimacy to the preemptive pro-capitalist "spin" placed on *Centesimus annus* by Richard John Neuhaus in the *Wall Street Journal* and picked up by other conservative commentators. Based on his own interpretations of *Centesimus annus*, John Paul is certainly no candidate for a ticker-tape parade down Wall Street in New York.

Increasingly John Paul II has also expressed reservation about capitalism's lack of ecological concern. This is clearly the case in the two most recent social encyclicals and it surfaced even more explicitly in his 1990 World Day of Peace message that focused on ecology. In that message the Pope said the following:

> It is manifestly unjust that a privileged few should continue to accumulate excess goods, squandering available resources, while masses of people are living in conditions of misery at the very lowest level of subsistence. Today the dramatic threat of ecological breakdown is teaching us the extent to which greed and selfishness—both individual and collective—are contrary to the order of creation, an order which is characterized by mutual interdependence.[33]

Two other themes have emerged in John Paul's writings of late. One is a growing concern about the relationship between militarization and the economy. Part of the Pope's strong objection to the Gulf War stemmed more from the continued negative impact of military spending on human development across the globe than from any direct application of just war criteria or from any concern for the church's strategic interests in the region. The importance given this theme in *Centesimus annus* is good evidence of this. The second theme is the developing focus in John Paul's writings on the dangerous effect of "capitalist-generated" culture on human consciousness. Cultural renewal is certainly necessary in the papal view if the capitalist system is ever to reach an acceptable moral standard internationally.

CONCLUSIONS

As we take a final look at the contour of papal teaching on economic justice for more than a century, we can say that it is definitely marked both by consistency and change. Some of the themes first proposed by the Fribourg Union and incorporated into *Rerum novarum* have remained constant with minor adaptations at best. The opposition to class struggle is a case in point.

In other areas definite shifts are visible. One is certainly with regard to a specific Catholic model for the economy. While the first two social encyclicals promoted one such model, subsequent papal writings have been rather adamant in rejecting the notion of a specifically Catholic model. John Paul II went to great lengths to make this point in *Sollicitudo rei socialis* and in his Riga address. There has also been a clear shift of focus from a dominant emphasis on the economic problems of Europe to a far more global perspective. Methodologically the basic argument of the social encyclicals has tended to move away from the earlier emphasis on natural law to a more central stress on human dignity.

Ambiguities surely remain in the official Catholic position. One major one concerns the role of the state. John Paul II, at least in *Centesimus annus*, seems to move back to generalities in this regard, unlike Paul VI who was somewhat more specific and hence more controversial. But since John Paul II retains the centrality of state intervention, more will have to be done to make it concrete if it is to be a useful principle.

Perhaps the most trenchant analysis of the social encyclicals with regard to ambiguities is to be found in Mary E. Hobgood's *Catholic Social Teaching and Economic Theory: Paradigms in Conflict*. She argues that there exists a continuing clash between a more radical socio-economic analysis (especially in Vatican II's *Gaudium et spes* and the encyclicals of Paul VI) and a more cautious (i.e., "liberal") analysis found in other encyclicals, which is on occasion interspersed with pieces of the more radical critique. She believes the church continues to sanction the idea of private wealth accumulation because of a mistaken judgment that it is necessary for the effective ordering of society and that those who hold such wealth are capable of being transformed (i.e., "converted") toward reformed distribution patterns and general benevolence. She likewise faults church leaders for holding the notion that the state can represent the common good and that those who enjoy economic privilege will voluntarily moderate it for the sake of the common good.[34]

In my estimation her critique is overdrawn despite some important points. John Paul, for example, has made it rather clear that he does not support an unrestrained form of liberal capitalism and his strong emphasis on the participation of all in economic decision making certainly reduces the dominant role of the state. In emphasizing the role of the state John Paul is looking for a way to counterbalance the power of private wealth. It may not always work, but it is as least one response to the issue of entrenched power. In supporting the "market economy" John Paul should not be interpreted as favoring capitalism as a whole. Hobgood offers no real alternative model to the market economy that few question today as a starting point for a just economy. The dispute is over controls and participation once that economy is set into motion. Perhaps the strongest point made by Hobgood concerns the issue of entrenched economic power. The encyclicals' persistent opposition to class struggle has failed to offer a clear-cut alternative for dealing with such economic power beyond personal conversion. But is that sufficient? I personally doubt it.

The papal social encyclicals clearly contain a mandate for worldwide Catholic support for, and participation in, a fundamental restructuring of the global economic system and the culture it has generated. There is little doubt the first two encyclicals had a major role in bringing about improved conditions for the working classes of Western Europe and North America. Whether the more recent ones can do the same for the global poor remains an open question. In part, success or failure will depend on how much the Vatican is willing to make these encyclicals a major criterion for ministerial leadership in the contemporary church. Thus far there is not too much evidence that such an all-encompassing commitment exists. But its basis has been firmly established and in certain places it is in fact being implemented.

Notes

1. David M. Byers, ed., *Justice in the Marketplace: Collected Statements of the Vatican and the United States Bishops on Economic Policy, 1891-1984* General Introduction and Document Introductions by John T. Pawlikowski, O.S.M., (Washington, D.C.: USCC Publications, 1985).

2. Cf. David O'Brien and Thomas Shannon, eds., *Renewing the Earth* (Garden City, N.Y.: Doubleday, 1977), 21-22.

3. The ideas of the Fribourg Union received papal approval in a January, 1888, meeting between Union leaders and Leo XIII.

4. Norman J. Paulhaus, "Social Catholicism and the Fribourg Union," *Selected Papers—1980* (The Society of Christian Ethics), 79.

5. Cf. *Acta apostolicae sedis*, 193, 185; 211.

6. As quoted by George Higgins, "Religion and National Economic Policy: A Catholic Perspective," in Eugene J. Fisher and Daniel F. Polish, eds., *Formation of Social Policy in the Catholic and Jewish Traditions* (Notre Dame, Ind.: University of Notre Dame Press, 1980), 85.

7. David Hollenbach, *Claims in Conflict: Retrieving and Renewing the Catholic Human Rights Tradition* (New York: Paulist Press, 1979), 157.

8. Andrew Greeley, "American Catholicism: 1909-1984," *America* 150 (June 23-30, 1984): 487-92.

9. John Coleman, *An American Strategic Theology* (New York: Paulist Press, 1982), 102.

10. George Higgins, "Religion and National Economic Policy," 92.

11. Cf. Vincent A. Yzermans, *The Major Addresses of Pope Pius XII*, Vol. 2. (St. Paul, Minn.: North Central Publishing Co., 1961).

12. John T. Pawlikowski, "The Vatican and the Holocaust: Unresolved Issues," in Marvin Perry and Frederick M. Schweitzer, eds., *Jewish-Christian Encounters Over the Centuries: Symbiosis, Prejudice, Holocaust, Dialogue* (New York: Peter Lang, 1994), 293-310.

13. Cf. Joseph Gremillion, ed., *The Gospel of Peace and Justice* (Maryknoll, N.Y.: Orbis, 1975), 155-56.

14. Ibid., 154.

15. Ibid., 33.

16. Ibid., 505.

17. Paragraph #24.

18. Richard McCormick, "Notes on Moral Theology, 1981," *Theological Studies* 43:1 (March 1981): 92-95.

19. Michael Novak, "Creation Theology—John Paul II and the American Experience," *This World* 3 (Fall 1982): 93-94.

20. Ibid., 86.

21. The text of *Sollicitudo rei socialis* can be found in *Origins* 17:38 (March 3, 1988): 641; 643-60.

22. The text of *Centesimus annus* may be found in *Origins* 21:1 (May 16, 1991): 3-24.

23. Michael Novak, "Creation Theology."

24. George Weigel, "The New, New Things. Pope John Paul II on Human Freedom," *American Purpose* 5:5 (May-June 1991): 33-40.

25. Cf. Pontifical Justice and Peace Commission, "An Ethical Approach to the International Debt Question," *Origins* 16:34 (Feb. 5, 1987): 601; 603-11.

26. J. Bryan Hehir, "Reordering the World: John Paul II's *Centesimus annus*," *Commonweal* CXVIII:12 (June 14, 1991): 394.

27. Paragraphs #15; #40.

28. Cf. David M. Byers, ed., *Justice in the Marketplace*, 348-52.

29. Ibid., 359-61.

30. Ibid. 355; also Gregory Baum, "The Anti-Cold War Encyclical," *The Ecumenist* 26:5 (July-August 1988): 65-74.

31. Cf. Catholic News Service. "Pope, criticizing Capitalism, laments widening rich-poor gap, ecological damage," *National Catholic Reporter* 27:31 (May 31, 1991): 8.

32. John Paul II, "What Church Social Teaching Is and Is Not," *Origins* 23:15 (Sept. 23, 1993): 257.

33. John Paul II, "Peace With All Creation," *Origins* 19:28 (Dec. 14, 1989): 465-68.

34. Mary E. Hobgood, *Catholic Social Teaching and Economic Theory: Paradigms in Conflict* (Philadelphia: Temple University Press, 1991), 236-37.

Catholic Social Thought on Property: An Urgent Need for Extension and Renewal

DANIEL RUSH FINN

> *The proposition that men are under moral obligation to give away the greater portion of their superfluous goods or income is, indeed, a "hard saying." Not improbably it will strike the majority of persons who read these pages as extreme and fantastic. No Catholic, however, who knows the traditional teaching of the Church on the right use of wealth . . . will be able to refute the proposition by reasoned arguments.*[1]
>
> John A. Ryan

Introduction

Monsignor John A. Ryan's judgment about the likely reaction of his readers is no doubt even truer today than it was seventy-five years ago. It is not simply the unchurched who are averse to the traditional view of the obligations of private property but a significant number of modern Catholics as well. Of course, a sizable portion of this problem arises from the near absence of adult catechesis in the contemporary Catholic church. The focus in this essay, however, will be on a particular intellectual obstacle to the acceptance of the traditional Catholic doctrine of property in the modern world, one tied to the modern notion of human personhood and creative labor. In particular, a challenge proposed by John Locke some three-hundred years ago remains to be addressed adequately in a contemporary doctrine of property.

There is, however, a preliminary problem in addressing the traditional doctrine of property at all: an unfortunate ignorance of most Catholics concerning the development of moral teaching. Many have casually assumed that because there have been "reversals" of church teaching, particularly concerning the Scholastic condemnation of usury, this whole tradition of economic morality somehow deserves to be ignored. Part of this problem can be attributed to the reluctance of the church's magisterium to admit and cogently explain the developments of moral doctrine that have in fact occurred. Just as importantly, however, the conceptual asymmetries between the analyses of usury and property have not been widely enough noted. Modern economic insight completely reverses the Thomistic logic of the condemnation of usury (so that a modern Aquinas would himself defend the taking of interest), but requires only revisions—yet to be fully accomplished—in the analysis of property.

In part, the eclipse of the traditional view of property is attributable to the need for a conceptual development of the two fundamental tenets underlying that view. These are the dignity of the human person and the creaturely status of the material world, or, as Ryan phrased it,

> [o]n the one hand, . . . man's intrinsic worth, his essential needs, and his final destiny; and on the other hand, . . . the fact that nature's bounty has been placed by God at the disposal of all his children indiscriminately.[2]

The traditional perspective must be extended to account more adequately for the outcome of productive processes where human creativity and hard work transform nature's bounty to produce forms of wealth—goods and services—that cannot in any simple way be said to have been "placed by God" in the creation of the earth.

The Development of Social Doctrine

The first difficulty facing a renewal of the traditional Christian view of property is the widespread misunderstanding of the historical development of moral teaching. This section will very briefly employ the example of usury to illustrate the development of social doctrine in an attempt to overcome the popular presumption that because the

Scholastic condemnation of usury has been abrogated, other teachings from that era—particularly those concerning property—are without weight today.

Thomas Aquinas begins his discussion of usury—the charging of an additional payment when money is lent and subsequently returned—with a distinction taken from Aristotle. Thomas argues that there are two kinds of goods in the world: those that are used up when they are used and those that are not.[3] Wine and wheat are his examples of the former. We consume wine when we use it and thus, he says, "the use of thing must not be reckoned apart from the thing itself." A house is the prime example for the second kind of good because it can be used without being consumed.

Looking at these two from a commercial point of view, Thomas observes that it would be wrong for someone to sell wine separately from the use of the wine because that would entail the sale of the same thing twice or "selling what does not exist." It simply makes no sense to charge someone for using the wine and then to expect a second charge if they also wanted to own it. This makes it immoral to sell the two separately; they are simply inseparable. Extending the argument to the issue of a loan, Thomas's argument is that upon loaning someone a bottle of wine for an evening dinner party, one should not expect to receive in return anything more than the bottle of wine itself. When the borrower returns that bottle of wine, or an equivalent bottle purchased in the meantime, it would be immoral for the lender to also charge an amount for the use of the wine. It makes no conceptual sense, he argues, and would be immoral. The extra charge would constitute selling something that doesn't exist, a form of fraud.[4]

On the other hand, one could reasonably sell a house but reserve the use of it for a time or, Thomas observes, the owner might grant to another the use of a house for a time while retaining ownership. Unlike the situation with the wine, it makes perfectly good sense to distinguish use of the house from a transfer of ownership of the house and thus the sale of one or the other but not both is perfectly justifiable. In traditional parlance, the house produces "usufruct" while the wine does not; in contemporary terms, the house is a productive asset (or a capital good) while the bottle of wine is a consumption good.

The connection to usury comes when Thomas observes that money is like wine and not like the house. In Thomas's terms, "money . . . was invented chiefly for the purpose of exchange, and, consequently, the proper and principle use of money is its consumption or alienation."

The purpose of this gold coin is using it up by giving it away in a commercial transaction in exchange for goods that I wish to buy. Just as it would be wrong to loan someone a bottle of wine and then upon the return of an equivalent bottle of wine, charge an extra amount for its use, so the loan of money ought not be accompanied by any extra charge when the money is returned.

We should note that Thomas's argument against the taking of interest on a loan is in no way dependent on a concern for the poor, even though this is an obvious motivation of the prohibition against usury in the Scriptures. In the Bible the focus is on the injustice done by wealthy lenders to the poor when the latter are forced by circumstance to borrow money in hard times. Thomas implicitly shifts concerns about poverty to the doctrine of property, to which we will turn presently. Instead he makes a more general conceptual argument about usury based on the classical view of the nature of money.

Odd Langholm, John Noonan, and a host of others have traced the developments in the Scholastic analysis of usury and we need not review that literature here.[5] To make this long story very short, we might say that the "reversal" of the church's teaching on the morality of usury comes not from a change in moral principle but from a change in the understanding of money. Simply put, modern people understand money to be more like the house than like the bottle of wine. Money is not simply a consumption good, in spite of the appearance of a gold coin in Thomas's day. Rather, money is now understood to be a claim upon assets and, like the house, it is perfectly intelligible to speak of the use of such a claim for a time without necessitating a consumption of those assets during that time.

Thus, what looks superficially as a contradiction of an earlier position is actually consistent with an affirmation of the earlier moral analysis, simply recognizing the change in the underlying cultural notion of money. A modern Thomistic analysis would no longer view usury as wrong in principle. This recognition that the development of a doctrine can occur in continuity, even amidst apparent discontinuity, is a critically important insight through all of moral theology and Christian theology generally. However, here we need only note the importance of such development when there are changes in the cultural understandings that form the foundation for Catholic social thought. An analogous shift in the foundation of the doctrine of property has occurred but the doctrine has yet to be adequately revised in response.

The Traditional View of Property

The Scholastic view of property was rooted in earlier biblical and theological traditions. Its ultimate foundation was the doctrine of creation: God created the earth and gave it to humankind, authorizing humans to use it but only as stewards rather than absolute owners. This view was rooted in the covenant of the Hebrew Scriptures and was exemplified in the restrictions on property identified in the Torah, such as the requirement not to harvest the corners of the field or make a second pass through a vineyard to harvest what had been left at first. These were to be left for the widow, the orphan, and the stranger in the land.[6] This fundamental view of property remains a part of Jesus' teaching on the danger of riches and his appeal for simplicity. It is developed somewhat in the Patristic period.

The leaders of the early church wrote and spoke with great energy in stressing the limitations of property ownership. Ambrose of Milan argued that "God has ordered all things to be produced so that there should be food in common for all, and that the earth should be the common possession of all."[7] So strong is the obligation imposed by the intention of the creator that Augustine taught that "the superfluous things of the wealthy are the necessities of the poor."[8] He adds "those who give something to the poor should not think that they are doing so from what is their own."[9]

It is no surprise that Christian social thought was affected by the Hellenization of Christianity. In making these arguments about the obligations of property owners, quite similar to many in the Hebrew Scriptures, church leaders such as Clement of Alexandria begin to identify the Christian doctrine of creation with Greek notions of what is "natural." Thus Clement writes, "Just as the foot is the measure of the sandal, so the physical needs of each are the measure of what one should possess."[10] Appealing as did the Stoics to such "natural facts," Clement argues that it would be foolish to buy sandals too large for your feet because this is "unnatural"; it doesn't make sense. Similarly, he argues that the standard of human needs is the appropriate measure for the amount of property that one should own. Here he appeals both to the Stoic value of self-sufficiency (*autarkeia*), "which anyone can acquire by a few things," and to the obligations toward those around us whose material needs are unmet.

Thomas Aquinas's development of a natural law approach to property is, of course, an extension of this earlier effort to associate

Judeo-Christian morality with Greek philosophical insight. Thomas founded his analysis of property on a theory of natural law: a fruitful marriage of the biblical doctrine of creation with the Greek notion of structure to the universe. He argues that God's intention in creating each creature is "built into" the structure of being. Because God intended the material world to meet the needs of humans, it is fully appropriate for humans to use and have dominion over material objects.[11]

The core of Thomas's argument about property is based, as all his arguments seem to be, on a critical distinction. He asserts that there are two different sorts of things humans do in dealing with "exterior things." The first is to make decisions about them or, as Thomas phrased it, "the power to procure and dispense them." The second is the actual use of those objects. Distinguishing these two is not intuitively obvious to the modern mind but Thomas's analysis is revealing.

In analyzing the power to procure and dispense material goods, Thomas argues that in this regard it is moral for humans to possess private property. He argues that having individuals, rather than an undifferentiated humanity, make these decisions about procurement and dispensation of goods is "necessary to human life" for three reasons.[12]

The first is that every individual is "more careful to procure what is for himself alone than that which is common to many or to all." This might strike us as a very "modern" reason based on insight into human incentives. Thomas points out that "each one would shirk the labor and leave to another that which concerns the community, as happens where there is a great number of servants." Clearly the argument is that the sinful self-interest of humans would prevent people from making prudent provision for the future because the benefits of such efforts may go substantially or even totally to others.

The second reason is that affairs are more orderly when it is clear that a particular person, the owner, is responsible for taking care of a material object, "whereas there would be confusion if everyone had to look after any one thing indeterminantly." Putting this more concretely, you might ask yourself what would occur if all the families on your block owned all their automobiles jointly. Because no one person had responsibility to change the oil in a particular car, there is a greater danger that maintenance will not occur than if cars are owned individually.

The third reason is that "a more peaceful state is insured to man if each one is contented with his own." Thomas opines that quarrels occur more frequently when things are owned in common.

These three reasons justifying private property in regard to "the power to procure and dispense" are what we today would call "efficiency" reasons. In many situations, it simply makes good common sense that individual owners make decisions about procurement (the decision to make or purchase a thing) and decisions about dispensation (the decision as to who gets to use these goods, and when). To the modern ear, this argument—especially the "power to dispense"—seems to imply a rather strong version of private property. However, Thomas's true meaning becomes clear when he moves to the second thing competent to humans concerning external goods: their use.

Here, in regard to the use of external things, Thomas argues that "man ought to possess external things, not as his own, but as common, so that, to-wit, he is ready to communicate them to others in their need."[13] In a shock to modern consciousness, Thomas makes a perfectly reasonable distinction: individuals may own property privately and thus possess authority to make decisions about that property, but the individual is not thereby authorized to make those decisions in any way he or she pleases. Rather, as always, those decisions must respect the nature of each privately owned material good as an object intended by God to meet human needs.

It is out of this analysis that Thomas draws a principal nearly identical to that articulated in the Patristic era a thousand years earlier. If I as an owner of property have more than I need (I own "superfluous goods") and if you have less than you need, then I am under an obligation in natural law to meet your needs with those superfluous goods.[14]

Following this logic, Thomas arrives at a nearly revolutionary conclusion. If someone is in dire need and "if the need be so manifest and urgent that it is evident that the present need must be remedied by whatever means at hand (for instance, when a person is in some imminent danger and there is no other possible remedy)," then the power to procure and dispense ordinarily enjoyed by the owners of material objects is suspended and the person in dire need is morally justified in taking the owner's property to meet that need.[15] Thomas's argument here is not that the person in dire need has the "right" to take the property; rights language is a modern phenomenon. Rather, the argument is that the nature of the objects owned is to meet human needs. This intention of the Creator, built into the material world, is the bedrock of Thomas's moral argument about property.

We might note the status of private-property claims in the natural law analysis. Thomas recounts an objection to private property based on the traditional awareness that according to the natural law all things are common property. Thomas answers that holding goods in common has traditionally been ascribed to the natural law "not because the natural law dictates that all things should be possessed in common . . . but because there is division of possessions, not according to the natural law, but rather according to human agreement, which belongs to positive law." He reminds his readers that nature did not provide humans with clothes but people invented them. In the same sense, although nature did not provide the "distinction of possessions" inherent in private property, this was "devised by human reason for the benefit of human life."[16] Thus, private property is "not contrary to the natural law but an addition thereto devised by human reason."[17]

This view of private property has continued in Catholic social thought up to the current day and is the foundation for John A. Ryan's conviction articulated in the opening quote to this article. Still, we can see in the modern period at least two significant instances of a shift or development in meaning in the Roman Catholic doctrine of private property. While these will not be the ultimate focus of this paper, it is helpful to identify them here.

The first arises in the work of Leo XIII and Pius XI in their defense of private property against the perceived threats of the socialists of their day. Leo downplays Thomas's basic distinction between procuring/dispensing and use and instead stresses the role of labor, arguing that the working man labors in order to obtain property that he is free to dispose of in providing for his family's needs. While the Popes do not employ John Locke's argument that labor is the source of an individual's moral claim to goods taken from the commons, they include the earning of property by labor as a distinct part of their moral analysis.[18]

The second major extension of the doctrine of property in the modern era arises from the broader "turn to the subject" that has characterized not only Roman Catholic but nearly all of modern thinking. What Thomas had understood as an obligation of property owners rooted in the nature of the material goods owned (that they were intended by God to meet human needs) the modern mind also understands as a claim vested in persons (i.e., a "right") over the goods of the earth. Thus while the modern papal encyclicals still speak of a "social mortgage" of property quite similar to Thomas's notion of the owner's obligation, they also include a list of "economic rights," intending to refer to the same set of obligations but this time from the point of view of the recipient of assistance.

In each of these two cases we should note that the underlying doctrine of property is extended but not fundamentally controverted. An additional extension still needs to be made.

JOHN LOCKE'S UNANSWERED CHALLENGE

Political philosophy in the English-speaking world is universally understood to have been transformed by the work of Thomas Hobbes and John Locke. At the dawn of the modern era these two thinkers shifted political attention toward the individual and undermined the traditional consensus that legitimated the rule of monarchs and undergirded social morality in the West.

In chapter 5 of his Second Treatise on Government, Locke turns to the notion of private property and employs the same heuristic fiction there that he used in thinking through political organization: the state of nature. In order to understand property ownership in his own day, Locke asks first what it would mean to take—as private property—items that exist in the commons. He agrees with his predecessors that God gave the world to humanity in common for the use of all. Yet unless an individual expropriates the apple from the tree in the commons, that individual (and, similarly, all individuals) will starve. Thus, Locke asks, "What warrants the moral claim to those apples and other fruits of the earth which God clearly intends individuals to have and consume?" Locke's famous answer is that it is the labor of the person in harvesting the fruit that makes the fruit, formerly unowned in the commons, now the property of the harvester.

The person's own body and labor are property of the person, Locke observes, and anything taken from the commons has been joined to this labor. Because of this joining "the harvester can have a right to what that is once joined to."[19] The argument applies equally to consumption goods (justly picking apples from trees growing in the commons) and to land itself (justly taking ownership of land formerly in the commons if one's labor is used to till it).

We should note that Locke attaches two kinds of limits to what can be rightfully taken from the commons. On the one hand, there should be "enough and as good left in common for others," and on the other hand, any goods taken from the commons must not be allowed to spoil because those goods would not be used, a violation of God's intention in giving the world for humanity's use. There are a number of conceptual problems with these stipulations, but they are not our focus here and will go unexamined.

Rather, we need to take note of a less controversial contribution of Locke in his attempt to offset a common-sense objection: since nearly all land in England in his day had already been taken out of the commons and made into private property, there clearly did not seem to be "enough and as good left over in common." The key argument Locke makes at this juncture is that there is another way in which labor "should be able to over-ballance the Community of Land."[20] He argues that because the production from an acre of well-tended land is so much greater than the production from an acre of land lying in the commons, it is obvious that "the improvement of labor makes the far greater part of the value" of products grown in the soil. He adds that

> of the *Products* of the Earth useful to the Life of Man, nine-tenths are the *effects of labour*: Nay, if we will rightly estimate things as they come to our use, and cast up the several Expenses about them, what in them is purely owing to *Nature*, and what to *Labour*, we shall find that in most of them 99/100 are wholly to be put on the account of *labour*.[21]

The argument here, then, is that although there is an original claim of all humanity to all land, because the labor exerted on the land produces 99% of the value of the products of the farm, whatever claim the rest of humanity may have on the products belonging to the farmer, that claim certainly does not entail more than 1% of the farmer's annual produce. Even this 1%, Locke presumes, is justifiable through his argument about labor legitimizing possessions taken from the commons. He seems to be adding here that, to the extent this argument is not compelling to his readers, they should note that it is still an argument over a tiny sliver of the total production of the farm. And of course if this is true for agriculture, it will apply even more cogently to other kinds of production.

Implicit here is the argument that all of the Scholastic analysis of property—dependent upon God's gift of the world to humanity in common—is really a debate concerning 1% of the value of what persons own in the modern world. This is Locke's unanswered challenge.

It is, of course, true that few moderns quote Locke regularly and that some of the modern challenges to the traditional doctrine of property are made on grounds completely unaffected by this argument about the productivity of labor.[22] However, this argument is used both directly and indirectly in a number of situations. Robert Nozick, in *Anarchy, State, and Utopia*, bases his argument on Locke's analysis and explicitly depends on this large difference between the value of the ultimate product and the value of the "untransformed raw materials" embodied in it.[23] Broadly dependent upon this argument is the claim by a number of neo-conservatives in the last quarter century that the true creative force in production is human intelligence.[24]

The Challenge for Catholic Social Thought

Is Catholic social thought on property vulnerable to John Locke's 99% argument? It is no surprise that in its pre-modern form the traditional doctrine does not anticipate Locke's insight.

Prior to the modern world—before the rise of economics as a discipline—very little was written about how wealth and prosperity come about. The explanation for this lacuna seems quite direct. Throughout most of human history, the fundamental source of human wealth was agricultural productivity. The wealthy were those who owned and controlled large tracts of land. It is not surprising that the leaders of the early church, for example, presumed that the wealthy either had taken wealth from others or, as Augustine phrased it, had "found it here."[25] When nearly all wealth is based in agriculture, it seems clear that God's gifts—the earth, sunshine, and rain—are the direct causes.

With further reflection—and the rise of what came to be the social sciences—writers like Locke and Adam Smith constructed social and economic theories that recognized the critical importance of applying human intelligence and hard work within production processes. This became most vividly clear in the industrial revolution when, for example, cotton could be spun into thread and threads woven into cloth far more quickly and at lower cost through industrial processes than had been possible in traditional handicraft. Even looking back on productive farming in the ancient world, it became obvious that the knowledge and work of the farmer, both in the improvement of the land and tending of the crop, were heavily influential in the outcome.

Consider even so ordinary an appliance today as the household telephone. There is little doubt that the cost of the unharvested raw materials in it—iron and copper ore, petroleum to produce the plastic—

is a tiny portion of the cost of production. The rest of its value goes to those who took those natural resources from the earth, transported, and transformed them, and to that multitude of others who took those products and further altered them in a myriad of ways to produce the scores of separate elements that go into a telephone. Any analysis of modern kitchen appliances, the family car, your favorite bedside novel, and even the wooden chairs around the dinner table would yield a similar result. The value of the unharvested natural resources that eventually went into each of these products is probably not exactly 1% but it is doubtless very small in comparison with the "value added" by human ingenuity and hard work in the production process.[26]

Thus we must ask what it means to say that God has given the earth for the use of all and that this entails an obligation on the part of those who claim to own part of that gift.

There are several possible responses to the 99% challenge presented by Locke and others since. The most immediate is that even though the current market value of those resources is but a tiny portion of the total market value of the end products, those products would be impossible without the underlying natural resources and thus the importance of the resources far outweighs their economic value. This argument will be more appealing to those highly critical of an economic understanding of the world than to others, but even there it simply dulls the point of Locke's argument and, debatably, simply reduces the 99% estimate to a lower fraction. Surely some sizable portion of the value of the product is attributable to creativity and hard work rather than to the physical resources naturally occurring on the earth. Thus, this response does not answer the objection fundamentally. This is particularly true if we were to consider intellectual property, such as that protected by copyrights and patents.

There are also a number of responses that set this issue of property aside and instead ask the broader socioeconomic question as to why there are poor people in dire need in a world with great wealth. This response is often accompanied by a critique of the reigning economic systems in the world. While systemic responses such as these are critically important, they usually take for granted rather than help to demonstrate that the unmet needs of the poor stand as an indictment against the superfluous prosperity of the well-to-do. The issue at hand, for both Aquinas and modern Catholic social thought, is whether and why those who hold more goods than they need—even if they came by those goods justly—are obliged to share with those who hold less than they need.

Other critics on the left will assert that the wealth of the rich is indeed more attributable to human labor than to natural resources, and for this reason that wealth is seen as having been expropriated from countless workers. Once again, however, this argument begs the question at hand in favor of a different one: whether and to what extent commercial agreements between capitalists and employees are just. Those convinced of a Marxian "labor theory of value" will recognize in that analysis a far stronger tool for the indictment of the wealthy than the Catholic doctrine of property. According to the labor theory of value, only human labor creates new value; natural resources transfer their value to the final product and capital goods transfer the value of their depreciation.[27] As a result, the owners of capital goods—the machines and factories—do not have a rightful claim to their profits but instead expropriate the value created by their employees. However, even though Catholic social thought denies the libertarian presumption that the voluntary nature of a commercial agreement guarantees justice,[28] it has rejected the labor theory of value.[29] Ryan himself makes this clear.[30] As a result, the narrower question of the rights and responsibilities of property owners remains critical.

Thus, John Locke's 99% argument remains as a challenge to the traditional Catholic view of private property. Humans may face the obligation of common use of the goods of the natural world given by God, but value created by human ingenuity and hard work would seem amenable to a stronger claim of ownership by the person who creates it. Is there not a more personal relation and a stronger moral claim to control between a person and the things he or she creates than between a person and an ore deposit or an acre of grazing land or a creek that flows through one's property?

If any sizable portion of modern human wealth has a different moral status than that of the natural world created by God, then the traditional doctrine of property, because it ignores this difference, is put into question.

An ultimate resolution of this question and an adequate answer to Locke's three-hundred-year old challenge lies beyond the scope of this essay and the competence of this author. The solution will have to be developed from resources (many already at hand) within Christian anthropology and will need to be founded in fundamental moral theology for a renewal of the doctrine of property. Whatever the outlines of such a resolution will be, it will stand as a challenge to a fundamental conviction of many moderns that human autonomy warrants very strong versions of private property. While this essay can provide no complete solution, the final section outlines elements likely essential for a solution, awaiting scholars better grounded in other theological disciplines for a more adequate response.

Outlines for a Revision of the Doctrine of Property

Attention must be directed, I judge, at the fundamental point where Locke's own argument first breaks with the traditional doctrine of property. (It is significant that this is also the point where Locke's approach allows a libertarian interpretation, such as that provided by Robert Nozick.)

Locke begins with the traditional assumption "that God . . . has given the earth to the children of men, given it to mankind in common."[31] This, of course, we saw in Aquinas. Locke goes on, however, in a way inconceivable to Aquinas and his intellectual forebears:

> Though the Earth, and all inferior Creatures be common to all Men, yet every Man has a *Property* in his own *Person*. This no Body has any Right to but himself. *Labour* of his Body, and the *Work* of his Hands, we may say, are properly his.[32]

The argument proceeds, as we have seen, that because humans have this property in their own labor they make the fruits of the earth their own when they "mix" those fruits with labor in harvesting them from the commons. The point here, however, is the view of the human person articulated by Locke. Locke's anthropology views each person as owning—in the sense of owning property—one's own person and owning one's own person in an absolute manner, in that "no Body has any Right to it but himself."[33] It is this bold statement of individual autonomy that led C. B. McPherson to label Locke's view "possessive individualism."[34]

It is interesting to note that in Locke's text God's intentions appear in the paragraphs immediately preceding and following paragraph 27, but there is no mention of God's intention in this critical section where the right of property over one's own person is cast in an absolute sense. There the argument is that "no Body" and "no Man" can justly make a claim against each person's "Property in his own Person." He does not ask whether God makes such a claim. The question that Christians need to press is why Locke would be attentive to the intention of God in creating "the world" but inattentive to the parallel question of God's intention for how humans understand themselves and their own labor.

The answer that Christian theology has given, of course, is that human life and personhood are themselves gifts from the Creator and thus humans do not own themselves in an absolute sense. (The traditional prohibition against suicide, something that makes no sense to libertarians, is based on this insight.) Contemporary Christians do indeed need to endorse rights of the person strong enough to obviate slavery, ensure equality, guarantee the prerequisites of human dignity, and encourage human flourishing. Nonetheless, the notion that humans have an absolute property in themselves is a clear violation of the Christian doctrine of creation, and it simply cannot provide an adequate basis for Locke's subsequent argumentation on the character of private property more broadly.

Once we phrase the problem this way we can see that Locke's argument on property in fact begs the question. He sets out to investigate the meaning of property and begins with the question of "how men might come to have a property" in material things that God originally gave to humankind in common.[35] However, in answering this question and deciding upon the obligations attendant to such property relations, Locke starts with a very strong and, at least in his own work, unexamined presumption about what property in one's own person means and uses this unwarranted presumption to then answer the question of what a property right in material goods would mean. The circularity here is apparent.

Even though we can recognize the weakness in Locke's argument concerning the absolute ownership of oneself, we are nonetheless left with the problems caused by Locke's more compelling observation that 99% of modern wealth is the product of human labor. Especially in an era when theology itself has been transformed by the "turn to the subject," we need to improve on the tradition's simple presumption that all property, all wealth, is of a single kind: given by God in the creation of the world.

It would seem that there are four primary resources that need to be woven together in this movement from a renewed Christian anthropology to an updated fundamental moral theology to a doctrine of property more adequate to modern insight. These are an application of the traditional standard of property to the fruits of labor, an appreciation of humanity's role in God's ongoing creation of the world, the integration of modern moral discourse about economic rights into the traditional doctrine of property, and the insights of the sociology of knowledge in understanding human creativity.

The first element of a likely solution has already been mentioned: because human personhood and creativity are themselves gifts from God, persons do not "own" themselves in any absolute way and the fruits of human creativity and labor stand under requirements of justice as do other material goods. An authentic sense of the gift-character of one's own creative abilities leads the Christian to recognize obligations in the exercise of those capacities. This would seem to be a partial answer to Locke's challenge, but it is not a complete one because the role of human effort in assessing what any person morally deserves has long been recognized. We saw how Pope Leo relied on work to warrant the laborer's claim to wages earned. John Ryan himself listed efforts, sacrifice, and productivity among the canons of distributive justice.[36] The U.S. Catholic Bishops explicitly argued in favor of some degree of inequality in the distribution of income and wealth out of a concern to provide incentives.[37] Thus while this extension of the Thomistic paradigm of ownership to the fruits of labor eliminates the radical libertarian option, it does not address the important moral difference that contemporary Christian anthropology would seem to recognize between two kinds of relationships: the relation between an owner and a privately owned but naturally occurring resource and that between a person and the result of his or her creativity and labor. While similar in some respects, the two relations would seem to be different enough to entail a difference in the rights and responsibilities of ownership.

The second intellectual resource likely to be part of an adequate view of property will be founded on the role of human action in God's ongoing creation of the world. This will be an important addition to the first element that plays a primarily negative and limiting role in focusing on the responsibilities attendant to the gift of personhood. A well-articulated doctrine of human action as, at its best, a part of the ongoing creation of the world puts such limitations in a broader and more adequate context, viewing human creativity and labor as a part of God's plan for the ongoing creation and transformation of the world. There are, of course, risks in this view as it could uncritically endorse, for example, the destruction of the biosphere if not limited by other theological principles. Nonetheless, the inclusion within a doctrine of property of the modern appreciation for human creativity requires this sort of theological grounding.

The third element in the resolution of this matter is an integration of "rights" language into the traditional doctrine of property. The most important shift for moral theology in the turn to the subject in the modern world has been the endorsement of the language of rights. Thomas concluded that the owner's obligations are rooted in the nature of those goods. Modern thought, including modern Catholic thought, articulates the same set of moral relations from the point of view of the persons involved, recognizing rights of owners and rights of those in need. The lists of "economic rights" that are now taken for granted in conciliar, papal, and episcopal documents stand as ample evidence of this shift. Thus even if the traditional doctrine of property has difficulty in addressing Locke's 99% challenge, the notion of economic rights, based on the intention of the Creator, focuses attention on claims of needy people that must be respected regardless of our construal of the relation of ownership.

Although there have been important gains in shifting the argument to rights language, there has been a significant loss as well. In Thomas's view each holder of wealth could justify owning superfluous property only if there were no persons with unmet needs around them. Each property owner had a personal obligation. The modern notion of economic rights recognizes the moral claims of individuals and a general societal obligation to meet those claims, but the immediacy of obligation of particular owners of property is muted. What is needed, it would seem, is a theory of property that recognizes Locke's 99% objection but that is internally related to the notion of economic rights.

The fourth element in a resolution of these issues will likely come from the sociology of knowledge, specifying more adequately the social context within which human creativity and labor occur. While there is a strong tendency in the modern world to view human creativity and effort in individualist terms, the insights of modern sociology and psychology make clear the communal character not only of human action but even of human knowing and language. Thus the inventor-entrepreneur, the darling of the libertarian economic story, in reality owes debts to an untold number of persons who never get mentioned in the novels of Ayn Rand or in the philosophical analyses of Robert Nozick. The reason, of course, for this sort of blindness is the libertarian presumption that gifts freely given entail no obligations on the part of the recipient. Other than the prohibition against causing harm to another's person or property under the law of nature,[38] obligations to others, they assert, arise only out of voluntary agreement. This is not the place to launch a broad critique of libertarian views, but it is clear that such a perspective eclipses the social world as it is understood and experienced by the Catholic tradition and, I would argue, by most people today.

Instead of this denial of obligations, a more adequate assessment would identify a long list of gifts—and attendant responsibilities—without which human creativity and hard work itself could not exist. It is helpful to recall some of these: personal character formation in our families of origin and elsewhere; our conceptual and practical knowledge of the world rooted in the history of daily experience and of the sciences, the humanities, and the arts; a social system that provides the stability, structure, and institutional nurturance within which human creativity can occur; and even the language upon which we all depend for understanding and communication. Libertarians rarely advert to those gifts but could, if pressed, simply assert that these are either explicit donations from others or are assets existing in the intellectual commons that we can take and benefit from without further obligation. This view is simply inadequate. The typical silence about these socially-provided advantages bespeaks an inadequate empirical grasp of the sociality of human life. In addition, those whose faith rests in a provident God do not recognize an option to reap a harvest sown by untold others who came before us without consequent responsibility to those around us and to follow.

Conclusion

Whatever the particular resolution, these four elements will need to be integrated within a robust vision of a very traditional Catholic concern: the common good. As Robert Bellah and his associates have argued articulately in *Habits of the Heart* and elsewhere, the overly individualistic language that characterizes so much public and private discourse today underrepresents the reality of communal ties in daily life.

John A. Ryan was correct seventy-five years ago, and it is even truer today, that many contemporary persons would regard the traditional obligations concerning superfluous goods as "extreme and fantastic." A sizable portion of that reaction is due to an inappropriate integration into the modern religious imagination of too individualistic a view of life. Nonetheless, a portion of that aversion is attributable to a fully appropriate modern appreciation of the character of human creativity and labor, an appreciation that the traditional doctrine unfortunately does not take into account.

A renewal of the doctrine of property stands, then, as a task within the broader retrieval of the notion of the common good, a retrieval to which John A. Ryan dedicated himself so creatively. It also offers the hope that a more adequate conceptual foundation for property ownership will itself challenge the extreme individualism to which so many today are inclined and will assist in its own way in our efforts to secure the common good.

Bibliography

Aquinas, Thomas. *Summa Theologiae.* Translated by Fathers of the English Dominican Province. New York, N.Y.: Benziger Bros, 1948. Hereafter referred to as *ST.*

Dempsey, Bernard W. *Interest and Usury*. Washington, D.C.: American Council on Public Affairs, 1943.

Divine, Thomas F., S.J., *Interest: An Historical and Analytical Study in Economics and Ethics*. Milwaukee: Marquette University Press, 1959.

Gilder, George. *Wealth and Poverty.* New York: Basic Books, 1981.

Langholm, Odd. *The Aristotelian Analysis of Usury*. Bergen: Universitetsforlaget AS, 1984.

Locke, John. *Two Treatises on Government*, ed. Peter Laslett. New York: New American Library, 1960.

Lustig, Andrew. "Natural Law, Property, and Justice: The General Justification of Property in John Locke." *The Journal of Religious Ethics* vol. 19, no. 1 (Spring 1991): 119-49.

Marx, Karl. *Capital.* New York: International Publishers, 1967.

McPherson, C. B. *The Political Theory of Possessive Individualism: Hobbes to Locke*. Oxford: Oxford University Press, 1969.

National Conference of Catholic Bishops. *Economic Justice for All: Catholic Social Teaching and the U.S. Economy*. Washington D.C.: United States Catholic Conference, 1986.

Noonan, John T., Jr. *The Scholastic Analysis of Usury*. Cambridge, Mass.: Harvard University Press, 1957.

Nozick, Robert. *Anarchy, State, and Utopia*. New York: Basic Books, 1974.

Ryan, John A. *Distributive Justice: The Right and Wrong of Our Present Distribution of Wealth*. New York: Macmillan Co., 1916.

Notes

1. John A. Ryan, *Distributive Justice: The Right and Wrong of Our Present Distribution of Wealth* (New York: Macmillan Co., 1916), 314.

2. Ryan, *Distributive Justice*, 30.

3. *ST*, II-II, Q. 78, a. 1.

4. The modern mind recognizes a dimension to the loan of the bottle of wine to which Thomas does not refer. If I borrow a bottle of wine from you for my dinner party but don't use it, I have still benefited from the flexibility that its temporary presence in my house provided. My guests might have asked for wine and thus the loan provided a very real service to me even though, as it turned out, my guests chose to drink something else. It would seem that Thomas may have ignored this added dimension simply because he considered it morally irrelevant. As he argued (*ST* II-II, Q.77, a.1) in discussing the just price of an article, although a seller may charge more than the item "is worth in itself" when the seller will incur an additional loss due to circumstance, the seller "ought not to raise the price [if] the advantage accruing to the buyer is not due to the seller but to a circumstance affecting the buyer." Applying the same logic to the loan of wine, you the lender would be unjust to charge me the borrower due to any advantage I receive from having the bottle of wine available at the dinner party.

A completely different issue is raised if you the lender would in some way be inconvenienced by the absence of this bottle of wine from your house this evening. Again, Thomas does not address thc issue, but if I prevailed upon you to lend me the bottle of wine when we both had dinner parties this evening and it was your only bottle (and thus you yourself would experience a real disadvantage from its absence), the just price argument would seem to allow you to charge me to offset the loss you would incur. It seems throughout the Thomistic analysis of usury (and of lending more generally) that the lender is presumed to have a more than adequate supply of whatever is lent, and thus would not have any particular loss from a temporary loan.

5. See, for example, Odd Langholm, *The Aristotelian Analysis of Usury* (Bergen: Universitetsforlaget AS, 1984); John T. Noonan, Jr., *The Scholastic Analysis of Usury* (Cambridge, Mass.: Harvard University Press, 1957);

Bernard W. Dempsey, *Interest and Usury* (Washington, D.C.: American Council on Public Affairs, 1943); Thomas F. Divine, S.J., *Interest: An Historical Analytical Study in Economics and Ethics* (Milwaukee: Marquette University Press, 1959).

6. Deut. 24:19-21; Lev. 19:9-10.

7. *De Officiis Ministrorum* 1.28 PL 16:62.

8. *Psalmum* 147 12, PL 37:1922.

9. *Sermon* 50 1.2, PL 38:326.

10. *Paidagogos* 3.7, PG 8:609.

11. *ST* II-II, Q.66, a.1.

12. *ST* II-II, Q.66, a.2.

13. Ibid.

14. Ibid.

15. *ST* II-II, Q.66, a.7.

16. *ST* II-II, Q.94, a.5.

17. *ST* II-II, Q.66, a.2.

18. See, for example, *Rerum novarum*, para. 4-5.

19. John Locke, *The Second Treatise on Government*, ed. Peter Laslett (New York: New American Library, 1960), para. 25.

20. Locke, para. 40.

21. Ibid.

22. For example, recent debates in the United States about the "takings" clause of the Constitution pertain to ownership of unimproved natural resources and thus would be unaffected by this portion of Locke's argument.

23. Nozick quotes David Friedman to use a 95% figure where Locke had used 99%. Robert Nozick, *Anarchy, State, and Utopia* (New York: Basic Books, 1974), 177.

24. See, for example, George Gilder, *Wealth and Poverty* (New York: Basic Books, 1981).

25. *Sermon* 124 5.5, PL 38:686.

26. A full analysis would have to include the capital goods that assisted in the production process, but here too the same argument holds: only a tiny portion of their value is attributable to the unharvested natural resources embodied in them.

27. While David Ricardo used a labor theory of value in a limited sense, the full-blown theory, and the one that survived, is that of Karl Marx, best outlined

in *Capital* (New York: International Publishers, 1967), vol. 1, chap. IX, sect. I, 204ff.

28. *Rerum novarum*, 34.

29. *Rerum novarum*, 15 and 35.

30. Ryan, *Distributive Justice*, chap. X, 145-51.

31. Locke, *Second Treatise,* para. 25.

32. Locke, *Second Treatise*, para. 27.

33. We should note that Locke's use of the term "property" is multivalent. Throughout most of the *Second Treatise* he uses the word to refer more generally to "Lives, Liberties and Estates" (para. 123). Commentators generally agree, however, that he limits that word to the more ordinary material possessions in the critical chapter on property discussed above. See, for example, Peter Laslett's lengthy introduction in John Locke, *Two Treatises on Government* (New York: New American Library, 1960), 115ff.

34. C. B. McPherson, *The Political Theory of Possessive Individualism: Hobbes to Locke* (Oxford: Oxford University Press, 1969). As with a number of other important issues concerning Locke's work, we do not here have space to investigate the dispute as to whether Locke should be seen as the champion of possessive individualism as McPherson argues or as a reaction against that trend, represented by the property arguments of Hugo Grotius, as others have argued. See Andrew Lustig, "Natural Law, Property, and Justice: The General Justification of Property in John Locke," in *The Journal of Religious Ethics* vol. 19, no. 1 (Spring 1991): 119-49.

35. Locke, *Second Treatise*, para. 25.

36. Ryan, *Distributive Justice*, 246-48.

37. National Conference of Catholic Bishops, *Economic Justice for All: Catholic Social Teaching and the U.S. Economy* (Washington D.C.: United States Catholic Conference, 1986), para. 185.

38. Even this is something of an overstatement of the libertarian notion of obligation. Nozick, for example, does not view the prohibition against harm to others as an obligation to those others. He sees it as a requirement of "the law of nature."

Business Implications of John A. Ryan's Thought

John A. Ryan believed that businesses played a critical role in manifesting the common good in society, that is, in creating conditions that would foster human welfare. Critical in accomplishing the common good is the cooperation between employer and employee. Ryan was concerned that the animosity between the two would cause significant damage to their hearts and souls, blocking a lasting industrial peace. The "cash or contract nexus" between employer and employee, Ryan argued, must be supplanted by a human relation based on participation and cooperation that "will make the latter feel like a partner and less like an antagonist" (*A Better Economic Order*, 165). The role of participation and cooperation was not to increase productivity and quality, although Ryan believed that it would do this as well, since ethics and expediency are compatible. Instead, the real goal was to bind people together in a way to realize their full humanity. The first three articles in this section examine this general theme.

David W. Lutz's article "Christian Social Thought and Corporate Governance" points out that the idea of a community of work Ryan desires cannot be governed by a predominantly individualistic philosophy. Such a philosophy separates the property relationship of shareholders and boards of directors from the social relationship of the community. Formed by the Christian social tradition, Lutz argues, Ryan has the philosophical foundations that provide an alternative social philosophy for defining the nature of business as an intermediate economic and social body within the economy, and whose governance is wedded to the "economic common good," as an act of contributive justice.

It is precisely this notion of governance as virtue that M. J. Platts picks up in his article "Limited Liability." Contrasting the tradition of virtue in Confucian, Islamic, Jewish, and Christian thought with the Anglo-American utilitarian view of virtue, Platts explores the relationship of these traditions to the notion of "limited liability" in corporate ownership. Platts sees as disastrous the combination of Franklin's utilitarian notion of virtue as informing the leadership of companies whose ownership structures are described in terms of "limited liability." The whole relationship between management and the corporation is instrumentalized to achieve maximum efficiency, productivity, and profitability. The manager in this utilitarian tradition is seen as an adventurer who views work "as a source of opportunistic deals." This is radically different from German and Japanese companies who have been influenced by Christian and Confucian virtue traditions. Here the manager views work as a "craftsman" called to a life of virtue to create organizations where people can develop.

Michael J. Schuck and Francis T. Hannafey's article "Entrepreneurs and Markets: Contemporary Entrepreneurial Practice and Morality in Relation to the Thought of John A. Ryan" explains an often overlooked aspect of Ryan's thought: his appreciation for the entrepreneur. Ryan is often known as a champion for labor, but as Schuck and Hannafey point out, Ryan recognized the irreplaceable role of the entrepreneur for a just economy. His writings provide a coherent and feasible vision for the entrepreneur to deal with issues of distribution of profits and losses, promotion, investments, and product development.

Although Ryan was concerned with the general relationship between employer and employee, he spent much of his time focusing on the wage dimension of that relationship, an issue of special relevance in light of the growing wage disparity between executives and employees. Ryan recognized the truth of the comment by the English clergyman Charles C. Cotton (1822): "Our incomes are like our shoes; if too small, they gall and pinch us; but if too large they cause us to stumble and trip." A critical part of human development was economic development through wages that allowed people to live decent human lives. As an agent of the whole, Ryan argued that "The employer has obligations of justice, not merely as the receiver of a valuable thing through an onerous contract, but as the *distributor* of the common heritage of nature" (*Distributive Justice*, 279-80). Ryan placed the wage question squarely in terms of its morality. Just as there are no atheists in fox holes, there are no relativists in pay determination.

The last four articles examine the responsibility of the employer to pay a living wage. Regina Wentzel Wolfe's article "John A. Ryan and Women's Wages: Still a Radical Stance?" argues for the relevance of Ryan's views on wages for today. Wolfe observes that with today's minimum wage woefully inadequate for a living wage and the gap between women and men's wages still unacceptable, social and structural barriers still prevent women from acquiring just wages. She maintains that John A. Ryan, the Catholic social tradition, and their anthropological starting point can help to dismantle such barriers.

Georgia Keightley's article, "Catholic Social Teaching on Women's Work and Wages: A Feminist Critique," provides a feminist rethinking of Catholic social ethics as it relates to wages. She argues that a development of Catholic social thought should occur in understanding better the role of women in the workplace. According to Keightley, the church's social teaching has wedded itself too closely to an organic model that placed women in overly static and defined roles and that contributes to the low wages women receive.

David Krueger's article "Can Ryan's Economic Ethic Work for a Global Economy?" examines the feasibility of applying Ryan's thought to the international market economy. Using Ryan's ethical method, Krueger points out the failure of present wage systems to meet a living wage. He explains that Ryan's ethical method provides "important moral directives toward structural reform in global economic policy."

The authors of these essays provide a great service for business ethics, especially in the area of human resources. They retrieve Ryan's thought and bring it to bear on managerial issues today. In light of the growing wage disparity of "Marie Antoinette proportions," and the apparent growing detachment of corporate property from the common good, the retrieval of Ryan's thought provides a unique Christian perspective that has been dominated by classical liberal categories and analyses.

CHRISTIAN SOCIAL THOUGHT AND CORPORATE GOVERNANCE

DAVID W. LUTZ

In *Distributive Justice* (1916, 1927, 1942) and *A Better Economic Order* (1935) Msgr. John A. Ryan advocates an alternative to the existing economic orders of his day. This better order would be characterized by social justice, which "impels both individuals and public officials to promote the common good; that is, the common welfare, taken distributively as well as collectively; the good of the community, not only as a unified entity, but as composed of social groups and individuals."[1] It would feature cooperation, which Ryan defines as "that joint economic action which seeks to obtain for a relatively weak group all or part of the profits and interest which in the ordinary capitalist enterprise are taken by a small and different group."[2] It would include industrial democracy, and would make it possible for labor to share in management, profits, and ownership. Ryan understands this alternative to be the same as the proposal of Pope Pius XI (and Oswald Von Nell-Breuning, S.J.) in *Quadragesimo anno* (1931).

VIA MEDIA OR THIRD WAY?

Msgr. Ryan believes that this better economic order would be a virtuous mean between two vicious extremes: "Coöperation is a golden mean between individualism and Socialism. It includes all the good features and excludes all the evil features of both."[3] Again: "The industrial system proposed by the Pope [Pius XI] would occupy a middle ground between capitalism and Communism, between individualism and Socialism."[4]

I submit that while this alternative is indeed distinct from the vices of individualism and socialism, it does not lie *between* these extremes. Aristotle himself found difficulties with his doctrine that virtues are mean states between vices of excess and deficiency:

> Not every action or feeling admits of the mean. For the names of some automatically include baseness, e.g. spite, shamelessness, envy [among feelings], and adultery, theft, murder, among actions. All of these and similar things are called by these names because they themselves, not their excesses or deficiencies, are base.[5]

It is remarkable that in a world as complex as ours, we so often think of our political, social, and economic options as all falling somewhere on a one-dimensional spectrum or continuum ranging from extreme individualism at one end to extreme socialism at the other. We think in terms of "right" and "left," "conservative" and "liberal." Anyone whose beliefs are near neither of these poles must be a "moderate" or a "centrist"—or must be confused. Many writers have found it difficult, for example, to determine Pope John Paul II's position on this continuum, because on some issues he sounds like a "conservative," while on others he sounds like a "liberal." We identify large numbers of American voters as "economically conservative and socially liberal," without asking whether the fact that someone could be both a "conservative" and a "liberal" does not suggest that our model is too simple. I submit that an accurate positioning of our options would require a multidimensional framework, and that the optimal political, social, and economic order is neither that of John Locke, nor that of Karl Marx, *nor any compromise between the two.*

The words of John Paul himself, in *Sollicitudo rei socialis*, suggest that he may see the situation in this manner: "The Church's social doctrine *is not* a 'third way' between *liberal capitalism* and *Marxist collectivism*, nor even a possible alternative to other solutions less radically opposed to one another: rather, it constitutes a *category of its own*."[6] One possible interpretation of this passage is that Catholic social doctrine, on one hand, and capitalism and Marxism, on the other, are incommensurable, because the domains in which they exist do not intersect.

A quite different view of whether the church's social doctrine is a *via media* is offered by Michael Novak:

> Since Leo XIII condemned socialism and criticized capitalism [in *Rerum novarum*, 1891], many concluded that the Catholic Church must be propounding a "middle way." A great deal of effort went into the search for this elusive middle way. This was a futile search, however, for it overlooked the asymmetry between capitalism and socialism. Socialism is a moral, economic, and political system all in one. But capitalism is the name only of an economic system which, for its full and free development, requires a democratic polity and a humanistic and pluralist culture. Indeed, the threefold *combination* of democracy, capitalism, and religious liberty *is* the "middle way" between socialism and capitalism.[7]

On Novak's account, even though socialism is a moral-economic-political system and capitalism is only an economic system, the two are commensurable, and are related to one another in such a way that we can speak, at least in relative terms, of the distance separating them. Additionally, when capitalism is combined with democracy and religious liberty, the product is also commensurable with both capitalism and socialism. Furthermore, the position of this moral-economic-political combination relative to capitalism is in the direction of, and approximately half the distance to, socialism. I do not believe that Novak himself would accept this implication. And whether we agree or disagree with him at other points, neither should we accept it.

If we look at the context within which the above passage from *Sollicitudo rei socialis* is found, we find evidence that Catholic social doctrine is commensurable with options such as liberal capitalism and Marxist collectivism: "The church does not propose economic and political systems or programs nor does she show preference for one or the other, provided that human dignity is properly respected and promoted, and provided she herself is allowed the room she needs to exercise her ministry in the world."[8] But if any further clarification were needed, John Paul states clearly in *Centesimus annus* that neither unrestrained capitalism—"a system in which freedom in the economic sector is not circumscribed within a strong juridical framework which places it at the service of human freedom in its totality and which sees it as a particular aspect of that freedom, the core of which is ethical and religious"[9]—nor Marxist socialism properly respects and promotes human dignity, nor allows the church room to exercise her ministry in the world.

Furthermore, John Paul has some specific things to say about the economic and political features of the proper "goal of the countries now making efforts to rebuild their economy and society"[10] in the aftermath of the collapse of the Soviet Union. Whatever label we choose for it, it is "an economic system which recognizes the fundamental and positive role of business, the market, private property and the resulting responsibility for the means of production as well as free human creativity in the economic sector."[11]

I submit that we can best make sense of these various passages by understanding Catholic social doctrine to be indeed a *third way*, but not a third way *between* individualistic capitalism and Marxist collectivism. To push the spatial metaphor to the limits of its usefulness, individualism, Marxism, and Catholic social doctrine are the three corners of a triangle; none of which lies between the other two.

Ryan explains why he understands the better economic order to be a mean between the vicious extremes of individualism and socialism:

> On the one hand, it demands and develops individual initiative and self-reliance, makes the rewards of the individual depend upon his own efforts and efficiency, and gives him full ownership of specific pieces of property. On the other hand, it compels him to submerge much of the selfishness and indifference to the welfare of his fellows which characterize our individualist economy. It embraces all the good that is claimed for Socialism because it induces men to consider and to work earnestly for the common good, eliminates much of the waste of competitive industry, reduces and redistributes the burdens of profits and interest, and puts the workers in control of capital and industry. At the same time, it avoids the evils of an industrial despotism, of bureaucratic inefficiency, of individual indifference, and of an all-pervading collective ownership.[12]

But rather than simply being a compromise, with many of the strengths and few of the weaknesses of individualism and socialism, Catholic social doctrine possess attributes belonging to neither vicious system. Instead of compelling persons to submerge selfishness and indifference to the welfare of others, it teaches that true self-love is inseparable from concern for the welfare of others. Rather than seeing pursuit of individual good and pursuit of common good as activities between which one can choose or which should be balanced with one another, it teaches that the individual good and the common good cannot be divorced from one another. Furthermore, at its core is a principle found in neither individualism nor socialism, the principle of subsidiarity, according to which the primary sphere for the conjunction of individual good and common good is the community, not a large political body.[13] My intention in this section is not to quibble, but to give Ryan's theory more credit than he himself gives it; it is better than a compromise between two vices.

STOCKHOLDERS AND STAKEHOLDERS

I now shift from Christian social thought and its rivals, understood as theories about the macro economy as a whole, to social philosophies for the governance of particular corporations operating within the macro economy. Although the connection between these two subject matters is seldom noted, it is important. Within a macro economy governed by a predominantly social-democratic or Marxist social philosophy, the governance of individual business corporations is seen primarily as the governance of operating segments of the macro economy having little autonomy. The means of production are viewed as governmental entitlements. Within a macro economy governed by a predominantly individualistic, laissez-faire social philosophy, in contrast, corporate governance is usually viewed as the governance of autonomous entities having little or no responsibility to the overall economy, so long as they do not violate the rather minimalist laws that apply to its operations. The assumption is that the individual initiative of each business corporation is the only relevant consideration impacting its governance, and that there is little or no reason to consider the firm's impact on the overall economy and the common good, beyond legal compliance and the operation of the invisible hand.

The tradition of Christian social thought, within which John Ryan writes, represents a distinct, third social philosophy pertaining to the governance of business corporations. Within this tradition, the governance of a particular business corporation, viewed from the perspective of social philosophy, is both a matter of individual initiative emanating from those who manage and comprise the corporation as an extension and expression of human dignity and the economic needs that result therefrom, and a matter of a close relationship to the limited economic common good of that corporation, viewed as an intermediary economic body within the economy and as an important contributor to the economic common good of the economy as a whole. Thus a fundamental issue in corporate governance within the tradition of Christian social thought is the nature of the business corporation as an intermediate economic and social body within the economy, in which those comprising and managing its corporate operations take both of these dimensions into consideration.

Within the Christian social thought tradition, this same dual perspective applies also to the governance of nonprofit-services-sector corporations (labor organizations, higher-education institutions, foundations, industry associations, pension trust organizations, etc.) and government-sector corporations (local economic development corporations, governmentally owned public utility corporations, airport commissions, the federal reserve system) that, taken as a whole, play at least as great a role as business corporations in our national and global economies. The point here is that the Christian social thought tradition, within which John Ryan is writing, views the subject of corporate governance within the context of a broader social philosophy that places a primary emphasis upon the multiple roles and contributions of the vast array of intermediary economic bodies that contribute to the economic good of society as a whole. This is much too broad a subject matter to address in depth here; but these are basic considerations that should be noted as being relevant to the subject of corporate governance in the context of social philosophy.

Within the tradition of Christian social thought, business corporations, like nonprofit-sector and governmental-sector intermediary economic and social bodies, must be viewed and analyzed as distinct moral and legal persons providing economic functions important to human dignity, human economic needs, and the economic common good, but not primarily a part of or subsumed within government-sector activity. And within the tradition of the virtues, managers of corporations in all three sectors must be persons of character who recognize their role as stewards of the resources entrusted to their care and upon which the good of all depends. They must define their own missions in such a manner that they meet their responsibility as "dispensers of justice."[14] Discussions of corporate governance in other traditions of social philosophy do not begin to address adequately or properly either the complexities or the importance of corporate governance viewed from this classical virtues perspective.

Although Ryan does not address the issue of corporate governance explicitly, it is implicit in his discussion of labor participation in management, profits, and ownership. The governance of corporations with publicly-traded shares is more complex than that of sole proprietorships and partnerships, because the set of managers and the set of owners are not identical. In such corporations, a board of directors is responsible for the management of the firm. Its role is important in cases where the activities of the managers, if ungoverned, would differ from those that other parties prefer. And one complicating factor in the governance of corporations is that the key actors within the board of directors are often the key actors within the firm's management team.

In a 1991 *America* article entitled "The Unfinished Business of Reforming Corporate Government," T. R. Martin and Richard D. Roberts state that in 80 percent of large corporations, the chief executive officer of the corporation is also the chairman of its board of directors.[15] This article was sparked by the recent savings and loan debacle, and the burden to be borne by taxpayers because boards of directors failed to meet their responsibility to ensure that managers managed prudently. But discussions of corporate governance are more commonly concerned with the challenge of directing the behavior of managers toward the economic interests of a firm's shareholders in cases where the economic interests of managers and shareholders diverge.

One assumption of much corporate-governance literature, and indeed of much business literature, is that managers should direct their efforts toward increasing the wealth of shareholders, because managers are agents, shareholders are principals, and agents are obligated to act in the interests of their principals. The challenge, then, is to get managers to act in the interests of (one group of) other persons. Given another common assumption, that managers always act to maximize their own utility, the challenge is to design a control system such that the utility-maximizing behavior of managers approximates owner-wealth-maximizing behavior.

One problem with this approach is that the initial assumption is false. The managers of a corporation are indeed agents, but are agents of the *corporation*, not of its owners. The explanation of the common mistake of understanding managers to be agents of owners is that, in our post-Hobbesian, individualistic culture, human societies and smaller human organizations are nothing more than aggregates of individual persons. The more traditional, contrasting view is presented by Heinrich Rommen: "Each human society is not an amorphous aggregation, a mere mass, but a *unitas ordinis;* it has a constitution, a framework of rules by which the *ordo* and the *unitas* of the wills of the individuals are produced and their functions are integrated to an organic whole."[16]

The modern, liberal view of human society as a mere aggregate of human individuals has now become the philosophy of the business corporation. This can be seen clearly in one of the classic works of "agency theory": Michael C. Jensen and William H. Meckling's "Theory of the Firm: Managerial Behavior, Agency Costs, and Ownership Structure." These authors write: "It is important to recognize that most organizations are simply *legal fictions that serve as a nexus for a set of contracting relationships among individuals*."[17] They then tell us that corporations are included among this set of organizations:

> The private corporation or firm is simply one form of legal fiction that serves as a nexus for contracting relationships and is also characterized by the existence of divisible residual claims on the organization's assets and cash flows, which can generally be sold without permission of the other contracting individuals.
>
> • • •
>
> There is in a very real sense only a multitude of complex relationships (i.e., contracts) between the legal fiction (the firm) and the owners of labor, material, and capital inputs and the consumers of output.[18]

Jensen and Meckling then draw some implications of their position:

> Viewing the firm as the nexus of a set of contracting relationships among individuals also serves to make it clear that the personalization of the firm implied by asking questions such as, What should be the objective function of the firm? or, Does the firm have a social responsibility? is seriously misleading. *The firm is not an individual.* It is a legal fiction that serves as a focus for a complex process in which the conflicting objectives of individuals (some of whom may "represent" other organizations) are brought into equilibrium within a framework of contractual relations.[19]

Jensen and Meckling are not the first scholars to view the corporation as a fiction. E. Merrick Dodd, Jr. wrote in 1932 of "the widely prevalent theory that the corporate entity is a fiction."[20] If "the personalization of the firm" were understood to mean the transformation of the corporation into an individual human being, these authors' point would, of course, be well-taken. But "a corporation is an entity created by law that exists separately and distinctly from the individuals whose contributions of initiative, property, and control enable it to function."[21] It is "an association of individuals created under the authority of state laws that recognize it as a separate entity having its own rights, privileges, and liabilities, distinct from those of its members."[22] Furthermore, a corporation "is considered, for some purposes, a person."[23]

Our present philosophical condition, in which a corporation cannot have moral properties, because it is understood to be a legal fiction, nothing more than an aggregate of individual persons, contrasts sharply with that of Plato, who described at some length in the *Republic* the relationship between the virtuous human individual and the virtuous city-state. And Pope John Paul II explicitly recognizes business corporations as communities: "The purpose of a business firm . . . is to be found in its very existence as a community of persons who in various ways are endeavoring to satisfy their basic needs and who form a particular group at the service of the whole of society."[24]

Recent "business ethics" literature includes criticism of the claim that the sole objective of a business corporation is to increase shareholder value. An alternative to the shareholder or stockholder approach has been proposed, and is most commonly called the "stakeholder" approach. But while this alternative maintains that owners are not the only individuals whose interests should be considered by managers, it does so within the same post-Hobbesian, social-contract tradition. Human society is an aggregate of human individuals bound together by a bundle of explicit or implicit contracts.

This can be seen in a question posed by R. Edward Freeman, one of the pioneers of the stakeholder approach to business ethics: "Is the corporation to be understood solely as a means to the creation of wealth for stockholders, or can it be understood as a social contract among stockholders, customers, suppliers, employees, and communities?"[25] Freeman prefers the latter understanding of the corporation. But an unsolved problem for stakeholder theories is determining how the clashing interests of the various groups of stakeholders are to be balanced. I believe that we have in Msgr. Ryan's works at least the outlines of an alternative superior to both agency theories and stakeholder theories of corporate governance.

Just Corporations

Msgr. Ryan minimizes the distinction between stockholders and bondholders. He writes that four classes of persons contribute to the products of industry: "landowners, capitalists, undertakers or business men [in a corporation, managers], and laborers or wage earners."[26] Corresponding to each class is a type of income: rent, interest, profits, and wages, respectively. There seems not to be a place in this schema for shareholders (who are not also landowners, managers, or laborers). Their income is not interest, the type corresponding to capitalists. And profits correspond to managers, which they are not. But Ryan includes shareholders among the class of capitalists and treats their dividends as a species of (fixed-rate) interest, equal to the "interest on capital" or "pure interest" that bondholders receive, plus insurance against risk:

> The annual income from a railway bond is interest on lender's capital, and consequently pure interest. Ordinarily the bondholder is adequately protected against the loss of his capital by a mortgage on the railroad. On the other hand, the holder of a share of railway stock is a part owner of the railroad, and consequently incurs the risk of losing his property. Hence the dividend that he receives on his stock comprises interest on capital plus insurance against loss. It is usually one or two per cent higher than the rate on the bonds. Since the officers and directors are the only shareholders who perform any labor in the management of the railroad, only they receive wages of management. Consequently the gross profits are divided into interest and dividends at fixed rates, and fixed salaries.[27]

Because Ryan's terminology varies, it may be worthwhile at this point to complete the schema. To determine a corporation's profit for some period of time, several categories of costs must be subtracted from its total revenue:

Total Revenue
- – Rent (to Landowners)
- – Wages (to Laborers)
- – Other Costs of Production: Materials, Repairs, Replacement, Depreciation, etc.

= Gross Profits or Gross Returns
- – Pure Interest or Interest on Capital (to Bondholders and Stockholders)
- – Insurance against Risk or Insurance against Loss (to Stockholders)

= Net Profits
- – Wages of Management or Wages of Direction or Salaries (to Managers)

= Surplus Profits or Surplus Interest (to Stockholders, or to Managers and Laborers?)

In addressing the question of whether the practice of receiving interest can be justified morally, Ryan explores two avenues of approach: "Is interest justified immediately and intrinsically by the relations existing between the owner and the user of capital? Or, is it rendered morally good by its effects upon social welfare?"[28] He considers three "intrinsic or individual grounds upon which the capitalist's claim to interest has been defended . . . : productivity, service, and abstinence,"[29] and concludes that receiving interest cannot be conclusively justified on either of the first two grounds: "It is impossible to demonstrate that the capitalist has a strict right to interest because his capital produces interest, or because it renders a service to the laborer or the consumer."[30] Some interest can, however, be partially justified on the ground of abstinence:

> A part, probably a small part, of the interest now received can be fairly justified by the title of sacrifice. Some present owners of capital would not have saved had they not expected to receive interest. In their case interest may be regarded as a just compensation for the sacrifice that they underwent when they decided to save instead of consume.[31]

Ryan next considers alleged social and presumptive justifications of interest. He concludes that for a variety of reasons, and "in view of the manifold and grave uncertainties of the situation, it is practically certain that modern States are justified in permitting interest."[32] He also softens his position on individual justifications of interest: "We have not contended that the intrinsic factors of productivity and service are certainly invalid morally. We have merely insisted that the moral worth of these titles has never been objectively demonstrated."[33] The conclusion of his discussion of the justification of interest is that it is probably not immoral for capitalists to receive interest (including stockholders' dividends) "as long as the present industrial system endures."[34]

Within his discussion of the third class of contributors and the corresponding third species of income—managers and profits—Ryan identifies six canons of distributive justice "that have been or might be adopted in distributing the product of industry among those who participate actively in the productive process."[35] He rejects the canon of arithmetical equality, because people with different degrees of need require different quantities of external goods in order to attain the same level of welfare, and because it is to the benefit of society as a whole that persons with above-average abilities have incentives to be more productive. The canon of proportional needs is also found to be deficient because it ignores the relative magnitudes of different person's contributions to the products of industry, because there is no practical way to determine accurately each persons needs, and because, like the canon of equality, it would reduce the incentive to be more productive. Ryan also finds the canon of efforts and sacrifices to be unsatisfactory because it ignores differences in needs, because it ignores the fact that different persons achieve different levels of productivity with the same level of effort and sacrifice, and because effort and sacrifice cannot be accurately measured. Ryan then makes a division within the set of canons: "The three rules already considered are formally ethical, inasmuch as they are directly based upon the dignity and claims of personality. The two following are primarily physical and social; for they measure economic value rather than ethical worth."[36] The canon of comparative productivity is problematic because it ignores differences of need, effort, and sacrifice, because persons are not personally responsible for many of the qualities that make them more or less productive than others, and because there is often no way to compare the productivity of persons engaged in different kinds of work. According to the canon of relative scarcity, persons with abilities for which the demand exceeds the supply should be compensated more than persons with abilities that are not scarce. Ryan finds this principle to be inadequate because some persons acquire such abilities through great effort or sacrifice, while others are given such abilities. Nevertheless, Ryan concludes that neither in the case of greater productivity nor in the case of scarcer ability for which the agent is not personally responsible "can the demand for and the receipt of superior rewards be proved immoral."[37]

The sixth canon is that of human welfare or social justice. It "includes and summarizes all that is implied in the five other canons,"[38] and is found by Ryan to be acceptable. He writes of this canon:

> It requires that all human beings be treated as persons, as possessed of natural rights: this is equality. It demands that all industrial persons receive at least that amount of income which is necessary for decent living and reasonable self-development: this is a recognition of needs. The canon of human welfare declares that some consideration must be accorded to manifestations of good will by those who take part in the processes of industry: this is a recognition of efforts and sacrifices. And it gives reasonable recognition to the canons of productivity and scarcity.[39]

In addition to his discussions of the justification of interest and the canons of distributive justice, Ryan provides three fundamental ethical principles upon which any economic system must rest if it is to be just:

1. The earth and its potentialities belong to all members of the human race without distinction.[40]
2. Men are morally obliged to use the goods and opportunities of the earth in accordance with the laws of justice and charity.[41]
3. Industrial society is an organism, every part of which is subordinate within certain limits to the whole and is obliged to promote the well-being of the whole.[42]

Following his discussions of ethical canons and principles, Ryan turns to the question of distribution of surplus profits, that is, profits remaining after rent, wages, salaries, interest, dividends, and all other expenses of production have been paid. The practice in capitalistic economies, according to Ryan, is to give this surplus to a corporation's stockholders. He argues, however, that it should go instead to the firm's laborers and managers, in proportion to their regular wages and salaries. He believes we have made a mistake in understanding the analogy between business corporations, the dominant form of business organization in developed nations today, and the sole-proprietorship, which was dominant in earlier centuries:

> Our conception of property has not taken account of the changes in the functions of the proprietor. Because the small farmer, the small shop-keeper, the independent artisan, obtain all the profits of their business we have assumed that this variable share should likewise be taken by the non-working stockholder in a corporation. We have permitted him to obtain not only the normal rate of interest or dividend, but an additional percentage from surplus profits.[43]

Ryan argues that, according to the canon of human welfare or social justice, these profits should go to the managers and laborers, not to the stockholders:

> A corporation which, with fair methods of competition, obtains surplus gains is evidently more efficient than its competitors. Instead of awarding the fruits of this superior efficiency to the stockholders, it would be more economic and more scientific to distribute them among the active workers, from the president of the concern down to the humblest day laborer. This arrangement would return the surplus to those who had created it and would prove a powerful stimulus to sustained and increased efficiency. The stockholders, as such, do not produce the surplus. If they receive guaranteed and cumulative dividends, they have sufficient incentive to place and keep their money in the business. To pay them more than is necessary to attain

> these ends, is unprofitable and socially wasteful. It is contrary to the canon of human welfare.[44]

Ryan's analysis of the ethics of economic distribution provides not only an alternative to the current, orthodox theory of the firm, according to which the supreme objective of a business corporation is the maximization of shareholder wealth, but also an alternative to stakeholder theory, according to which a corporation is a bundle of contracts (most of them implied). The fact that "agency theory" is understood to require the maximization of shareholder value (within the constraints of other laws) stems from the inability to see human organizations as anything more than aggregates of human individuals. If managers are agents of the corporation, but a corporation is nothing more than a legal fiction, managers must really be agents of those who own the corporation. And since the relationship of most corporations to most of their stockholders involves little more than buying and selling shares and receiving dividends, the agents of the stockholders must be obligated to maximize the wealth of the stockholders.

Within the philosophical and theological tradition to which Ryan belongs, however, "neither political nor economic society is a mere collection of individuals."[45] And this is true not only of society as a whole, but also of the intermediate organizations called for by the principle of subsidiarity. But if human organizations are more than mere aggregates of individuals, they, like Plato's ideal city-state, can have their own character traits, including virtues and vices. And what greater objective could corporate executives have, *qua* corporate executives, than to manage their corporations in such a manner that they become virtuous, and specifically just, corporations?

If Ryan's proposal were adopted, the problem of corporate governance would be radically changed. According to today's orthodoxy, the board of directors of a business corporation "should be regarded primarily as a governance structure safeguard between the firm and owners of equity capital."[46] Adopting Ryan's alternative would not eliminate all problems. But the unsolved problem of compelling managers to maximize shareholder value, rather than their own utility, would no longer remain. And if our range of options is not limited to a one-dimensional continuum between Marxism and laissez-faire capitalism, the now-undeniable failure of Marxism need not mean that we must be satisfied with our present economic order.

CONTRIBUTIVE JUSTICE

But even if Ryan's proposal is better than our present way of doing business, it has inadequacies of its own. One problem is that he focuses on only one species of justice, and says little about the others. Aristotle distinguishes three species of the virtue of justice.[47] Commutative or exchange justice is the only one of the three taken seriously by the mainstream of present-day microeconomic and management theory. "Commutative justice considers persons as equals before the law and regulates their relations, their exchanges, and services from the standpoint of equality of the exchanged goods or of the remunerations for services."[48] If human associations are fictions, nothing but aggregations of individuals, then justice is justice among individuals. As Josef Pieper makes the point, for the consistent individualist, "when an individual confronts the social totality, *one* individual confronts *many* individuals. For him the social whole is not a reality of a special order. Therefore he admits of only one single type of justice—commutative justice—because individuals always have to do with other individuals."[49] Heinrich Rommen maintains that "the fundamental error of Rousseau is . . . the application of the rules of commutative justice to the relations between government or political authority and the governed."[50] And Clarence C. Walton notes the historical relationship between commutative justice and the theoretical foundations of capitalism: "Because exchange justice prevails more fully when markets are genuinely competitive and entry relatively easy, Adam Smith used this definition in his apologia for market capitalism: a competitive market was the best mechanism humans could contrive to meet the twin imperatives of justice and equality."[51] But when exchanging parties must bargain from significantly unequal starting points, commutative justice is insufficiently just.

Addressing adequately the justice of relationships among owners, managers, and laborers in Ryan's day (and probably in any other day) requires a discussion of distributive justice. And this is, of course, the species upon which he focuses. Given the unequal starting points of workers relative to investors and managers, commutative justice alone is insufficient. But labor's position today is not what it was in Ryan's day; it is now necessary to consider a third species of justice: legal or contributive justice. What are the responsibilities of investors, managers, workers, and corporations to the economic common good of society? Ryan says little about this matter, because he presupposes a pool of wealth in a static society. In presenting what he believes to be a just distribution of a firm's profits, he fails to discuss the role of internally-generated capital, retained earnings, in developing new products. But subsequent writers in the Christian social thought tradition have made progress in addressing issues of contributive justice. Pope John XXIII, in *Mater et magistra*, writes:

> Any adjustment between wages and profits must take into account the demands of the common good of the particular country and of the whole human family.
>
> What are these demands? On the national level they include: employment of the greatest number of workers; care lest privileged classes arise, even among the workers; maintenance of equilibrium between wages and prices; the need to make goods and services accessible to the greatest number . . . .
>
> The demands of the common good on the international level include: the avoidance of all forms of unfair competition between the economies of different countries; the fostering of mutual collaboration and good will; and effective co-operation in the development of economically less advanced communities.
>
> These demands of the common good, both on a national and a world level, must also be borne in mind when assessing the rate of return due as compensation to the company's management, and as interest or dividends to investors.[52]

When deciding how to distribute the fruits of a corporation's labors, its directors and officers must consider contributive, as well as commutative and distributive justice. And there are no simple answers to questions about how great a share of surplus profits to give to shareholders, workers, and themselves, and how great a share to retain for expanded operations. Making such decisions requires the virtue of seasoned professional competence or *prudentia*.

In a chapter of his *Better Economic Order* titled "Industrial Democracy," Ryan calls for a "new status for labor: sharing in management, in ownership, and in profits."[53] This paper has focused on an increased share for labor of profits. But it is worth observing that labor's greatest increases since Ryan's day have been in their share of the ownership of corporations. The dominant owners of corporate America today are not wealthy capitalists, but pension funds. Franz H. Mueller wrote in 1963: "What is the essential difference, if any, between the manager of a 'capitalistic' corporation, possibly owned by a pension or welfare fund, and the manager of a government-controlled enterprise in Russia?"[54] And the role of pension funds is much greater today than it was when Mueller wrote.

This situation differs from the one Ryan envisioned. He wanted laborers to own shares of the particular corporations for which they work. Today's workers, instead, own small shares of many corporations, with which they have no other relationship. One advantage of this distribution of wealth is the security of diversification. If workers owned only shares of the corporation for which they worked, failure of that corporation would mean not only loss of employment, but also loss of savings. The position of workers is more secure today.

But the disadvantage of the rise of pension funds as dominant owners of corporations is that investors are more interested in the growth of the fund than in the good of the many corporations in whose shares the fund is invested. We have made progress in distributive justice since Ryan wrote. But now that laborers own the country, they must think about the character of the organizations they own and must meet the demands of contributive justice.

Much work remains to be done in understanding what it means for an economic order and for corporations and persons within them to be just. But I believe the works of Msgr. Ryan and others within his tradition deserve careful scrutiny and are a good place to begin that work. And I am confident that extending this tradition into new territories is far more likely to bear fruit than pursuing the "stakeholder" approach of expanding the bundle of contracts within and around the corporation.

BIBLIOGRAPHY

Aristotle. *Nicomachean Ethics*. Trans. Terence Irwin., Indianapolis: Hackett, 1985.

Dodd, E. Merrick, Jr. "For Whom Are Corporate Managers Trustees?" *Harvard Law Review* 45 (1932): 1145-63.

Freeman, R. Edward, ed. *Business Ethics: The State of the Art*. New York: Oxford University Press, 1991.

Jensen, Michael C. and William H. Meckling. "Theory of the Firm: Managerial Behavior, Agency Costs, and Ownership Structure." *Journal of Financial Economics* 3 (1976): 305-60; revised version, *Economics and Social Institutions: Insights from the Conferences on Analysis & Ideology*. Ed. Karl Brunner. Boston: Martinus Nijhoff, 1979, 163-232. (Citations in this paper are of the revised version of Jensen and Meckling's article.)

John XXIII. *Mater et magistra*. Rome, 15 May 1961.

John Paul II. *Sollicitudo rei socialis*. Rome, 30 December 1987.

_____. *Centesimus annus*. Rome, 1 May 1991.

Madden, Richard B. "The Large Corporation as a Mediating Structure." *Democracy and Mediating Structures: A Theological Inquiry*. Ed. Michael Novak. Washington, D.C.: American Enterprise Institute for Public Policy Research, 1980.

Martin, T. R. and Richard D. Roberts. "The Unfinished Business of Reforming Corporate Government." *America* Vol. 164, No. 5 (9 February 1991): 117-21.

Mueller, Franz H. "The Church and the Social Question," in *The Challenge of Mater et magistra*. Ed. Joseph N. Moody and Justus George Lawler. New York: Herder and Herder, 1963.

Novak, Michael. *Catholic Ethic and the Spirit of Capitalism*. New York: Macmillan, 1993.

Pieper, Josef. *The Four Cardinal Virtues: Prudence, Justice, Fortitude, Temperance*. New York: Harcourt Brace Jovanovich, 1965; Notre Dame, Ind.: University of Notre Dame Press, 1966. Pieper's *Justice* was translated by Lawrence E. Lynch, and originally published as *Über die Gerechtigkeit*. Kösel-Verlag, 1955.

Pius XI. *Quadragesimo anno*. Rome, 15 May 1931.

Rommen, Heinrich A. *The State in Catholic Thought: A Treatise in Political Philosophy*. St. Louis: B. Herder, 1945; repr., New York: Greenwood, 1969.

Ryan, John A. *A Better Economic Order*. New York and London: Harper & Brothers, 1935.

_____. *Distributive Justice: The Right and Wrong of Our Present Distribution of Wealth*, 3rd ed. New York: Macmillan, 1942.

Smith, Len Young, Richard A. Mann, and Barry S. Roberts. *Business Law and the Regulation of Business*, 4th ed. Minneapolis/St. Paul: West, 1993.

Walton, Clarence C. *The Moral Manager*. New York: Harper & Row, 1988.

Williamson, Oliver E. *The Economic Institutions of Capitalism: Firms, Markets, Relational Contracting*. New York: Free Press, 1985.

Notes

1. Ryan, *Distributive Justice*, 188.
2. Ibid., 151.
3. Ibid., 168.
4. Ryan, *A Better Economic Order*, 183; *Distributive Justice*, 342.
5. Aristotle, *Nicomachean Ethics*, 1107a9-13.
6. John Paul II, *Sollicitudo rei socialis*, ¶ 41.7.
7. Novak, *The Catholic Ethic and the Spirit of Capitalism*, 147.
8. John Paul II, *Sollicitudo rei socialis*, ¶ 41.1.

9. John Paul II, *Centesimus annus*, ¶ 42.1.

10. Ibid., ¶ 42.

11. Ibid., ¶ 42.1.

12. Ryan, *Distributive Justice*, 168-69.

13. The classic statement of the principle of subsidiarity, which takes its name from the Latin word *subsidium*, meaning "support," "help," or "assistance," is found in *Quadragesimo anno*, ¶ 79: "As history abundantly proves, it is true that on account of changed conditions many things which were done by small associations in former times cannot be done now save by large associations. Still, that most weighty principle, which cannot be set aside or changed, remains fixed and unshaken in social philosophy: Just as it is gravely wrong to take from individuals what they can accomplish by their own initiative and industry and give it to the community, so also it is an injustice and at the same time a grave evil and disturbance of right order to assign to a greater and higher association what lesser and subordinate organization can do. For every social activity ought of its very nature to furnish help to the members of the body social, and never destroy and absorb them."

14. Walton, *The Moral Manager*, 218.

15. Martin and Roberts, "The Unfinished Business of Reforming Corporate Government," 118.

16. Rommen, *The State in Catholic Thought*, 184.

17. Jensen and Meckling, "Theory of the Firm," 170-71; emphasis in the original.

18. Ibid., 171; emphasis in the original.

19. Ibid., 171-72.

20. Dodd, "For Whom Are Corporate Managers Trustees?" 1145-46.

21. Smith, Mann, and Roberts, *Business Law and the Regulation of Business*, 746.

22. Madden, "The Large Corporation as a Mediating Structure," 107.

23. Smith, Mann, and Roberts, *Business Law and the Regulation of Business*, 747. These authors elaborate: "Whether a corporation is a 'person' within the meaning of a constitution or statute is a matter of construction based on the intent of the lawmakers in using the word. For example, a corporation is considered a person within the provisions in the Fifth and Fourteenth Amendments to the U. S. Constitution that no 'person' shall be 'deprived of life, liberty, or property, without due process of law' and in the Fourteenth Amendment provision that no state shall 'deny to any person within its jurisdiction the equal protection of the laws.' A corporation also enjoys the right of a person to be secure against unreasonable searches and seizures, as provided for in the Fourth Amendment. On the other hand, a corporation is not considered

to be a person within the Fifth Amendment clause that protects a 'person' against self-incrimination," 748.

24. John Paul II, *Centesimus annus*, ¶ 35.2.

25. R. Edward Freeman, *Introduction to Business Ethics*, 4.

26. Ryan, *Distributive Justice*, 3.

27. Ibid., 88.

28. Ibid., 121.

29. Ibid., 126-27.

30. Ibid., 134.

31. Ibid., 134.

32. Ibid., 140.

33. Ibid., 142.

34. Ibid., 146.

35. Ibid., 180.

36. Ibid., 183.

37. Ibid., 187.

38. Ibid., 187.

39. Ibid., 197-98.

40. Ryan, *A Better Economic Order*, 148.

41. Ibid., 149.

42. Ibid.,, 153.

43. Ibid., 167.

44. Ryan, *Distributive Justice*, 192.

45. Ryan, *A Better Economic Order*, 153.

46. Williamson, *The Economic Institutions of Capitalism*, 298.

47. Aristotle, *Nicomachean Ethics*, Book V.

48. Rommen, *The State in Catholic Thought*, 185.

49. Pieper, *The Four Cardinal Virtues*, 73.

50. Rommen, *The State in Catholic Thought*, 320.

51. Walton, *The Moral Manager*, 135.

52. Pope John XXIII, *Mater et magistra*, ¶¶ 78-81.

53. Ryan, *A Better Economic Order*, 160-74.

54. Mueller, "The Church and the Social Question," 136-37.

Limited Liability

M. J. PLATTS

The trader sees work as an undesirable cost in an opportunistic deal (the adventurer model). The craftsman sees work as a creative enrichment process for both craftsman and client *(a calling).* The history of the development of western civilization is the history of successive waves of people who have dedicated themselves to this enrichment process. Two characteristics define this work. First, their labor is not just an act of communication but an act of communion. Their actions definitively carry life's meaning. There is, second, an ascetic self-control in their behavior. Whenever channels are dedicated, the Light comes through and humanity grows. So they *sacrifice* their work—make it a channel for the Light—*make it sacred.* This formative self-control is not negative but positive. In western history the development of the capacity to transmit Light is a well-known path. It is described as the Way of Virtue—from the Latin "*virtus,*" meaning "strength."

Any work can be made a channel. What matters in its formation is its dedication. What matters in its operation is constant openness, constant inner listening for guidance. Any limit on liability closes the channel. Meaning comes from insight, insight comes from inner work, inner work comes from commitment, and commitment comes from the experience that it is indeed true that inner effort results in meaningfulness. The cycle of commitment and confirming experience is continuously tested. At every step the commitment has to be made alone, and in the face of fears and desires. Only then is the meaningfulness revealed. To turn from that commitment, because of fear or desire, does not remove the emotion. It simply becomes invisible, as does the meaningfulness which lay beyond it. That emotion then radiates out through you at others, whom you seek to control with it. Through fear and desire life is demeaned. *Power* is not *service.*

Fountain of Virtue

Four lines of Light came out of twelfth-century Spain (fig. 1), each forming a Way of Virtue.

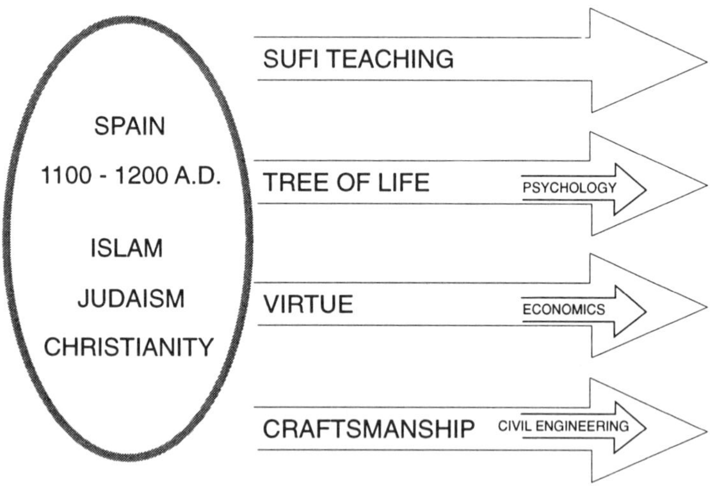

FIG. 1

One was the Sufi line, which had brought understanding to Spain in the first place. In the conflux and intermingling of Islamic, Jewish, and Christian thoughts in the universities of Spain it took new shape and acquired new strength, emerging in Ibn El-Arabi, "The Greatest Sheik," to return east, in due course to revitalize Islamic teaching. Too often ignored in the west, this line is today perhaps most accessibly represented in the works of Idries Shah.[1] It is too easily forgotten how in twelfth-century Spain people who were renowned in Europe as Christian mystics, under Christianized names, were at the same time renowned in the Islamic world as Sufi teachers under their own names.

Thomas Aquinas benefited as much from studying their commentaries on Aristotle as on the translations of Aristotle that they provided. To give honor where honor is due is also to remember that honor is not mere lip service. We can benefit as much from studying their work today as Aquinas himself did then. In the exposition of the necessary practical details of self-development they are unsurpassed.

The second line is the Jewish way of knowledge called "Kabbalah," which means "to receive." Often acting as translators and intermediaries, and intimately intertwined in the developments in Sufi and Christian mystical thinking, Kabbalah itself underwent a transformation. The Tree of Life, a meditative glyph known from ancient times and given embodiment in the shape of the seven-branched candlestick by Moses, took on its modern western form in this period in Spain. Most completely and accessibly represented today by the work of Z'ev ben Shimon Halevi,[2] this line is important because modern psychology is derived from it. The Tree of Life provides a very powerful map of the psychological and spiritual structure necessary for any organization to transmit the Light.

The third line is the line of which Aquinas himself is a key part and for which the Friars Preachers, and in a different way the Friars Minor, were for centuries the conduit.[3] It is the line from which all the modern universities emerge, the line of philosophical study. There is an antecedent to this line, in western Europe, in the monastic movement beginning with Patrick in Ireland and spreading first to Scotland with Columba and then, through the fifth, sixth, and seventh centuries steadily throughout Europe.[4] It is hard to imagine the completeness of the illiteracy of the Dark Ages after the collapse of the Roman empire. To those Irish monks is due the honor of regenerating the skill of reading and writing, and the practice of personal reflective study that goes with written material. The material and practices that come from Spain in the twelfth century moved this study to a completely different level. The detailed discussion of virtue, particularly as articulated by Aquinas, became the core of the subject known as moral philosophy and studied for centuries in Europe's universities. What has been a failure is that over the centuries these universities, all of which are in origin religious institutions, have slid into discussion of the virtues as remote, academic, abstract entities, when they should have been sustaining the teaching of the practicalities of the process of *developing* the virtues. This is no small failure when it is realized that Adam Smith was professor of moral philosophy at Glasgow University and had written

"The Theory of Moral Sentiments" twenty years before he wrote "Wealth of Nations." Economics as a subject is a subset of the study of moral philosophy and, at their best, all modern economists are serious philosophers. Much has been lost, and when Frederick Hayek, in the last chapter of his last book, laments that society has lost the input that religious awareness used to give, that lament needs to be heard and answered, not in empty rhetoric, but in the elucidation and demonstration of practical methodologies.[5] The extent of seeking for guidance has increased significantly since Hayek's lament, and open discussion of the virtues is beginning to be possible now in economic circles (as for instance in Gertrude Himmelfarb's recent book *The Demoralization of Society*).[6] A similar call is slowly emerging in corporate management circles.

The fourth line again intertwines two threads, of theory and practice, and similarly suffers today, from the over-abstraction of the theory from the practice by the same universities' over-commitment to a scientific paradigm that views knowledge as something to be written down and treated academically, not as a practice to be lived. In the universities, this path has been taught as the study of natural philosophy, and has evolved into modern science. However its origins are the translation of the Zij of al-Khwarizmi (which was a book on astronomy, but which contained sine tables and introduced the use of Arabic numerals and Arabic mathematics to the west) and Euclid's geometry, in 1126, by Adelard of Bath.[7] These were not taken up in any abstract way at all but were picked up by the master masons who built the cathedrals and became the core of Masonic teaching of technique, out of which grew modern engineering. While Arabic numerals were in use for engineering in this way, three hundred years later cathedral accounts were still being done in Roman numerals. Yet by this time, and partly inspired by the Islamic Qurmations,[8] who amongst other things built the Dome of the Rock, Masonic teaching had acquired a spiritual teaching vocabulary and methodology, still extant today (though often debased) and known as the Way of the Craftsman.[9]

The Protestant Work Ethic

What is of particular interest, and represents the root of modern manufacturing industry, is the confluence of the good features of both these two last lines (fig. 2), in the seventeenth century, in a new line of Light emerging out of the struggles of the Protestant movements, to find meaning. One particular group colloquially known as Quakers but whose full organizational title is the Religious Society of Friends of Truth, stand as heirs in many ways to the Franciscan tradition, a reoccurrence of it so to speak, but this time carrying their spirituality out into the world through their manufacturing activities, rather than via retreat alone. The nature of this development of spiritual action is well described in Max Weber's *The Protestant Ethic and the Spirit of Capitalism.* Writing in Germany in 1904, Weber accurately pinpoints two approaches to capitalism that identify the source of the modern problem. Of one group he says:

> And in truth this peculiar idea, so familiar to us today, but in reality so little a matter of course, of one's duty in a calling, is what is most characteristic of the social ethic of capitalist culture, and is in a sense the fundamental basis of it. It is an obligation which the individual is supposed to feel and does feel towards the content of his professional activity, no matter in what it consists, in particular no matter whether it appears on the surface as a utilization of his personal powers, or only of his material possessions (as capital).[10]

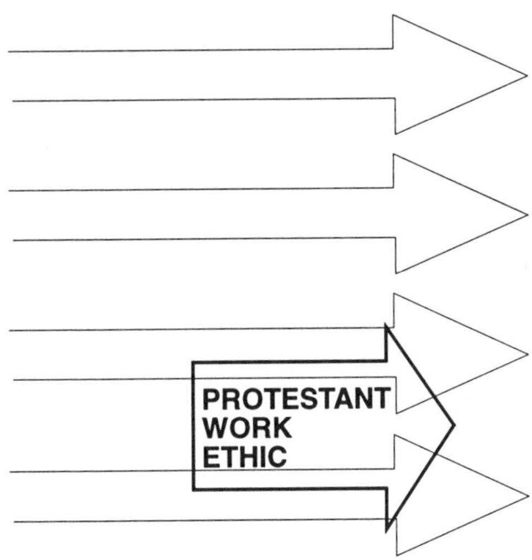

FIG. 2

Of the other group he says:

> Capitalistic acquisition as an adventure has been at home in all types of economic society which have known trade with the use of money

> and which have offered it opportunities, through *commenda*, farming of taxes, State loans, financing of wars, ducal courts and office-holders. Likewise the inner attitude of the adventurer, which laughs at all ethical limitations, has been universal. Absolute and conscious ruthlessness in acquisition has often stood in the closest connection with the strictest conformity to tradition. Moreover, with the break-down of tradition and the more or less complete extension of free economic enterprise, even to within the social group, the new thing has not generally been ethically justified and encouraged, but only tolerated as a fact. And this fact has been treated either as ethically indifferent or as reprehensible, but unfortunately unavoidable. This has not only been the normal attitude of all ethical teachings, but, what is more important, also that expressed in the practical action of the average man of pre-capitalistic times, pre-capitalistic in the sense that the rational utilization of capital in a permanent enterprise and the rational capitalistic organization of labour had not yet become dominant forces in the determination of economic activity. Now just this attitude was one of the strongest inner obstacles which the adaptation of man to the conditions of an ordered bourgeois-capitalistic economy has encountered everywhere.[11]

The seeds of that first approach are easily found in early Quaker behavior. In 1654 George Fox, writing about a group of businessmen who had come to live by their consciences, said:

> many Friends, being tradesmen of several sorts lost their custom at first; for the people would not trade with them nor trust them, and for a time Friends that were tradesmen could hardly get enough money to buy bread. But afterwards people came to see Friends' honesty and truthfulness and 'yea' and 'nea' at a word in their dealing, and their lives and conversations did preach and reach to the witness of God in all people, and they knew and saw that, for conscience sake towards God, they would not cozen and cheat them, and at last that they might send any child and be as well used as themselves, at any of their shops.
>
> So then things altered so that all the inquiry was, where was a draper or shopkeeper or tailor or shoemaker or any other tradesman that was Quaker; insomuch that Friends had double the trade, beyond any of their neighbours. And if there was any trading they had it, inasmuch that then the cry of all the professors and others was "If we let these people alone they will take the trading of the nation out of our hands."[12]

And they did. Ironmaking, steelmaking, canals, railways—machines of every description came out of these people—and *meaningful work.*

In that line came the gatherings that eventually became the first professional engineering institution in the world, The Institution of Civil Engineers (1821), so named because they were not military engineers. They knew what they were building.

And concerning the creative use of capital, William Penn, the Quaker statesman, contemporary, and friend of George Fox, wrote in *Some Fruits of Solitude* in 1693:

> Lend not beyond thy Ability, nor refuse to lend out of thy ability; especially when it will help others more than it can hurt thee.
>
> If thy Debtor be honest and capable, thou hast thy Mony again, if not with Encrease, with Praise: If he prove insolvent, don't ruin him to get that, which it will not ruin thee to lose: For thou art but a Steward, and another is thy Owner, Master and Judge.
>
> The more merciful Acts thou dost, the more Mercy thou wilt receive; and if with a charitable Imployment of thy Temporal Riches, Thou gainest eternal Treasure, thy Purchase is infinite: Thou wilt have found the Art of Multiplying indeed.[13]

In these two passages is captured the ethic of an era, and also the streak of jealousy that is its enemy. It is well to remember that the industrial revolution in Britain was built on a hundred percent personal liability before man and before God. It is a Sufi story that tells of a Sufi master one day giving each of his pupils a chicken and telling them to go somewhere where they would not be seen and kill it, and then report back. They all set off, thoughtfully, except one, who sat where he was, tears streaming down his face, who then knelt forward, still nursing his chicken, and put his head on the ground in sobbing prayer. One by one the others returned. When all were gathered, the Sufi master asked each in turn where they had gone, then said to the sobbing student "and you?" Still sobbing he cried "Master, I cannot do as you ask. There is nowhere I can go where I am not seen."

Throughout Islamic teaching Allah says "I am closer to you than your jugular vein." We answer for all we do. There is no such thing as limited liability. When that is known inwardly, and carried inwardly, it bears fruit.

Unfortunately there are flaws in both the British and American makeup. The adventurer element is strong in American history, with a determined avoidance of liability. Max Weber observes of Benjamin Franklin:

> Now, all Franklin's moral attitudes are coloured with utilitarianism. Honesty is useful, because it assures credit; so are punctuality,

> industry, frugality, and that is the reason they are virtues. A logical deduction from this would be that where, for instance, the appearance of honesty serves the same purpose, that would suffice, and an unnecessary surplus of this virtue would evidently appear to Franklin's eyes as unproductive waste. And as a matter of fact, the story in his autobiography of his conversion to those virtues, or the discussion of the value of a strict maintenance of the appearance of modesty, the assiduous belittlement of one's own deserts in order to gain general recognition later, confirms this impression. According to Franklin, those virtues, like all others, are only in so far virtues as they are actually useful to the individual, and the surrogate of mere appearance is always sufficient when it accomplishes the end in view. It is a conclusion which is inevitable for strict utilitarianism. The impression of many Germans that the virtues professed by Americanism are pure hypocrisy seems to have been confirmed by this striking case.[14]

The German view is expressed clearly in Oswald von Nell Breuning's words of 1934, here with a surrounding comment by Michael Naughton, which directly speaks of virtues:

> Munificence, like courage, strives "for what is arduous and difficult." Whereas courage may jeopardize one's life, munificence may jeopardize one's resources. Because the virtue of munificence directs resources toward the good of the community as well as profit, the munificent person acts courageously by incurring greater financial risk. Munificence is an expression of public co-operation, incorporating both market criteria and the good of society.
>
> Oswald von Nell Breuning calls munificence "a genuine capitalistic virtue," that is, "a virtue for the entrepreneur." He explains that only the entrepreneur who "gives first thought to service and second thought to gain" practices the virtue of munificence. Nell Breuning explains that munificence is manifested in that person
>
>> who in his enterprise and in his means of production employs his working men for the creation of goods of true worth; who does not wrong them by demanding that they take part in the creation of futilities, or even harmful and evil things; who offers to the consumer nothing but useful goods and services rather than, taking advantage of the latter's inexperience or weakness, betrays him into spending his money

> for things he does not need, or that are not only useless but even injurious to him.

> Products should not be produced only for the purpose of fulfilling market whims; the choice of products has an ethical and even a spiritual character that can never be reduced to simple economics.[15]

The echoes between Oswald von Nell Breuning's words and those of George Fox and William Penn two and one-half centuries previously are obvious. What forms a continuum through them and marks the difference between them and the (ultimately egocentric) utilitarianism of Benjamin Franklin is the difference between affirmation and assertion, a difference enshrined in British law by the early Quakers. They observed that any assertion is inevitably power based. It is based on one's will. If one affirms something, however, it is because one acknowledges the truth of something that stands in its own right beyond oneself. An affirmation is the result of reflective observation, experience followed by reflective thought. One affirms a truth because it has achieved indelible meaning. One therefore acknowledges that one understands (stands under the influence of) it and can do no other. It is a statement of humility. Sadly, but perhaps consistent with Max Weber's observation of Benjamin Franklin's utilitarianism, which will steal the appearance of virtue for personal ends, the word "affirm" has been hijacked in America. Affirmative-action programs are visibly assertive, because of a failure to understand this crucial difference between something being outwardly visible and something being inwardly visible. This is not so in Germany, where still today there is no notion of limited liability, either in company ownership or in civic conduct, and that liability is carried inwardly. Thank heaven.

Echoes in the East

In Japan the same sort of inner awareness and sense of responsibility is established, from a Confucian starting point. Business journals from the Pacific Rim will now sometimes refer to the Confucian work ethic. The writings of Confucius, Lao Tzu, and Sun Tzu taken together provide a very substantial and articulate core of meditative material guiding leaders toward seeking meaning rather than seeking power.[16] The common saying "when the best leader's work is done the people say it happened naturally" (or, as it is sometimes rendered, ". . . the people say we did it ourselves") is after all a translation from Lao Tzu. The I Ching is equally useful meditative material toward the path of virtue. Through the Tokugawa period in Japan (1600-1868) some of the key elements of the Japanese religious thinking evolved, to develop in the people an attitude towards their work as a *calling* very similar to that found by the Protestants in Europe. In particular towards the end of that period the Shingaku movement, and the teaching of its leader Ishida Baigan, were very influential in this direction.[17] This made it possible for the Meiji restoration to give engineering leadership a social significance it previously did not have (Tokyo University's School of Engineering was founded in 1867) and for a very high proportion of the samurai to move to it as their warrior leadership status was being dismantled. The steady development of society as a moral community, through this century, is inspirational work of the highest order, in which semibureaucratic organizations such as the Kyochokai (The Co-operation and Harmony Society, established in 1919) played a significant role.[18] It is entirely natural as a consequence that whereas America, with a long history of slavery, should bequeath to the manufacturing world a view of a company that consists only of the capital, and of managers that have responsibility only toward the owners of that capital, are entirely detached from the subject matter of the work, and manage people by detailed control of their actions (scientific management, the Taylorist, Fordist approach) reminiscent of slaves; in Japan, as in Germany, manufacturing companies are invariably led by engineers, who see their responsibility as a very wide social remit and who have bequeathed to the world myriad managerial practices all to do with developing sensitivity and awareness and providing instant, direct, and visible communication of meaning between people (listening to the customer, kan ban, kaizen, Quality circles, Taguchi analysis, Ishikawa diagrams, etc). These have brought more people closer to heaven than all the guns in America.

The Problem of Duality

Britain is an interesting case because it has a dual identity. It is often forgotten that in 1066 England was a conquered country and that still in 1400 the language of the ruling aristocracy was Norman-French, not Anglo-Saxon. The south of England, and Parliament, was all to do with control, with control of military capacity on the one hand (the Navy in particular) and control of trade on the other. It is perhaps hard for Americans to understand that in 1776, when they were fighting for independence from a parliament in which they were ridiculously under-represented, the north of England and Scotland were equally pathetically represented, but fighting was not a possible option (the 1745 Scottish uprising had been very harshly put down). Developing a peaceful but nevertheless protest-ant display of their own worth was a key driver of the industrial revolution. These unkind overlords would *not* stand between them and God, and they would find a way to get the Light through.[19]

The whole of the industrial revolution is founded on this and it was driven through—all the industrial heritage Britain has was created—on 100 percent personal liability. Limited liability did not arise as a possibility in company ownership until 1862 and only slowly came into use in the following decades. But it allowed the other half of Britain to change the rules in its favor. *Chambers' Encyclopaedia* commented in 1889:

> Upon the whole the statute of 1862 has been beneficial in the development of trade; but it has also produced a great mass of dishonest speculation, with which the common-law doctrines of fraud and misrepresentation have not been adequate to deal. The law will shortly be amended so as to take further securities for the substantial character of business and for the punishment of dishonesty.[20]

While the north was the fountain of industry the city of London had long been the trading capital of the world. It still controls one of the largest international investment portfolios in the world, conservatively estimated at twice the total capital invested in U.K. businesses.[21] During the nineteenth century the city itself was rampantly growing.[22] In any complete ownership model, ownership implies long-term responsibility for meaningful leadership. It is necessary to have a mechanism for transferring shares in companies, but this is very secondary to ownership, as is the case with the small European stock exchanges, and in the Far East. Unfortunately the introduction of limited liability in Britain opened up the shares market to the buying and selling, deal-making opportunism of the city.[23] With this one stroke capitalism in the U.K. moved from the first of Max Weber's categories to the second; upper management moved away from identification *with* the work to manipulation *of* it. Only in the Anglo-American world are there business schools that teach management as a separate skill, and only in the Anglo-American world is accounting, similarly, taught and revered as a separate skill. And both vocabulary and activity changed. Only in Anglo-American companies does one get competitive takeover bids, with "dawn raids" on shares, all the strategies and vocabulary of battle and always, always the vocabulary of competition. Companies of the other school know, that if you find what is the right thing to do, that is, if you find something latent in the collective unconscious and unlock it honorably, people will grow because of (and through) that work—your activity will be blessed. There is no greater success. To play combat games with the meaningfulness of other people's lives, and think it a clever thing to do, is the gateway to hell, manned by people who have not yet grown up. It consistently demeans the Way of the Craftsman and any concept of the Way of Virtue.

Knowing the Difference

Writing not particularly in an industrial but more in a total economic and social context (but isn't that what industry is?), Gertrude Himmelfarb has recently laid out very well the slow de-meaning of the way of virtue in Anglo-American society through this century. What has to be retrieved (and here it *is* an industrial issue) is the teaching of that path again; and this is not abstract, academic teaching about "the virtues" as something that is of nominal interest because it seemed to mean something to somebody else a long time ago and in a different place. What needs revitalizing is the teaching of the *process* of *achieving* virtue, *now*. Figures 3 and 4 are meditative pointers in this direction. Figure 3 is an ascending ladder of virtues, sequential in the sense that in a genuine way each one above depends on the established practice of the one below, fully resiliently and so established as to be an automatic habit beyond thought. That list uses the word "charity" in the way that William Penn uses it, which is rather the way Oswald von Nell Breuning uses the word "munificence." This ascending sequence fits side by side with (but goes beyond) Abraham Maslow's hierarchy of human needs.[24] Figure 4 transcribes it onto the Tree of Life, into which teaching it fits naturally, as it fits naturally into the teaching paths of any of the lines mentioned throughout this paper.

As with all these paths it is material for reflective thought and meditation. At root, assertive liability limitation is a process of anaesthetizing—desensitizing—whereas every step of the ascetic path not only increases sensitivity but instantly recognizes the understanding it brings, the pattern of meaning it makes inwardly visible, which then indelibly shapes subsequent action, which quietly affirms, that is, makes inwardly visible to others, the inherent truth of that pattern of meaning . . . so all respond.

VIRTUE: ABILITY TO TRANSMIT MEANING

COURAGE	:	Will commit oneself
CHARITY	:	Will commit resources
JUSTICE	:	Will hold to what is right
SERVICE	:	Will do what comes to you to be done
HUMILITY	:	Put oneself under the hand of Providence
PRUDENCE	:	Good custodianship, Balance, Integrity
HONESTY	:	Independent of emotions
MODESTY	:	Independent of attention
PATIENCE	:	Independent of time
MODERATION	:	Independent of things

FIG. 3

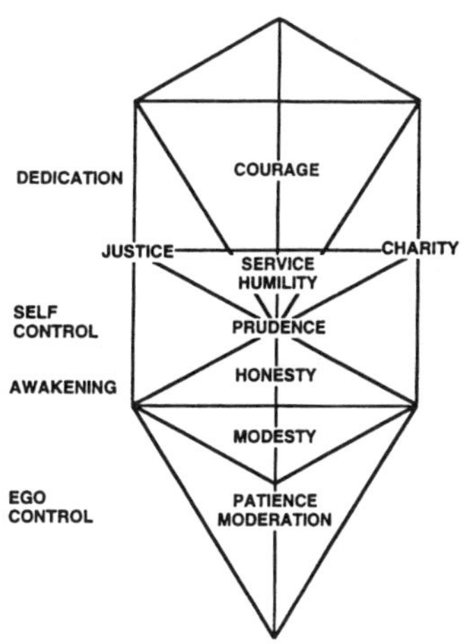

THE VIRTUES ARE MEASURES OF MANAGERIAL COMPETENCES

FIG. 4

Notes

1. Idries Shah, *The Sufis* (Anchor, 1971); *Learning How to Learn* (Octagon, 1983).

2. Z'ev ben Shimon Halevi, *Tree of Life* (Rider, 1972); *Kabbalah and Psychology* (Gateway, 1986).

3. C. H. Lawrence, *The Friars* (Longman, 1994).

4. T. Cahill, *How the Irish Saved Civilization* (Hodder & Stoughton, 1995).

5. Friedrich A. von Hayek, *The Fatal Conceit* (Routledge, 1988).

6. Gertrude Himmelfarb, *The De-moralization of Society* (Institute of Economic Affairs, 1995).

7. L. Cochrane, *Adelard of Bath—The First English Scientist* (British Museum Press, 1994).

8. J. J. Robinson, *Dungeon, Fire and Sword—The Knights Templar in the Crusades* (Michael O'Mara Books, 1994), 68.

9. W. K. McNulty, *Freemasonry—A Journey through Ritual and Symbol* (Thames and Hudson, 1991).

10. Max Weber, *The Protestant Ethic and the Spirit of Capitalism* (George Allen and Unwin, 1976), 54.

11. Ibid., 58.

12. George Fox, *Journal of George Fox* (Religious Society of Friends, 1975), 169.

13. William Penn, *Some Fruits of Solitude* (Friends United Press, 1985), 12.

14. Weber, *Ethic*, 52.

15. Michael Naughton, "Who Managers Become when They Manage: The Importance of Virtue in Management," *Journal of Applied Manufacturing Systems* 7 (1994): 27-31.

16. M. J. Platts, "Confucius on Leadership," *Journal of Strategic Change* 3 (1994): 249.

17. R. N. Bellah, *Tokugawa Religion* (Free Press, 1957).

18. W. D. Kinzley, *Industrial Harmony in Modern Japan: The Invention of a Tradition* (Routledge, 1991).

19. M. J. Platts, "Levels of Thought in Strategic Thinking" (Working paper, Cambridge, 1992).

20. *Chambers' Encyclopaedia*, Vol. 3 (1889), 390.

21. W. Jamieson, "Britain: The £1,400 Billion Global Investor," *Britain and Overseas* 25 (Economic Research Council, 1995): 3.

22. D. Kynaston, *The City of London*, Vol 1: *A World of Its Own 1815-1890* (Pimlico, 1994).

23. D. Kynaston, *The City of London*, Vol 2: *Golden Years 1890-1914* (Chatto & Windus, 1995).

24. Abraham Maslow, *Motivation and Personality* (Harper & Row, 1987); *Toward a Psychology of Being* (Van Nostrand Reinhold, 1968).

Entrepreneurs and Markets: Contemporary Entrepreneurial Practice and Morality in Relation to the Thought of John A. Ryan

MICHAEL J. SCHUCK and FRANCIS T. HANNAFEY, S.J.

Entrepreneurs are the heartbeat of the market economy. The other organs of economic production—laborers and capitalists—cannot substitute for the entrepreneur. The innovation, information gathering, foresight, and risk-taking involved in entrepreneurial activity provide the pulse behind new products and processes brought to the market. The two-hundred-year history of market system dominance in Europe and the Americas is, in many ways, a history of entrepreneurs.

The history of modern Roman Catholic social thought has paralleled the rise of the market system. As such, economic issues have been a dominant moral concern inside the social encyclical tradition of the modern papacy. Since Pope Benedict XIV's 1745 encyclical *Vix pervenit* on usury and dishonest profit, at least sixteen encyclicals have focused exclusively on economic morality.

Given the centrality of entrepreneurs to the market economy and the attention paid to economic morality in papal teaching, it is remarkable that two hundred years of modern Roman Catholic social thought has produced scant reflection on the entrepreneur. There are reasons for this lacuna; however, this is not the topic of our paper.

Instead, our focus is on a notable exception to Roman Catholicism's intellectual silence on the entrepreneur. That exception is Msgr. John A. Ryan. People aware of Ryan's work rightly identify him as a champion of labor. Few also recognize him as a champion of the entrepreneur. This may strike us today as incongruous, but it did not strike Ryan that way. He understood and appreciated the role of the entrepreneur no less than he understood and appreciated the role of the laborer.

In his 1982 book *The Entrepreneur: An Economic Theory*, Mark Casson offers a serviceable definition of the entrepreneur. The entrepreneur, he says, "is someone who specializes in taking judgmental decisions about the coordination of scarce resources" (Casson, 23). This definition has five parts requiring brief comment.

First, the entrepreneur is a person. Only a person can trigger the imagination, coordinate resources, negotiate with suppliers and fabricators, and make the quick decisions necessary to move a new idea to market. No team, committee, organization, or computer program can accomplish this creative task.

Second, an entrepreneur is a specialist. Not every player in the market economy has the ability—or the desire—to imagine new product options and the foresight to anticipate the many variables involved in bringing a new idea to reality. These skills are difficult (if not impossible) to learn in business school. As such, entrepreneurs have a comparative advantage over many otherwise powerful players in the market when it comes to creating change.

Third, entrepreneurs make judgmental decisions. Entrepreneurial decisions are calculated risks. The calculations flow from judgments about product possibilities, opportunity costs, projected public demand, and creditor patience. Everyone makes decisions in a market economy; not everyone makes the judgmental decisions characteristic of an entrepreneur.

Fourth, the entrepreneur is a coordinator. He or she puts the factors of production together in a new way. More than allocation, this involves reallocation of resources. It is this kind of coordination that makes entrepreneurs agents of change in the market.

Finally, entrepreneurs work within the context of scarce resources. Everyone operates in the market under conditions of scarcity, but the entrepreneur's situation is distinct. They are not primarily laborers, though entrepreneur's may work long and hard; nor are they identical with capitalists, because someone else typically finances an entrepreneur's idea.

Since entrepreneurs challenge conventional wisdom in the economic system, they often function on the fringes of business life. The nature of entrepreneurship, which is difficult to categorize in economic theory, make the ethical decision-making environment of entrepreneurs all the more challenging. In an informative 1992 essay entitled "Entrepreneurship through an Ethical Lens: Dilemmas and Issues for Research and Practice," J. Gregory Dees and Jennifer A. Starr identify four types of moral dilemmas facing entrepreneurs. They call these promoter, relationship, and innovator dilemmas; also included is a final category of "other" kinds of dilemmas confronting entrepreneurs. I will comment briefly on each of these dilemmas.

Promoter dilemmas occur as entrepreneurs coordinate the resources necessary to launch new products or processes. Entrepreneurial success depends on the ability to garner support from venture capitalists, fabricators, distributors, and consumers. In this context, moral issues surface concerning disclosure and manipulation of information, impression management, and deception. According to Dees and Starr, it is necessary to "distinguish harmless puffery, customary influence, and bargaining tactics, and effective salesmanship . . . from immoral distortion and deceptive practices" (Dees and Starr, 98).

Relationship dilemmas emerge as entrepreneurs seek the capital and labor necessary to launch their idea. The entrepreneur, who is required to market and promote new products or services, must constantly manage relationships with resource controllers. To cite a famous example, business ethics literature has documented the alleged deception used by Philippe Kahn, computer software entrepreneur and founder of Borland International, Inc. Referred to by many as "The Borland Scam," in November 1983 the hard-charging entrepreneur Kahn convinced a salesperson from *Byte* magazine to run a crucial ad for Borland on favorable credit terms. As the story goes, Borland was founded on an alleged deception. The Borland case illustrates the kinds of promoter dilemmas faced by entrepreneurs. The entrepreneur struggles with the legitimate business need for effective bargaining and goals-oriented sales strategies. This same entrepreneur must also face built-in promoter dilemmas which can lead to potentially unethical situations of outright dishonesty, immoral distortion, and deceptive practices.

Since financing is difficult to receive from strangers, entrepreneurs often turn to family and friends for support. As Dees and Starr observe, "the transformation of social and kinship networks into instrumental business relationships raises possibilities for conflicts of interests due to conflicting roles" (Dees and Starr, 99, italics in the original). Similarly, there is a temptation for entrepreneurs to attract laborers with initial promises only to pare those costly promises back when the venture is operational. Entrepreneurs need to manage prior and continuing relationships, often with friends, family members, and business associates. Not unlike promotion dilemmas, the entrepreneur's need for resources can raise questions of trust and credibility in business relationships (Dees and Starr, 98). And as such business relationships develop, roles, expectations, and ethical obligations typically change along with them. When a family member or friend becomes an investor in a new enterprise, the entrepreneur must deal with the potential strain resulting from the unclarity of roles in the new relationship.

Innovator dilemmas involve the possible social costs of a new venture. The lure of market success often conflicts with an honest assessment of the side effects, or negative externalities, the venture could bring to the community. These concerns include product safety, environmental impact, and effect on community stability. Highly innovative entrepreneurs very often challenge the status quo in business with new ideas and organizations. The result is often the forging of new institutional infrastructures and values (Dees and Starr, 100). For example, recent discussions in bioethics have wrestled with a new startling dilemma concerning international medical entrepreneurs who have sought to create a market to facilitate the purchasing of human organs to be used in transplant surgeries. It is a bit startling to even imagine the complex ethical issues that arise when an entrepreneur in the medical industry considers such an "innovative" market opportunity. Dees and Starr aptly summarize the nature of entrepreneurial innovative dilemmas by observing that "[i]nnovation can create new types of ethical problems to which there are not ready answers" (Dees and Starr, 101).

In addition to promoter, relationship, and innovator dilemmas, entrepreneurs must often address a variety of other ethical problems in the course of doing business. For example, entrepreneurs are regularly required to grapple with distribution challenges common in any ongoing enterprise. Entrepreneurs must develop a fair approach to the distribution of profits and losses resulting from cooperative business efforts (Dees and Starr, 102). A crucial question is often "how" to distribute the shares of profits, losses, and other organizational goods and obligations among stakeholders in a new enterprise.

I noted earlier that Roman Catholic social thought is conspicuous in its silence on the entrepreneur. One must also point out that, historically, conventional neoclassical economic theory has likewise been bereft of sustained reflection on this topic. Broad-based attention to the function and morality of the entrepreneur by professional economists has only occurred in the last fifteen years. This makes Msgr. Ryan's understanding and appreciation for the entrepreneur all the more remarkable.

Reading the works of John A. Ryan, American Catholic priest, author, and educator, one is surprised to discover in the writings of this tireless defender of working women and men a uniquely favorable view of the entrepreneur. An attentive reading of Ryan's two most influential works, *A Living Wage* (1906) and *Distributive Justice* (1916), reveal a unique and surprisingly advanced understanding of the entrepreneur. Ryan's perspective is especially exceptional considering the limited treatment afforded the entrepreneur in Catholic social thought, a tradition that inspired Ryan throughout his long career.

In a variety of Ryan's writings, the entrepreneur is referred to as an "undertaker," a "director of industry," or a "business man" (*Distributive Justice*, 237). In *A Living Wage*, Ryan's doctoral dissertation, those who serve a business enterprise as owners, directors, or as risk takers are "variously called the employer, the entrepreneur, the undertaker, the business man" (*A Living Wage*, 207). When considering the nature of business profits, Ryan frequently uses the older term "undertaker" to refer to the entrepreneur whose profits are understood to "constitute the share of the undertaker" (*A Living Wage*, 207). For Ryan, the entrepreneur is one who takes financial risks, the organizer, the person who makes things happen in business.

Ryan's recognition of the importance of the entrepreneurial function in business activity is evident throughout *A Living Wage* and *Distributive Justice*. For example, in *A Living Wage* the entrepreneur/employer, whether efficient or inefficient, is in most cases "a more important productive factor than any single laborer" (*A Living Wage*, 247). When considering profits in competitive markets, in *Distributive Justice* Ryan suggests that large profits earned by successful entrepreneurs/business persons may be "justified by the canon of human welfare" (*Distributive Justice*, 255). The more one studies Ryan's writings, the clearer it becomes that he uniquely appreciated the role of the entrepreneur who has a valuable and necessary role to play in the economic life of society.

According to Ryan, the entrepreneur is essentially the one who "organizes, directs, and takes the risks of the industrial process, finds a market for the product, and receives in return neither rent nor interest but only profits" (*Distributive Justice*, 238). Ryan pays a good deal of attention to innovative contributions made by the successful entrepreneur. For example, in *Distributive Justice*, he writes:

> [t]he exceptionally efficient undertakers, those possessing the imagination, foresight, judgment, and courage to take full advantage of the recent improvements in the industrial arts, and in the methods of production generally, seem to have advanced in wealth and income more rapidly than any other class that has been subject to the operation of competition. (*Distributive Justice*, 240-41)

Creativity, imagination, the courage for risk taking, and good business judgment are all part of Ryan's conception of the successful entrepreneur. For Ryan, an innovative entrepreneur who is an effective manager contributes to human welfare, a key concept throughout Ryan's writings.

In *A Living Wage*, Ryan similarly values the exceptional ability, skill, and contributions of the entrepreneur. For example, Ryan writes that:

> [t]he undertaker's share of the product of industry is evidently a variable one. Its size will depend on his ability to forecast the demand for his goods and his success in putting the latter on the market at a minimum cost. The more accurately he can gauge the tastes and purchasing power of the public, and the lower he can reduce the outlay for capital and labor, the greater will be his net profits. . . . [u]ndertakers having exceptional ability or exceptional opportunity will sell their goods at the common price, and therefore obtain exceptional profits. (*A Living Wage*, 208-9)

Ryan is ahead of his time in recognizing the importance of marketing information to the entrepreneur. According to Ryan, a major task of the entrepreneur "is to estimate the public demand for goods, and to organize, direct and pay for the capital and labor required to meet the demand" (*A Living Wage*, 207). Without using contemporary consumer behavior research terminology, Ryan saw that the entrepreneur must possess keen marketing information, timely instinct, and precise judgment in order to make practical business decisions to meet constantly shifting consumer demand. For Ryan, "ability and opportunity" are the essential professional and personal qualities of the successful entrepreneur (*A Living Wage*, 209).

Ryan's favorable view of the entrepreneur is particularly discernible in his treatment of profits in a competitive market economy. According to Ryan, "profits are that share of the product of industry that goes to the business man [sic]" (*Distributive Justice*, 254). In *Distributive Justice*, Ryan defines profit (or net profit) when considering the economic role of the entrepreneur/business person. Profit is "the return for his labor of organization and direction, and for the risk that he underwent" (*Distributive Justice*, 238). Ryan himself admits that this definition can be artificial as it does not include an entrepreneur who is also a capitalist or landowner "in addition to his function as director of industry" (*Distributive Justice*, 238). Therefore, Ryan's definition of "profits" here does not include interest on capital and rent on land. Rather, profit is understood strictly "as comprising merely that part of the business man's returns which he takes as the reward of his labour, and as insurance against the risks affecting his enterprise" (*Distributive Justice*, 239). For Ryan, profits naturally and rightly belong to the entrepreneur.

According to Ryan, the entrepreneur/business person is "the residual claimant of industry" since profits are determined at "the end of the productive period" (*Distributive Justice*, 239). The profits of entrepreneurs are therefore also "residual" until the shares due to other agents of production (land, labor, capital) have been determined. Not surprisingly, Ryan recognizes the necessity of business profitability and the need for "superior business management" in the functioning of a just market economy (*Distributive Justice*, 258).

While Ryan observes that profits in most competitive free markets will usually tend toward what he terms a "normal or minimum rate," the potential profit rewards to successful entrepreneurs who manage scarce resources effectively can at times be quite large (cf. *A Living Wage*, 208-9). On this subject, Ryan argues that such "exceptional profits" are morally justifiable based on the "exceptional ability" of talented entrepreneurs. In *Distributive Justice*, Ryan accepts the general rule that business persons "who face conditions of active competition have a right to all the profits that they can get, so long as they use fair business methods" (*Distributive Justice*, 255). According to Ryan, the "Canon of Human Welfare" and the "Canon of Efforts and Sacrifice" may justify "the freedom to take indefinitely large profits" (Ibid). For Ryan, when entrepreneurs have satisfied ethical obligations for wage and distributive justice, room remains for the moral justification of "exceptionally large profits" (Ibid). This is especially true for profits earned by successful entrepreneurs "which can be traced specifically to that unusual ability which is exemplified in the invention and adoption of new methods and processes in progressive industries" (Ibid). However, for Ryan exceptionally large profits are only morally justified when full wage justice obligations have been met by business managers.

While Ryan does not provide us with a developed theory of the entrepreneur, the writings of this great American Catholic thinker do offer a rich resource for moral reflection on the role of the entrepreneur in economic and social life. A careful review of Ryan's writings suggest that his thought can assist with some of the specific kinds of ethical dilemmas which confront entrepreneurs daily. In particular, Ryan may be helpful in providing assistance with many of the relationship, innovator, and distributive ethical dilemmas cited by Dees and Starr. Since many of Ryan's writings deal more directly with systemic and organizational ethical issues in the economic sphere, it is initially difficult to apply his ethical thought to the highly interpersonal concerns that are much a part of promoter dilemmas. However, given Ryan's favorable and sophisticated understanding of the entrepreneur, his work has great potential to speak in specific ways to entrepreneurial relationship, innovator, and distribution dilemmas.

Entrepreneurs enter into many different relationships when beginning a new enterprise. They must manage newly developing relationships with employees, investors, banks, business associates, competitors, consumers, and others. In *A Living Wage* and *Distributive Justice*, Ryan provides practical ethical guidelines that can assist entrepreneurs with employee issues of fair treatment and just wage compensation. For example, Ryan's principles of wage justice can inform entrepreneurs of their ethical obligations concerning wages. Ryan's guidelines for ethical employee relationships might prove useful to the many entrepreneurs who struggle with cash flow and debt servicing problems common in new business ventures.

In other writings (for example, the articles on stock speculation and public utility valuation), Ryan treats the moral obligations entrepreneurs/business persons have to investors. For Ryan, honest and fair financial reporting is a must for entrepreneurs in relationships with investors. Further, entrepreneurs must always be vigilant in protecting the well-being of consumers. In *Distributive Justice*, the "Canon of Human Welfare" may offer guidance as entrepreneurs evaluate their relations with consumers. For example, entrepreneurs might often ask themselves whether or not new products or services contribute to or harm human welfare? Concerns with consumer safety are obvious practical applications.

In modern business environments, entrepreneurs frequently are required to deal with distribution dilemmas. *Distributive Justice*, perhaps Ryan's most original and influential work, offers a great wealth of practical guidance in ethical questions concerning distribution. Beyond legal requirements, entrepreneurs must determine how profits and losses are to be ethically distributed to stakeholders in a new enterprise. Ryan's canons of distributive justice may prove especially useful in these questions. For example, the "Canon of Efforts and Sacrifices" and the "Canon of Productivity" may provide the much needed grounding for ethical criteria to assist entrepreneurs in reaching ethical distribution decisions.

Externalities (for example, social costs, pollution, and safety issues) represent a perplexing innovator dilemma faced by entrepreneurs and society at large. In addition to profit and benefit distribution, Ryan's *Distributive Justice* may be practically useful in ethical distribution decisions concerning negative externality cost allocation. To cite a much debated recent example, how should society at large in partnership with business finance the huge costs of dealing with the disposal of nuclear waste or the cleanup of toxic waste sites? Ryan's canons of distributive justice may provide assistance with these and other enduring problems of externalities that are the result of highly innovative entrepreneurial activity. Technology frequently creates external costs that must be absorbed by society at large. While society generally welcomes the positive contributions made by the innovative entrepreneur to economic growth, it is often at a loss in deciding how to distribute the sometime sizable costs to society of these new technologies and new products. Ryan's "Canon of Human Welfare" may offer some guidance in dealing with externalities that arise from the activities of the entrepreneur. Any entrepreneurial ethic must be adequately adaptable to deal reasonably with the quickly changing environments in which entrepreneurs conduct business. A careful consideration of John A. Ryan's major writings demonstrates that his ethical thought appears to be flexible enough to provide general guidelines if not some basic norms to aid the ethical decision making of the business entrepreneur.

In conclusion, this study of the economic and moral dimensions of the entrepreneur in the thought of John A. Ryan reveals that: (1) Ryan offers a uniquely favorable perspective on the entrepreneur and (2) that Ryan's thought can serve as an important resource for moral reflection in the field of entrepreneurial ethics. Further, these two findings are all the more noteworthy considering that: (1) Roman Catholicism has been virtually silent on the subject of the entrepreneur and that (2) neoclassical economic theory throughout most of its history has said little about the nature and function of the entrepreneur in a market economy. Considering the more recent attention given the entrepreneur in economic theory and business ethics, Ryan's thought on this important subject is deserving of further consideration and study.

References

Casson, Mark. *The Entrepreneur: An Economic Theory*. (Totowa, N.J.: Barnes and Noble Books, 1982).

Dees, J. Gregory and Jennifer A. Starr, "Entrepreneurship Through an Ethical Lens: Dilemmas and Issues for Research and Practice," in Donald L. Sexton and John D. Kasarda, eds. *The State of the Art of Entrepreneurship*. (Boston: PWS-Kent, 1992).

Ryan, John A. *A Living Wage: Its Ethical and Economic Aspects*. (London: Macmillan, 1906). (1912 Edition)

Ryan, John A. *Distributive Justice: The Right and Wrong of Our Present Distribution of Wealth*. (New York: Macmillan, 1916.) (Reprint Edition 1978 by Arno Press)

John A. Ryan and Women's Wages: Still a Radical Stance?

REGINA WENTZEL WOLFE

> . . . it is evident that those women who are forced to provide their own sustenance have a right to what is a Living Wage for them. Since they have no other way of living but by their labor, the compensation therefore should be sufficient to enable them to live decently. Again, women doing the same work with the same degree of efficiency as men in occupations where both sexes are employed, have a right not merely to a woman's Living Wage, but to the same remuneration as their male fellow workers. Distributive justice requires that equally competent workers be rewarded equally. Moreover, when women receive less pay than the men the latter are gradually driven out of that occupation. Unless we hold that an increase in the proportion of women workers is desirable, we must admit that social welfare would be advanced by the payment of uniform wages to both sexes for equally efficient labor.[1]

The above quotation provides a fairly succinct summary of John Ryan's position on women's wages. Given the social context in which this challenge was made I am led to conclude that, for its time, it was a radical position to adopt. Were a similar call to be made today, it would be difficult, at least on the surface, to claim any degree of radicalness. In fact, in view of the many changes in American society since Ryan's day, particularly in the demographic makeup of the population, many would be likely to dismiss it out of hand as dated and out of touch with the reality of contemporary life. I believe that such a dismissal would be regrettable. The continued disparity between men's and women's wages in this country must be addressed. Ryan's underlying belief in the dignity of the human person as a basis upon which to determine wage levels, as well as his sharp sense of justice, present us with two themes that ought to be part of any consideration of the issue of equity in women's wages in our day.

In examining Ryan's position it is important to note that he makes two distinct appeals in terms of women's wages. One focuses on a woman's living wage. The other focuses on equal pay for equal work. In calling for all employed women to receive a living wage Ryan was concerned with what he called a personal living wage. That is a wage that would ensure that the wage earner—in this case a working woman—is able "to live in a manner consistent with the dignity of a human being."[2] There are two reasons in particular that this position seems to me to be radical for its day. First, Ryan's understanding of a wage sufficient for a decent living went well beyond that of many of his contemporaries. He was not speaking of a mere subsistence wage. Rather he was concerned with women being able to live a dignified life. In general, he understood a dignified life as one in which a person could obtain food, shelter, and clothing as well as other conventional needs. These latter included the financial ability to engage in recreational activities, to join associations, to purchase reading material, and to provide for health care, possible disability, and old age.[3] For Ryan, working women's wages should be sufficient "to maintain them away from home, because a considerable proportion of them live in this condition."[4] Apparently Ryan was willing to make his claims based on the actual lived experience of women, something we should continue to do today.

Second, Ryan was clear that the right to receive such a wage was not dependent on a woman's family status. "[T]he wage of all working women should be determined by the cost of living outside the parental precincts."[5] His rationale for this position was a concern that employers would hire only those women who, because they were perceived as having fewer needs as a result of living at home, could be paid lower wages thus placing on society the burden of maintaining those women unable to provide for their own sustenance. While Ryan may not have been alone in expressing concern for the single working woman, his call for the wages of all women to be determined by the needs of those women who lived independently was arguably a radical stance. His was a time of wide societal acceptance of the cult of true womanhood and belief in separate spheres of influence[6] that not only understood the proper role of women to be that of wife and mother but also assumed that women living in family situations received support from rather than provided support to other family members.[7] These underlying assumptions about women's roles in society, the source of women's income, and the use to which women put their earnings continue to be important in any discussion of the wage gap.

Ryan's second contention—that women doing the same work as men should receive the same wage as their male colleagues—was also radical for its day. Though some—particularly women in the socialist labor movement in the early part of this century—argued for equal pay for women, this was a minority position that they were unable to attain. In fact the "Protocol in the Dress and Waist Industry" a contract signed by the International Ladies' Garment Workers Union in 1913 not only "formalized the trade's division of labor by gender, reserving the more skilled, more highly paid jobs for men,"[8] it also stipulated that "the lowest paid male worker was to earn more than the highest paid female. Men were to be paid more even when they did the same work."[9] It was not until fifty years later with passage of the 1963 Equal Pay Act that some of the inequities began to be addressed in concrete ways.

Women's Wages Today

Despite discrepancies between women's and men's wages that still exist today, many have argued that the Equal Pay Act, coupled with other antidiscrimination statutes and affirmative action programs, have rendered concern for equity in women's wages a nonissue. Women and other minorities are protected from unfair and discriminatory wage practices by legal sanctions. In addition, minimum wage laws that are perceived to be gender neutral and seen to "protect the humanity of workers and emphasize the doctrine that labor is not just another commodity"[10] are considered to be a safety net for all workers. The gap between men's and women's earnings that has persisted throughout this century is understood to result from market forces and/or differences in skill levels, educational backgrounds, and personal choices.

Cursory acceptance of the above views might lead to the conclusion that Ryan's concerns for women's wages have been answered. Closer analysis, however, places doubt on such a conclusion. First, and most obvious, the minimum-wage laws do not ensure earnings that are sufficient to support a lifestyle that is in keeping with the human dignity of the worker and those for whom he or she is responsible.[11] Second, many neoclassical economic explanations for the wage gap neither account for the entire difference between women's and men's wages nor address the possibility that underlying social attitudes and structures—over which women have little or no control—might be contributory factors to that gap.

Answers to questions about the wage gap often rely on differences in the personal characteristics of employed men and women in explaining inequalities in earnings. As Alice Kemp has found, "the literature on male-female earnings inequality frequently contains assertions and claims that women's labor market characteristics (education, training, skills) are inadequate. Furthermore, women's presumed lack of commitment to the labor market affects their tenure, quit rates, and subsequently justifies their lower wages."[12] Quite obviously differences in personal characteristics play a part in any explanation of wage inequalities. However, the reasons for those differences require examination. In addition, it is important to realize that differences in women's personal characteristics do not account for the complete difference in the earnings gap. Combining Department of Commerce data with the findings of Treiman, Hartmann, and Roos, Kemp notes that even "though education, job training, attachment or commitment to working, and job tenure are important for men's and women's earnings these [personal] characteristics leave unexplained between 35 and 66 percent of the wage gap."[13]

Differences in structural characteristics account for some of this unexplained gap in earnings. Kemp's research indicates that:

> family status, labor market characteristics such as the dual economy model, and indicators of the time spent in household work represent some of the structural characteristics found important for explaining women's lower earnings. When summary analyses include structural characteristics as well as individual characteristics, approximately 60 percent of the gap can be explained . . . . Nevertheless, a portion remains unexplained that is partly attributable to occupational segregation and to discrimination.[14]

Explanations for the persistence of occupational segregation and the lower wages associated with women's work are ambiguous. As noted above, market forces such as supply and demand coupled with personal characteristics and choices of individuals are cited by some as determining factors in women's decisions about occupational preference. Women are understood to be acting as rational beings making individual choices about labor force participation based upon their personal situations, needs, and desires. These views are sometimes coupled with traditional understandings of women's roles as wives and mothers that view women as secondary wage earners who, when they do participate in the labor force, tend to choose occupations more "naturally" suited to them. That such occupations happen to be low-paying occupations is coincidental.

Critics of these views argue that they are unhelpful abstractions that neither reflect the economic theory upon which they are based nor the reality of women's situations and experiences. Sandra Christie notes that "gender-typing of occupations seems to be an integral part of our economic system, though it violates one of capitalism's basic premises, obtaining the best person for the particular job."[15] Kemp argues that "a tautology occurs when women's choice of low-skill, dead-end jobs is justified with the traditional division of labor in the home . . . [by maintaining on the one hand] that women have fewer and more limited opportunities in the labor market because they have family obligations, and [on the other hand that] they are assigned the family obligations because they have fewer opportunities in the labor market."[16] Kessler-Harris is concerned that abstract explanations can "obscure differences among women."[17]

In all, such critics highlight the complex nature of the issue of women's wages both in terms of the difficulty of identifying the reasons for inequities in women's wages and in terms of the challenge of finding appropriate means of rectifying those inequities. With them I question those who respond that women's wages are simply a reflection of women's personal choices. While not denying that women do in fact make personal choices about labor-force participation, I would argue that, despite the progress women have made since Ryan's day, there still exist social and structural barriers that unjustly limit and control those choices. If women who participate in the workplace are to be treated equitably, particularly in the area of wages, those barriers must be identified and dismantled.

Ryan's Legacy Lives On

But where to begin such a seemingly insurmountable and complex task? I am not sure there is a starting point, at least not in a linear sense. Many perspectives have been and continue to be brought to the discussion of equitable treatment of women in the workplace. Ryan's legacy lives on in contemporary Catholic social thought and its consideration of wages and other economic issues. I would like to consider what Catholic social teaching can bring to the current discussion as the struggle for equity in women's wages continues. It will be helpful to consider briefly a few key themes that inform this perspective.

Catholic social thought is quite clear about the inherent dignity and worth of all human beings and the duty to respect all persons, to acknowledge their essential equality, and to recognize their interdependence and mutuality. Being created in the image of God not only commands respect and demands just treatment, it also places an obligation on all people to participate in the human endeavor of developing a society that enables all its members to become conscious of their dignity and self-worth and to become more fully human.[18] One of the ways in which such human development is facilitated is through work.

Pope John Paul II has been particularly insistent about the place and meaning of work in human life. The principle of the priority of labor over capital for which he argues highlights the subjective dimension of human work that recognizes that actions undertaken by human beings in the process of work aid them in realizing their full human potential. This goes beyond Ryan's perspective by "showing that the basis for determining the value of human work is not primarily the kind of work being done, but the fact that the one who is doing it is a person."[19] Work is more than a means to a livelihood. Work—understood to be constitutive of the human person—assists individuals in following their call to be truly human and to participate in communal efforts to promote the common good and improve society.

The realization and development of an individual's personal life require mutual relations with others in the reciprocating interaction of life in society. Social life is not something accidental to humans. It is through society and its various organizations, including work, that people develop their potential and are able to respond to their vocation and shared responsibility for the world around them. If the social systems and structures in which people find themselves are dehumanizing or otherwise disrespectful of human dignity, people's growth and development is hampered as is their ability to expand their ties with others and meet their obligation to work toward the common good.

Ryan was arguing for a living wage in order that the worker could live a dignified life. His view of work and its meaning and place in human life was much narrower than the view of work held by John Paul II. Ryan's call for a just wage was based on his understanding of work as the source of the economic means to lead a life that would be fulfilling.[20] While Pope John Paul II also calls for just wages, his insistence on work as constitutive of the human person goes beyond Ryan and presents different challenges to the manner in which human work is organized. The Pope reminds us of our obligation to insure that no individual is precluded from work as well as our obligation to insure that such participation enhances both the life of each worker and the life of the broader society.

A Call To Restructure

What is radical about the challenge is that by focusing on the dignity of the person and the manner in which that dignity is understood vis-a-vis the workplace, the call is really a call to restructure the system making full and equitable participation of all persons—including women—integral to it. The workplace must be organized in a way that places persons first and underscores the fact that the place and meaning of work in human life has primarily to do with the development of human potential rather than with the production of any particular product or the profitability of any given business enterprise.

The practical implications and concerns arising from such a revisioning—particularly as they address the issue of equitable treatment of women in the workplace—might not be very different from those suggested by others who are concerned with women's earnings and various related issues. In their pastoral *Economic Justice for All* the American bishops condemned discriminatory practices in employment, particularly those that lead to occupational segregation, low wages, and limited opportunities for personal advancement for women.[21] Pope John Paul II has also condemned discriminatory practices toward working women making it clear in his recent "Letter to Women" that in terms of the personal rights of women "there is an urgent need to achieve real equality in every area: equal pay for equal work, protection for working mothers, fairness in career advancement, equality of spouses with regard to family rights and the recognition of everything that is part of the rights and duties of citizens in a democratic state."[22] Such condemnation and assessment of the implications of both discrimination and structural barriers in the workplace are echoed by others who are concerned with upholding these rights of women. But condemnation and assessment are not sufficient. As the Pope noted:

> Progress in achieving full respect for women and their identity involves more than simply condemnation of discrimination and injustices, necessary though this may be. Such respect must first and foremost be won through an effective and intelligent campaign for the promotion of women, concentrating on all areas of women's life and beginning with a universal recognition of the dignity of women.[23]

It should be remembered, however, that the Pope, bishops, and others working from the perspective of Catholic social thought have no unique strategies, methods, or programs for a campaign to achieve these rights. Their suggestions are similar to the suggestions of others. In terms of women's personal characteristics these revolve around debunking myths and changing attitudes that perpetuate stereotypical responses to and by women in the workplace, particularly as they are related to inadequacies—real or perceived—in women's personal backgrounds, inadequacies that are often cited as justifications for the devaluation of women's wages.[24] They are concerned, as are others, with preventing discrimination in the training and education of women in order to insure that women are not at a competitive disadvantage in terms of entry to and advancement in the labor force, particularly in high–wage, highly skilled occupations.

This concern goes beyond attempts to enhance women's own personal development. It also focuses on ways to remove structural and systemic barriers that impede equal participation in the workplace and place women at an economic disadvantage as a result of lower earnings potential. The complexity of adequately addressing some of the structural barriers, whether from the private sector or through public policies, is touched upon by Grossman and Chester. While acknowledging an increase in studies on women and their experiences in the workplace they observe that:

> much of this research tends to rely on data generated through government census bureau and social science research centers. Unfortunately these large data sets are often used to imply that women's lot as workers has been improved greatly with regard to opportunities, conditions, and pay. Such conclusions can create a false optimism about women worker's experiences that can be particularly damaging for minorities, the poor and/or single parents. This is particularly problematic given that data produced through large survey polls are frequently the basis for policy decisions regarding how and where public money and energy are directed.[25]

When women are treated as a homogeneous group, which is often the case in such surveys and data sets, the likelihood of statistical discrimination is increased. The uniqueness, worth, and dignity of individuals is either diminished or altogether denied when "the average characteristics of particular groups"[26]—in this case women seeking participation in the labor force—are used as the basis for determining responses to and treatment of particular members of the group. In addition, policies intended to alleviate discriminatory practices and other injustices often fall short of the mark. An ideal correction would be to respond to the uniqueness and individuality of each woman who desires to participate in the labor force. A more pragmatic approach might be to adopt the principle of subsidiarity in an attempt to better account for differences among women in a way that enables them to have a voice in the formulation of policies that affect them. Again, it is important to recall that this type of strategy is not unique to Catholic social thought. Grossman's and Chester's book, *The Experience and Meaning of Work in Women's Lives*, is intended to give voice to the myriad of experiences of women in an effort to better understand the social and structural barriers to equitable participation in the workplace with which they are confronted.

A Different Framework

Quite clearly those working from the perspective of Catholic social thought suggest remedies for overcoming personal and structural characteristics that hamper women's participation and advancement in the workplace that are not substantially different from remedies suggested by those addressing the same issues from other perspectives, be they economics, sociology, education, or psychology. The obvious question then is what does Catholic social teaching have to offer? The answer, I think, is that it offers a different framework based on a different starting point—the human person. To understand how radical this difference is, it will be helpful to look at one or two examples of others' justification for changes in the workplace, particularly as they impact on women's wages.

In her book *Breaking with Tradition*[27] Felice Schwartz challenges business to wake up and realize that it must respond to women's needs and restructure the way it organizes work in order to insure full and equal participation of women. From her perspective it is in the interest of business to do so. While she is concerned for women and the problems they face, she supports her challenge by arguing that companies and corporations that continue to devalue women's work and refuse to facilitate women's ability to work to their full potential will lose out. Such companies will be at a competitive disadvantage. From Schwartz's perspective it is in the economic self-interest of business to respond positively to concerns about equal access and fair treatment.

Others demand change based on their sense of justice. Whether their arguments stem from liberal theories, socialist theories, or feminist theories, they are clear that the rights of women to full and equal participation in the life of society are at stake. There can be no doubt that Catholic social thought supports such demands for economic justice. However, it goes beyond such demands, for it is not simply that women have the right to full and active participation in social endeavors, including work. Catholic social teaching is clear about the fact that women have a duty and obligation to engage in such participation. This is so not only because work assists in our own personal growth and development but also because, as John Paul II reminds us, we are "called to transform the face of the earth. In this task . . . man and woman alike share equal responsibility from the start."[28] If we recognize this obligation and yet fail to engage in the complex and arduous task of restructuring the workplace and other social institutions that impact on women's ability to engage in meaningful participation in that workplace, we are complicit in the resulting discrimination and injustices that women endure. Some of the responsibility and the blame for the inequitable treatment women receive is ours.

It is very easy to deny any personal complicity—to picture ourselves on the moral high road or to see ourselves as inconsequential and unable to effect meaningful change. Yet, I would argue that the success of any campaign whose goal is attaining parity in wages through the just treatment of women in the workplace will require an honest assessment of our own perceptions and biases coupled with a willingness to correct our misconceptions and overcome our prejudices. This is a formidable task that presents many pitfalls even for the most well-intentioned among us.

To illustrate my point, I return to the Pope's recent "Letter to Women." As noted above he is adamant in contending that the question of fairness for women goes beyond assuring that their economic rights are upheld. Fairness for women is also a matter of enabling them to respond to their vocation to share fully in the obligation to create a social environment, including a work environment, that fosters the ability of all persons to enrich their lives by participating in all aspects of society. Yet, from my perspective, the Pope seems to qualify—and so diminish—the force of his own position by adopting an idealized view of women. He identifies women's contribution to society as "primarily spiritual and cultural in nature"[29] and expresses regret at the "spiritual impoverishment of humanity" that has resulted because women "have often been relegated to the margins of society."[30] Noting the tendency of progress to be measured by scientific and technological criteria he argues that social and ethical criteria are more important measures of progress. These latter criteria deal "with human relations and spiritual values. In this area, which often develops in an inconspicuous way beginning with the daily relationships between people, especially within the family, society certainly owes much to the 'genius of women.'"[31] From the Pope's perspective it is "in giving themselves to others each day, [that] women fulfill their deepest vocation. Perhaps more than men, women acknowledge the person, because they see persons with their hearts. They see them independently of various ideological or political systems. They see others in their greatness and limitations; they try to go out to them and help them."[32] It is precisely "the feminine genius"[33] imbued with spiritual values and morals that the Pope hopes will be brought to bear on society and its institutions—including its economic institutions—when women are "fully integrated into social, political and economic life."[34]

While the last thing I would want to argue is that women do not have values and morals, I am uncomfortable with the notion of some type of "feminine genius." Rather than being grounded in an anthropology that emphasizes inherent equality this notion is reminiscent of the separate-sphere theory that understands women as the keeper of values and morals and calls upon them to "save the world" by bringing those values and morals to the forefront of public discourse and policy development. The problem here is manifold. First, it idealizes women and their so called "moral nature" while implying that men are somehow not capable of being moral or ethical in matters of the world. Second, it maintains the separate-sphere theory thus making it difficult if not impossible to bring about any meaningful structural changes. This is because it imputes to women a reason for engaging in the affairs of the world that differs from the reason or reasons cited for men's engagement in affairs of the world. In fact, studies show that women are engaged in work for the same reasons that men are engaged in work: they are supporting themselves and their families; they are providing meaning to their lives; they are engaged in productive work for the good of society; they enjoy the power and prestige of the work they perform. Finally, history would suggest that women's participation in social institutions does not necessarily render them more moral or just. We need only remember those who based their arguments in favor of women's suffrage on women's moral superiority and ask whether much has changed in the political sphere in the past seventy-five years.[35]

If we accept that women work for the same reasons that men work, that women are no more or less moral than men, that women are no more or less capable of productive activity than men, then on the basis both of women's inherent worth and human dignity and of the demands of justice, women's treatment in the workplace particularly as it relates to the complex issue of wage parity must be addressed. And here I would argue that the key words are "complex" and "parity." Discussions about the wage gap are often formulated in ways that do not take seriously the vast differences that exist among working women. Working women are not members of a homogeneous group. And yet the culturally ingrained understanding of working women as either single self-supporting women or married women who are simply working for "pin money" persists. Such undifferentiated views of women manifest a lack of concern for the particularities of women's situations and needs that can only be addressed by dismantling structural barriers.

As John Ryan did in his day, we must be willing to engage in public discourse in an effort to effect needed change. We—men and women together—have an obligation to bring the values and morals that we have inherited from the Catholic social tradition to this public task. If we understand the depth of that tradition we will understand that this entails much more than participating in policy debates. It is a challenge to recognize the place and meaning of work in the lives of all persons—men and women alike. It is a challenge to recognize our own complicity in building and maintaining a system of organized work that precludes women's full and meaningful participation, thus limiting possibilities for their human growth and development. It is a challenge to examine and change our attitudes so that we might begin the process of breaking down unfounded justifications that perpetuate injustice. In other words, it is the ever-radical call to conversion.

Notes

1. John A. Ryan, *A Living Wage: Its Ethical and Economic Aspects* (New York: Macmillan, 1906), 108.

2. Ibid., vii.

3. Ibid., 132–36.

4. John A. Ryan, *Distributive Justice: The Right and Wrong of Our Present Distribution of Wealth* (New York: Macmillan, 1916), 373.

5. Ibid., 373.

6. For a discussion of the cult of true womanhood and the theory of separate spheres of influence as they impact women's roles in society see Linda L. Lindsey, *Gender Roles: A Sociological Perspective* (Englewood Cliffs, N.J.: Prentice Hall, 1994) and Alice Abel Kemp, *Women's Work: Degraded and Devalued* (Englewood Cliffs, N.J.: Prentice Hall, 1994).

7. For a discussion of the way in which women's wages were affected by the assumption that family support was given to rather than received from working women living at home see Alice Kessler-Harris, *A Woman's Wage: Historical Meanings & Social Consequences* (Lexington, Ky.: The University Press of Kentucky, 1990). It should be noted that Kessler-Harris argues that "Ryan failed to acknowledge that in attributing to women 'average conditions' that reflected social myth rather than reality he undermined his own cause" (Kessler-Harris, 11).

8. Carol Hymowitz and Michaele Weissman, *A History of Women in America* (New York: Bantam Books, 1978), 253.

9. Ibid., 253.

10. J. Philip Wogaman, *Economics and Ethics: A Christian Enquiry* (Philadelphia: Fortress Press, 1986), 86.

11. Annual earnings for an individual working a forty-hour week at the minimum wage is $8,840. Families of two or more persons with a sole wage earner receiving the annual minimum wage fall below the 1993 poverty levels by family size. According to the "Current Population Reports" published by the Bureau of Census in February, 1995, the poverty level for a family of two persons is $9,414, for three persons it is $11,522, and for four persons it is $14,763. Only a one-person family would be above the poverty level, which is $7,363.

12. Kemp, 194.

13. Ibid., 195.

14. Ibid., 104. For a fuller discussion of the dual economy as it has developed in the United States see Kemp, 200ff.

15. Sandra Christie, "Women, Work, and the Workplace" in Lindsey, *Gender Roles*, 252.

16. Kemp, 75. For a discussion of the simple neoclassical model and its "circular reasoning" see Francine D. Blau and Marianne A. Ferber, *The Economics of Women, Men, and Work*, 2nd ed. (Englewood Cliffs, N.J.: 1992), 34ff.

17. Kessler-Harris, 127.

18. For a comprehensive description of the human person see the documents of Vatican Council II, especially *Gaudium et spes,* nos. 12, 15, 16, 18, 22, 29, 30.

19. Pope John Paul II, *Laborum exercens*, no. 6.

20. For Ryan this meant sufficient income to enable a man to support a wife and family. Ryan held that "the chief means of normal self-development" was through marriage;" " . . . the laborer has a right to a family Living Wage because this is the only way in which he can exercise his right to the means of maintaining a family, and he has a right to these means because they are an essential condition of normal life" (Ryan, *Living Wage*, 118).

21. National Conference of Catholic Bishops, *Economic Justice for All: Pastoral Letter on Catholic Social Teaching and the U. S. Economy* (Washington, D.C: United States Catholic Conference, 1986.) See chapter 3 "Selected Economic Policy Issues," particularly nos. 147 and 179.

22. Pope John Paul II, "Letter to Women," *Origins* Vol. 25, No. 9 (July 27, 1995): 140.

23. Ibid., 140–41.

24. For an interesting discussion of the relationship between traditional understandings of behavior appropriate for women and the barriers to success that women who have internalized such attitudes often exhibit, see Susan Schenkel, *Giving Away Success*, 2nd ed. (New York: Harper-Collins, 1991).

25. Hildreth Y. Grossman and Nia Lane Chester, eds., *The Experience and Meaning of Work in Women's Lives* (Hillsdale, N.J.: Lawrence Erlbaum Associates, 1990), 5.

26. Kemp, 72.

27. Felice N. Schwartz, *Breaking with Tradition: Women and Work, The New Facts of Life* (New York: Warner Books, 1992).

28. Pope John Paul II, "Letter," 141.

29. Ibid., 141.

30. Ibid., 139.

31. Ibid., 141.

32. Ibid., 143.

33. Ibid., 143.

34. Ibid., 140.

35. For a discussion of this element of the prosuffrage movement earlier this century, see chapter 5 in Hymowitz and Weissman.

Catholic Social Teaching on Women's Work and Wages: A Feminist Critique

GEORGIA KEIGHTLY

That today's U.S. Catholic women want—and need—the help and support of their church in their efforts to combat the discrimination they encounter in all aspects of their lives is well documented in the first draft of the ill-fated pastoral letter on women, "Partners in the Mystery of Redemption."[1] Here, in their own voices, Catholic women cite the variety of ways they experience second-class citizenship in both church and society. In chapter 3, they enumerate the many injustices they encounter in the workplace: the all-too common failure to recognize that today women work out of need, not selfishness; the discrimination they encounter on the job that takes the form of low pay, job segregation, racism, limited opportunity for advancement, lack of benefits, and on-the-job training.[2]

"Partners" recognizes that women look to the church to take up their cause: it says, "Women welcome the church's efforts to emphasize [their] essential worth while extraordinary changes are taking place in society."[3] The text also acknowledges that the women consulted in the document's preparation "pointed repeatedly to four main realms where they sense strong support from the church: economic justice; education; homemaking and motherhood; and resistance to exploitation."[4]

The extent to which the bishops actually implemented the proposed initiatives with which they concluded the pastoral's final version—

downgraded and issued some four years later as an Ad Hoc Committee Report titled, "One in Christ Jesus,"—remains unclear.[5] Recent events, however, strongly suggest that the Vatican intends to make a serious commitment to women's cause for justice. In his June 29, 1995 "Letter to Women" in anticipation of the UN Fourth World Conference on Women, Pope John Paul II spoke of "the urgent need to achieve real equality in every area." Among those needing attention he cited "equal pay for equal work, protection for working mothers, fairness in career advancement, equality of spouses with regard to family rights."[6] Perhaps even more remarkable and telling of Vatican commitment was the announcement that it would not allow its positions on abortion and birth control to detract from discussion of the Beijing Conference's central themes—equality, development, and peace.[7]

A significant resource for helping women achieve political and economic justice is that body of teaching of the Catholic social tradition. Catholic feminists, however, cite the inherent ambivalence of this teaching as regards to women. While on the one hand, equality and the attainment of full civil, political, and economic rights is claimed for all persons, there are nonetheless many texts where women's appropriation of these rights is compromised. Catholic feminists argue that the tradition's ambiguity arises from the patriarchal perspective and bias that shapes it. Thus Maria Riley calls for a feminist revisioning of Catholic social thought in order that a truly liberating ethic, one pointing the way to social structures of mutuality and solidarity might ultimately emerge.[8] Lisa Sowle Cahill indicates that this "feminist revisioning" of Catholic ethics necessitates "full attention to the personal and social experience of women." Above all, it must give recognition to the fact that

> justice for women means to regard women as the moral and social equals of men and to support their equal participation in the social roles that contribute to the common good, as well as their equal share in those benefits comprised by it.[9]

This study aims to contribute to this feminist revisioning of Catholic social ethics. To this end, it will make explicit how and in what ways the tradition tends to contradiction on the subject of women and in so doing, actually compromises the claims to justice it would make on their behalf. By way of illustration I will examine teaching that relates to the subject of women's waged work.

To help pinpoint and explore the tensions within church positions here, I will refer to theses developed in Mary E. Hobgood's *Catholic Social Teaching and Economic Theory: Paradigms in Conflict.*[10] My analysis will not only indicate how in Hobgood's terms, paradigms in conflict create ambiguity in church teaching; I will also argue that the same sort of paradigm conflict exists within economic theory, particularly in its assessment of women's participation in U.S. economic life. This means that if Catholic social teaching is to offer a meaningful critique of women's disadvantage in the workplace, it must take into account the feminist assessment of economic theory. But at the same time, if the Catholic tradition is to point the way to effective, transformative public policy, then a feminist corrective of Catholic social teaching itself will also be required. Only once these things are done will an ethical stance, one capable of directing the way to the achievement of justice for women in the area of waged work, finally take shape.

Hobgood's Thesis

In *Catholic Social Teaching and Economic Theory*, Mary Hobgood argues that Catholic social thought relies on three different models to analyze and critique modern socioeconomic reality.

These are 1) the *organic* model that derives from feudal social relations; 2) the *orthodox neoclassical* model of capitalist society and 3) what Hobgood calls the *radical* model of structural analysis.[11] While each model has something in common with the others, each actually represents a fundamentally different approach to understanding society, to interpreting complex social and historical processes, and for the interests of this paper, for explaining socioeconomic realities.

Hobgood explains that these different, competing sets of theories about economic life arise out of different worldviews, and embody distinct "perspectives, norms, or assumptions" about such things as the nature of persons, work,and how social life ought to be ordered.[12]

It is her thesis that because the documents of the Catholic social tradition incorporate these models in an unexamined and thus, in an indiscriminate and uncritical way, their analysis of important social problems is frequently flawed. She also argues that because assumptions implicit to the worldviews associated with the models are also uncritically presumed, this too creates tensions within as well as compromises important ethical positions. As a result, the public policy strategies church documents recommend regularly "fail to frame a coherent agenda." More to the point, this skewed analysis stands in the way of the formulation of an adequate ethic on which to base appropriate social change.[13] It is for this reason then that Hobgood concludes that when addressing twentieth-century economic realities, "the Catholic hierarchy exhibits a divided mind."[14]

Hobgood's Thesis as Applied to Catholic Social Teaching

Hobgood's work suggests that the contradictions found in the tradition pertaining to women can be attributed to inconsistent use of the three models and the assumptions implicit to them. For example, the perspective on women associated with the organic model is presupposed in many contemporary church documents, documents that also espouse liberal and/or radical positions and attitudes.

In organic social theory, society is compared to the human body and because the well-being of the organism takes precedent over the individual limbs, the hierarchical ordering of social relationships, manifested in terms of status and relations of subordination/domination is seen as beneficial. In Catholic thinking, such social organization—especially the subordination of women to men—has been seen as being part of the divine order of things.

As Hobgood observes, "the organic view of the social order had the patriarchal family as the model for the institutional church and all other social entities, including labor unions and the state."[15] While this model presumes—and depends on—the benevolence of the privileged in economic affairs to "prevent a grossly unequal income distribution," it also assumes the "existence of social stratification as natural and necessary" and as being completely in accord with the natural law.[16] In an important aside, Hobgood proposes that it is precisely because "capitalism generates socio-economic hierarchies in both the economy and the family" that Catholic social thought has regularly been able to affirm "the moral acceptability of the capitalist system and the assumptions of economic liberalism."[17]

One of the primary ways in which the hierarchical, dualistic elements of the organic model manifest themselves in Catholic social thought has to do with the way in which woman's nature is conceived and how this has been allowed to determine her social performance.

Indeed, a central task of Catholic feminist scholars has been to challenge the understanding of woman's nature that has so long shaped church teaching and practice. This view, which originates in interpretations of Genesis, presents woman's nature as being essentially different from that of man. Review of the tradition reveals that historically, this difference was also construed as constituting woman's natural inferiority to man and for this reason, her subordination to him was also a logical outcome. At the same time, this dualistic anthropology substantiated the view that this difference of nature rendered a woman fit for certain occupations and unfit for others.[18] In other words, woman's role in both church and society were inscribed in, as well as circumscribed by, the intrinsic demands of her biology.

While prior to the encyclicals of Pope John XXIII, "women were seldom mentioned in social documents except implicitly under generic statements regarding the dignity of 'man,'"[19] there are instances where woman's essential, natural difference is emphasized. The most outstanding example of this perhaps is Pius XI's remark concerning coeducation. He says:

> There is not in nature itself, which fashions the two [natures] quite different in organism, in temperament, in abilities, anything to suggest that there can be or ought to be promiscuity, and much less equality in the training of the two sexes.[20]

It is to be observed, however, that this emphasis on the distinctiveness of feminine nature, "the genius of women"[21] as he calls it, is a theme regularly reprised in the writing and teaching of the present pope.

As subjects of Catholic social teaching, women normally appear only in discussions pertaining to family. Hobgood notes that both *Rerum novarum* and *Quadragesimo anno* emphasize "the organic model of the patriarchal family where women belong at home in economic dependency."[22] Thus Leo XIII and Pius XI accepted domestic labor and childbearing as being woman's proper role; papal concern for the worker and payment of the just wage had in view the protection and economic well-being of his wife and children and others who may be dependent on him.

Ambiguity arising out of a conflict of models initially appears in the work of John XXIII. In *Pacem in terris* for instance, the pope introduces the radical notion that societies must value women in the same way as men, thus according them the same privileges, rights, and duties.[23] In other instances, however, John follows his predecessors, asserting that woman's nature consigns her to childbearing and housekeeping within the patriarchal family.[24]

One finds a similar ambiguity in *Gaudium et spes*. On the one hand, the council fathers deliberately use the word *homo* (rather than *vir*) to refer to the human person; by so doing they clearly intend to say that women no less than men are in possession of a fundamental human dignity.[25] Yet at the same time that they denounce every kind of discrimination, but especially those of sex and race,[26] they also take an uncritical view of woman's participation in culture, namely, that this must be "in accordance with [her] own nature"[27] to ensure that "this domestic role of hers must be preserved."[28] Likewise, in *Octogesima adveniens*: While he affirms full economic, social, and political rights for women, Paul VI denounces "false equality" that would deny women's true nature and "proper vocation."[29]

Alongside a growing recognition by church officials that women too must be accorded basic human rights, one also begins to see greater apprehension of the reality of women's lives. For example, the *Puebla* document notes the virtual exclusion of women from participation in public life because of "male predominance, unequal wages, deficient education, etc."[30] And here, for a first time, Catholic social teaching acknowledges the reality of women's "double day," that in addition to their domestic duties, the majority of women are also obliged, for survival's sake, to participate in the labor force.[31] But *Puebla* too reiterates traditional themes: it cites woman's specific aptitude for serving others; it acknowledges her "fundamental role . . . as mother, the defender of life and the home educator."[32]

Organic and radical perspectives are also juxtaposed in the U.S. bishops' pastoral, "Economic Justice for All." On the one hand, the bishops resort to structural analysis to show that, rather than being randomly located throughout the population, poverty and unemployment are in fact concentrated among women and minorities. And, at the same time that they acknowledge the tremendous cultural and social pressures that make life in family so tenuous and difficult today,[33] the bishops remain steadfast to the ideal of the western nuclear family and recommend that women remain at home with their children.[34]

The clearest example of a conflict of paradigms relating to women and work, however, appears in the writings of John Paul II. In *Laborem exercens,* which extols work as a means of expressing personal creativity, the pope adopts an essentially radical view. Work is seen here as a means of manifesting, even increasing, one's personal dignity. Besides being a God-given duty, work is understood as a primary way to becoming more human;[35] seen in this light, sin is a matter of the laborer's alienation from his work. On the basis of such argument, the right to employment and thus participation in economic life is presented as being an inviolable human right.[36]

But that this right extends fully, equally to women is immediately called into question as the pope proceeds to argue that the principle criterion of the just wage is "a single salary given to the head of the family for his work, sufficient for the needs of the family *without the spouse having to take up gainful employment outside the home*."[37] Following upon this, the pontiff asserts that having to "abandon" the tasks of motherhood "in order to take up paid work outside the home is wrong from the point of view of the good of society and of the family."[38] A subsequent document *Familiaris consortio*, written only months later, appears to rescind altogether women's right to participate in the labor force. Here it is stated that "the true advancement of women requires that clear recognition be given to the value of their maternal and family role, by comparison with all other public roles and all other professions." The document further declares that "society must be structured in such a way that wives and mothers are not in practice compelled to work outside the home."[39]

As the above examples show, the confusion of paradigms, the failure to clarify associated assumptions, all serve to undermine important points of Catholic social teaching, especially where women are concerned. Because of admitted natural, inherent differences, it seems to be the case that women and men can be said to have a quite different set of rights and duties as far as society is concerned. Or, as Maria Riley so pointedly asks: "Can a person having a proper role and vocation, pre-determined by her nature and needing special protection, still be independent and have equal rights?" especially when compared to "a person who has no such qualifying and limiting definitions pre-determined by his nature."[40] Furthermore, doesn't the difference in nature imply that such values as fairness, justice, and equality have different definitions and applications as far as women and men are concerned?

For her part, Hobgood argues that the church's continuing insistence that woman's nature is other than, incomplete and/or complementary to man's plus its corollary, that is, that woman's primary social role relates to family and home, actually serves to legitimate gender segregation in the workplace.[41]

Such an assumption also lends credence to the view that since a woman's waged work is but secondary and supplementary to that of her husband, compensation due her falls outside the criterion of the just wage cited above. It has, in fact, been common practice to pay women less than men, yet today's statistics show that more than ever, women are obliged to work and to share responsibility for their family's support.[42] Statistics also reveal that the perduring wage gap is largely responsible for the phenomenon, the feminization of poverty, highlighted by the U.S. bishops. But even as recently as June 1995 it was reported that "women still receive 71 cents for every dollar earned by men."[43]

Finally, because of its presumptions and its failure to address the actual situation of U.S. women, Hobgood concludes that, for this particular context, Catholic social teaching actually endorses "the injustice of women's double day of work in the market place and at home."[44]

Hobgood's Thesis as Applied to Economic Theory

This Catholic feminist critique of the church's social ethic is highly significant given the coincidence it has at many points with the feminist critique of economics.

According to economist Barbara Bergmann, women are disadvantaged in today's workplace in two basic ways: these have to do with the wage gap and the occupational segregation that is largely responsible for the pay differential that exists between women and men.

She notes: "The division of labor based on sex is and has been common to all societies." But even in today's technological workplace, jobs continue to be identified by gender and what distinguishes a "man's" from a "woman's" job is that the former tends to pay better, it allows for some independence of action, it has fewer boring duties, and can lead to still better jobs.[45] While some economists argue that women's inferior position in the workplace has very little to do with unfairness or with sexist prejudices of employers, that the labor market operates on the classic principle of supply and demand, the fact is, statistical data and judicial opinion have established that discrimination is a key factor in disadvantaging women in the workplace.[46]

It is striking that many of the explanations economists offer to account for women's situation in the labor market reflect notions found in the Catholic documents cited above. In a survey article, Bergmann notes that some economists view occupational segregation as "dictated by biology and that women's comparative advantage in home tasks is a matter of natural differences between the sexes in talent, aptitude and taste."[47] Other economists argue that women deliberately select jobs that will not interfere with their home responsibilities: they choose jobs "in which exit and subsequent reentry are relatively easy and in which overtime, travel, locational transfer, and demanding duties are not required."[48]

Alice Kessler-Harris in her study, *A Woman's Wage: Historical Meanings and Social Consequences,*[49] finds the same kind of logic at work in the development of wage structure. While here too some economists would argue that wage rates are simply "a product of more or less rigid laws," Kessler-Harris argues that the wage actually encodes "a set of gendered instructions that speak to men and women and to the relations between them."[50] In her historical review, the author shows that both the "living" and the "family" wage presume that woman's well-being and support resides with the male head of her family; and both assume her primary social responsibility to be that of full-time service to home and family.

While the advent of the minimum wage witnesses to the growing reality of female independence made possible by industrialization, the fact is, the minimum wage was intended to supply merely what was necessary to the lone woman's bare upkeep, the presumption being that she would receive some basic level of support from her family. The wage's amount was determined by her employer according to his estimate of what she needed to live; but the employer also could, and did, adjust the wage downward by taking into consideration such other factors as race and ethnicity.[51] According to Kessler-Harris, the minimum wage "prescribed a spartan life-style, sufficient, it was hoped, to preserve morality for those destined to earn but not so generous as to tempt those in families to live outside them."[52] And so while "men came into occupations at a wage paid for the job," women's wages were based on their personal need and what employers, influenced by social custom, found acceptable to pay.

Both the Bergmann and Kessler-Harris studies confirm that Hobgood's methodological insights also have important application for the Catholic ethicist's analysis of women in U.S. economic life. First of all, her initial premise, namely, the central role of socially articulated meanings and values (such as those constitutive of worldviews) in defining/shaping what appear to be impersonal, abstract social systems and institutions, becomes obvious in the discussions of both job segregation and wage structures. Again, while orthodox theory holds that as far as jobs and wages are concerned, the market's law is simply that of supply and demand, Bergmann shows that discrimination against women is very much a matter of agreed-upon meanings and is socially rooted. She shows that jobs construed as being "man's work" have superior status, involve more interesting work and greater monetary reward and that is exactly why women seek them. But, she notes, men fear that once their jobs are opened to women, image, status, and wages will decline. For their part, employers worry what effect on productivity women's presence will have. Resentment, the presence of feminine competition, the possibility of having a female supervisor, plus other compatibility issues—all have the potential to disrupt the work environment. Bergmann shows that in light of these concerns, firms keep job segregation intact by means of personnel policies, by controlling promotional and training opportunities, and by permitting both overt and covert tactics of harassment.[53]

Kessler-Harris concludes her study by stating that as problems, neither job segregation nor the wage gap are to be strictly attributed to market malfunction. Socially-defined attitudes about what women can do and how they should live have also been influential here.

"As it functions in the daily lives of people, [the market] is not independent of the values and customs of those who participate in it. Justice, equity, and fairness have not been its natural outcomes. Rather, market outcomes have been tempered by customary notions of justice or fairness. The specific forms these take have been the object of struggle. And just as ideas of fairness influence our response to the market, so, too, do they influence how the market works."[54]

Secondly, the Bergmann/Kessler-Harris studies also support Hobgood's thesis about the ethicist's need to be aware of paradigm conflict, not only in the Catholic social tradition but within economic theory itself. For example, these authors' discussions of the minimum wage and the pay equity debates highlight instances where the lack of coherence between models challenges the formulation of appropriate policies and realistic strategies for change.

Kessler-Harris notes that in 1926, the Supreme Court denied the constitutionality of a Washington, D.C. law that provided minimum wages for women and minors. It did so on the basis of the concept of freedom of contract, that is, the individual's freedom to contract to sell her/his labor without restraint or state interference, a principle fundamental to the orthodox neoclassical model of economics.[55] This decision was a logical one, given the prevailing view of the market; it was also consistent, given the fact that the concept of a minimum wage derives from an organic view of society that presumes society's right to intervene on behalf of women and minors in those instances where "conditions detrimental to their health and morals, resulting from wages which are inadequate to maintain decent standards of living."[56] While the court eventually reversed itself in 1937 and extended the same protection to men, Kessler-Harris notes that this episode illustrates the difficult struggle involved in creating public policy when two "competing paradigms" are involved; yet at the same time, she observes, it also illustrates the degree to which social needs and interests were able to overcome theory and get institutionalized into law and public policy.[57]

The debate over pay equity involves a conflict of paradigms as well. First of all, that the worker receives pay equal to the value of her labor is implicit to the orthodox model of economics; however, the effects of discrimination reflected in the statistics cited above confirms that historically the market has not actually operated in this way.

Bergmann herself indicates that the employer's right to segregate jobs by sex and to attach lower salaries to women's jobs is consistent with a strict laissez-faire approach to the market.[58] She herself not only argues in favor of legislation against discrimination in hiring; she also advocates government action to require wages that meet comparable-worth standards. In taking such positions however, she steps outside the neoclassical paradigm and inserts a notion of equity that is more in keeping with either a liberal or radical viewpoint.[59]

For their part, radical theorists argue that capitalist markets require racism and sexism to sustain themselves.[60] While orthodox theory holds that market pressure actually tends to erode discrimination for the reason that, whatever her/his background, the most productive worker will be hired at the prevailing wage in the interests of maximizing profits, feminists argue that a segmented labor market provides an essential safety valve for capitalism. And, this it does in several ways.

For one thing, the underpaid wage labor of women is obviously a boon and benefit to the economy as a whole. One effort to quantify this concluded that in 1970, "approximately 23 percent of all manufacturing profits [were] attributable to the lower wages paid to women."[61] For another, sexism provides a reserve supply of labor to be used in expansive periods but that can be let go during recessive periods, and with minimal political ramifications. Finally, capitalist societies are thoroughly dependent upon the unpaid domestic labor of women in that such supports and attends to the physical and emotional well-being of the entire work force; and of women's work here too, business is a direct beneficiary.[62] Hobgood aligns herself with the radical consensus that until such time as "women's unvalued work at home" is reassessed and revalued, the undervaluing of their work in the marketplace simply will continue.[63]

Feminist scholars also agree that given the stratification of the labor market, such liberal remedies as subsidies to employers for on-the-job training, educational programs aimed at developing human capital are only superficial solutions and will in the end have minimal results. They point out that while the educational levels of women and minorities have risen, neither group has made significant, sustained progress in either area of wages or jobs. Other theorists question that job creation programs offer a viable solution; the restructuring of the U.S. economy currently underway suggests that in the future, availability of jobs will not be the issue. Rather, the problem will be that the type of jobs now being created will be similar to those women and minorities have traditionally filled—service-sector jobs that involve few skills, are poorly paid, have little responsibility attached to them, and provide no benefits or job security.[64]

In these instances, per Hobgood, because the policies recommended do not derive from and/or are inconsistent with the way in which the market is structured and operates, they will prove to be ineffectual solutions.

Conclusion

This review shows the points at which the Catholic perspective can and must address the bias women experience in the workplace, specifically in terms of job segregation and wages.

But it has also shown that unless the Catholic tradition's own ambiguity concerning women can be overcome, church teaching will never be able to mount an adequate critique in respect to these issues nor will it be able to bring about justice for women or contribute to their advancement in U.S. society. And, while Monsignor John A. Ryan has not been the subject of this study directly, his work does provide the overall context and background for its project.

First of all, his entire body of work illustrates the thoroughgoing and rigorous type of analysis of social problems that is absolutely essential to the development of Catholic social ethics. Indeed, his own contribution to analysis and critique of U.S. political and economic life was a major one. The church documents cited above, however, provide examples of the contradictions and incoherence of ethical teaching that results when analysis is not so rigorous, when fundamental assumptions of worldviews and competing paradigms go unexamined. To this end, the work of Catholic feminists—and their appropriation of feminist theory—provides an essential and indispensable corrective. For as I have tried to show in the instance of women's waged work, church teaching simply can not and will not be capable of promoting justice for women until such time as the theological anthropology that undergirds it is brought into line with the tradition's declaration of personal dignity, the call for full human rights, and the demand for justice and equality—commitments that have arisen out of the church's concern and practical engagement with the poor and marginalized in each place and time.

What Ryan's work exemplifies is the sort of careful analysis necessary to achieve insight into the basic structural relationships and interconnections within social systems, as well as the meanings and values that order and legitimate such institutions. As one of his students said of him, it was Ryan's constant practice to view things in their causal relationship to one another. More to the point, he demonstrated the theologian's need to be familiar with disciplines other than her own if she is to engage in the critical, ongoing dialogue between the gospel and modern culture.

Perhaps the finest description of Ryan's approach to his work was provided in the funeral oration delivered by his former student, Bishop Francis J. Haas. The bishop said:

> Theologian though he was, [Ryan] had a passion for facts. He took the perfectly rational position that no one can pass valid judgment on industrial or other questions unless he is acquainted with the facts concerning them. "The general principles," he wrote, "are true, indeed, but they are practically useless unless they are applied specifically to the actual conditions and relations of industry."[65]

By way of confirmation, Haas cited one reviewer's assessment of Ryan's book, *Distributive Justice*:

> Few ethical authorities have sufficient knowledge of economic facts to adapt ethical principles to the economic field; few economists are

> abreast of the best modern work in ethics. To this rule, the most notable exception is Dr. Ryan. His economic scholarship is unimpeachable.

Another important thing to be learned from Ryan is that good analysis, even in and of itself, still is not enough. For the Catholic, ethical analysis must lead to explicit action and the transformation of society to the benefit of the common good. As theologian Joseph Komonchak remarked in a recent address at Marquette University, the church becomes what it is—namely, the means by which Christ's reconciling, redeeming love becomes a presence to the world—in the everyday decisions and activities of its members who in their own lives embody the implications of the Christ event for all aspects of human existence.[66] By and through his own powerful and effective advocacy for a variety of complex social issues, Ryan made Christ's church a redeeming, reconciling presence in his own time. In his spirited defense of such issues as minimum-wage legislation, unemployment insurance, child labor laws, and in supporting the right of labor to bargain and organize, Ryan confirmed the claim, recently sounded, that "the work of public advocacy is a holy thing."

There is perhaps a lesser known, but no less important legacy of Monsignor Ryan and that relates to the many years he spent in the classroom at my institution, Trinity College in Washington, D.C. From 1916 with few interruptions until his death in 1945, he taught young Catholic women the principles of economics and political science. Majors in these disciplines became very popular according to the college's records, suggesting that this was due in no small part to the great impact Monsignor Ryan had on his students as he helped them to understand and appreciate what responsible citizenship required of them. But the record shows that Trinity alumnae also took from him a deep sense of social responsibility; many of these young Catholic women—even against their time—went on to become lawyers, doctors, teachers, and social workers.

Given his considerable experience working with Trinity women then, it is not surprising to find that he tended to be more generous in his estimate of the wage due single-women workers or to learn that he testified in support of the Equal Rights Amendment before the Senate Judiciary Committee.[67] Nor, I believe, would it seem strange or inappropriate to him now that a feminist ethical perspective—one that regards women as the moral and social equals of men—should be brought to bear on Catholic social teaching.

The 1940 *Trinilogue* described Monsignor Ryan as "beloved by those who knew him" and as one "who plays a vital role on Tuesday and Thursday mornings at Trinity." But perhaps the highest compliment he received from students that year was this one: "Monsignor Ryan is in the most perfect sense a priest, a scholar and a democrat."

Notes

1. "Partners in the Mystery of Redemption: A Pastoral Response to Women's Concerns for Church and Society," *Origins* 17:45 (April 21, 1988).

2. Ibid., #s 137-52.

3. Ibid., #129.

4. Ibid.

5. It should be noted that among the twenty-five initiatives the report sets forth, only five specifically address women's issues having to do with social justice. The majority center on improving women's situation within church life; an inordinate number also are directed to sexual issues.

6. "Letter to Women" dated June 29, 1995 in *The Tablet* 249: 917-18.

7. "Vatican Will Not Contest Language on Abortion," *Washington Post* September 7, 1995, A29.

8. Maria Riley, *Transforming Feminism* (Kansas City, Mo.: Sheed and Ward, 1989), 76-77.

9. Lisa Sowle Cahill, "Feminism and Christian Ethics" in *Freeing Theology: The Essentials of Theology in Feminist Perspective*, ed. Catherine Mowry LaCugna (San Francisco: Harper Collins, 1993), 212.

10. Mary E. Hobgood, *Catholic Social Teaching and Economic Theory: Paradigms in Conflict* (Philadelphia, Pa.: Temple University Press, 1991).

11. Ibid, 6-7. Hobgood describes organic *theory as having its origins in assumptions taken from Aquinas and feudal social relations and derives from the theologian's "appropriation of Aristotle in which the social and natural world are viewed on the same continuum"(98). It views social reality in hierarchical, communitarian and dualistic terms. The orthodox* and *radical* paradigms "offer different analyses of the interrelationships of the primary social structures within late twentieth-century capitalism." The two perspectives offer different explanations "about the way that production, government policy and spending and social institutions . . . are related." Each claims to provide the best analysis of "the origins, manifestations, and potential solutions to problems generated by the political economy of capitalism"(8-9).

12. Ibid., 11.

13. Ibid., 227. For example, she notes on p. 7 that "competing assumptions from the organic social model . . . have split the hierarchy's loyalties between orthodox and radical perspectives and their contradictory interpretations of capitalist political economy."

14. Ibid., 7.

15. Ibid., 101.

16. Ibid.

17. Ibid., 6.

18. Aquin O'Neill, "The Mystery of Being Human Together" in *Freeing Theology*, 149.

19. Riley, 81.

20. *Divini illius magistri*, Dec. 31, 1929. Cited in O'Neill, 149.

21. John Paul II, "Letter to Women" (June 29, 1995) in *The Tablet* 249 (1995): 919.

22. Hobgood, 121.

23. *Pacem in terris*, #41.

24. See for example excerpts taken from speeches cited in *The Teachings of Pope John XXIII*, ed. Michael Chinigo (New York: Grosset and Dunlap, Inc., 1967), 179-80, 181-82.

25. Riley, 82.

26. *Gaudium et spes*, #29.

27. Ibid., #60.

28. Ibid., #52.

29. *Octogesima adveniens*, #13.

30. *Puebla document*, #834.

31. Ibid., #837.

32. Ibid., #s 846, 845.

33. *Economic Justice for All*, #s 3, 16, 18, 175-70, 209.

34. Ibid., #207.

35. *Laborem exercens*, #9.

36. Ibid., #18.

37. Ibid., #19. This theme is also reiterated in *Centesimus annus* #15.

38. Ibid., #19.

39. Ibid., #23.

40. Riley, 84.

41. Hobgood, 143, 186. And, of course, Catholic teaching tends to ignore the fact that for minority women and for most of the world's women, work outside the home has consistently been an utter necessity, not a choice.

42. Per "Facts on Working Women" No. 93-2 (June 1993), U.S. Department of Labor, Women's Bureau, "working wives contribute substantially to family income. In March 1992, 59 percent of wives in married-couple families were labor force participants. In 1991, the median income of married-couple families with the wife in the labor force was $48,169, compared with $30,075 for those without the wife in the paid labor."

43. "Women's Pay Stagnates Despite Rapid Growth in the Workforce," *HRFocus* 72 (1995): 11.

44. Hobgood, 143.

45. Barbara Bergmann, *The Economic Emergence of Women* (New York: Basic Books, 1986), 87.

46. A classic study of wages done in 1979 by Mary Corcoran and Gregory Duncan ("Work History, Labor-Force Attachment, and Earnings Differences Between the Races and Sexes," *Journal of Human Resources* XIV (1979): 3-20) concluded that a difference in worker characteristics could account for only 45 percent of the difference in men's and women's salaries. This suggested that the remaining 55 percent could probably be attributed to discrimination.

47. Barbara Bergmann, "Women's Roles in the Economy: Teaching the Issues," *Women's Studies Quarterly* 3/4 (1990): 9.

48. Ibid.

49. Alice Kessler-Harris, *A Woman's Wage: Historical Meanings and Social Consequences* (Lexington, Ky.: University Press of Kentucky, 1990).

50. Ibid., 2.

51. Ibid., 16.

52. Ibid., 13.

53. Bergmann, *Economic Emergence*, 92-117.

54. Kessler-Harris, 117-18.

55. Ibid., 31, 38.

56. This was the justification for enacting the D.C. minimum-wage law, cited in Kessler-Harris, 35.

57. Ibid., 55-56.

58. Bergmann, *Economic Emergence*, 183.

59. Paula England, *Comparable Worth: Theories and Evidence* (New York: Aldine de Gruyter, 1992), 260.

60. Hobgood, 53.

61. Quoted in Hobgood, 56.

62. Ibid., 56-57.

63. Ibid., 57.

64. "Introduction," *The Reshaping of America: Social Consequences of the Changing Economy*, ed. D. Stanley Eitzen and Maxine Baca Zinn, (Englewood Cliffs, N.J.: Prentice-Hall, 1989), 6-7.

65. "Monsignor John A. Ryan," Sermon delivered at funeral of Rt. Rev. Msgr. John A. Ryan, D.D., at St. Paul Cathedral, St. Paul, Minn. September 19, 1945, by Most Rev. Francis J. Haas, D.D. Bishop of Grand Rapids, Mich., reprint from the October, 1945 issue of *Catholic Action*, monthly publication of the National Catholic Welfare Conference.

66. Joseph A. Komonchak, "Mission and Identity in Catholic Universities" unpublished address given at conference on theological education held at Marquette University, August 1995.

67. Richard J. Purcell, "John A. Ryan, Prophet of Social Justice," *Studies* (1946): 169.

Can John Ryan's Economic Ethic Work for a Global Economy?

DAVID A. KRUEGER

In this paper, I consider whether John Ryan's natural law, economic ethic can be reappropriated within the new global, capitalist economic context in order to make judgments about and prescriptions for modern economic life. This task is potentially valuable, for Ryan's economic ethic may constitute the most comprehensive, systematic, detailed evaluation of a capitalist economy within the tradition of modern Roman Catholic social ethics, certainly within North America.[1]

First, I highlight notable benchmarks in Ryan's work, both methodologically (e.g., use of natural law, uses of economic theory) and substantively (e.g., advocacy of a living wage, defense of private property and capital), in his attempts to evaluate and make conclusions about the U.S. economy of his day. Rather than offer a comprehensive overview of Ryan's ethical method and analysis of early twentieth-century U.S. capitalism,[2] I focus on his development and application of the concept of the living wage to illustrate the evaluative and prescriptive character of his economic ethic. Second, I consider the applicability of Ryan's ethic to the contemporary economic context, which is both similar to and different from Ryan's own. I suggest how these continuities and discontinuities provide opportunities as well as challenges for the attempt to use Ryan's thought for the ethical evaluation of contemporary global market capitalism. In effect, the moral task is to determine whether and how Ryan's ethical norms can be embodied within the contemporary market practices, organizations, and systems of a global economy in order to achieve the same kinds of ethical goals and economic outcomes that Ryan envisioned for the relatively self-contained, domestic U.S. economy of his day. As a test case in the reappropriation of Ryan's ethic, I use Ryan's ethical method to consider whether a universal living wage is a practical moral demand that should be applied to the contemporary global market economy.

I. Ryan's Economic Ethic: A Conditional, Natural Law Defense of Early Twentieth-century U.S. Capitalism

Ryan's work was a self-conscious attempt to apply the general theological framework and moral principles of *Rerum novarum*, (cf., *A Living Wage*, 1906) and later of *Quadragesimo anno*, (cf., *A Better Economic Order*, 1935; *Distributive Justice*, 1942), to the specific context of the U.S. economy in the early twentieth century. Ryan not only concluded that a capitalist economy, when meeting certain minimal moral requirements, was morally defensible for the U.S. society of his day, but also offered various detailed prescriptions for reforming the character of U.S. economic practice. That economy was characterized by rapid industrial growth and also by a distribution of wealth and income in which the majority of workers did not receive "a decent livelihood"—remuneration sufficient to guarantee what Ryan considered to be the minimal economic standard of living required by human dignity within the particular social context of his day. Ryan also understood this economy to be broadly capitalistic insofar as its constitutive features included private ownership of the means of production, a relatively free market in which the factors of production (land, capital, management, and wage labor) were valued and remunerated largely according to their relative scarcity (their supply and demand), and a system of production in which the majority of workers received their livelihood in the form of wages.

Ryan's economic ethic, consistent with early modern papal social thought, was grounded in a Thomistic theological anthropology. As such, human nature, rightly ordered, is understood to be directed toward ultimate human ends—union with God and the development and perfection of personality. This intrinsic end grounds the moral claim of universal human dignity, unconditioned by any social factors (cf., 1944).

Because this ultimate telos requires the instrumental satisfaction of certain basic human needs, Ryan concludes that God's intention for the material goods of creation is that they be distributed in such a way as to sustain all humans: "God created the earth for the sustenance of all His children" (1942: 270; cf. also 1923: 14; and 1935: 148). As such, access to the material goods of the earth becomes a natural right, based upon essential human nature. In sum, these two general moral norms—universal human dignity, and the universal destination of creation to sustain all persons—serve to order virtually all of Ryan's economic ethic and specific prescriptions for early twentieth-century, U.S. industrial life. Consistent with this framework of human nature and natural rights, Ryan develops a normative understanding of economy and its proper role in the attainment of human purposes. Economic life involves the production and distribution of external goods, more precisely, material goods and services for human use. A rightly ordered economy attempts to provide all individuals those external goods owed them by natural right through maximizing the production and distribution of goods and services instrumentally necessary for humans to attain their proper ends of self-perfection and salvation. Concretely, that requirement is embodied in the provision of a decent livelihood:

> Since God has imposed upon [the individual] the obligation of attaining his eternal end, his eternal salvation, God wishes him to have the means which are adequate for that purpose. Now a human being will not have the means to attain his salvation, will not have the means to live a reasonable life, unless he has that minimum amount of material things and opportunities which is equivalent to a decent livelihood. (1920: 69)

This right to a decent livelihood entails the duty to ensure that all individuals have "reasonable access" (and "reasonable terms") to those material goods minimally necessary for basic, human well-being. Hence, "the men [sic] who are in present control of the opportunities of the earth are obliged to permit reasonable access to these opportunities by persons who are willing to work" (1916: 360; see also 1923: 10). What "reasonable access" concretely implies is unspecified in this general articulation of principle and might vary from system to system. Its moral force is universal and, as such, functions as a moral criterion for assessing any economic system. Furthermore, the concept of "a decent livelihood" provides a "moral minimum" requirement regarding the distribution of national economic product.

Ryan proposes a "living wage" as that right specific to a capitalist economy that fulfills the general and abstract requirement of a "decent livelihood" and as such satisfies the minimal material requirements of human dignity as dictated by a natural-law metaphysic and ethic. This "remote" conclusion of the natural law is deduced from the primary right to subsist upon the bounty of the earth through a decent livelihood. As a specification of this primary right, a living wage is a natural right owed the worker, male or female,[3] within the context of a capitalist wage-based economy. Within the context of early twentieth-century U.S. life, Ryan believed a living wage should be sufficient to sustain the following kinds of material and social needs: food, shelter, and clothing sufficient to maintain a worker and his or her family, the means for some recreation, the means for participation in community and religious life, access to education, and modest unemployment and social security (1920: 65-66). Clearly, Ryan intends this living wage to be concrete and measurable. Indeed, he calculated an annual living wage to be $601.03, which would sustain a worker and his/her family with the above kinds of modest material conditions of life in 1905 (1906: 123-50). (One notes here illustratively the detail and precision that pervaded Ryan's attempt to create a natural-law economic ethic for U.S. society.)

Ryan's argument for a living wage is not yet sufficient to conclude that the U.S. economy of his day was duty-bound in practice to provide a universal living wage. Ryan has made an abstract, metaphysically based moral claim—the universal right to a decent livelihood. He has specified the contingent, historical form that this right would take in his own social context—a living wage. He must also argue empirically for its practicality. This economic viability requires that the aggregate U.S. domestic economic product be large enough to sustain a universal living wage, which he claims is the case empirically, and that a proposed method of reform can create an economic state of affairs that actually embodies the moral objective and that avoids unintended economic consequences that may be less morally desirable than the original state of affairs. In other words, he must provide evidence that there is a "large enough economic pie to provide enough to go around" and that there is an institutional means to accomplish such an objective.

At this point, Ryan's economic ethic demonstrates dependence upon economic theory to provide warrant for the efficacy of the general ethical principle. To support his proposal of a universal living wage,

Ryan utilizes the "underconsumption and oversaving theory" of his contemporary, English economist John A. Hobson. This theory argued that depressions (and in particular the Great Depression of 1929) are generally caused by overproduction of capital goods (primarily through savings and investments by the wealthy) and the underconsumption of consumer goods due to lack of purchasing power primarily on the part of the masses of the laboring classes. Hobson provides the necessary economic theory to back Ryan's moral argument for a universal living wage for all U.S. workers. With this theory, Ryan can argue that the consequence of a living wage—a redistribution of purchasing power so that those who have the need and desire to spend for consumption will also have the means to do so—in all probability will generate positive outcomes for the economy at large and real gains for wage-earners in particular.

Within a wage-based economic system, Ryan argues that the obligation to pay a living wage falls upon employers directly because they are in control of the process of production. While he asserts that it is the employer's direct responsibility to provide a living wage, he believes this cannot be attained voluntarily or solely through market forces of supply and demand. Neither benevolence nor competitive market conditions can insure voluntary compliance; neither can it be instituted through labor unions, given their limited membership (1919: 81, 100-151). Because he believes the general function of the state is to promote social welfare, he sees it as the state's legitimate function to enact legislation that requires employers to pay a minimum wage and that employs the coercive powers of government to penalize noncompliance. Furthermore, if the economic situation is such that employers cannot pay living wages, Ryan cites *Quadragesimo anno* to argue that the state is obliged to do what it can to create the necessary conditions that make feasible the fulfillment of this duty (1942: 280-81).

His discussion also articulates economic factors that create morally permissible exceptions to the employer's concrete obligation to provide a living wage (e.g., inefficiency and low productivity, the prior obligation of the employer to provide oneself and one's family with a decent livelihood) (1920: 52; 1942: 276-81). While Ryan does not elaborate at length on these exceptions, in practice they could entail considerable latitude in exemptions from the general moral imperative to provide a living wage. For instance, one might liberally apply low productivity to attempt to exempt considerable numbers of workers from the obligation to provide a living wage. One can infer, though, that Ryan means this list of exemptions to involve exceptional cases, not large segments of the work force. We will return to this set of exceptions below when we consider the applicability of Ryan's ethic to the contemporary global economy.

In sum, Ryan argues that the provision of a universal living wage for all U.S. workers was a minimum moral requirement for the U.S. economy of his day. This is the primary minimum moral requirement for the treatment of wage labor—one of four basic "factors of production"—that provides the structural framework for Ryan's comprehensive analysis of U.S. capitalism. Ryan's economic ethic goes on to argue for other minimum moral requirements with respect to the other three factors of production and their remunerations—land/private property and rent, capital and interest, and management and profits. He proposes various other institutional reforms with respect to the other three factors of production to make their functioning and distributions better to cohere with the demands of human welfare and of distributive justice. These reforms are to take place within the basic institutional framework of capitalism, a moral conclusion made largely upon empirical and comparative analysis that no other known economic system can better approximate his general theological and ethical norms. In addition, Ryan articulates moral criteria that go beyond minimal criteria to specify maximal ethical criteria for "complete economic justice" (cf., 1942) and whose discussion would move well beyond the scope of this essay.

II. Can We Apply Ryan's Economic Ethic to Contemporary Global Market Capitalism?: A Universal Living Wage as a Test Case

Can Ryan's economic ethic be reappropriated for application to contemporary global market capitalism? At least two shifts must be addressed in such an effort: changes in the field of ethics and changes in economic life since Ryan's day.

Much has transpired in Roman Catholic ethics and in the broader field of Christian social ethics since Ryan's day, trends that have been treated and analyzed by many (cf. Gremillion, 1976; Pawlikowski, 1986; Hehir, 1991). I cite briefly only a few of the more obvious. Most relevant for Ryan's work is a shift away from primary dependence upon the framework of classical natural law toward a focus on scripture and more explicit theological language and motifs to ground ethical norms and prescriptions, a trend that develops stronger continuities between Roman Catholic and Protestant ethics (cf. Gustafson, 1978; 1989). Roman Catholic natural law theory itself has seen methodological shifts and developments, for example, to a more person-centered approach that acknowledges greater dependence upon human sciences and empirical verification, trends for which Ryan's work shared a strong early affinity. Furthermore, Catholicism's increased interaction not only with Protestant ethics but more recently and profoundly with other world religions has challenged and tempered its own natural law assumptions about the universalism of its truth claims, resulting, in some circles, in a greater appreciation for historicity as well as cultural, religious, and ethical diversity.

It is beyond the scope of this essay fully to reconstruct Ryan's ethical method to account adequately for all the shifts within the tradition. For current purposes I merely note them, acknowledging as well important thematic weaknesses and gaps in Ryan's thought, for example, strongly hierarchical assumptions about gender relationships, virtually no attention to sin, an absence of ecological stewardship. Nevertheless, I propose that central ethical concepts in Ryan's thought—human dignity, the universal destination of the goods of creation, the framework of natural rights—have enduring value not only within the field of Christian social ethics, but also within the large public discourse about civil society. One can commend the basic methodological intent of Ryan's natural law foundation—to develop general, objective, universalizable ethical norms grounded theologically in assertions about the nature of reality that provide comprehensive principles of evaluation capable of evaluating the relative merits of specific systems, institutions, and practices of political economy. Also noteworthy is Ryan's careful attention to economic theory, description, and analysis that serve to provide clarity about social context as well as strategic and policy arguments to support his moral arguments.

More significant are the dramatic changes in social context that have occurred within economic life. It is to these shifts that we must turn for their potential to challenge the enduring efficacy of Ryan's economic ethic. Despite numerous changes, many aspects of contemporary economic life are continuous with those that Ryan analyzed in the early twentieth-century U.S. economy. Its capitalist institutional framework remains essentially the same, defined in terms of the four factors of production that order Ryan's analysis. Private property remains the primary form of ownership. Labor's remuneration remains essentially in the form of wages. Capital allocations remain predominantly in the private sector. Firms compete in competitive markets. Prices are generally free and determined by supply and demand.

Three significant changes are notable since Ryan's time. First, an even more extensive system of government regulation has developed within industrialized democracies like the United States. New Deal legislation was taking place only late in Ryan's career. Since then, new waves of and some modest counter-reactions to government regulation of business have taken place. Second, viable systemic alternatives to capitalism have destroyed themselves from within. This is significant for Ryan's ethical method in that Ryan's affirmation of U.S. capitalist structures was largely comparative and empirical. Capitalist institutions and practices were affirmed insofar as they satisfied ethical criteria better than actual (and sometimes hypothetical) systemic alternatives. This nearly global rejection of socialist economic assumptions and institutions would provide additional moral weight in favor of capitalist institutions and performance for a method like Ryan's. In other words, history itself seems to validate Ryan's natural law conclusion that capitalist economic practice has sustained and promoted human welfare better than the alternatives. The third change is the dramatic shift toward globalization—the slow but steady integration of domestic and regional economies around the world into a single, integrated global economy that inexorably links the economies of most nation-states. This has occurred largely through the expansion of global trade and the steady dismantling of trade barriers. Ryan's own work includes no discussion of a global economy, with virtually no references even to the reality of global trade or multinational corporations. His discussion focuses exclusively on a domestic context, within the confines of a single nation-state, the United States, whose economy centered more heavily on manufacturing than is the case today.

So, here is our question: Would Ryan argue for a universal living wage in the global economy at the end of the twentieth century as he did the U.S. economy at the beginning? I will consider whether Ryan's own ethical method would conclude that the abstract and general right to a decent livelihood entails the actual embodiment of a universal living wage within today's global economy.

First, Ryan's method would identify and evaluate any competing theories of wage justice. Here I presume that Ryan's arguments against various competing theories would continue to apply. Indeed, his rejection of socialism's labor theory of value would carry further weight given the collapse of socialist, centrally planned economies. Second, Ryan would articulate a theory of wage justice that satisfies conditions of human dignity and welfare. Within a capitalist economy, this would take the form of a living wage. Third, Ryan would consider empirically whether the actual system of global capitalism satisfies this ethical demand. Empirical evidence unambiguously demonstrates that this demand is not fully satisfied. While global economic output has expanded dramatically through most of the twentieth century, raising the standards of living of millions across the globe well above the poverty line to approximate at least what Ryan envisions with the living wage, widespread poverty nevertheless still exists. Most demographic accounts categorize at least a billion people globally as desperately poor and/or malnourished. In sum, it is incontestable that a large portion of persons around the globe do not receive decent livelihoods, due to unemployment, underemployment, or inadequate income, generally in the form of low wages.

Fourth, having demonstrated that the global economy fails to satisfy this minimum moral criterion, we must consider whether it would be practically feasible to do so. In other words, would it be possible to provide all, or nearly all, workers around the globe with a living wage? This step is perhaps the most critical in Ryan's ethical method, for the universal right to a decent livelihood remains an abstract, unembodied right that does not become a concrete, actual right until an empirical analysis can demonstrate its economic viability. As Ryan asked whether the U.S. economy's national economic product was sufficiently large to sustain a universal living wage, so must we ask whether the global economic product is also sufficiently large to provide a truly universal living wage. If not, then the process of moral argumentation has ended with the conclusion that the moral requirement of a living wage is not actual and concrete. In this case, we might nevertheless examine the global economy with a smaller unit of analysis than the totality itself, such as nation-states or regional economic units such as the European Union or North America (with NAFTA). We might conclude that those smaller economic units with sufficient economic product do have an actual and concrete duty to provide a universal living wage.

For the sake of argument, though, I will make the empirical assumption that there is sufficient global economic product to provide a universal, or nearly universal, living wage. Large regional exceptions would undoubtedly apply, though, such as regions in Africa and parts of

Asia and South America. In this case, our analysis would proceed to the empirical question of whether a viable economic strategy can be devised to implement a successful universal living wage within a global economy. In effect, the ethicist must become an economist and provide evidence that a proposed method of reform within the global economy would create an economic state of affairs—a universal living wage—that actually embodies the moral objective and that avoids unintended economic consequences that may be less morally desirable than the original state of affairs.

At this point, one must acknowledge the different empirical factors in social context that impinge upon Ryan's ethical method to shape our practical conclusions. One involves the social agent who could be responsible to provide a decent livelihood. Ryan's earliest and most substantial thinking about a living wage occurred before the growth of the welfare state initiated by Roosevelt's New Deal. In the absence of a welfare state where government becomes a possible provider of livelihood, Ryan's assignment of moral responsibility to the employer functioned as an argument of moral last resort. No other social actor was able to provide a decent livelihood; thus it fell to the employer. Nevertheless, Ryan acknowledged that mandatory legislation, and not voluntary action, would be necessary to ensure employer compliance. In the late twentieth century, though, many industrialized nations still have an adequate welfare state apparatus in place to permit the possibility that government could provide something approaching a decent livelihood for citizens in the form of welfare, making a living wage unnecessary. Still, most nation states in the global economy, especially those where most poor people reside, do not have public sector resources sufficient to provide adequate levels of welfare for its citizens. Indeed, global trends in Third World government monetary and fiscal policy (e.g., IMF-initiated structural adjustments) will make such possibilities even more remote in the future.

Global competition among the economies of various nation-states also complicates the question of policy and strategy in implementing a universal living wage. Within the domestic economy of Ryan's day, his proposal that government legislation was necessary to mandate a universal living wage was a recognition of the problem of the "free rider." Legislation was necessary to create a "level playing field" that prevented some employers from offering a lower wage in the face of unemployed workers who would consent to work for such a wage. In effect, any nation-state without wage-rate legislation acts as a "free rider" in an integrated global economy in which production moves across borders to seek the lowest wage rates relative to productivity. Hence, nothing short of transnational legislation across nation-states would be necessary to create the kind of level playing field that would approximate what Ryan had in mind in his economic ethic. Such a structural reform is clearly impractical in the foreseeable future, although some regional governmental collaboration moves in this direction, such as the shift toward unified economic regulation in the European Union.

Although not the case, let us assume for the sake of argument that there is substantial political will across the globe to create universal living wage legislation. If so, Ryan would still demand that we utilize economic theory to support a policy mechanism that would be successful in creating a living wage that would have the intended beneficial effect—increased standards of living for the poor—and not some unintended harmful social effect, such as no real increase in standards of living or even decreased standards of living. In his own work, Ryan utilized John Hobson's "underconsumption theory" as well as microeconomic price theory to argue that increased wages would likely result in some real income gains for workers. In other words, the increased wages would not be completely eroded by the inflationary tendencies of living-wage legislation. Whether such noninflationary assumptions would hold in today's global economy seems dubious, where the scale of persons receiving less than living wages is not in the millions but perhaps more than a billion. Indeed, multinational lending to less developed countries in the 1970s and 1980s suggests that hyperinflation would be a strong probability to any massive and rapid initiatives intended to increase wages globally. In addition, Ryan's various exemptions from the employer's duty to provide a living wage would also apply on a wide-scale basis. For example, Ryan argues that employers are not duty-bound to provide a living wage to workers with low productivity. In fact, low productivity is a primary cause for low wages in parts of today's global economy, especially in less-developed countries.

CONCLUSION

In sum, it would appear that Ryan's ethical method demonstrates that the various conditions necessary for a universal living wage are not fully satisfied in today's global economic context. Hence, the abstract, natural right to a living wage is not yet actual and concrete on a universal basis in today's global economy. Nevertheless, Ryan's ethic could provide important moral directives toward structural reform in global economic policy. While the universal right to a living wage is not yet actual, the general natural right to a decent livelihood for all workers is valid and should be directive for public policy and private sector policy. As such, public policy is properly ordered to create the necessary conditions for the eventual embodiment of a decent livelihood for all. This directive would embrace the goal of increasing global economic output, especially in less developed countries, with a special focus on the poor. It could include governmental collaboration across nation-states that aims toward eventual agreements on wage legislation. It would also involve directives and reforms in the other three factors of production that Ryan discusses, but that have not been fully addressed in this essay. Those initiatives could include policies that encourage widespread ownership of private property, facilitating a growth in the numbers of entrepreneurs and managers especially among less-developed nations, and encouraging widespread growth in ownership of financial capital especially among the poor, including programs that support the development of cooperatives.

With respect to corporate policy and the behavior of private-sector firms, the moral imperative of a decent livelihood would mandate a living wage where legislated. It would provide a strong moral presumption against anything less than a living wage unless various empirical conditions are not satisfied as discussed above. With respect to multinational corporations doing business in less-developed countries, it would provide a strong moral presumption in favor of providing living wages globally, even where legislation is absent and even where market wage rates might fall below levels necessary to sustain a decent livelihood. The argument here would be one of capability. More generally, global corporations in less developed countries would face a moral presumption in favor of creating and sustaining those types of activities and relationships that enhance long-term economic development rather than discourage or hinder it. Such activities would include technology transfer, infrastructure development, and skill development of those employed from poor nations, all with the aim of creating the necessary long-term conditions for economic and social development that would eventually support the practice of a decent livelihood for all.

REFERENCES

Beckley, Harlan
1992 *Passion For Justice: Retrieving the Legacies of Walter Rauschenbusch, John A. Ryan, and Reinhold Niebuhr.* Louisville: Westminster/John Knox Press.

Curran, Charles
1982 *American Catholic Social Ethics.* Notre Dame: University of Notre Dame Press.

Gearty, Patrick
1953 *The Economic Thought of Monsignor John A. Ryan.* Washington, D.C.: The Catholic University of America Press.

Gremillion, Joseph
1976 (editor) *The Gospel of Peace and Justice: Catholic Social Teaching since Pope John.* Maryknoll, New York: Orbis.

Gustafson, James M.
1978 *Protestant and Roman Catholic Ethics: Prospects for Rapprochement.* Chicago: University of Chicago Press.
1989 "Roman Catholic and Protestant Interaction in Ethics: An Interpretation," *Theological Studies* 50: 44-69.

Hehir, J. Bryan
1991 "The Social Role of the Church: Leo XIII, Vatican II and John Paul II." Unpublished paper for a conference entitled *One Hundred Years of Catholic Social Teaching,* University of Notre Dame, April, 1991.

Krueger, David A.
1988 "The Economic Ethics of John A. Ryan and Gustavo Gutiérrez." Ph.D. Dissertation (unpublished). The University of Chicago.

Pawlikowski, John
1986 "Modern Catholic Teaching on the Economy: An Analysis and Evaluation," *Christianity and Capitalism: Perspectives on Religion, Liberalism and the Economy.* Edited by Bruce Grelle and David A. Krueger. Chicago: Center for the Scientific Study of Religion, 3-24.

Ryan, John A.

1906 *A Living Wage: Its Ethical and Economic Aspects.* New York: Macmillan.

1916 *Distributive Justice: The Right and Wrong of Our Present Distribution of Wealth.* First edition. New York: Macmillan.

1919 *The Church and Socialism and Other Essays.* Washington, D.C.: The University Press.

1920 *Social Reconstruction.* New York: Macmillan.

1923 *The Christian Doctrine of Property.* New York: Paulist Press.

1935 *A Better Economic Order.* New York: Harper.

1942 *Distributive Justice: The Right and Wrong of Our Present Distribution of Wealth.* Third edition. New York: Macmillan.

1944 *The Norm of Morality Defined and Applied to Particular Actions.* Washington, D.C.: National Catholic Welfare Conference.

Notes

1. I am indebted to James M. Gustafson for introducing me to Ryan's thought. Indeed, his passing reference to Ryan in *Protestant and Roman Catholic Ethics* (1978) and his treatment of Ryan's work in the classroom have served to introduce many students of ethics, both Protestant and Roman Catholic, to Ryan's thought.

2. For more comprehensive treatments of Ryan's economic ethic see, for instance, Gearty (1953), Curran (1982) Krueger (1988), and Beckley (1992).

3. While Ryan's understanding of gender relations is traditional, patriarchal, and hierarchical—he assumes family life as normative with the male as primary economic provider and the female primarily as domestic caretaker—he does argue against any wage discrimination against women and/or unmarried workers. The alternative would be a two-tiered wage system that would place married male workers at a competitive disadvantage in the labor markets and therefore would compromise their capacity to receive a living wage (1942: 283-84). "His right to [a living wage] is directly based neither upon the needs nor the rights of his family, but upon his own needs, upon the fact that family conditions are indispensable to his own normal life" (1942: 283-84; see also 1906: 119).

John A. Ryan and Public Policy

A theme uniting the essays in this section is, "If Ryan were alive today, with what public policy issues would he be concerned?" As a person deeply committed to progressive social reform, democracy, and dialogue with non-Catholics, his legacy lies not only in his specific policy recommendations but also in the spirit with which he addressed social concerns. The following set of essays responds to this legacy of Ryan.

Christine Firer Hinze relies on a concept of "ecology" to characterize Ryan's work. In the first part of her essay she argues that Ryan appreciated the "complex, interconnected physical and social landscapes within which human economic activity occurs." Ryan's approach to economic problems illustrates his respect for the complexity of such issues. While he recognized the need for public policy and was an advocate of an activist form of government, he also held that other social entities had a significant role to play in social reform. In the second part of her essay, Hinze considers the dramatic changes in economic life that have occurred since Ryan's time and invites a discourse between Ryan's work and three issues in contemporary economic relations: ecological economics, the option for the poor, and the work-family nexus.

William J. Byron, S.J., brings Ryan's driving concern for a "more equitable distribution of material blessings" to bear on what Byron refers to as "two new social questions," namely the appropriate uses of molecular medicine and the health care finance reform. Byron describes the latter issue to be the major question of distributive justice for our day. In the tradition of Ryan, Byron presents a detailed economic and ethical consideration of the three dominant models proposed for health care-finance reform.

John A. Coleman, S.J., narrates the historical development of American believers' citizenship as it relates to social justice from Ryan's day to our own. He presents "three snapshots" in this history: beginning of the twentieth century, mid-century, and the new century ahead. Coleman describes three characteristics of the contemporary context highlighting the "new paradenominational action groups" that "include the full ecumenical gamut in their constituency and cover a broad range of social justice issues." He concludes the essay with five theses about the relationship between citizenship and discipleship.

Diana L. Hayes highlights Ryan's work in the defense and promotion of human dignity. She argues that it is this element of Ryan's thought that needs to be reemphasized in our contemporary debates about social concerns. Although, as Hayes admits, Ryan did not speak out on issues of race and sexism, in many ways he was ahead of this time on other social issues. Thus his work laid a foundation for Christian social action in our contemporary "culture of disbelief."

Margaret O'Brien Steinfels's reflection on the life and work of Ryan leads her to propose three points concerning the work of justice. First, doing justice requires real thought and real action. Ryan's work is a model of this. He brought reason and sound argument to justice issues. Her second point is that justice is a social responsibility. Society, in part through the state, has responsibility to promote social good. Finally, she writes, the work of justice is for all members of the community.

John Berkman invites the reader to consider what might be called John Ryan's "family values." As Ryan, in his analytical way, came up with the exact requirements of a living family wage, he must, suggests Berkman, address the question of family size. Ryan argues for the importance of a large family and the values a large family instills against those whom he called the "neo-Malthusian" industrialists. Berkman argues that Ryan's emphasis on the social role of the family is not present in contemporary Catholic discussions on regulating family size.

Patricia McNeal shifts the conversation from economics to international relations as she narrates the history of American Catholic responses to war from the outbreak of World War I to the end of World War II. Ryan was deeply involved with matters of international justice and the roles that the Catholic church and the U.S. government ought to play in insuring justice. McNeal presents the development of Ryan's thought on issues of justified war, revolution, and pacifism as well as his relationship with the Catholic peace movement in Europe and in America.

John A. Ryan, Public Policy, and the Quest for a Dignified Ecology of Work

CHRISTINE FIRER HINZE

Introduction

In its most common usage, the term "ecology" alludes to the web of interdependent biosystems within which the human species is enmeshed, and on which it depends. At other times, "ecology" is used to refer to the pluriform but interdependent social systems—political, cultural, and economic—that compose the noetic environment for human life.[1] In either case, the ecological lens is the lens of the big picture, but the big picture composed by and dependent upon the vital interactions of many smaller, local systems.

In a profound way, the realm we call the economic mediates between our physical and social environments by means of a crucial activity: work. The "ecology of work" thus takes in the complex, interconnected physical and social landscapes within which human economic activity occurs. Like the biotic ecosphere, the ecosphere of work exhibits a dizzying scope of relationships and operations, ranging from the simple and local, to the highly complex and global.

This essay considers the legacy of John A. Ryan through a look at his quest for a dignified ecology of work. Though "ecology" is not a term that would have been familiar to Ryan, it is compatible, I think, with the Roman Catholic moral and social tradition he represented, and that many of us attempt to carry on today. Modern Roman Catholic social thought has favored organic imagery that depicts humans as persons embedded in webs of social relations. The venerable concept of the common good fosters a religious and social sense of connected parts within a whole. Most recently, Catholic social thought has highlighted the dignity of each individual person. Yet it has continued to uphold the traditional natural law assumption that interdependent communal settings, in particular the family, the economy, and the polis, are natural to humans, and necessary for their survival and thriving.

Making connections, moreover, was one of Monsignor Ryan's great talents. He ably combined Americanism, Catholicism, and professional expertise in economics. He grasped interactions between theory and practice, facts and values, the religious and the mundane in the political and economic spheres. From early on he perceived his own vocation in terms of building bridges between religio-moral ideals and concrete economic practice. He writes: "I wanted to examine economic life in the light of Christian principles, with a view to making them operative in the realm of industry. It seemed to me that the salvation of millions of souls depended largely upon the economic opportunity to live decently, to live as human beings in the image and likeness of God."[2] Throughout his long career, Ryan's concern for the salvation of souls was expressed through ministrations on behalf of everyday workers' rights to economic conditions that honored their dignity and status as human beings, and as children of God.[3]

In the years since Ryan's death, tremendous changes have occurred. Yet in our altered milieu, the life's work that engaged Ryan—articulating a coherent, practical, vision of socioeconomic reform for the sake of the genuine well-being of everyday people—continues to press on us. And Ryan, who understood so well the need to "think together" the different facets of society and economy, offers us the lineaments of an approach that engages the resources of the Roman Catholic tradition to address the distinctive situation of the late 1990s.

What follows focuses on the wholistic theological and moral vision that underpinned Ryan's economic theory and reformist practice. This is by no means to ignore Ryan's genius as a public policy analyst and activist. Yet, with Ryan, I believe that sound policy advocacy depends upon a sound normative picture of "good work" in its macroscopic and local settings. U.S. Christian economic ethicists indebted to Ryan must articulate, in contemporary idiom, a religio-moral worldview and ideology capable of propelling dynamic, genuinely Christian and humane, economic policy making. And, as Ryan also saw, attaining a decent livelihood for our most vulnerable citizens and families must be the practical center of Christian economic concern, the criterion for adequate public policy, and the measure of theoretical and practical success.

The essay proceeds in three parts. Part I sketches the normative ecology of work envisioned by Ryan, and the role he envisioned for public policy in achieving it. In Part II we turn to the landscape of work in the U.S. today, noting changes that have taken place since Ryan's death in 1945. Using three of these changes as focal points, I will then suggest an ensemble of encounters between Ryan and the contemporary scene. In so doing, I hope to show that Ryan provides U.S. Christians with basic coordinates for a contemporary program for socioeconomic renewal, and to indicate ways his contribution requires revision if it is to serve us well today.

I. Ryan's Vision of a Dignified Ecology of Work

General Description

Ryan drew on Catholic natural law theory, papal teachings, progressive political and economic theory, and the evidence of his own observation to fashion a vision of a "good economy" whose aim was the protection and fostering of the material conditions for the genuinely human welfare of all its members. Human beings, wrote Ryan, "are intrinsically sacred, and essentially equal by nature in their claims to a reasonable livelihood from the common heritage of the earth." "A reasonable livelihood" meant that minimum amount of goods and opportunities "necessary for rational existence . . . supplying those needs connected with humane living."[4] The natural right to a decent livelihood was normally actuated by the expenditure of reasonable amounts of honest labor, to be remunerated in industrial economies by a "family living wage."

Ryan's arguments for workers' rights to a decent livelihood acquired through work, the obligations of employers to provide it, and the role of government in assuring it, are framed by religiously inspired strictures against greed and the idolatry of material acquisition or success.[5] His claims rest, most fundamentally, on a theological affirmation of the place of human beings in God's bigger, teleological economy. Ryan's Thomistic anthropology portrays humans as created in God's image and likeness, who, as social beings, are meant to cooperatively develop their spiritual personalities, toward the proximate end of temporal flourishing, and the ultimate end of the beatific vision. The economy plays its part by providing the necessary material conditions for the pursuit and realization of these divinely ordained, human ends.

To fulfill its purpose, according to Ryan, any economic system must be founded on certain basic ethical principles.[6] The first, frankly religious principle, was one he frequently reiterated: the earth and its potentialities were divinely created and intended for the sustenance of all God's children. Though unequal situations warrant differential treatment, "Equal claims upon the bounty of the earth do . . . comprise [a right to] at least those minimum amounts of goods and opportunities which are required for reasonable life and development."[7]

Second, "men are morally obliged to use the goods and opportunities of the earth in accordance with the laws of justice and charity." Ryan draws several implications from this claim: Private property is a moral institution because it is necessary for human welfare. Holders of private property are morally obliged to act in such a way that the nonowners will have access to these things on reasonable terms. And ownership implies stewardship for the common good.[8]

The final ethical principle acknowledged by a good economic order is that "industrial society is an organism, every part of which is subordinate within certain limits to the whole and is obliged to promote the well-being of the whole." Individual liberty in the use of private property ceases to be morally valid, not when it begins to encroach upon the equal liberty of others, but as soon as it begins to violate the moral claims arising from either economic charity or economic justice.[9]

Ryan thus specifies the interacting bonds and obligations between God, the earth, and the human community—the big picture—within which particular economic systems must situate themselves. This complex, religiously grounded, ecological-economic vision is predicated on answers to fundamental teleological questions. Human beings, while ends *in se*, are created for a larger purpose. Similarly, the earth, families, the polis, and the economy, while maintaining their own distinctive internal processes and identities, have interconnected purposes in relation to humanity and to God's wider purposes for creation.

Oikonomia *and the Ecology of Work*

In order to grasp more fully the theological horizon of Ryan's Catholic natural law understanding of economy, it is useful to recall the term's derivation from the ancient Greek *oikonomia*, recently explored in Methodist theologian M. Douglas Meeks's book, *God the Economist.*

Modern economics focuses on production, consumption, labor, capital, and profitmaking in the context of competition for scarce resources. But economics in its fuller, classical sense is the science whose concern is gathering, cultivating, and distributing the earth's material resources, with a view to the survival and thriving of human communities. Thus understood, economy, *oikonomia*, mediates between physical ecology on the one hand, and the *oikoumene* (from which the English word "ecumenical" is derived) of human interconnected community on the other.[10]

The Christian tradition situates all these spheres within an even greater and more profound understanding of *oikonomia*, as God's own creative, redeeming, and reconciling work, the "divine householding" that sustains and renews the physical-ecological, economic, and ecumenic-civic households. The fundamental relatedness of these different *oikoi* is in this way even more clearly revealed. Meeks writes, "The integrity of God's righteousness and of human justice holds these three concerns together as mutually interdependent. Economic justice includes the question of justice for the land and justice for the peoples on the land. [Hence,] every economic question is also an ecological and ecumenic question and vice versa."[11]

Besides linking human work to the supreme economy of the Kingdom of God, the language of *oikonomia* sheds light on work's local ecology by signaling links between the public economy and the household economy, and among the various household relations that make up the mundane economy of family and work for most people. The dignified economic ecology Ryan pictured entails work as not simply a means to ever greater monetary reward, status, or wealth, but rather as useful expenditure of effort through which modest material prosperity is attained, human potentials are expressed and developed, and the community is served.[12]

Gender and the Ecology of Work

Ryan's Catholic social vision accorded women and men equal dignity, and equal claims on a decent livelihood attainable through their labor.

Ryan's substantive economic vision, however, like Leo's and Pius's, harbored a particular gender subtext.[13] Ryan assumed as valid the complementary gender roles he had experienced as a child on a farm, and that had evolved in laboring—and middle-class—families into the widely accepted "male breadwinner/female homemaker" distinction. Women's central role in the home, and men's in the workplace, were thought to reflect natural differences between men and women. From Ryan's teleological vantage point, women and men are potential partners, but are designed for different economic and familial purposes; they are, in some basic ways, *for* different things.[14]

This particular division of masculine and feminine economic roles had become more pronounced with the emergence of the modern market economy. Meeks points out that in the modern period, the ruling metaphor, and moral goal, of the economic realm shifted.

The classic normative picture of economy as the public household through which *access to livelihood* was to be mutually pursued, was supplanted by a vision of capitalist economy as competitive marketplace where scarce goods are *exchanged for profit*. In the process, many facets of the human pursuit of livelihood, including work, talent, time, collaboration, and achievement, were reduced to exchangeable commodities. The result was a degradation of work and workers that threatened to infect the entire ecology of work both inside and outside the familial household.

At least partly, if implicitly, in response to this perceived danger, a rather ingenious compromise developed in middle- and working-class cultures of the late-nineteenth and early-twentiuth centuries. Gender-role ideology was used to distinguish, and then reconnect, the older household and newer market economic paradigms.[15] Men were delegated into the public wage-earning sector, where the logic of the exchange market ruled. Women, buttressed by a newly energized cult of "womanhood" and "motherhood" also reflected in papal teachings, became the conservers and carriers of the older relations of *oikos* as collaboration for livelihood, relegated now to mores and practices within the confines of the private household. Unlike the biblical householdwoman praised in Proverbs 31, however, female-centered households in market capitalism increasingly lost their productive functions, and were treated and encouraged to behave as "units of consumption." Against this trend, the ideal of homemaker charged women with a most significant mission: to defend humanizing and religious values, to cherish and nurture children and the frail, and to preserve a more people-oriented rhythm of life. Sensing the stakes, even when disagreeing about their proper articulation, twenthieth-century women have struggled to maintain families as more than simply consumption enterprises, and economic activity more than interest-maximizing exchanges. Hindsight reveals that what was at risk was not simply a quaint but outdated way of life, but the traditional, fundamental meaning of *oikonomia* as humanizing livelihood. Seen in this light, the near-sacred character of the roles attributed to women as mothers and homemakers, and the deep emotions that have been stirred as these roles have come under question, become more understandable.

Many women, especially unmarried, younger women, did work in the industrial sector of Ryan's day. The promise of a wage, the experience of community and friendship among coworkers, and a measure of freedom from the parental domicile drew many young women to factory work in the early part of the century. Yet, as Leslie Tentler and others show, women were nearly always confined to lower-paying jobs that assured maximum tedium, but minimum skill-building, room for advancement, or power. The ironic upshot was that women's experiences in the workforce reinforced stereotypical female roles; passivity at work was encouraged, "and a lack of self confidence in any but the most familiar roles." This contributed, among female workers, to a push toward marriage and domesticity as a means to escape factory life.[16] During the Second World War, women entered the workforce in great numbers to fill jobs left by men in military service. In these circumstances, day-care centers and other accoutrements of working motherhood were initiated. But workplace participation by women through the postwar years continued to be couched within a widely shared ideological climate that gave primacy to women's domestic role.[17]

For Ryan, to be profamily, proworker, and genuinely prowoman, demanded that one advocate public policy and economic practices that freed women to focus principally on the home, while assuring men jobs at a wage that would support their wives and dependent children. Both Ryan's understanding of the objective "nature of women" and his perception of wage-earning women's own concerns led him to champion special protective legislation for women, and to regard the paycheck of a male breadwinner as the normal channel by which a woman would receive her living wage. He assumed that woman's place was in the home, and therefore the proper ecology of work ought to conduce to that end.

Public Policy: A Necessary, but not Sufficient Means

Ryan's Catholic ecological view of society led him to perceive an important role for public policy, but a role balanced and limited by the integrity and proper domains of other social entities, of the church, and of the legitimate freedom of individuals and their families.

Adumbrating what later theology would call the "option for the poor," Ryan contends that a fundamental redistribution of power must occur, favoring those in the industrial capitalist system with the least voice or leverage—the most vulnerable wage earners. Specifically, worker empowerment would be comprised by "sufficiency, security, and status": Sufficiency for labor in the present through a family living wage; security for labor in the future through savings and social insurance; and a new status for labor that includes sharing in management, profits, and ownership.[18]

The key features of Ryan's vision of socioeconomic reform were a universal living wage for workers and their families and the establishment of industrial democracy. The principal means for attaining these were to be the enactment of social reform legislation; the empowerment of workers by means of a new status in industry; and the promotion of a strong, interdependent, multigroup economic order.[19] For attaining these, Ryan maintained a generally activist view of the role of public policy and the state. "When the economic organization fails to enforce [the] obligations of the property owner," he wrote, "the task must be assumed by the State." In this regard, Ryan never tired of quoting the words of Leo XIII: "Whenever the general interest, or any particular class, suffers or is threatened with injury which can in no other way be met or prevented, it is the duty of the public authority to intervene."[20]

While advocating state intervention where needed, Ryan insisted on a concomitant, more fundamental effort to reform economic morals. If the U.S. economy failed to develop along the necessary lines, he warned, there will ultimately be one villain. "We perceive that if . . . efforts to establish a better economic order are unsuccessful, the main cause of the failure will be a very ugly and very ancient vice. It is the vice that we call avarice or greed."[21] In this linkage of the kind of economy we want with the kind of people we need to be, we discern another example of Ryan's sound ecological instincts.

Throughout his career, Ryan argued for a dual line of attack in the battle for socioeconomic reform.[22] A first means, "moral suasion," appeals to the hearts and consciences of individuals, but does not shrink from using moral and spiritual sanctions in the process. In this Ryan saw religion and the church as playing a direct role. A second means, "social effort," involved the activity of private associations, such as labor unions, and of the state. Ryan criticized both those who underestimated the potential impact of religious and moral suasion, and those who assumed that persuasion alone could assure economic justice.[23] Ryan was aware that false consciousness often kept "good Christians" in thrall to the foreign, and ultimately inhumane ethical standards of the competitive marketplace.[24] In the face of this, effective moral suasion requires "earnest, continuous, enlightened activity on the part of public teachers and molders of public opinion." But, he added, "organized effort will add very materially to the results that can be accomplished through moral suasion addressed to individuals. This very obvious general truth is superlatively true in our time, when man's social relations have become so numerous and so complex."[25] This combined effort promised the most positive outcome for the laboring class, especially its poorest-paid members.[26]

II. Retrieving and Extending the Ryan Legacy: "A Dignified Ecology of Work" Today

In many ways, the tasks before those of us wishing to articulate and enact a humane and Christian vision of good economy and good work are the same as those that faced Ryan. But important changes over the past fifty years have made the place where we now stand quite distinct from Ryan's situation. Developments in economy, society, and in the Catholic church have conspired to transform the context for thinking about and acting toward economic justice at the end of the century.

An Altered Landscape

First, we have moved economically from the heyday of the modified, national-economy-based capitalism that Ryan promoted, to an era of increased global competition and vastly larger conglomerate enterprises. In this new stage, called by some national-security industrial capitalism, by others, advanced global capitalism, the state has now become to the world market what the corporation once was to the national market, and before that, the family firm to the local market. "The state is now charged, not only with moderate economic regulation within the boundaries of the national economy, but with streamlining the whole national system for efficient transnational competition."[27]

With the transnationalization of capital and the emergence of new computer-based technologies, some economic entities have dramatically increased their size and power, by means of a proliferation of transnational and multinational corporations, mergers, and takeovers.[28] Yet, as Joseph LaBarge points out, "The underside of this unprecedented expansion of power by the few has been a pervasive feeling of powerlessness by the many."[29] There have been profound repercussions for the everyday life of millions of wage earners, including increasing job insecurity, declining real wages, and decreasing benefits.

Second, the years since 1945 have witnessed the conscientization and mobilization of groups traditionally marginalized or subordinated in the public economy. In 1963, Pope John XXIII went so far as to identify these developments as the distinguishing characteristic of our age, observing that the working classes, women, and dominated peoples and nations have increasingly begun to claim their dignity and power, and their rightful place and participation in economic and public affairs.[30] In the United States, especially, changes in the social and economic participation of women have had far-reaching effects and consequences.

Third, the ecclesial and theological context for reflection on economy and public policy has also shifted. These years have witnessed the Second Vatican Council and the reorientations of Catholic theology, teaching, culture, and practice that are being hammered out in its wake. In the United States since 1945, the Roman Catholic church has become a majority religious community, divided between a largely white, suburbanized middle-class membership, and a burgeoning urban membership consisting mostly of poorer people and people of color.[31] These demographic shifts have thrown U.S. church's traditional ties to the working class and labor unions into transition.

The body of modern Catholic social teaching to which Ryan appealed has, to be sure, maintained some striking continuities during these years. The writings of John Paul II on labor, work, and economy reflect the lineage of Leo and Pius in their concern for an objective order of justice, in their focus on laborers, in their insistence on a legitimate role for state intervention on behalf of the poor and less powerful, with the dignity of the human person as the motive and end of all manner of economic reforms. Also perduring in recent Catholic social teaching is a tradition of organic, cooperative economic thinking that attempts to steer a path between collectivist socialism and capitalist individualism.

Yet significant developments in Catholic economic teaching have taken place. Since Vatican II, popes and the U.S. bishops have been at pains to enunciate a more biblically and explicitly theological critique and evaluation of the economy.[32] Translating such assessments into public policy arguments has proven more challenging than was the case for the philosophical, natural law language to which Ryan, Leo, and Pius XI most often appealed. Also in these writings, the overarching principle of human dignity has begun to be mediated through a new theme—that of the "preferential option" for the poor and less powerful.[33] Finally, Catholic social teaching has undergone a certain evolution in its treatment of the roles of women in the public sphere. Beginning with Pope John XXIII, one finds explicit arguments supporting the equal social, political, and economic rights of women.[34] Pope John Paul II has extended these claims within a theology and philosophy of male-female complementarity, simultaneously insisting on women's rights to social and economic participation, and warning that society must not force a woman to abandon her special mission and role in the home with her children.[35] Echoes of the public/private, breadwinner/homemaker gender division strongly reverberate through this pontiff's writings. The implication remains that men are indispensable as breadwinners, and appreciated in, but not primarily meant for, the domestic role. For women, the reverse is assumed.[36]

With these changes and continuities in mind, I would like to conclude by identifying several loci for dialogue, debate, and mutual pedagogy between Ryan and Christians who today strive to promote conditions for a dignified ecology of work. I will touch on three: First, the movement in society and church into a more explicit ecological consciousness and ethics; second, liberation theology's option for the poor; and third, debates among contemporary North American feminists and familists concerning struggles of 1990s families to maintain a fruitful balance between home life and work.

Three Points of Encounter

Ryan's Legacy and an "Ecological Economics." Ryan's Thomistic appreciation for the interconnectedness of all aspects of created reality creates in his thought a receptivity to the recent upsurge in ecological thinking within Catholic social teaching and the society at large. His typically Catholic inclusivist interest in individual, local communal, as well as larger systemic economic and political matters awaits connection with the wider ecological framework just beginning to be advanced in recent papal and episcopal teachings.[37] On this issue, a writer like Wendell Berry, who speaks of the need to acknowledge the all-encompassing setting of creation, "The Great Economy," amidst which any "little economy" is inevitably set, would find Ryan a promising dialogue partner. Berry's critiques of a gluttonous and acquisitive culture and society are also closely akin to Ryan's concerns about the virtues and vices associated with false and true conceptions of human economic welfare. As early as 1919, Ryan was waxing eloquently on the idolatrous evils of consumerism and unlimited material acquisition. In his eyes, the connections between personal frugality, social well-being, and spiritual flourishing were patent. Though Ryan remained myopic regarding the connections between human economies and physical ecological systems, the scaffolding for that development is firmly laid in his progressive, Leonine Catholic thought.

A charge some sympathetic critics level against strands of the contemporary environmental movement is also germane. Many, they observe, are attracted to the notion of a cosmic, ecological consciousness today, and may themselves engage personally in so-called "green behavior," such as recycling. But these same people too often remain clueless about ways to effect change in the vast region between the cosmic and the personal, the arena of mediating cultural, political, and economic institutions.[38] For addressing this lacuna, Ryan's work is instructive. He had no patience with moral suasion bereft of efforts on the public policy front. He castigated those who eschewed concrete proposals and public policy initiatives, whether out of "intellectual helplessness, academic hyper-modesty, or practical agnosticism."[39] And he himself modeled the combination of clearly articulated moral principle, tenacious attention to the empirical facts, and gutsy specificity that will be required in order to move from general ecological sensitivity to effective institutional renovation.

Ryan's Legacy and the "Preferential Option for the Poor." By insinuating itself into official church documents on social and economic justice, the notion of solidarity with the poor and oppressed, or the "preferential option for the poor," a bequeathal of liberation theology, has introduced what Rebecca Chopp calls "a radical interruption" into earlier Catholic natural law descriptions of economy and polis.[40] So saying, Chopp, a Methodist, perceives something in recent Catholic economic teaching that we Catholics ourselves have tended to miss: insofar as it seriously embraces an option for the poor, the goals of a Catholic economic ethics are transformed, perforce, from reform to radical reorganization. Given the statistics cited by the U.S. bishops on domestic and world poverty, deep changes in the status quo, from family and neighborhood locales to a global scale, are demanded. As Chopp points out, however, the correctivist strategies typically advanced by U.S. church leaders belie the transformationist implications of their rhetoric. This gap between rhetoric and strategy was adumbrated in Ryan's own work, and locates a persistent tension in contemporary Catholic economic thought and practice.[41]

At the same time, Ryan's passionate concern with the most vulnerable in the economic system, and his recognition that minimal economic justice for all would require what amounted to a massive redistribution of power and wealth, constitute strong points of contact with the discourse on solidarity with and for the poor that marks recent official social teaching.[42] The beginnings of fruitful cross-fertilization of liberationist solidarity and Ryan's principle of human dignity is detectible, for example, in David Hollenbach's articulation of the priority principles that emerge from the Catholic human rights tradition, and in the moral priorities for the nation developed by the U.S. bishops in their pastoral letter on the economy.[43]

Ryan, Contemporary Feminism, and the Work-Family Nexus. Since 1945, more and more of women's energies have been transferred into the public workforce. Unlike the men who left agricultural for nonhome-based employment in earlier generations, these wage-earning women and their families have had no one staying behind to "keep the home fires burning." This crucial difference has led to a serious crisis in the domestic-public economic arrangement that had pivoted on a gender-role compromise struck nearly a century before.

In the 1960s, women's advocates criticized the hidden sexism that had glorified women's role at home while denying it public value. These liberal feminists fought on behalf of women's right to participate on equal footing with men in the competitive public marketplace. As this meant women would spend less time in the home, the logical solution seemed to be to commodify and to purchase services formerly performed by the homemaker. But advocates of such measures failed to perceive clearly enough what was noted earlier, that the homemaker-breadwinner arrangement had also functioned to preserve the practices and values of traditional *oikonomia*. Insofar as this crucial fact was overlooked in the push for equal rights, the solutions forged during these years were bound to fall short. And with insufficient cultural and institutional support for men and women to fashion genuine partnerships in both the public and domestic economic spheres, the livelihood of the home often suffered and deteriorated.[44]

Between the 1970s and the 1990s, two new responses emerged among feminists, each finding representatives among Christian thinkers. "Profamily" feminists criticize the women's movement of the 1960s for its liberal individualist, antimotherhood, and antifamily tendencies.[45] A second group, "liberationist" feminists and womanists, also decried liberal feminists' white, middle-class, and superficial reform agendas, and call for the inclusion of marginalized voices, deeply-cutting critique, and structural transformation.[46] Each group directs similar criticisms to the culture at large.

Profamily and liberationist feminists disagree about many things. But they share a hesitance to deny all differences between men and women, and a desire to seek ways to accommodate differences without jettisoning the great liberal insight that a just society must honor the distinctiveness and the shared humanity of each of its citizens. Further, since both feminist perspectives pierce through the illusion that gender equality means simply inserting women into current workforce structures, each of these groups, in their different ways, augurs a deeply cutting agenda for social and economic transformation.

Recent Catholic social teaching shares much in common with the postliberal feminist agenda just described. Yet, carefully examining home and work crisis from both familist and liberationist feminist perspectives calls into question the gender subtext that is subtly continued in recent official writings on the ecology of work. This subtext is detectible, as well, within nonreligious discourse concerning that crisis.

One small illustration may help clarify the complex area of concern to which I refer. Two short articles appeared side by side in the Autumn, 1994 issue of the University of St. Thomas alumni magazine. One is a review of Harvard economist Juliet Schor's 1992 book, *The Overworked American: The Unexpected Decline of Leisure*, written by a St. Thomas M.B.A. by the name of Margaret George. The reviewer accurately details Schor's argument—that the late twentieth century, despite increased technology and "labor saving" devices, has witnessed an unprecedented increase in hours spent at work, especially among women. Schor attributes this surprising development to the fact that Americans have inadvertently fallen into a trap—we are caught in a work and spend cycle that becomes like the squirrel wheel; we keep running faster but just get more firmly caught. Ms. George, the reviewer, concurs with Schor's analysis. She expresses skepticism, however, about Shor's proposed solutions, which focus on government and public policy intervention. In the reviewer's opinion, the changes Schor advocates will be more effectively pursued by grass-roots movements.

Sharing a page with this review is an inset column that tells the story of alumni Phil and Deb Davis, parents of two young children. After a number of years coping quite successfully with the stresses of a two-career family, the Davises "downsized" in 1992 to a one-career family. The precipitating crisis for this change was a three-month period when Deb fell ill, and had the opportunity to step back and reevaluate. "As she reflected on her life," the article reports, "Deb realized that her family was most important. She quit her job." Two years later, the whole family is extremely happy with the change. Deb says, "I have come to believe that to take care of a family and do it well is a full-time job, if you are lucky enough to be able to do that. So I've really changed from the driven career woman I was in my 20s and 30s. . . . We're really enjoying our lives." Along with volunteering, Deb "now consults about eight hours a week for the St. Thomas Management Center and continues herself lucky to be able to continue using her professional skills." Phil, an associate college dean who has always undertaken a big share of the parental and household tasks, agrees that now there is a much better balance between work and family. "They're not competing anymore."

I was intrigued, and yet also somehow disturbed, by the side by side placement of the Schor review and the story of the Davis family's resolution to the challenge of establishing a dignified ecology of work for the 1990s—a drama being played out, in one way or another, by families throughout our society today. Schor's thesis is clearly explained and persuasive. The Davis's story, and the obvious moral and religious integrity of this young Catholic family, are inspiring.

Yet several other messages, subtle but potent, are communicated by these pages. Message number one is that there is, indeed, a crisis of time and energy for working families that threatens the well-being of parents and children in our culture, a crisis that educated Catholic laypersons are called upon to address. Second, though well-meaning, public policy-level solutions are not the primary solution to this crisis. Third, individual families can and should find ways to alter the detrimental cycle of the "work and spend" rat race. Fourth, the wife and mother both experiences the burden of the two-career family more heavily, and, in seeking a solution, is most likely to want to and/or decide to find ways to distribute a greater proportion of her attention and energy to the home front. As the story of the Davis family suggests, by rededicating herself to her vocation as "hub" or "heart" or "anchor" of the family, an individual woman with her family can, at the grassroots, counteract many of the ills described by Schor.

These intertwining messages pinpoint, I believe, an interpretive tendency or evaluative mood affecting many middle-class, Euro-American Catholic young people and their families (and no doubt many other young people and families) today. It is a mood I frequently encounter among my undergraduate students at Marquette University. However, the light shed by a Ryanesque Catholic social perspective, and by a postliberal feminist critique, illumines serious moral and practical questions about this line of interpretation.

On the one hand, Ryan would sharply disagree with the suggestion that it is mainly or only at the grass roots that the crisis of time and attention of two-job families must be addressed. Ryan had a keen sense of the need for public policy-level solutions, insofar as economic problems were social and institutional, and not just personal and familial in nature. As we have seen, his Thomistic understanding of the state as the arbiter and protector of the common good led Ryan, along with modern Catholic social teaching as a whole, to a fairly activist understanding of democratic governance. By contrast, mainstream public opinion today is marked by widespread resistance to government interference into family and economy, support for increasing female labor-force participation, yet a lingering assumption that the familial, domestic economy is primarily women's domain and responsibility. These frequently clashing attitudes create a confusing ambience for families struggling to do right by their members and to make ends meet.

The message that women are mainly responsible for the quality of life at home does find reinforcement in Ryan's work, and, to some degree, in the writings of every modern pope. Among familist and liberationist feminists, the primacy of women's domestic calling over against that of men is nearly always rejected in favor of norms of partnership. This disagreement highlights a perplexing conundrum. A major societal reevaluation of the question of gender difference in relation to home and work is underway, but it is by no means completed. Yet public policy, the economy, and family life goes on apace, and willy-nilly must reflect some answers to the questions, what are men for? what are women for? in each sphere. So, too, must Catholic social ethics.

One other dimension of our contemporary circumstance relevant to the challenge of fashioning a dignified ecology of work deserves mention. The seismic shifts in work-home and gender relationships that confront families today plainly cry out for reflection, analysis, and response. Yet, consumer culture's genius at multiplying, marketing, and home delivering new forms of distraction (also known as "entertainment") designed to appeal to the fatigued worker, continues to breed not engagement, but inertia in the cultural arena, in the polis, and in the workplace. A "culture of distraction" too often isolates people, enervates them, and deteriorates their powers of personal and communal attention.[47] The capacities to recognize and accurately analyze the conditions of our economic ecology (including the vexed questions surrounding gender) and the energies required to act for the common good, are thereby bled from the body politic.[48] As Ryan would certainly agree, promoting practices that cut through this manufactured lethargy must be among the major objectives of an effective Christian social ethics for the new millennium.

Conclusion

Ryan bequeaths to U.S. Catholics a legacy of intelligent, active engagement in response to the economic crises of his time. Fifty years after his death, we, too, often seem to be carried along by economic forces we can barely understand, much less control. Connected to the machinations of global economics and the rising threat of ecosystemic degradation is a crisis that hits North American families "where we live," a crisis in the domestic economy of material resources, time, attention, and balance. As we seek to address these interrelated challenges, Ryan's fundamental regard for the big economic picture and its roots in divine *oikonomia*, and his joining of a comprehensive public policy agenda with a campaign for reoriented personal values, exemplify the needed approach. Certain policies proposed by Ryan, particularly the shorter workweek, and specific vices he decried, especially greed and consumerism, are also on target for us today.[49] But a contemporary U.S. Catholic vision of a "better economic order" will require a paradigm shift and vital institutional and cultural commitment to women's and men's right, responsibility, and indeed vocation to be active partners in *both* the public and domestic households. Public policy strategies for enacting this commitment to economic partnership must be shaped and refined by two other norms: an environmental norm of ecological justice, and a social norm of practical solidarity with the poor. Animated by this religious and moral vision, Catholic families and workers must join their fellow citizens in a crucial task: the practical quest for a pluralist, institutionally rich ecology of work wherein men and women are able to make a dignified living together, and take their place, humbly and responsibly, amid the interdependent economies of family, of workplace, of the polis, and of the earth.

Notes

1. The U.S. bishops' 1991 document, "Renewing the Earth," inaugurates official U.S. Catholic reflection on environmental issues in light of basic themes of Catholic theology and social teaching by making plain this link between physical and social ecology. "Above all," they stress, "we seek to explore the links between concern for the person and for the earth, between natural ecology and social ecology." U.S. Catholic Bishops, "Renewing the Earth" (Washington, D.C.: U.S. Catholic Conference, 1991), 2.

2. John A. Ryan, *Social Doctrine in Action: A Personal History* (New York: Harper & Row, 1941), 59. Cited in Joseph M. McShane, S.J., *Sufficiently Radical: Catholicism, Progressivism, and the Bishops' Program of 1919* (Washington, D.C.: The Catholic University of America Press, 1986), 29.

3. See Charles E. Curran, *American Catholic Social Ethics* (Notre Dame, Ind.: University of Notre Dame Press, 1983), 30-34; Harlan Beckley, *Passion for Justice* (Louisville, Ky.: Westminster/John Knox Press, 1992), 117-27; Richard Gaillardetz, "John A. Ryan: An Early Revisionist?," *Journal of Religious Ethics* 18 (Fall, 1990): 111-14. Leo XIII's *Rerum novarum* provided Ryan with authoritative, religious approbation for his pursuit of economic reform. Forty years later, Pius XI's *Quadragesimo anno* seemed to Ryan and many others to be a vindication of his life's work.

4. Ryan summarizes the elements of a decent livelihood as "Food, clothing and housing sufficient in quantity and quality to maintain the worker in normal health, in elementary comfort, and in an environment suitable to the protection of morality and religion; sufficient provision for the future to bring elementary contentment, and security against sickness, accident, and invalidity; and sufficient opportunities of recreation, social intercourse, education and church-membership to conserve health and strength and to render possible the

exercise of the higher faculties." Ryan, *Distributive Justice: The Right and Wrong of Our Present Distribution of Wealth* (New York: Macmillan [1916] 1942), 273.

5. These last are most evident in Ryan's several essays treating "false versus true understandings of welfare," and minimum and maximum standards of living. See John A. Ryan, "The Fallacy of Bettering One's Position," *Catholic World*, 1907; "False and True Conceptions of Welfare," in *The Church and Socialism*, (New York: Macmillan, 1919); *Distributive Justice* [1916, 1927, 1942] (1942, Chapter 18, "The Duty of Distributing Superfluous Wealth," esp. 242-45); "Minimum and Maximum Standards of Living," in *Declining Liberty and Other Papers* (New York: Macmillan, 1927), 315-29.

6. "Lacking these, the system can exemplify only partial, pragmatic and irregular justice." John A. Ryan, *A Better Economic Order* (New York: Harper & Brothers, 1935), 148.

7. Ibid., 148-49. The priority of needs as a partial rule for wage justice ultimately rests, explains Ryan, on three fundamental principles "regarding man's position in the universe:" 1) God created the earth for the sustenance of *all* His children; therefore, all persons are equal in their inherent claims upon the bounty of nature; 2) the inherent right of access to the earth is conditioned upon, and becomes actually valid through, the expenditure of useful labor. 3) "The men who are in present control of the opportunities of the earth are obliged to permit reasonable access to these opportunities on reasonable terms." Every man willing to work has an inborn right to sustenance from the earth on reasonable terms and conditions. Ryan, *Distributive Justice*, 3rd ed., 270-73.

8. Ryan, *Better Economic Order*, 150-51.

9. Ibid., 153.

10. See M. Douglas Meeks, *God the Economist: The Doctrine of God and Political Economy* (Minneapolis: Fortress Press, 1989). Jewish and Christian faith has consistently rendered God in relation to *oikos*, most especially for Christians within the *oikonomia tou theou*—the economy of God, by which is understood the creative, judging, and redeeming relations of God to humankind in history. Meeks's work suggests that attention to *oikonomia* among Catholic social ethicists may disclose similarly illuminating links between theology and economic life. For a concise synopsis of his argument, see M. Douglas Meeks, "The Holy Spirit and Human Needs: Toward a Trinitarian View of Economics," in Kenneth Aman, ed., *Border Regions of Faith* (Maryknoll, N.Y.: Orbis Books, 1987), 474-86.

11. From the perspective of biblical traditions, Meeks tells us, *oikos* may be understood as, first, the household in which God wants to give people access to life: this is the deeper theological meaning of "economy," whose traditional concern has been livelihood. Second, *oikos* may refer to the household of

creation in which God wants God's creatures to live together in interdependence: here is the religious ground for "ecology," whose concern is mutual and beneficial relatedness with nature. In a third usage, *oikos* refers to the world that God wants to make into a home by establishing divine justice and peace among the peoples and nations. Meeks connects this usage to the root meaning of *oikoumene*, "ecumenics"—the inhabited world drawn close together, whose concern is "mutually recognized and supportive habitat in peace." Meeks, *God the Economist*, 34-35. Cf. Letty Russell, *Household of Freedom: Authority in Feminist Theology* (Philadelphia: Westminster, 1987).

12. Similar moral understandings of work are articulated in later official teaching, e.g., Pope John Paul II, *Laborem exercens* (Boston, Mass.: Daughters of St. Paul, 1981), #6, #9, #10; U.S. Catholic Bishops, *Economic Justice for All* (Washington, D.C.: National Conference of Catholic Bishops, 1986), esp. #72, #97.

13. In the papal social teaching Ryan knew, men's and women's familial roles were differentiated. Fatherhood was discussed most often in terms of a man's right to fulfill his role as head of the family by supporting it financially. Pope Pius XI warned women strongly against pursuing an "exaggerated liberty which cares not for the good of the family; [the order of love] forbids that in this body which is the family, the heart be separated from the head," for this unnatural condition puts the family at grave risk, and betrays woman's glorious vocation as well. "For if the man is the head, the woman is the heart, and as he occupies the chief place in ruling, so she may and ought to claim for herself the chief place in love." Pope Pius XI, *Casti connubii*, "Christian Marriage in Our Day," 1930, #27. In Joseph Husslein, S.J., ed., *Social Wellsprings*, Vol. II, Eighteen Encyclicals of Social Reconstruction by Pope Pius XI (Milwaukee, Wis.; The Bruce Publishing Co., 1942), 134.

14. Ryan observed the middle-class, Euro-American feminist movement, just as the struggle to gain the vote for women was finally being won. Ryan insisted that women performing work equal to men's ought to receive equal pay, and he acknowledged that some women were forced by circumstances to take up full-time employment outside the home. Yet his normative views neatly coincided with the hierarchical, domestic-workplace division, gender ideology of the era. Ryan found the equal-rights feminists of his day grating and wrongheaded. He greeted women's suffrage with resignation, declaring that Catholic women had never wished for the vote, but urging women to exercise their conservative family-values influence on the political arena. He scathingly described the well-educated, middle-class leaders of the Women's Party, whom he found to be hypocritical and out of touch with the concerns and desires of working-class women. See "Woman Suffrage," in John A. Ryan, *The Church and Socialism* (Washington, D.C.: University Press, 1919), 236-45; "Equal Rights for Women," in John A. Ryan, *Declining Liberty and Other Papers* (New York: MacMillan, 1927), 101-14.

15. See Arlie Hochschild, with Anne Machung *The Second Shift* (New York: Avon Books, 1990), 239-56; Clare B. Fischer, "Liberating Work," in *Christian Feminism: Visions of a New Humanity*, ed. Judith L. Weidman (San Francisco: Harper & Row, 1984), 123-24.

16. Leslie Woodcock Tentler, *Wage-Earning Women: Industrial Work and Family Life in the United States, 1900-1930* (New York: Oxford University Press, 1979), 185, passim.

17. Susan Householder Van Horn has recently demonstrated that workforce participation actually continued to rise in the postwar years. However, women's decisions about working were framed by a widespread belief in "the primacy of the home." See Susan Householder Van Horn, *Women, Work, and Fertility, 1900-1986* (New York: New York University Press, 1988), ch. 9, esp. 124-25.

18. Ryan called for an end to the "industrial dependence" that keeps wage earners passively in thrall to employers who pull all the strings in a given business concern. Such dependence is un-American and inhumane, abnormal and against human welfare. It is also inefficient. Labor needs to be made an active collaborator in the direction of business, without denying differences in status and training. Underlying this is a recognition of the need for work that is intrinsically valuable, and that intrinsic value does not come simply from quantifying the amount of a worker's output. See "Democratizing Industry," in Ryan, *Declining Liberty*, 224-38.

19. Curran, *American Catholic Social Ethics*, 49-60. For a more extended treatment of Ryan's thought on this matter, see also, Christine Firer Hinze, "John A. Ryan: Theological Ethics and Political Engagement" *Proceedings of the Catholic Theological Society of America*, 1995.

20. Ryan, *Better Economic Order*, 153, 154.

21. Ibid., 190.

22. To determine a just economic policy measure, Ryan believed that one must educate oneself in the enduring principles of Catholic social thought, and conscientiously study the "facts" of the particular economic problem at hand in order to determine a potential course of action. One then must consider two questions: "Is this measure in conformity with right reason and Catholic teaching?" and "Is it prudent to advocate this reform at this time?" If the answer is yes, then every available avenue of legitimate influence ought to be used to promote that change. Ryan, *Social Reconstruction*, 213-14.

23. "We are not infrequently assured that, 'only religion will solve the labor question.' Most certainly it will not be permanently and adequately solved *without* religion, that is, without the aid of religious agencies and a larger infusion of the religious spirit in the minds and hearts of men; but neither will religion suffice in the absence of a detailed application of moral principles to the

relations of employers and employees." Ryan, *A Living Wage* (New York: Macmillan [1906] 1912), 329.

24. "Men may be religious in the ordinary meaning of the term, and yet remain so thoroughly dominated by the ethical code of unlimited competition that they are blind to the many forms of moral wrong which that code sanctions. There are thousands of employers in every church organization who wish to live up to the standards of their respective denominations, and believe that they are succeeding fairly well, who nevertheless feel no conscientious scruples when they pay their employees much less than a Living Wage. They see no wrong in this, for are they not paying the current rates? In other words, they conform to the standard of business ethics, instead of to the standard of Christian ethics." Ibid., 329-30.

25. Ibid., 331.

26. Ibid., 330-31.

27. Joe Holland and Peter Henriot, *Social Analysis: Linking Faith and Justice*, rev. and enlarged ed. (Maryknoll, N.Y.: Orbis Books, 1984), 81, cited in Joseph A. LaBarge, "Economic Systems and the Sacramental Imagination," in Joseph F. Gower, ed., *Religion and Economic Ethics*, Annual Publication of the College Theology Society, vol. 31 (Lanham, Md.: University Press of America, 1990), 156.

28. LaBarge, "Economic Systems," 155, 159.

29. Ibid., 159.

30. See Pope John XXIII, *Pacem in terris*, #39-41.

31. In the mid-1980s, most Catholics still lived in urban areas. George Gallup and Jim Castelli, *The American Catholic People*, (1986), 5. But *de facto* segregation of many parishes along racial and socioeconomic lines persisted and, with white flight to the suburbs, at times had increased. Some analysts perceived a trend toward a two-tiered church: "One level is white, middle-class, and suburban; the other is brown and black, lower-class, and urban. Neither one talks very much to the other and the lower-class church feels especially alienated from the rest of the American Catholic Church." Jay Dolan, in Jay Dolan et al, *Transforming Parish Ministry*, (Notre Dame, Ind.: University of Notre Dame Press, 1994), 309.

32. See, e.g., William C. Spohn, S.J., "The Use of Scripture in Catholic Social Ethics," in Judith A. Dwyer, ed., *The New Dictionary of Catholic Social Thought* (Collegeville, Minn.: Michael Glazier), 861-74.

33. See, e.g., Donal Dorr, *Option for the Poor: One Hundred Years of Vatican Social Teaching* (Maryknoll, N.Y.: Orbis, 1983), esp. chs. 8-10; Stephen J. Pope, *The Evolution of Altruism and the Ordering of Love* (Washington, D.C.: Georgetown University Press, 1994), 19-34.

34. See Pope John XXIII, *Pacem in terris*, 41; cited in Maria Riley, O.P. "Women," Dwyer, ed., *The New Dictionary of Catholic Social Thought*, 986-91.

35. "True advancement of women," he writes, requires that women should "not have to pay for their advancement by abandoning what is specific to them and at the expense of the family, in which women as mothers have an irreplaceable role." Pope John Paul II, *Laborem exercens*, On Human Work (Washington, D.C.: Daughters of St. Paul, 1981), #19

36. Not surprisingly, such formulations have had a mixed reception across the ideological spectrum of the U.S. Catholic community. Some have hailed the pope for prophetically affirming truths that modernity has obscured, but some feminist theologians contend that the official papal view teeters over into a dual anthropology of separate "natures" for men and women. See Margaret A. Farley, "Family," in Dwyer, ed., *New Dictionary of Catholic Social Thought*, 371-81; also Barbara Hogan, "Feminism and Catholic Social Thought," in ibid., 394-98; Official pronouncements of the U.S. bishops, while never rebutting the pope's proposals concerning gender differences, have declined to underscore them. See, e.g, U.S. Catholic Bishops, *Economic Justice for All*, #206-208.

37. Indeed, the U. S. bishops' 1991 statement on ecology notes eight themes of Catholic social teaching that, they argue, express integral dimensions of ecological responsibility: *a God-centered and sacramental view of the universe*, which underpins human accountability for the fate of the earth; a consistent *respect for human life*, which extends to respect for all creation; a worldview affirming the ethical significance of *global interdependence and the common good*; *an ethics of solidarity* promoting cooperation and a just structure of sharing in the world community; an understanding of *the universal purpose of created things*, which requires equitable use of the earth's resources; *an option for the poor*, which gives passion to the quest for an equitable and sustainable world; and a conception of *authentic development*, which offers a direction for progress that respects human dignity and the limits to material growth. U.S. Catholic Bishops, *Renewing the Earth*, 5-6.

38. This is the criticism raised by Robert N. Bellah, et al, *The Good Society* (New York: Random House Vintage Books, 1991), 14-15.

39. Ryan, *Distributive Justice* 1942 ed., 302. He continues: "If there exist moral rules and rational principles applicable to the problem of wage justice, it is our duty to state and apply them as fully as we can. Obviously we shall make mistakes in the process; but until the attempt is made, and a certain (and very large) number of mistakes are made, there will be no progress. We have no right to expect ready-made applications of the principles from Heaven."

40. Rebecca Chopp, "Making the Poor the Rich: Rhetoric vs. Strategy in the Pastoral Letter on the Economy," in Gower, ed., *Religion and Economic Ethics*, 263-70. Chopp's interpretation stands in contrast to Dorr's thesis that the

option for the poor has been a consistent thread in modern Catholic social teaching. Dorr, *Option for the Poor.*

41. I believe that this tension suggests the need for articulating a "radically transformative" ethical posture that combines thoroughgoing critique and transformative goals, with practical engagement with existing structures geared toward advancing those changes. For more on a "radically transformative" ethics, see Christine Firer Hinze, "James Luther Adams and U.S. Liberationists: Mutual Pedagogy for a Radically Transformative Ethics," *Journal of American Philosophy and Theology*, 1995.

42. See, e.g., Pope John Paul II, *Sollicitudo rei socialis*; U.S. Catholic Bishops, *Economic Justice For All*, #51-52.

43. Hollenbach writes that to counteract patterns of privilege and marginalization that prevent persons from realizing their basic needs, freedoms, and relationships, Catholic social ethics must translate basic normative standards into three strategic priority principles for public policy: 1. The needs of the poor take priority over the wants of the rich; 2. The freedom of the dominated takes priority over the liberty of the powerful; 3. The participation of marginalized groups takes priority over the preservation of an order that excludes them. David Hollenbach, S.J., *Claims in Conflict: Retrieving and Renewing The Catholic Human Rights Tradition* (Mahwah, N.J.: Paulist, 1979), 204-5. See also, U.S. Catholic Bishops, *Economic Justice for All*, #85-95.

44. Feminist theologian Bonnie Miller-McLemore [*Also A Mother: Family and Work as Theological Dilemma* (Nashville, Tenn.: Abingdon, 1994), 164-74] argues that, while children need less pure self-sacrifice than an earlier ideal of selfless motherhood had assumed, children today need *more "caring labor"* than they often receive, from parents and from a wider support network of kin, community, and society. Support for the special role played by the family, she argues, requires that our society, recover its "parental instincts," thereby reinvolving the community in shared responsibility for the well-being of children. Policy proposals will not have lasting impact without "a personal and cultural crusade to deconstruct and restructure adult generativity" along lines of gender egalitarianism and partnership. Ibid., 194.

45. Prominent representatives of this perspective are political philosopher Jean Bethke Elshtain, legal scholar (and leader of the 1995 Vatican delegation to the United Nations Conference on Women in Beijing, China) Mary Ann Glendon, and economist Sylvia Ann Hewlett.

46. Liberationist feminists are frequently Christian theologians. North American representatives include Beverly Wildung Harrison, Elizabeth Johnson, Rosemary Radford Ruether, and Sharon Welch.

47. On democracy and institutions as organized patterns of attention and distraction, and democracy as paying attention, see Bellah, et al, *The Good Society*, 254-86.

48. Miller-McLemore suggests ways that churches can assist their members in gathering together to address common issues around family and work today in *Also A Mother*, ch. 8.

49. A recent effort along the lines suggested in this paper is the set of policy analyses and proposals recently coming from the New Party. See esp. Juliet Schor, *A Sustainable Economy for the 21st Century*, New Party Paper 1 (Westfield, N.J.: Open Magazine Pamphlet Series, 1995). From the Christian ethics side, see James A. Nash, "Toward the Revival and Reform of the Subversive Virtue: Frugality" (Paper presented at the Annual Meeting, Society of Christian Ethics, Washington, D.C.: January 7, 1995)

Two New Social Questions: The Uses of Molecular Medicine and The Reform of Health Care Finance

WILLIAM J. BYRON, S.J.

According to his biographer Francis L. Broderick, the young John A. Ryan considered the social question to be virtually the same the world over. It was a quest, in Ryan's words, for "a more equitable distribution of material blessings." Throughout his entire life, John A. Ryan raised that question in various shapes and forms, but his response always reflected a concern for more equitable economic conditions in human life.

Broderick finds the "young Mr. Ryan . . . in the winter of his second year of theology," defining the social question in three articles written for the *Northwestern Chronicle*.

> The social question, he said, was almost identical the world over—the quest for "a more equitable distribution of material blessings." The question was fraught with possibilities for good or for ill, for "the masses will not be satisfied today with homilies on the emptiness of human life, and the blessedness in store for them beyond the clouds." People were weary of these "drafts upon eternity." Past remedies no longer satisfied: "We must bear in mind that the discoveries of physical science and the tendency toward the elimination of the

> supernatural from religion have given the world—the here and now—an importance not realized before."[1]

The title I chose when invited to deliver the 1993 Pope John XXIII Lecture at the Columbus School of Law of The Catholic University of America, was "The Future of Catholic Social Thought."[2] I was to deliver that lecture shortly after the centenary of *Rerum novarum*, so I was interested in speculating on the shape of what the Catholic tradition calls "the social question" might take over the next one hundred years. I framed the social question at the most general level for that audience in these words: "How can the human community of persons and nations live together in peace secured by justice?" This, in my judgment, is the "canopy" statement of the overarching, perennial social question of how persons are to develop in full human dignity and live in true human community. Under this canopy, significant social questions will keep emerging in every age and sphere of social life. We should not, I think, be searching for solutions to "the" social question. Our time and energy will be better spent identifying and attempting to solve the multiple social questions that arise out of the ever-changing human condition.

I will discuss here two new social questions without attempting to argue that they are the most urgent, or, in some absolute sense, the most important. Each, however, is significant. Each is worthy of consideration in the spirit of John A. Ryan's respect for science, his concern for the here and now, and his sense of social justice.

I want first to turn to questions emerging from the field of molecular medicine and gene therapy. Then, I want to look at both the ethics and economics of the question of health care-finance reform.

I acknowledge these are just two of the many social questions that call for a response today from the tradition that John A. Ryan advanced in his day. If he were with us now, he would be involved in these issues, I suspect; and I know that we can honor him by raising these important questions now. They are social questions because they define problems that affect vast numbers of human beings, and because their solution cannot come from isolated individuals but only from society itself.

Molecular Medicine

In approaching the new questions in the area of molecular medicine, I want to adopt the framework set by Pope John Paul II in his 1995 encyclical *Evangelium vitae*. This encyclical letter on "The Gospel of Life" has implications that are profound relative to the future of

Catholic social thought. As I read through the document, I noted some sections that could be useful reference points or benchmarks for discussions in the Catholic health care community, particularly as they relate to any possible Catholic future for research in molecular medicine. (If there is no future for a Catholic presence there, then, in my view, there will be no future at all for Catholic medical education and research.) Here are a few of the sections I highlighted in the encyclical letter.

Nos. 75, 76, and 77 function as preamble to Part IV, which is a call to promote life, to work "for a new culture of human life." Negative moral precepts, says the pope in No. 75, "have an extremely important positive function." In No. 76 he says, "The commandment 'you shall not kill' . . . leads us to promote life actively and to develop particular ways of thinking and acting which serve life." And in No. 77 he adds: "It is therefore a service of love which we are all committed to ensure to our neighbor, that his or her life may be always defended and promoted, especially when it is weak or threatened. It is not only a personal but a social concern which we must all foster: a concern to make unconditional respect for human life the foundation of a renewed society."

In Part IV, principles are articulated that flow from the "Gospel of Life" proclaimed in this encyclical. The task for those who are moved by the encyclical is "to bring the Gospel of life to the heart of every man and woman and to make it penetrate every part of society" (No. 80). Among other things, this involves "making clear all the consequences of this Gospel. These can be summed up as follows" (No. 81) and here is where, in my view, the "principles" emerge that could guide Catholics in health care:

> *Human life, as a gift of God, is sacred and inviolable.* For this reason procured abortion and euthanasia are absolutely unacceptable. *Not only must human life not be taken, but it must be protected with loving concern.* The meaning of life is found in giving and receiving love, and in this light human sexuality and procreation reach their true and full significance. Love also gives meaning to suffering and death; despite the mystery which surrounds them, they can become saving events. *Respect for life requires that science and technology should always be at the service of man and his integral development.* Society as a whole must respect, defend and promote the dignity of every human person, at every moment and in every condition of that person's life. (Italics are mine.)

I suggest that the italicized words are capable of standing apart from the rest of the document and serving as general principles to guide what Catholics in biomedical research might be doing in the future. Here again are the principles: (1) Human life, as a gift of God, is sacred and inviolable. (2) Not only must human life not be taken, but it must be protected with loving concern. (3) Respect for life requires that science and technology should always be at the service of man and his integral development.

With reference to the whole question of how Catholic health care will fit into the molecular medicine future, I turn to No. 89 of *Evangelium vitae*:

> A unique responsibility belongs to health care personnel: doctors, pharmacists, nurses, chaplains, men and women religious, administrators and volunteers. Their profession calls for them to be guardians and servants of human life. In today's cultural and social context, in which science and the practice of medicine risk losing sight of their inherent ethical dimensions, health care professionals can be strongly tempted at times to become manipulators of life or even agents of death. In the face of this temptation their responsibility today is greatly increased, Its deepest inspiration and strongest support lie in the intrinsic and undeniable ethical dimensions of the health care profession, something already recognized by the ancient and still relevant Hippocratic oath, which requires every doctor to commit himself to absolute respect for human life and its sacredness.
>
> Absolute respect for every innocent human life also requires the exercise of conscientious objection in relation to procured abortion and euthanasia. "Causing death" can never be considered a form of medical treatment, even when the intention is solely to comply with the patient's request. Rather, it runs completely counter to the health care profession, which is meant to be an impassioned and unflinching affirmation of life. Biomedical research too, a field which promises great benefits for humanity, must always reject experimentation, research or applications which disregard the inviolable dignity of the human being and thus cease to be at the service of people and become instead means which, under the guise of helping people, actually harm them.

Experts say that, relative to the future of medicine, we are today where Wilbur and Orville Wright were, relative to the future of air and space travel, in 1903. What is "new" today is in the field of molecular medicine and in the possibility of gene therapy for diseases previously beyond the reach of medical science. All of this poses an immediate challenge and an enormous opportunity for Catholic health care, which has to stake out a public position that is grounded without compromise in a Catholic identity (and in *Evangelium vitae*), so that Catholic institutions, physicians, and scientists can wholeheartedly engage with the rest of the medical community in "gene therapy and the retooling of human life," to borrow the subtitle Jeff Lyon and Peter Gorner put on their new book *Altered Fates* (Norton, 1995).

I have no competence to frame the specific bioethical guidelines for research and experimentation conducted under Catholic auspices in this dawning new world of molecular medicine. Nor am I competent to provide practical directives for any cooperation Catholic centers might have with other research centers or activities like the Human Genome Project. If all those in a Catholic health care center—researchers, practitioners, ethicists, chaplains, and administrators—will accept the sections of *Evangelium vitae* that I have highlighted earlier in principle form, there will be institutional common ground on which to take measured steps into the future of medicine. Recall the third principle: Respect for life requires that science and technology should always be at the service of man and his integral development. This is a principle of action, not inaction. What can we, as Catholics, do? What are we going to do?

A major problem for Catholics relates to the practice of in-vitro fertilization (IVF) in genetic research. There are the moral questions of how the semen is collected, what to do with nontransferred embryos once IVF takes place, and the question of possible abortion in cases of multiple pregnancies resulting from implantation after IVF. Should Catholic moral restrictions on collection of semen and impeding the development of a fertilized ovum, together with a Catholic moral commitment to respect human life in all its forms—including embryonic—preclude Catholic medical and scientific involvement in any form of IVF for any possible reason (including reasons of deepest respect for human life)? Should genetic risk ever foreclose an embryonic future?

To frame the social question in this new context, I will simply quote from the Introduction to *Altered Fates*:

> As scientists begin to apply the principles of gene therapy—an umbrella term we use here to signify the fruits of molecular medicine in their many forms—to the understanding, diagnosis, and treatment of various human diseases, the outlines of the golden age of medicine

> to come are slowly taking shape. We have tried to trace the contours of this fast-approaching millennium and—because it cannot be ignored—to consider how the technology will most likely be applied, for better or worse, to a panoply of traits outside those that relate to illness.

The art of manipulating human genes, of deliberately altering the fates of individuals and—inevitably, it seems to us—of the species as a whole, is the incarnation of utopian longings that have captivated humanity for eons. The quest for eternal youth, the Faustian myth of abrupt reversal of fortune, and our own country's flirtation with the perfectibility of man are themes that find realization in the modern alchemy of gene therapy. Yet, as always when fairy tales come to life, there is a dark side. Even in these first, hesitant days of human gene therapy, a period sure to be looked upon one day with the same amused nostalgia with which we view the initial flights of the Wright brothers at Kitty Hawk, many thoughtful people are frightened by the power of the tools that science has placed in our hands. Will we comport ourselves with grace and wisdom as we put them to use? Or will we create the same hash with them that we have made with other Promethean technologies (11-12)?

Health Care-Finance Reform

It is already obvious that the new medical technologies signal the advent of still higher costs for health care. There is need today for health care-finance reform in the United States not only to contain rising costs, but to expand coverage of health insurance to the estimated 37 to 40 million Americans who are not now covered. These twin issues—cost and coverage—constitute another major social question for our time. They represent a major question of distirbutive justice for our day.

The central issue in the framing of this particular social question is health care-*finance* reform. The public policy debate in the United States for the past few years is (or at least should be) about change in the way we purchase health insurance and put limits on what we as a nation pay for health care services.

A few years ago—when the public debate was raging and printer's ink was flowing freely to keep the nation informed, I made the following published comment on the op-ed page of the *Philadelphia Inquirer*:

> For want of a single word, proponents of healthcare reform might lose the most important public-policy debate of this decade. The central issue is healthcare *finance* reform. There is no crisis in the quality of healthcare services in this country; we clearly have the best in the world. There is, however, a crisis in healthcare finance—how we pay for insurance that will cover everyone, and how we contain the cost of services delivered.
>
> What a difference that one word makes! It sharpens the focus of the debate and shields it against emotion and hyperbole.

Well, as we all now know well, the proponents did indeed lose the debate. The reason for that setback was, in my view, the failure on the part of those who wanted reform to keep the policy debate focused on finance.

The debate revolves around two statistics: the estimated number of Americans who have no health care-insurance coverage—37 million (and growing); and the 14 percent (and rising) share of gross domestic product now going to health care. The twin goals of health care-*finance* reform are to make insurance coverage a reality for everyone and to reduce excessive outlays for care. Society has to decide what is "excessive," and all of us have to accept the fact that our medical destinies are subject to budgetary limits.

It is clear to those who view this debate from the social and ethical, as opposed to the purely economic perspective, that there are derivative effects from the way health care is *financed* on the way health care is *provided*. The issue of equitable distribution of health care services thus comes into the picture.

There are, as I have indicated, two broad issues in this debate. One is coverage; the other is cost. On coverage, the policy objective is universal health insurance that provides for a set of comprehensive benefits. No one, regardless of ability to pay, will go uninsured. President Bill Clinton framed the issue in his January 25, 1994, State of the Union address. Waving both his pen and the threat of a veto before the Congress, he said: "If you send me legislation that does not guarantee every American private health insurance that can never be taken away, you will force me to take this pen, veto the legislation and we'll come right back here and start over again." He did not then anticipate that just the reverse would happen. Congress "vetoed" his proposal and it is now an open question about when the issue will be back on the legislative table and how ambitious any new reform initiatives might be.

With respect to cost, the policy concern has to be how the nation can contain the growth of health care expenditures as a percentage of total national spending, and how, therefore, both the cost of insurance, and the cost of the care the insurance purchases, can be contained.

The coverage question admits of at least three policy responses. One is the "single payer" solution; the national government purchases—pays for—basic insurance coverage (leaving room, however, for private purchases of additional coverage). The second solution is a combination of government-provided vouchers (to those who cannot afford it) and tax credits (to those who can) for individual purchases of private health-insurance coverage. This solution would, presumably, be accompanied by a law requiring everyone to have insurance (in much the same way as automobile drivers in many jurisdictions are required to have insurance). The third solution goes by the name of "employer-mandate"—employers would be required to purchase insurance for employees. (The self-employed or unemployed would be covered in another way.)

If an economist were to follow the dollars involved in each of these three solutions, he or she would be likely to admire the simplicity of the single-payer option, but immediately point out the danger of excessive government presence and power in the insurance market, and warn against the effects of the massive redistribution of income involved. In order to pay the insurance bill, the government would have to levy significantly higher taxes—on incomes, or consumption spending, or both—than is now the case.

Looking at a federal initiative first to require and then assist—through voucher or tax credit—every citizen to have insurance, economists would be, for the most part, not too troubled by this encroachment on individual freedom (i.e., the freedom to remain uninsured), but they would note that the cost to government (and thus the impact on taxes) would be high.

The economic perspective on an employer mandate—on the requirement that employers must, within specified spending limits and with subsidies under certain circumstances, purchase basic coverage for all employees—would be one of split vision. Some would favor this because it keeps the matter private and thus holds down the impact on taxes. They would acknowledge, however, that the costs will not really be borne by employers; they will instead be passed along to consumers in the form of higher prices or swallowed by workers in the form of wage concessions. Private insurers would, of course, have a central role to play in meeting the demand for health insurance.

Some economists would see a threat to the survival of small business in the employer-mandate approach. Businesses that do not now offer health insurance benefits to workers would receive a jolt that might not be easily shaken off (or passed along) and they might go out of business; or, if they stay, they are likely to reduce the number of people they employ.

An ethical perspective on these policy options could begin with the question of whether it is just for an employer to hire anyone without providing health insurance. If wages or salaries were so generous that the employee might reasonably be expected to provide personally for his or her health insurance, no strong ethical case could be brought against the employer. But the opposite situation often occurs and with it comes the problem. Wages are low; employment is sporadic and insurance coverage is nil. The employer who takes from a willing worker employable time that cannot simultaneously be employed elsewhere, should not exploit that worker by taking time and energy without giving fair compensation in return. Fair compensation means compensation commensurate with human dignity, and human dignity demands some insurance against health care expenses. An employer who cannot afford this level of compensation cannot ethically continue to offer employment. This is another way of saying that a business that cannot afford a just wage cannot ethically continue to remain in business. We can expect arguments over what is "fair" and what human "dignity" requires in the matter of health care. It will be a challenge for the nation to resolve these arguments on ethical, not solely economic grounds. That challenge was hardly noticed, in my view, during the unfocused, emotional, and largely scrambled health care debate of the winter of 1994.

In the context of the second solution—the individual mandate—ethics would look to the individual and ask two sets of questions. The first set would be applicable to any part of the health care-finance debate because some of the costs can be controlled by behavioral choices. These questions would examine personal responsibility for health maintenance through appropriate nutrition, exercise, rest, and care, and disease prevention through appropriate behavior. Is it ethical to behave the way we do, given the impact of that behavior on personal health? In this context, many of those things that you know are "good for you" become considerations of ethical import.

The other set of questions applies to this second solution—the provision by government of incentives (vouchers and tax credits) to enable individuals to buy their own insurance. Is it ethical for an individual to take the risk of being uninsured against a reasonable range of health care needs? Is it morally permissible to expose oneself and family to risk in this way? If the answer is no, then the ethical framework widens to include society and its obligation to assist or fully provide for those who cannot afford to insure themselves. There is ethical justification for governmental action that would encourage the insurance of everyone in this way; there is ethical justification for the corresponding cost to government. This conclusion rests on an understanding of the "common good" that may not be universally shared. Perhaps a national debate on the meaning and implications of our notion of the common good would be a productive preamble to any resumption of the health care debate on a national level. It is, in my opinion, nothing short of alarming that consideration of the common good had such minimal impact on the American conscience when universal coverage was debated in the policy arena in the first two years of the Clinton administration.

An economic argument can be invoked to add weight to the ethical justification of universal coverage, namely, the excessive expenditures associated with providing emergency-room care for the uninsured, and the higher-cost care required to treat aggravated conditions resulting from long medical neglect, which, in turn, is the result of no insurance. Here, as in so many other situations, good ethics makes good economic sense.

What light does an ethical perspective shed on the single-payer solution? One beam of that light emanates from the classic Catholic social principle of subsidiarity: no higher level of organization (or government) should be the primary player in matters that can be attended to satisfactorily at lower levels. Solutions two and three are, by definition, "lower-level" remedies and would thus have to be found to be demonstrably unworkable or ineffective before the single-payer route is taken. Note, however, that "single-payer" does not mean sole provider of health care services. This is not socialism. It is not government ownership of hospitals and clinics; physicians would not be government employees under a single-payer system. The issue, remember, is health care-*finance* reform. Ethically speaking, the single-payer option would be acceptable if it is clear that the private insurers simply cannot meet the need; it would be ethically necessary if all other lower-level alternatives fail.

This opens another door. Enter the ethical question of whether or not the economic principles of casualty insurance are applicable to health insurance. Casualty insurers avoid high-risk categories, or charge extremely high premiums to cover them. If coverage is to be universal and affordable, the economics of casualty insurance cannot apply. The practice of preselecting insurable risks will end. Any person with any "precondition" will be insurable under a truly universal, comprehensive health care coverage plan. It may well be that private insurers will no longer be able to operate profitably in the business of health care insurance. The stage will then be set for invoking the principle of subsidiarity to introduce a single-payer system, with all this would imply for taxes and government presence. Given all the uncertainties now surrounding the health care industry, this could happen in America, in my view, within a decade or two.

Another ethical principle that would permit, and in certain circumstances promote, a single-payer system is the principle of solidarity. This is a notion that the writings of Pope John Paul II have framed into a moral category. For him solidarity suggests "that the good to which we are all called and the happiness to which we all aspire cannot be obtained without an effort and commitment on the part of all, nobody excluded, and the consequent renouncing of personal selfishness." He spells this out in his 1988 encyclical *Sollicitudo rei socialis* where he singles out "political leaders and citizens of rich countries" as having a "moral obligation . . . to take into consideration in personal decisions and decisions of government [the] relationship of universality, [the] interdependence which exists between their conduct and the poverty and underdevelopment of so many millions of people." These words, aimed at narrowing the income gaps between nations, are equally applicable within nations, specifically within our own nation where, as I mentioned earlier, an estimated 37 to 40 million people are not covered by health care insurance.

Here again a morally pluralistic culture will entertain different descriptions of "the good" to which we are called, and "the happiness" to which we all aspire. The pope cannot be presumed to be speaking for everyone, although what he says makes sense to many, particularly the poor and disadvantaged. Responsible participants in the policy debate should do all they can to assure that there will be sufficient room for reason in the policy arena. Reason, I assume all will agree, was not the dominant voice in the health care debate that stopped, but did not end, with the adjournment of the 103rd Congress.

Since the twin goals of health care-finance reform are to make insurance coverage accessible for everyone and to reduce excessive outlays for care, I want now to put the cost-of-care issue under both the economic and ethical spotlight.

Both the economist and the ethicist should be raising questions about the volume of spending, relative to spending for other needs, that the nation lays out for health care. Put another way, ethical and economic concerns are appropriately raised about the things we cannot buy, as a nation, because we are buying so much health care.

The economist would think first about eliminating waste from health care expenditures, and next about the efficiency of spending a disproportionate amount for care in the last few weeks or months of life, over against the amount spent for prevention of illness for all, and maintenance of health for those with much longer life expectancies. The economist would want to know why, on a macroeconomic scale, such vast sums of money are spent for relatively low-benefit health care (low relative to the total population, not necessarily to the patient-beneficiary in any given case).

Upon examination, the economist would see a fault line in the way the present system permits us to purchase health care. Given the presence of third-party payers (private insurance companies in particular, but also government through Medicare and Medicaid) to the transaction between a fee-for-service physician and an insured patient, there is no economic reason for either physician or patient to ask "how much will this cost?" when the "best available" medical service is requested or prescribed. (Economic considerations do prompt some providers to avoid Medicaid patients because the payments are too low and the paperwork too complicated.) From an economic perspective, the approach of the fully-insured patient to a ready provider is similar to the situation of a car buyer walking into an automobile showroom and coming to an agreement with the salesperson to purchase the "best available" transportation without any thought of price. Individuals, not insurance companies, pay for cars; sales commissions presumably rise or fall in proportion to the price of what is sold. So, the "sticker price" is a major concern to the parties on both sides of the car-purchase transaction, but not at all central to the health care-purchase decision. Economists wonder whether this makes sense; so they look for ways of creating cost-control arrangements that would serve as budget constraints within which the provision and purchase of health care services would occur.

Ethicists wonder about this too. Like the economists, they will follow the dollars to see if fair shares are being borne by beneficiaries who can afford to pay, and whether fair returns are going to the providers—health care professionals and hospitals. If the returns to professionals are excessive (but who decides what "excessive" means?) by ethical standards, ethicists would be prepared to penetrate the privileged sanctuary of the physician-patient relationship to look for evidence of abuses in the fee-for-service system. They would also examine the relevance of price to cost within health care organizations. If prices are set excessively high to offset losses due to uncompensated care, the ethical eye will look first to managerial efficiency and, assuming good management and no waste, then to society's obligation, normally discharged through government, to share the burden of uncompensated care with hospitals that provide it, particularly that portion of uncompensated care that is related to charity, not simply to unpaid bills by those who can afford to pay them. This could result in an ethical argument for higher taxes.

A strong argument for universal insurance coverage is, of course, the anticipated reduction, if not elimination, of the uncompensated-care burden now carried by socially responsible, health care organizations.

A major contributory factor to rising health care costs is the utilization of sophisticated and expensive medical technology. If someone else is paying for it, there will be a tendency toward excessive use. For understandable reasons based on accumulated evidence of jury decisions in medical malpractice suits, some physicians will practice defensive medicine by ordering tests to confirm a finding or detect a problem through the application of advanced and quite expensive technology to a given case where the probability of learning anything new is quite low. Absent tort reform and the setting of limits on monetary awards that judges or juries can require defendant-providers to pay to plaintiffs, this overutilization will continue. And another contributor to rising health care costs—malpractice insurance premiums—will continue to climb.

If fair shares, proportionate to family income and assets, are not being borne by patient beneficiaries, ethicists would look for ways to have the wealthy pay more for their service or insurance, or both, and would encourage the government to extract from the wealthy a reasonable share of the resources needed to insure the poor. Ethicists would also encourage taxation on consumer items like tobacco and alcohol (some would add handguns and ammunition), which add to the demand for health care services. Taxing them, and using the revenue to meet health care expenses, enables government to place, in effect, a "user fee" on those who will be contributing to a disproportionate demand for health care services.

Ethicists are looking at the issue of large expenditures of health care resources in the final weeks and days of life, as well as those cases of extraordinarily expensive procedures to prolong life by another year or two. The issues are examined within a framework of the tension between the benefit to the one over against the unmet health care needs of the many. Is the individual taking an unreasonable benefit at the expense of the many? Are the many being deprived of needed care because resources are diverted—purchased away—by the privileged few who can afford to pay? Is the remedy in rationing? Or, is price already at work as a rationing device that works only in favor of the wealthy? In any case, who can or should decide? The principles in Catholic health care ethics that deal with the use of ordinary and extraordinary means of medical treatment are useful—i.e., applicable by extension to medical payment. The ordinary-extraordinary question applied not to treatment but to financial outlay then becomes: Is it ethically acceptable for a society to permit the coexistence of extraordinary health care expenditures for the wealthy when ordinary amounts are not there to be spent for primary and preventative care of the impoverished? This is a major social question for our day.

The cost-control side of this great policy debate (cost as opposed to "coverage") has not gone unattended until now. Health Maintenance Organizations (HMOs) are not new; they provide stipulated services at a fixed fee and are enjoying dramatic increases in enrollments. Preferred Provider Organizations (PPOs) are also growing. They are private arrangements between insurance companies that have negotiated discounts with a network of providers (physicians and hospitals) who will be compensated at the agreed-upon rates by an insurance company for services rendered to persons enrolled in groups that purchase protection from that insurance company. In effect, the insurer says to the physician, "If you discount your fees to us, we will send you patients." The insured are free to select a hospital and physician from those who are not part of the PPO. If they do, they pay more.

Point of Service (POS) options give the patient more generous benefits if the patient's choice about the exact place (point) where the service will be rendered begins with a consultation with that patient's primary care physician (PCP), who, of course, belongs to the network. But the patient has options that permit direct approaches (at slightly higher cost) to specialists (as opposed to primary care physicians) who are in the network, and (at still higher cost) to out-of-network specialists. Incentives to deal directly with the in-network primary care physician are there to control costs.

There are also Individual Practice Associations (IPAs), sometimes called "HMOs without walls," which list independent physicians to whose private offices enrolled patients will go for care. Patients choose, from within the IPA network, a primary care physician who will make necessary referrals to specialists.

The most tightly organized form of managed care, of course, would be the group- or staff-model HMO—a clinic or group of clinics providing comprehensive care for a fixed, prepaid premium.

The purest form of the "managed-care" approach is an agreement between an insurance company and a physician with respect to specific diagnostic and therapeutic procedures. This, of course, raises the question of who is practicing medicine in a given case—the doctor or the insurance company.

The federal government, enjoying significant market power through Medicare and Medicaid spending, imposed the DRG system (the Diagnosis Related Group) on hospitals some years ago as a cost-control measure. This replaced cost-based payments to hospitals with a system of fees tied to the diagnosis made at the time of admission, thus creating an incentive not to extend the hospital stay.

All these are examples of efforts now being made to control the costs of health care delivery. It should be noted that they all raise quality-of-care questions as they attempt to contain costs of health care. The recent national health care debate moved beyond managed care (symbolized by the HMO) to the newer concept of "managed competition" in the quest for cost containment.

Good old-fashioned market competition is one thing; managed competition is something else. It is possible, of course, that more market competition—price competition—between and among insurers, as well as among providers, will emerge. But managed competition is different. It was a key feature in the earlier versions of the Clinton plan for health care-finance reform. It would work through a few large purchasing groups on one side of the insurance market and a set of private sellers of insurance, and their related provider plans, on the other. You will recall both the argument and the vocabulary from the national debate. Purchasing "alliances" would have power (a function of the large number of individuals they represent and the volume of insurance they purchase) to force insurers and providers to compete among themselves. The purchasing alliances would favor plans that eliminate services with low economic benefits. And if the law or laws that emerge from the reform movement do not already require it, the alliances will force insurers to accept any applicant or group.

A large and heavy step beyond managed competition would be the imposition by government of budget limits on hospitals, and controls on what physicians can charge.

In this policy debate sharp differences stand out on the issue of employer mandate vs. individual mandate in order to achieve universal coverage, although virtually everyone agrees that universal coverage is desirable. Sharper differences relate to whether or not we should have budget caps—national budget limits. Would they expand or curtail access to health services?

Are they consistent with the goal of maintaining and improving quality? Henry Aaron, a leading economist on health care issues, says that our present decentralized system of health care delivery, kept flexible by our present financing arrangements, "does not permit resources to be shifted from traditional modes of delivering acute care to nontraditional health care or health-related activities that are widely thought to have important advantages for particular population groups: school-based clinics for children, neighborhood health clinics for residents of poorly served communities, health guidance to pregnant teenagers and counseling to young mothers on raising healthy children, or subsidies to encourage providers to practice in underserved areas." Our present arrangements, he says, cannot "break down the financial walls between traditional acute care to alternative, nontraditional services." Some form of budget limit is "essential," Aaron would argue, if cost control is to be achieved. The chief arguments against budget caps, however, relate to their potential for bureaucratic rigidity. Recipients of budget allocations always fight to enlarge or, at the very least, retain their current shares. If, however, budgets for health care services are allocated geographically, there would be "an opportunity for considerable reorganization in the delivery of care." This reorganization is, of course, what a lot of people fear. Why?

Patients and providers alike are concerned about the possibility of diminished quality in health care. Others, physicians for the most part and, among them, specialists in particular, are concerned about diminished incomes. Private insurers, especially small- and medium-sized companies and the brokers that serve them, are concerned about their ability to remain in the health-insurance business. The prospects for the very large insurance companies in managed competition are more promising. Similarly, giant corporations, which now pay a lot in health benefits for both employees and retirees, saw a lot of good in the Clinton health care reform bill. Small businesses not now insuring their employees, have another point of view. Finally, not everyone is persuaded that increased government involvement will, in fact, reduce the rate of growth of health care spending.

If managed competition with managed-care components ever comes to characterize our national health care system, physicians will be much more like employed professionals and no longer self-employed, fee-for-service practitioners. Income for specialists will fall, while primary-care physicians will be likely to achieve gains, although not parity with specialists. Simply put, some providers and insurers will win, and some will lose—economically—if anything resembling the general lines of the Clinton reform ideas ever become reality. Small wonder, then, that there was so much debate on these complicated issues.

Recall that the debate turned on two statistics: 37 million—and rising—uninsured (the coverage issue); and 14 percent—and growing—of gross domestic product going to health care (the cost issue). Economists warn about the implications of the statistics; they suggest options for the consideration of policy makers. Ethicists can more easily and naturally set the quantitative considerations aside long enough to remind all participants in the debate that quality—quality of care—is an issue not to be forgotten. It seems to me that management, not medicine, is the variable to watch most closely here. There is no reason to expect that providers of health care will be less competent, nor will the materials, facilities, and technologies available to them deteriorate in quality. But if the *management* of managed competition is faulty; if the *management* in managed care is weak; and if mismanagement in the bureaucracy (private or governmental, institutional, regional, or national) robs the providers of time for direct patient care, the quality of health care will surely decline. And that is an ethical and social problem.

There are, in my view, many workable options for health care-finance reform if we, as individuals and interested groups, have the will to make them work. Reform will not happen if we resist acceptance of a notion of the common good that requires all of us to make some sacrifices for the good of the whole community.

My personal bias is toward the single-payer option with the preservation of the fee-for-service system and patient choice within that system. For this option to be workable, taxpayers (every one of whom will at some time or another be a patient) will have to accept the weight that redistribution will place on the shoulders of those who "have" (and thus pay taxes), in order to enable society to extend a Medicare-like coverage to those who "have not" (either coverage or the ability to purchase it). Additional private coverage should be available for private purchase by those who want it; fees charged against that coverage should be a matter of agreement between provider and the insured person.

Providers will have to accommodate, however, to a government-managed system of reimbursement for care of the vast majority of patients. Providers will have to participate personally, or through their professional associations, in the political processes that set *ranges of fairness* within which competitive fees can be set by the providers themselves, fees that will be public and made known to patients in advance of treatment.

Providers have the right to expect, and should certainly receive as part of any health care-finance-reform program, effective tort reform that will result in reduction of malpractice insurance rates.

Teaching hospitals and research centers will, under universal coverage, have their now quite heavy burden of uncompensated care significantly lightened. Having so many Americans now without coverage means not only high-cost emergency-room treatment for the uninsured, but uncompensated care for most of the hospitalized uninsured, as well as high levels of demand for expensive acute care when the bill for long years of medical neglect, consequent upon the absence of insurance, comes due in the fourth or fifth decade of life.

Funding for research will, I would hope, continue to come from private and public sources in response to ever-more-persuasive arguments explaining the importance of quality medical research for the advancement of the common good. And thus specialists interested in providing clinical service in a research environment, will continue to be attracted to teaching and research hospitals, where adequately insured patients can see them, where medical students and residents can train under them, and where they themselves can see the frontiers of medicine advance to points far beyond the range of our present limited vision.

Clouds from the dust stirred up by the Clinton-initiated national health care debate (in itself a good and healthy development for the nation) limit our vision now. Anxieties (and corresponding defenses) generated by that debate can obscure our judgment about the future. Some of those anxieties are principled (and thus directly related to professional and personal ethics); some are practical (and often related to economic status, if not economic security). Each of us has a lot to attend to ethically as our respective roles and responsibilities for the future of health care unfold. And, on the economic side, there are personal and professional issues of cost containment that cannot be ignored by any of us, if there is to be a health care future, consistent with the common good, somewhere out there for all of us.

So there you have two new social questions: the appropriate uses of molecular medicine, and the choices we have to make, as a society, relative to paying for health insurance and containing expenditures for health care. John A. Ryan would be right in the middle of the discussion of these issues if he were with us today. We can honor his memory by bringing his social-justice perspective to these questions in our own spheres of influence.

Notes

1. Francis L. Broderick, *Right Reverend New Dealer: John A. Ryan* (New York: The Macmillan Company, 1963), 23.

2. Byron, William J. "The Future of Catholic Social Thought" *Catholic University Law Review* 42, no. 3 (Spring 1993): 557-69.

BELIEVERS' CITIZENSHIP IN JOHN A. RYAN'S TIME AND TODAY

JOHN A. COLEMAN, S.J.

History is always prologue, often premonition, and usually a potent shaper of any present or future. Although someone as quintessentially American as Henry Ford once said something as foolish and typically American as "history is bunk," it may prove useful to see the future of a believers' citizenship in its typical face of ecumenism as it relates to social justice as we face the twenty-first century by first situating our present and future in the past. Thus, I suggest that we look at this topic of a believer's citizenship in the American case by taking three snapshot views, one at the beginning of the century when John Ryan began his career with the publication of his dissertation, *A Living Wage,* in 1906, one at the decades of mid-century when Ryan was ending his career and life, and one now at the edge of the twenty-first century. In each case we can ask: (1) Who are the principal interlocutors in the ecumenical movement?; (2) What was/is the main carrying vehicle of the ecumenical movement?; and (3) What was/is the social justice or citizenship agenda for ecumenism? The first two snapshots will help us both to locate our current situation and to place John Ryan's work in a larger context.

Snapshot # 1: Believers' Citizenship at the Twentieth-Century's Beginning

At the beginning of the twentieth century, the ecumenical movement was uniquely Protestant. It encompassed what is now called the quasi-establishment Protestant churches. Some referred to them then as the liberal or mainline churches. Martin Marty has suggested that they may now be the *old-line* churches. Harvard historian William Hutchinson calls them the seven sisters: Episcopalians, Presbyterians, Disciples, Congregationalists, Northern Baptists, Methodists, and Lutherans.[1] Already at the turn of the century, these mainline churches, if growing in population, were not keeping up with the even greater population growth of the nation.

There were strong links between the leading figures of the Protestant seven sisters or quasi-establishment and with the educational, business, and political establishment. A personal old-boys network (women were excluded from leadership) bound the various establishments together.

William Hutchinson notes that on Mount Desert Island, off the Maine Coast, year after year, "Browns and Peabodys of the religious establishment vacationed with Eliots, Rockefellers and Peppers"—that is, with the educational, business, and political leadership.[2] George Apley's poignant rumination in John Marquand's novel, *The Late George Apley,* is apt in capturing this world. "Sometimes here on Pequod Island and back again on Beacon Street, I have the curious delusion that our world may be a little narrow." Yet, as Hutchinson notes, "a good many summer colonies were playgrounds, and to some extent workplaces, for a tight and well defined social organization in which the leaders of mainline Protestantism were fixtures."[3]

In that narrow world, of course, no Jew or Catholic need apply. Blacks were off the map. As historian Edwin Gausted has noted, "Liberal Protestantism, always in danger of being an elite Protestantism, did not establish an enviable record with respect to blacks in the first sixty years of this century."[4] What would become the fundamentalist-evangelical movement in the teens and twenties, spinning off into separatist cultural enclaves, also was restive in this world. Their premillennialism did not sit well with the social gospel presuppositions and the openness to higher biblical criticism of the mainline churches.[5]

The main vehicle for the ecumenical movement and its citizenship agenda in the first decades of this century was the Federal Council of Churches of Christ, founded in 1908 around a mission statement that proclaimed itself to be "profoundly impressed with the present opportunity for coordinating the churches in the interest of wider and larger service to America and the kingdom of God."[6] The purposes of the Federal Council were to manifest Protestant unity and reform American sociey. In some sense, its vision was that of John Mott, founder of the YMCA (and close friend to President Woodrow Wilson): "the whole world Christian (a code word for Protestant, it did not at that time include Catholics) in our generation."

The Federal Council embodied the social gospel. It seemed in that sense to be reformist and to incarnate what H. Richard Niebuhr has called a Christ-transforming-culture stance. Later historians, however, have suggested that it was much more of a Christ-*of*-culture stance, assuming as it did that American society was already basically decent, Christian, and reformed. Critics of the Protestant establishment note that the liberal churches (now in great decline in numbers and influence) reaped what they sowed when they forgot that no culture is worthy of the gospel and the church is always in a mission stance in whatever culture it finds itself.

The Federal Council stood for a reform of morals in the Prohibition movement, endorsed the reform of democracy in the Progressive movement (which, however, had a nativist tint and disliked the immigrants and their urban-machine politics), supported granting the suffrage to women, and stood full square for an industrial democracy that allowed a cooperative arrangement between capital and labor. It championed settlement houses for the immigrants (mainly Jews and Catholics, toward whom, at first, it had a proselytizing attitude). The social justice agenda was clear in commissions of the Federal Council dealing with Negro churches (largely exhibiting a benevolent attitude of charity rather than a stance of justice), in concern for "Christian" relief in post-World War I Europe, and in the World Alliance for Promoting International Friendship through churches. The Council continued to advocate membership in the League of Nations long after most Americans had lost interest, and both disarmament and support for the world court became important Council themes.

That the Council frequently embodied a Christ-*of*-culture stance is caught in the remark of one historian who notes that "The Council was widely identified by friend and foe alike with the social and political liberalism *of any given decade.*"[7] President Franklin Roosevelt could quip, when charged with radicalism because of the New Deal, that he was about as radical as the Federal Council of Churches.

Roosevelt could depend no less on the fervent support of John Ryan, "The Right Reverend New Dealer." Catholics did not engage, in this period, in an ecumenical movement, as such, although Ryan had crucial contacts with the Protestant social-gospel economist Richard Ely who wrote a preface to Ryan's *A Living Wage.* The nexus between the Federal Council's social gospel and the Catholic-based, natural law thinking of Ryan lay in the Progressive movement.

Ryan embraced no less than the Federal Council of Churches the Progressive agenda of the day, although he was more likely than the Federal Council to give teeth to the notion of an industrial democracy and to be more ardent in his support of labor unions and immigrants. Ryan's earlier support for prohibition waned in the late 1920s when he began to urge a selective disobedience to this bad law. Like the Council, Ryan espoused internationalism especially through the Catholic Association for International Peace of which he was a cofounder. Ryan's great achievement during this period was that "he presented a theoretical framework for his agenda that could be understood in both Catholic and American terms."[8] The Progressive movement's vision was the heart of Ryan's Americanist program that linked his vision as, analogously, similar to that of the Federal Council of Churches.[9] The difference lay in Ryan's mute appeal to specifically religious resources. His theory of citizenship was clearer than any distinctive notion of discipleship. Indeed, Ryan's "ecumenism" was more likely to be expressed through secular organizations such as The American Civil Liberties Union (for which he served as a vice-president) than in a more theological context.

Snapshot # 2: Believers' Citizenship at Mid-century

Our second snapshot takes us to the decades of the mid-century. Now, the Federal Council, still largely a bastian of the seven sisters, although it began to include women in leadership and some token blacks (e.g., Benjamin Mays and George Haynes), was renamed The National Council of Churches and located in the famous God-box on Riverside Avenue in New York. By mid-century, the social agenda of the newly formed National Council was somewhat tamed. Moreover, the Orthodox churches had also joined the Council.

But the real vehicle for American ecumenism and its vision of social justice and citizenship was no longer the National Council. As Will Herberg caught it in his famous book of the 1950s, the new religious establishment in America was no longer mainline Protestantism but a *troika,* a tripartite alliance of Catholics, Protestants, and Jews (note, the term in Herberg's usage did not include the Orthodox who were more numerous than Jews, and tended not to include the evangelicals among the Protestants.)[10]

Catholics and Jews had achieved considerable social and political mobility, were well-organized through their own national service organizations and bureaucracies and were swept into the grand tripartite coalition as much by the national government (which wanted to unite the three, at first during World War II and, then, during the cold war). The government chose to deal directly or indirectly through the three religious groups that had achieved a national bureaucracy to deliver commitments. The Protestant ecumenical game in the postwar period was the famous Consultation on Church Unity that sought a merging of denominations into a Pan-Protestant superchurch, boldly announced by Eugene Carson Blake of the National Council in the pulpit of Bishop Pike's Episcopal cathedral in San Francisco. In time, this scheme came to nothing, partially because people realized, through the church-growth movement, that you build up members in a denomination less by an ecumenical stance than by a clear identity and providing a sense of community. This formulation, of course, represents a simplified summary of the Council's Dean Kelley's famous book of the early 1970s, *Why Conservative Churches are Growing.*[11]

The main vehicle for the real ecumenical game, however, that between Protestants, Catholics and Jews, was to be found in some organizations such as the National Council of Christians and Jews (this time around the term Christian did include Catholics!) and in *ad hoc* coalitions of Catholic bishops, Jewish rabbis, and Protestant ministers addressing an intercreedal citizenship cooperation in fighting the cold war, preserving freedom, and fostering anticolonialism. Vatican II, of course, also changed the ecumenical landscape as Catholics and Protestant theological elites, and Catholics and Jews, entered in new ways into both dialogue and cooperative movements. The vehicle for a believers' citizenship also became the social movements that culminated in the 1960s in the Civil Rights movement (where the black churches, long deep outsiders, became central to the movement), in the work for the farm workers in California and Texas, and in the movements opposing the Vietnam War. Addressing the American dilemma of race, fighting against exploitative imperialism by the American government, and working to bring about a more inclusive multicultural and just society became the new agenda for a believers' citizenship. This was more squarely a Christ-transforming-culture stance but, as time proved, the seven sisters paid a deep price for it, since they did not notice what sociologist Jeffrey Hadden had announced as a "*gathering storm in the churches*" because of a deep cleavage between the social justice agenda of the clerical elites in the denominational bureaucracy and the people in the pews.[12]

The chief ecumenical vehicle was no longer any denominational agency or the Council of Churches but either the social movement or *ad hoc* social arrangements that reflected the *de facto* tripartite religious establishment. Religious hegemony was now gone. The Council no longer spoke of America as a Christian nation or assumed that the political, economic and educational establishment was friendly to it. Already in the 1950s John Courtney Murray could speak of a fourth conspiracy in America, alongside Protestants, Catholics, and Jews: the secular enlightenment.[13] While the evangelical Protestant wing remained outside the ecumenical establishment, it was growing apace. Billy Graham could be welcomed to Union Theological Seminary in the late 1950s and Union's President, Henry van Dusen wrote, already in this period, that evangelicals represented a third force in Christianity. While the evangelicals eschewed much ecumenism with liberal Protestants or (God save us) with Jews or Catholics, they were very ecumenical among themselves.

The National Association of Evangelicals provided for the evangelicals the *cupola* organization that the National Council did for the mainline. Moreover, most of the vehicles for evangelical penetration and growth, from Campus Crusade for Christ, The Full Gospel Fellowship of Businessmen, the Navigators, World Vision, and others were paradenominational in character.

Snapshot # 3: Believers' Citizenship as We Face the Twenty-first Century

We turn now from a historical sketch to sociology of religion to see the restructuring of the American ecumenical landscape and the vehicles for social justice and ecumenism at the end of the twentieth century. If at the beginning and middle of the century, the ecumenical leaders could speak of this as, in Henry Luce's triumphalist and millennial and, therefore, very American pregnant phrase, "the American century," few would use that kind of language today. If at the beginning and middle of the century, Protestants could still speak of this nation as a "Christian nation," few except evangelicals (and not all of them!) would use that language today. How has the ecumenical and social justice landscape for a believers' citizenship been restructured and reconfigured ? I have four rubrics under which I will discuss this topic.

(1) The decline of denominationalism.
(2) The growth of special purpose paradenominational groups as the main vehicle for the public church.
(3) New Cultural Wars that pit two worldviews of Christianity and religion and their social agenda against each other. These wars now cut across and not between denominations and have led to new forms of ecumenism.
(4) The defining of discipleship and citizenship in America as the key arena for understanding future dialogue about social justice and ecumenism.

Limitations of space will not allow me to be expansive in developing these themes but I will sketch their importance for answering our three questions: (1) Who are the principal interlocutors in the ecumenical dialogue? (2) What are the principal vehicles for ecumenism? and (3) What is the vision of social justice to inform the believers' citizenship that is beginning to emerge?

The Decline of Denominationalism

The decline of denominationalism is a principal conclusion of Princeton sociologist Robert Wuthnow in his now classic study, *The Restructuring of American Religion.*[14] By almost every indicator, people identify less with their denominations. A Gallup poll in 1955 showed, for example, that only one of every twenty-five adults (or 4% of the population) no longer adhered to the faith of their childhood. Almost thirty years later, one of every three adults belonged to a faith other than the one in which they had been reared. Attitude studies show that Americans entertain mutually positive feelings toward those who belong to the major denominations. Interreligious marriages are on the increase. Studying social attitudes by denominations shows very little difference because of denominational climate. Denominational labels, increasingly, yield little of sociological interest or differentiation.

Many sociologists of religion point to the extreme difficulty of maintaining a discipline or pedagogy of distinctive religious identity and discipleship in our churches. How do we hold our church members to and inculcate in them the ethics of discipleship that is central to the gospel and central too to any inculturation or transformation of a purely secular concept of citizenship? Studies of mainline Protestant churches (and increasingly this is also true for Catholics) point to a very selective, individualistic adherence to the ideals of discipleship. As the sociologists Wade Clark Roof and William McKinney put it in their book, *America's Mainline Religion,* the enemy of religion in America is not so much secularism or atheism but "pick and choose Christianity."[15]

Our common culture tends to eviscerate any strong attempt to maintain separate communities of creed, cult, and behavior and to undermine all tradition—it disvalues tradition and thus makes traditioning, that is, the passing on of distinctive values and ideals, very difficult. On this account, there is an American crisis of discipleship. Some voices among the churches, one thinks of Stanley Hauerwas of Duke or Avery Dulles at Fordham, urge that we concentrate for the time on making disciples and let the issues of citizenship (and the social justice agenda implied in them) take care of themselves for the none.

The difficulty in maintaining a coherent sense of discipleship is brought home to us in Wade Clark Roof's recent study of the religion of the baby boomers, *A Generation of Seekers: The Spiritual Journeys of the Baby Boom Generation.*[16] Roof finds a generation that does not want to make final commitments to anyone or anything, a generation that is on a spiritual quest but suspicious of organized churches (spirituality as a code word is in, religion is out), a generation that when it returns to the church after being married and beginning to establish a family does not seek out groups that are creedal or doctrinal or related to the churches they belonged to as young men and women but rather churches that have congenial programs for the family and small groups that allow personal sharing about the Bible and personal experience and that encourage spiritual seeking and quest.[17] In many cases, these baby boomers incorporate belief, for example, in reincarnation, with membership in the Christian churches.

The religious individualism of America makes discipleship difficult to achieve. Almost every major denomination has cut its national budgets and staffs and become what Robert Bellah has called *caucus churches,* that is, a kind of umbrella holding company for very diverse special interest subgroups such as Presbyterians for Life or Divorced/ Remarried Catholics. Caucus churches tend to become paralyzed as vehicles for effective social action. They must, of necessity, balance off the interests of the varying subgroups and their final teaching stance is frequently similar to the horse-trading of political caucuses, giving something for everyone and coming up with a rather colorless collage.

The decline of denominationalism is coupled with the rise of the percentage of the population that is nonchurched (still an amazingly low 8 percent and not all of that sample 'secular' by any means) and the looming presence of a secular establishment, well educated, disproportionately present in our urban centers and in the media and educational establishments that do not favor any distinctive religious language or direct religious input into the wider agenda and discussions about citizenship. Stephen Carter reminded us of the doleful results of this secular amnesia about religion for the agenda of a believers' citizenship in his much discussed book, *The Culture of Disbelief.*[18]

In Carter's argument, there is a widespread assumption among political theorists of citizenship that disciples must leave their language and deepest identities behind them when they engage with fellow citizens who are nonbelievers or of other religions about the goods we pursue in common.

To give some sense of this consensus among contemporary political thinkers and legal theorists, we can consider the following examples. The legal scholar, Sanford Levinson, in remarks that questioned the propriety of former President Bush using public God-talk, stated: "That one has a legal right to articulate religious convictions in the public square does not mean that one ought to do so." He further explains, "Many religious theorists argue that one should voluntarily refrain from religious speech in a particular kind of liberal polity."[19] This kind of thinking led to remarks that found it inappropriate for Mrs. Hillary Clinton to wear a silver cross necklace in public!

Political philosopher Stephen Holmes proposes what he calls legitimate gag rules upon believing citizens. He states that, "in a liberal social order, the basic normative framework must be able to command the loyalty of individuals and groups with widely differing self-understandings and conceptions of personal fulfillment." For that reason, in his view, liberal theory must steer clear of irresolvable metaphysical or religious disputes. Public God-talk or discipleship metaphors do not meet this test. Disciples are asked to forego speaking about their deepest selves or motivation all in the name of equality, fairness and democracy![20] Gag rules become, in this sense a vehicle for democracy that makes any ecumenical or distinctively religious contribution to citizenship issues moot, unless, of course, they are couched in purely secular language. In this framework, disciples are bound in public to espouse only Christ-*of*-culture language. For Stephen Carter, of course, churches are sociologically interesting precisely as carriers of resistance to the state and the dominant culture.

This issue of God-talk in the public square was not of concern to John Ryan who, like most Catholics of his time, appealed very sparingly to specifically religious motifs and remained wedded to a scheme of "natural law" as the main source for thinking about citizenship. Now, however, Catholics appeal, increasingly, to explicit religious warrants in public with the rise of what historian David O'Brien has called an evangelical brand of public Catholicism.[21]

Meanwhile, evangelicals have also come squarely into the public market place, often enough with a different social justice agenda about parental rights, protection of families as contributors to the social good and with concerns about educational and religious freedom.[22] To a large extent, they have shed an earlier virulent anti-Catholicism and have accepted the inclusion of blacks.[23]

Special-purpose, Religious Social-action Groups

With the decline of denominationalism, the breakdown of the coalition among Protestants, Catholics, and Jews around the social justice issues that typified the sixties, and the loud silence from the God-box on Riverside Drive, the new vehicle for a believers' citizenship is now the many special-purpose, religious social-action groups that have sprung up apace in the last twenty years. Groups such as Bread for the World, Habitat for Humanity, Focus on the Family, Operation Rescue, Morality in the Media, various pro-life groups, The Christian Coalition, and church-based community action and organizing groups such as the *Industrial Areas Foundation* have become the new privileged vehicles of the public church in America.

In a sense, we might say that we have come full circle to the kind of voluntary societies, paradenominational in character but still in his time pan-Protestant, that Alexis de Tocqueville noted as the first of the political institutions of America in the 1840s.[24] These new paradenominational-action groups now include the full ecumenical gamut in their constituency and cover a broad range of social justice issues: peace, world hunger, pro-life advocacy, racial justice, economic democracy, public decency. Many have a constituency almost entirely from the churches such as Habitat for Humanity, Bread for the World, and the various community organizing groups. In her recent book on *The Quickening of America,* Francis Moore Lappe notes how many of these groups working to revitalize American citizenship, democracy, and social justice have been spawned out of religious motivation.[25] Indeed, in the present scene, maybe only the environmental movement and the woman's movement, among such citizenship activist groups, lacks conspicuously church-based religious leadership.

In any event, as Robert Wuthnow notes of these groups:

> The 7 percent that claims involvement in world hunger ministries is comparable to the 7 percent of the general public that lists membership in the nation's largest Protestant denomination (The Southern Baptist Convention). And the 5 percent that claims involvement in positive thinking seminars equals the proportion of the general population that holds membership in the nation's second largest Protestant denomination. Even the 2-3% involved in anti-nuclear coalitions, holistic health activities etc. is larger in absolute size than the membership of most denominations.[26]

What is remarkable about these organizations is that they are vehicles for a new kind of ecumenism: Catholics, Presbyterians, Lutherans, and Methodists in Bread for the World; Catholics, mainline Protestants, and Unitarians in Habitat for Humanity. As we will see there is a new kind of ecumenism and believers' citizenship abroad in the land at the turn of the century. Most notably, the evangelicals are no longer the carriers of a rabid anti-Catholicism (they ally with Catholics in the pro-life movement) or anti-Semitism.

New Cultural Wars in America

My third rubric that refers to new culture wars in America relies, of course, on James Davison Hunter's book, *Culture Wars.*[27] Based on survey data, Robert Wuthnow had already shown that religious America is almost equally divided into conservative and more progressive or liberal branches, roughly 42 percent apiece.[28] There is a close connection between a liberal or conservative *religious* stance and a liberal or conservative *political* stance on attitudes toward American foreign policy, the role of government in promoting social justice, openness to social justice changes, and in general, attitudes toward foreign aid, internationalism, and other important issues in a global economy.

Hunter picks up this lead to show that there are two very different attitudes, one he calls orthodoxy and the other liberalism or progressivism. Hunter notes that, unlike the beginning of the century, when the split between the mainline Protestants and evangelicals was brewing, or the mid-century when a Protestant establishment either fought Catholics or brokered their inclusion in a tripartite establishment, "the divisions of political consequences today are not ideological and ecclesiastical in character but the result of differing worldviews."[29]

The first party, the orthodox, have a moral vision rooted in a commitment on the part of its adherents to an external, definable, and transcendent authority. Evangelicals, some mainline Protestants, and some Catholics and Jews fall into this divide in agreeing that moral authority comes from above and, at least in some essentials, is for all time and cultures. The progressivists, in Hunter's reading, by contrast, see moral authority as defined by the spirit of the modern age, a spirit of rationalism and subjectivism. From this point of view, truth tends to be viewed as a process, as a reality ever-unfolding. As Hunter sees it, for the progressivists, "the binding moral authority tends to reside in personal experience or scientific rationality, or either of these in conversation with particular religious or cultural traditions."[30]

The new culture wars involve a struggle to define America by making sense of the battles over the family (does it include gays or not?), over art (are there any moral standards?), over education (can we allow a new form of political correctness and multiculturalism to become the values agenda in our schools?), over law (does the new intepretation of the First Amendment privilege the establishment clause over the free-exercise clause in such a way that it actually promotes secularism and penalizes religious believers?), and politics.

We are seeing, because of this new religious divide between a liberal and conservative religious America—where the divide is no longer *between* denominations but *within* them—many new forms of ecumenism. Evangelicals, Catholics, and Orthodox Jews in alliance over vouchers for religious schools, on pro-life issues, and against euthanasia versus secularists, some mainline Protestants, Jews, and some Catholics who are pro-choice on abortion, against vouchers, or for euthanasia. As one United Church of Christ document put it, in response to a euthanasia referendum in the state of Washington, euthanasia may be the more loving and Christ-like action. To the orthodox, this is anathema.

Hunter tends to call these new ecumenical alliances, which simply bypass denominations or suprachurch bureaucracies, as unnatural but pragmatically necessary. In the end, he states, they are justified by the simple dictum that "an enemy of an enemy is a friend of mine." I am less cynical. While I am not sure I would have signed the ecumenical statement between Catholics and evangelicals on joint action in the social order (written by Richard John Neuhaus and Charles Colson), it strikes me that the document had much theological substance and is worthy of a careful ecumenical assessment.

In summary, in answering our three questions about ecumenism and social justice in the twenty-first century in America, we can ask: Who are involved in the new ecumenical dialogue? There is no longer any one ecumenical establishment. Catholics have broken out of their earlier ghettoes or carefully brokered ecumenical contacts to go all over the lot. They are likely to be part of one ecumenical dialogue if they are progressivist, quite another if they are orthodox. But they are fully part of the dialogue and major actors in Bread for the World and in the peace movement, on the one hand, and/or in Morality in Media, Focus on the Family, the pro-life movement, or the educational voucher movement, on the other.

Evangelicals have been part of the ecumenical movement since at least the founding of the National Association of Evangelicals but only since the 1970s have they begun to cross the threshold of their own natural home of fellow evangelicals to embrace some common cause with Catholics, Jews, and mainline Protestants who are also orthodox. Mainline Protestants are dealing so strongly with declining numbers in their churches that ecumenism takes a back seat to a new emphasis on denominational identity (not likely to be very successful). Moreover, there is a new, stronger secularist voice that is sometimes sane and neutral on religion and sometimes antireligious. We are no longer a nation of a tripartite establishment. There is no establishment. Some might rejoice in this since now we have a rainbow coalition. But a religious conversation that has no center and/or centering mechanism (which is something else than hegemony) is unlikely to produce any distinctive ecumenical voice on anything, let alone justice or a common sense of citizenship.

The new vehicles for ecumenism are less the denominations (Americans tend to eschew big churches as they do big government) or ecumenical establishments but a more grass-roots ecumenism in small groups and in special-purpose religious but paradenominational organizations. Here I find some hope that expands on Hunter's perhaps too strident view of a current *kulturfampf* between religious conservatives and liberals. For in some current research I am doing on these special-purpose paradenominational groups we are finding some overlap across these constituencies in groups such as Habitat for Humanity, community organizing groups, etc. For example, in one community organizing group we are studying in Pensecola, the group is the major vehicle for bringing the black churches and the white churches together in ways that no explicit ecumenical conversation or consensus ever before achieved. In New Orleans, black churches join with evangelicals, Jews, and Catholics in fighting drugs and working for low-cost housing.

I would need a separate chapter or article to argue at some length my tentative conclusion that is that I think the privileged ecumenical agenda for the beginning of the twenty-first century in America on the issue of citizenship will be one that focuses squarely on the topic of the relation of discipleship and citizenship. I simply want to end with some capsule theses about these two realities in America today.

Thesis # 1:

Individualism is the way Americans go about citizenship. Conversely, individualism is the way Americans go about discipleship. There is a crisis of both in America today, although belonging to a church group tends to counteract individualism somewhat and to provide a more communitarian vision than is found in purely secular citizenship ideals.[31]

Thesis # 2:

At its best, discipleship provides cultural tools for making sense of and instilling meaning into the experience of citizenship that is increasingly a purely procedural and nonsubstantive reality. Conversely, at its best, citizenship keeps disciples rooted in their specific historical context and thus provides substantial matter for the faith to reflect upon. It introduces the agenda of citizenship in its particularities into the life of the faith.[32]

Thesis # 3:

A careful look at efforts to renew radical democracy in America today—economic democracy, citizen and neighborhood groups, etc.—would show that a disproportionate share of the leaders and participants come from the churches. What Francis Moore Lappe is calling the quickening of America (referring to the revitalizing of democratic critical movements of renewal) is also a new quickening of the ecumenical movement. In some of the new vehicles for social justice we do find some evidence of groups crossing the divide between the orthodox and progressivist worldviews that Hunter postulates.[33]

Thesis # 4:

As our culture of citizenship becomes more exclusively centered on rights and self-interest, it becomes difficult to combine citizenship and discipleship.[34]

Thesis # 5:

Citizenship in pluralist America will have to come to grips with its tendency to privatize religion and to force gag rules on disciples. It may be impossible, as Jose Casanova recently argued, to fulfill the "secular" emancipation agenda without the help of the communitarian thrust of religion.[35]

Much of the new ecumenism and its citizenship activism is still quite localist. Americans generally operate with a notorious anti-Federalist notion of citizenship. But new forms of ecumenical citizenship, for example that which Wade Clark Roof and his associates are showing in their studies of religious resources for rebuilding Los Angeles after the riots, reflect a kind of pragmatic localism. As a sociologist I am betting on this new way of acting locally as the privileged locale and agenda for ecumenism and social justice in the twenty-first century. This need not be either provincialism nor a turning inward, if the churches do the job they are always called to do, to connect the very local communion of transformation to the global context. Moreover, the new paradenominational organizations rely on the churches to do the discipling that provides the motivation and motor of energies for the volunteer citizenship activity.[36] Almost all the evidence of breakthroughs across the ideological divides in the new culture wars come less from national elites (who are often locked into the ideology partially to keep their constituencies and remain spokespersons for the cause) than at the local level where a pro-life and pro-choice group find some common cause in preventing teenage pregnancy or revitalizing the neighborhoods in our cities.[37] In this sense, as Tip O'Neil once said of politics, in the end all ecumenism and all social justice is, at heart, local.

Notes

1. William Hutchinson, "Protestantism as Establishment," in William Hutchinson, ed., *Between the Times* (New York: Cambridge University Press, 1989), 4.

2. Hutchinson, op. cit., 10.

3. Hutchinson, op. cit., 10.

4. Edwin Gausted, "The Pulpit and the Pews," in Hutchinson, *Between the Times*, 37.

5. For the emerging evangelical enclave see George Marsden, *Fundamentalism and American Culture* (New York: Oxford University Press, 1980).

6. Cited in Richard Schneider, "Church Federation in the Twentieth Century," in Hutchinson, *Between the Times*, 105.

7. Schneider, op.cit., 110.

8. Jeffrey M. Burns, "John Augustine Ryan," in Judith Dwyer, ed., *The New Dictionary of Catholic Social Thought* (Collegeville, Minn.: The Liturgical Press, 1994), 856.

9. That progressivism formed the heart of Ryan's Americanism vision is the thesis of Joseph Mc Shane, *'Sufficiently Radical': Catholicism, Progressivism and the Bishops' Program of 1919* (Washington, D.C.: Catholic University of America Press, 1986).

10. Will Herberg, *Protestant-Catholic-Jew* (Garden City, New York: Doubleday, 1960).

11. Dean Kelley, *Why the Conservative Churches are Growing* (New York: Harper and Row, 1972).

12. Jeffrey Hadden, *The Gathering Storm in the Churches* (Garden City, New York: Doubleday, 1969).

13. John Courtney Murray, *We Hold These Truths* (New York: Sheed and Ward, 1960), 130.

14. Robert Wuthnow, *The Restructuring of American Religion* (Princeton, N.J.: Princeton University Press, 1988).

15. Wade Clark Roof and William McKinney, *American Mainline Religion* (New Brunswick, N.J.: Rutgers University Press, 1987), 13.

16. Wade Clark Roof, *A Generation of Seekers* (San Francisco: Harper/Collins, 1993).

17. For small bible discussion groups see Robert Wuthnow, *Sharing the Journey* (New York: The Free Press, 1994).

18. Stephen Carter, *The Culture of Disbelief* (New York: Basic Books, 1993).

19. Sanford Levinson, "Religious Language and the Public Square," *Harvard Law Review* 105 (June 1992): 2061-63.

20. Stephen Holmes, "Gag Rules or the Politics of Omission," in John Elster and Ruth Stagstad, eds., *Constitutionalism and Democracy* (New York: Cambridge University Press, 1988), 20-21.

21. David O' Brien, *Public Catholicism* (New York: McMillan, 1989), 244-46.

22. David Harrington Watt, *A Transforming Faith* (New Brunswick, N.J.: Rutgers University Press, 1991).

23. James Davison Hunter, *Evangelicalism: The Coming Generation* (Chicago: The University of Chicago Press, 1987).

24. Alexis de Tocqueville, *Democracy in America,* vol. 1 (New York: Vintage Books, 1990), 300-318.

25. Frances Moore Lappe and Paul Du Bois, *The Quickening of America* (San Francisco: Jossey-Bass Inc. Publishers, 1994).

26. Wuthnow, *The Restructuring of American Religion*, 120.

27. James Davison Hunter, *Culture Wars* (New York: Basic Books, 1991).

28. Wuthnow, *The Restructuring of American Religion*, 145.

29. Hunter, *Culture Wars*, 128.

30. Hunter, *Culture Wars*, 124.

31. For the contribution of religion to communitarianism in American citizenship see Stephen Hart, *What Does the Lord Require: How American Christians Think About Economic Justice* (New York: Oxford University Press, 1992) and Robert Wuthnow, *Acts of Compassion* (Princeton, N.J.: Princeton University Press, 1991), 325.

32. For an expansion of this thesis see John A. Coleman, S.J., "The Two Pedagogies: Discipleship and Citizenship," in Mary Boys, ed., *Education for Discipleship and Citizenship* (New York: Pilgrim Press, 1989), 35-75.

33. Evidence for this assertion can be found in a report published by John Miller and Wade Clark Roof, *Politics of the Spirit,* a brochure treating their Los Angeles riots project, available from the Department of Religion, University of Southern California.

34. For rights language run amok, see Mary Ann Glendon, *Rights Talk* (Cambridge, Mass.: Harvard University Press, 1993).

35. Jose Casanova, *Public Religion in the Modern World* (Chicago: University of Chicago Press, 1994).

36. This is what I have found in my research on discipleship-citizenship paradenominational organizations where the paradenominational organization is sycophant on the energies created in the churches.

37. See James Davison Hunter, *Before the Shooting Starts* (New York: The Free Press, 1994), 231-34.

The Legacy of John A. Ryan for a Multicultural Church and Society

DIANA L. HAYES

Let me begin by setting forth the context from which my thinking on John Ryan arises. Although I am not an economist nor is the field of ethics the area that I work in predominately, as an African American lay Catholic female theologian who has come to maturity as well as to voice in the post-World War II United States, I have been shaped and formed by the social, political, economic, and religious ethos of this period and the myriad shifts it has brought. As a result, how I view life, my faith, my country, and their interrelationships, has been affected in ways that both challenge and, at times, frustrate me. In the courses I teach, I have attempted to enable my students to see that we, as human beings, are all connected in this world and in this society, whether we like it or not. Thus, what we do, how we live, and what we believe not only affects us personally and individually but also affects those others whom we may not even know.

As a result of this understanding, I find it of critical importance to at least attempt to incorporate some knowledge of economics and ethics into all of my courses as well as political science, anthropology, cultural studies, and so on in an effort to enable both my students and myself to not only recognize but also to grapple with the multiplicative impact that race, class, gender, and religion have had and continue to have in making us the individuals, church, and nation we are today.

One would have to be an ostrich to be unaware, in today's world, of the social, political, economic, and religious issues that have formed and continue to play an important role in the life, positively and negatively, of the United States. The history of our country has been one in which people from all races, ethnicities, and social classes have come together to participate in a vision of liberty that has not always been lived out in praxis. Since the end of the Second World War, we have witnessed and perhaps even participated in the coming to voice of peoples of color who, because of their race, ethnicity, class, or gender, have been historically relegated to the sidelines.

The 1950s and 1960s saw the evolution of movements that brought about radical change in this land: the Civil Rights movement, the Women's Rights movement, the movements of migrant farm workers, Asians, Hispanics, and Native Americans, among others. The critical factor at the core of these movements was both the recognition by the proponents of these movements and the eventual corresponding acknowledgment by dominant society that people of African, Native American, Hispanic, and Asian descent as well as women of all races and ethnicities were all created by the same benevolent God in God's own image and likeness but were being treated in ways that denied that creation.

The gradual yet still incomplete and too often grudging recognition of this has called forth a response, a demand, actually, that the basic human dignity of all peoples be recognized and affirmed and that they too be empowered to engage in the "pursuit of life, liberty, and happiness" promised in the founding documents of this country.

Sadly, we see today a mindset reemerging in government and private life at every level, in the ranks of Congress, federal, state, and local judiciaries, legislative bodies, the workplace, and even in the religious world, which seems bent on denying what they and their ancestors have consistently fought for, not simply over decades but over centuries. We see an increasing encroachment on the dignity of human life and a denial of the values, rights, and responsibilities concomitant to that dignity: a living wage, decent housing, reasonable access to health care and education, and the freedom to worship in accordance with one's faith.

Although Monsignor John A. Ryan did not participate in these later movements, his thought and efforts on behalf of the dignity of all human beings and the responsibility of both state and church to

Ryan was one of the first to clearly articulate human rights and responsibilities, not just for Roman Catholics but for all Americans, based on his understanding of their shared humanity. His somewhat unique circumstances as a Roman Catholic priest espousing views many, in his day, saw as profoundly radical, provided him with an entrée to the political and ecumenical worlds of his time that, prior to Vatican II, few Catholic scholars in the United States had.

Msgr. Ryan was able to synthesize the teachings of the church, most importantly the beginnings of the Catholic social teaching tradition as first espoused in Leo XIII's *Rerum novarum*, with an understanding of the relationship between church and state in the United States. Although, as has been noted by other scholars, he failed in many ways to fully integrate the supernatural and natural worlds, his perspective is still of critical relevance. Today we see a move away from state (especially federal) action on behalf of and responsibility for the poor and marginalized in this country toward an increasingly individualistic attitude that, too often, blames the victim while denying, at the same time, access to any viable means for improving his or her situation.

John Ryan was a social reformer. His emphases, although theologically informed, were specifically economic and political. He was comfortable with and influential in a role that many, both then and now, felt somewhat unsuitable to a man of the cloth—he was engaged in the world in every sense. He willingly worked across religious, political, and social barriers in an effort to improve the lives and working conditions for ordinary people whom many overlooked or exploited. For him, to be Catholic was a calling to serve both God and his fellow citizens. He, therefore, sought to bring Catholic principles and the economic and social systems of the United States into harmony by bringing out the best in them. Thus, for him, the Catholic church was, most importantly, the friend of the worker, of the poor, and of the social and economic reform of American society.

In many ways, it can be said that Ryan and Martin Luther King, Jr. shared a common perspective, namely, that their calling as ministers of God was a calling for the transformation of the world in the here and now by vocally challenging the consciences of their fellow citizens, Although King more fully integrated the theological themes of the active presence of God's grace, "the call to conversion and the recognition of the power of sin"[1] in human life into his political efforts, I believe Ryan, if alive today, would assert, as King did, that the church should be "not merely a thermometer that recorded the ideas and principles of popular opinion; . . . (but) a thermostat that transformed the mores of society."[2] For Ryan consistently attempted by his interpretation of papal and magisterial teachings "to get more Catholics involved in working for social justice" at every level of the church.[3]

Ryan's thinking, as a Roman Catholic, was based in natural law, whose basic principles "are known intuitively, based on the inclination of human nature itself—to do good and avoid evil as well as the principles of self-preservation, care of offspring, and social intercourse."[4] Thus, "the ultimate norm of morality is the divine reason or essence, but this is mediated through human nature and human reason."[5] As Charles Curran has noted, for Ryan:

> . . . the human person is an end in itself and can never be used as an instrument or as a means for any other end. The human person has inherent worth, sacredness, and dignity.[6]

This is an understanding that, I believe, is increasingly being lost sight of in today's debates over immigration, welfare reform, affirmative action, welfare reform, health care, and employment. Rather than the inherent worth and basic equality of all human persons, our actions seem to assert that certain persons have more value than others, that some are inherently more worthy of education, justice, decent housing, and a living wage while others are doomed to a partial or non existence without hope.

Rather than seeing the static, whether federal or local, as an intrusion on the private lives of humanity, Ryan saw it as a necessary entity that served the function of providing for the betterment of society.

As he noted in *The State and The Church*:[7]

> [The State] is a necessary society, a society which men are morally bound to establish and maintain. This obligation arises from the fact that without a political organization and government, men cannot adequately develop their faculties, or live right and reasonable lives. God has so made human beings that the State is necessary for their welfare. . . .[8]

The end or general purpose of the state, for him, therefore, is "the promotion of human welfare." He emphasized, however, that the state is not an end in itself to which both the individual and the citizenry as a whole were the mere means. Rather, the human person is endowed with rights that may not be violated for the sake of the state.

However, the state *is* concerned with the promotion of the common good. That "good" is defined as ". . . all the things that man needs for existence and development in this life. They comprise all these orders of goods, spiritual, intellectual, moral, physical, and economic."[9] However, because the State cannot recognize and aid each individual, it must rather "provide common properties" of which the individual must take advantage and use for his or her particular needs. He notes: "As a rule, therefore, the State promotes the common good by general laws and institution, not by particular benefits."[10]

In many ways, Ryan's thinking can be seen as supportive of those measures taken by the federal government in the 1960s and thereafter to ensure that common opportunities long withheld especially by state and local governments to persons of African descent were finally within their reach. For he acknowledges that although the state, by acting on behalf of the common good, may thereby promote the welfare of a particular class, such action is necessary in order to achieve the state's final end, namely the welfare of all.

> Since its competent individuals are grouped in different classes, economic and other, they necessarily have different interests. Unless these varying interests are recognized and adequately cared for by appropriate state action, some of the classes of the community will not be justly treated by the State.[11]

This is a recognition of human failings, both individual and structural, that, when left to their own purpose have too often resulted in actions that denigrate some while elevating others, denying rights and opportunities to many while providing them for the few. Although Ryan does not use the notion of personal or structural sin in his writings, understandings that developed later in Catholic social ethics, his writings do reveal his recognition of the limitations of finite humanity and of individualism. They serve as a foundation for and are certainly in keeping with the understanding of sin developed in the U.S. bishops' pastoral letters, especially *Brothers and Sisters To Us*, as well as John Paul II's, *On Social Concerns.* Social or structural sin, as the latter noted, rises from the personal sins of those "who are in a position to avoid, eliminate, or at least limit certain social evils but who fail to do so out of laziness, fear, or the conspiracy of silence."[12]

Slavery persisted in this country for almost three hundred years because of the greed, laziness, fear, or indifference of individuals including, sadly, many within the Roman Catholic Church itself. Today, new forms of slavery thrive in our midst, sweatshops in which immigrants, legal and illegal, are held captive, forced to live and work in squalid, unsanitary and unhealthy conditions, for ten to twelve hours or more at less than minimum wage to provide designer clothing sold in some of our most prestigious stores. They exist and persist for the same reasons—the personal sins that result in a societal lapse bordering on an active disdain for and denial of the basic humanity of our fellow human beings.

A turn to the individual is insufficient as modernists discovered in their turn to the subject because the individuals resorted to are usually too caught up in their own worlds to be concerned about the needs of others while those on the margins are not consulted about or involved in the changes that impact on them to a much greater extent than anyone else. They are robbed of their voice and forced to stand silently by while all that makes them human is systematically denied and destroyed. The state as the embodiment of all the people has the authority, given it by individual citizens, to promote the welfare of all. Granted, this may require sacrifice or a diminishment of profits for some but the result is the greater good of all, a purpose of which we, as a nation, are increasingly in danger of losing sight.

Msgr. Ryan's exposition of the role of the state can have significance for us today as we seek to reconcile warring individual and communal needs and desires.

> If the State is to promote the common good in an equitable and adequate degree, it must consider both the good of the whole and the good of the various classes. The common interests of all the citizens can be cared for through uniform and general legislation, . . . The varying interests of the different classes must be provided for by enactments which differ according to the different needs and deserts; . . . To avoid all class legislation will mean discrimination in favor of certain classes, namely, those that are exceptionally powerful. These will be left free to exploit the weaker classes.[13]

This is what is happening today as the clamor for less federal involvement and for the turning over of monies and responsibilities to local and state governments has increased.

Today's United States is, in many ways, vastly different from yet also similar to that of Ryan's time. Both immigration and natural reproduction has resulted in a country that is increasingly diverse racially and ethnically as well as pluralistic religiously. Sadly, Ryan did not engage himself deeply in the situation of African Americans or other peoples of color in this country. His comments, which were much in keeping with those of his day, urging patience and fortitude while counseling against violence, are at odds with the prophetic and challenging interventions he made in terms of distributive justice and a living family wage for workers. Nor did he stray very far from accepted church teachings on the role of women although he did support the Equal Rights Amendment of his time as well as a living wage for single women. We can only wonder, in light of the advances made by these groups and the shifts in understanding brought about by the Second Vatican Council, whether his views would have remained as muted and restrained or whether they would have engaged him as critical questions of the day requiring articulation and expression in keeping with Catholic principles.

On other issues, he was ahead of his time, presenting ideas and proposals that challenged the dominance of rights for a privileged few over the needs of the disheartened many. In his support for labor actions including strikes, boycotts, and closed shops and his pronouncements on private property that stressed the right of use over that of ownership, John Ryan did not merely echo the evolving Catholic social tradition but laid the path that it would follow, prophetically setting the stage for Vatican II and the ensuing magisterial pronouncements.

As we confront the beginning of the twenty-first century, what can be said of John Ryan's legacy for both our church and society? In a church that many predict will, by the middle of this century be one predominantly of persons of color, reflective of a nation that will also be of a darker hue, what lasting contributions has he made?

I would argue that Ryan has provided the foundation for viable action on the part of both our church and our nation on behalf of the least among us. His insistence on the cocreatedness of all humanity, which enabled him to cross religious and political boundaries in order to promote and preserve that human dignity that is a direct result of that creation, can serve as an entry point for our own self-exploration. Are we really willing and able to acknowledge that God created humanity in its great diversity and that diversity, in and of itself, is good, requiring neither a forced assimilation or a harsh segregation? Can we assert the power and authority of the Roman Catholic Church on social, political, and economic questions that challenge the very core of our understanding of ourselves as church and state?

John Ryan, as noted earlier, did not speak in terms of social or structural sin. Nor did he balance his emphasis on natural law with a concomitant recognition of the presence of grace and the need for a *metanoia*, a true conversion of the hearts and minds of all of us in these

United States. He called for a radical reconstruction of the economic and political mores of our society but these cannot be separated from the social and cultural. Nor will change come about without that conversion that enables a society and a people to recognize the nature of the sinfulness festering within itself and to find the courage to "pluck it out."

Times have changed. For many today, the roles of church and state are strictly separate and must remain so. In an increasingly secularized society, which Ryan would have difficulty recognizing as the United States he once knew, it is now almost an act of faith to be totally detached from any religious faith or, on the other hand, to be so attached that church and state are necessarily one. We are living today in a "culture of disbelief," as Stephen Carter has noted in his work of that name,[14] a society in which all religious debate, discourse, and even faith is relegated to the sidelines of everyday life. The United States has become, in Carter's eyes, a nation where "on the one hand, American ideology cherishes religions, as it does all matters of private conscience. . . . At the same time, many political leaders, commentators, scholars, and others are coming to view any religious element in public moral discourse as a tool of the radical right for reshaping American society."[15]

We have, seemingly, lost our ability to speak, as people of faith, on issues that profoundly affect us at every level of our lives. Rather, fearing labeling, we keep our faith on the shelves, hauling it out only on Sundays or holy days for a brief time. Although on the one hand, "one of the most religious nations on earth"; on the other hand, we require "our citizens to split their public and private selves." One can be religious but should not act publicly on that faith.[16]

Like Carter, I am concerned about the wall that seems to have been erected between church and state in the United States today to such an extent that any efforts at religious discourse in the political, economic, or even social arena is looked at with suspicion. Where once the voices of Catholic and other religious intellectuals, such as John Ryan, John Courtney Murray, and others, were prominent, bringing the teachings of their faith to bear on the critical questions of their day, there now exists a vacuum too often filled by those concerned not for the common good but for their own good, albeit clothed in the name of religion. This vacuum has enabled the emergence of a discourse that condemns while providing no means or source of redemption, that relegates classes of people to "living hells" and wasted lives while preaching salvation for the elect. We have lost sight of the principles that are the cornerstone of our faith and Catholic social teachings that proclaim the essential equality of all as set forth in *Gaudium et spes* (29):

> All . . . are endowed with a rational soul and are created in God's image; they have the same nature and origin and, being redeemed by Christ, they enjoy the same divine calling . . . and it must be given ever greater recognition.

The church fathers continue:

> Excessive economic and social disparity between individuals and peoples of the human race is a source of scandal and militates against social justice, equity, human dignity, as well as social and international.

Ryan asserted, in keeping with *Rerum novarum* and the social teachings of the Church, that there is clearly a "religious dimension" to the economic as well as political and social debate. As Bishop Rembert Weakland noted upon the passage of the U.S. bishops' economic letter:

> For us in the United States, the separation of the church and state cannot be interpreted to mean that there is a separation of economic issues from religious issues, but, rather, that we must have a concern for all those socio-economic issues that harm the quality of human life . . . We are concerned by what an economic system does to people and for people and how it permits people to participate in it.[17]

Ryan's work helped set the stage for what has come to be recognized as the "preferential option for the poor," an option that does not exclude those with wealth but that urges that "in responding to the long-range concern God has for all people, and . . . 'for liberty and justice for all,' one starts with an immediate concern for, and involvement with, the poor. To the degree that the cries of the poor are given priority over the complaints of the rich, there can be movement toward a society that is more, rather than less, just."[18]

As our alleged representatives in Congress push for a flat tax that will negatively impact upon and increase the burdens of the poor and middle class, the dismantling of environmental safeguards that will foreseeably lead to the further erosion of the quality of life for all but especially those with little economic or political power, and the dismantling of legislation that has provided a boost for those seeking better education, better jobs and, thus, a better future for themselves and their children, the question must be raised: As a people of faith, whose side are we on? Fence-sitting is not an option for indifference or so-called neutrality, which only results, as the Holy Father has noted, in the perpetuation rather than the eradication of evil.

The legacy of Msgr. John A. Ryan is a multivalent one that provides us not only with food for thought but a blueprint for action. In many ways, our economic situation today is reminiscent of that of his time, where unemployment is climbing, where employers reveal a callous indifference to the lives and needs of their employees in their search for higher profits, where the gap between rich and poor is increasing and where the workers, those who helped to make this nation into the leading power that it is today by the sweat of their brow's and the toil of their hands, are increasingly frustrated and alienated, not only from their work but from each other.

We are called by our Christian faith to stand on the side of those wrongly accused and fraudulently condemned simply because of the color of their skin, their gender, or the type of work they do. For a time we, as a nation, moved in harmony, seeking the common good for all. Today, we seem bent on destroying that harmony by seeking the good for only a few. For John Ryan, today's American society would seem an increasingly inhumane and unjust one, out of harmony with the laws of God and the needs of humanity. The church, in fulfillment of its social mission, is called upon to live out its teachings in the world. More importantly, all of the faithful who, as the People of God are the Living Church, are called and commissioned to live out Christ's ministry in their own lives, by loving God *and* their neighbor, seen as all of humanity regardless, as themselves and by being proactive rather than passive in their faith.

As one person, we are perhaps weak, but as a collective voice, we are strong indeed. John A. Ryan was one voice, yet that voice echoes down the ages calling us to take responsibility for that new world abornin' where all people are treated in accordance with the dignity that makes them human.

I close with his words, taken from his work, *Social Reconstruction*:

> Radicalism and conservatism are mere catchwords. Personally, I don't want to be called either . . . because I find most people who boast of their conservatism are simply reactionaries, and most persons who prides themselves on their radicalism are extremists. It is not necessary to be tagged with either designation. The important thing is to know all the facts that are available, to acquire a good knowledge of the principles, and then to advocate remedies or reforms in the light of those facts and principles. . . . I ask myself, first, "is this measure

in conformity with right reason and Catholic teaching?" Second, "is it wise and prudent to advocate this reform at this time?"[19]

I believe that Msgr. John A. Ryan would recognize today that the time is right and the cause is just. The wise and prudent amongst us must not only speak out but also act in accordance with our Catholic faith and our Catholic convictions to right the wrongs being perpetrated in our society today.

Notes

1. Charles E. Curran, *American Catholic Social Ethics: Twentieth Century Approaches* (Notre Dame: University of Notre Dame Press, 1982), 85.

2. Martin Luther King, Jr., "Letter From A Birmingham Jail."

3. Curran, 90.

4. Ibid., 30-31.

5. Ibid., 31.

6. Ibid.

7. John A. Ryan and E. Millar, *The State and the Church* (New York Macmillan, 1922).

8. Ibid., 195.

9. Ibid., 204.

10. Ibid., 205.

11. Ibid., 206.

12. John Paul II, *Reconciliatio et paenitentia*, 16.

13. Ryan, *State and Church*, 206.

14. Stephen Carter, *The Culture of Disbelief* (New York: Basic Books, 1993).

15. Ibid., 3.

16. Ibid., 8.

17. "How to Read the Economic Pastoral," *Catholicism in Crisis* (March, 1986).

18. William K. Tabb, ed. *Churches in Struggle: Liberation Theologies and Social Change in North America* (New York: Monthly Review Press, 1986), 8.

19. John A. Ryan, *Social Reconstruction* (New York: Macmillan, 1920), 213.

THE CONTEMPORARY IMPORTANCE OF MONSIGNOR JOHN A. RYAN AND CATHOLIC SOCIAL THOUGHT

MARGARET O'BRIEN STEINFELS

I am particularly delighted to help remember and honor the work of a man whose thinking, writing, preaching, and teaching made a critically important contribution to our country, to our church and to American Catholics. I don't think these are separate species, but sometimes it does seem that the interests of Rome and those of American Catholics, while always going in the same direction, toward the kingdom, aren't always on the same bus. I think John A. Ryan did a great deal to help keep us all on the same road.

Writing this essay gave me an incentive to read again some of Monsignor Ryan's work. As an undergraduate at Loyola University in Chicago in the early sixties I took a required course in Papal Encyclicals. It was selective: we skipped the encyclicals on Americanism and Modernism and spent much of our time on *Rerum novarum*, *Quadragesimo anno*, and the newly minted *Mater et magistra*. In the mind and syllabus of our teacher, Father Robert Ryker, the course we were taking was Papal Social Encyclicals and Catholic Social Teaching. The bishops' 1919 statement on social reconstruction figured very prominently in that course as did John A. Ryan. Father Ryker was a wonderful priest and activist, deeply committed to the idea that lay people were to do the work of the church in their jobs, in their neighborhoods, and in their families and parishes. He was also extremely alert to the needs of young people even then, for subversive thought and activity. Bob Ryker agreed to be the chaplain for our renegade, quasi-underground YCS group. He was a priest of the Archdiocese of Chicago and among that fraternity, Reinhold Hillabrandt, George Higgins, Cantwell, and Jack Eagan, drew example and inspiration from John Ryan as I'm sure many did here in St. Paul. I took this course in the spring of 1961 as sit-ins and the Civil Rights movement were moving north. And there was cause at Loyola to think about these matters, for our YCS group had discovered that black women students were not allowed to use the swimming pool at the Catholic Women's Club available to white women students. In our Saturday morning class there were sisters from a variety of religious communities, and after some discussion of the problems and issues it became clear that their presence on a student picket line, if not exactly ordered by the Pope, would be absolutely appropriate by the lights of Catholic social teaching, the considered judgment of Father Ryker, the sisters own sense of responsibility, and the students' very considerable enthusiasm. And so what quickly became a cliché, "Nuns in Habits on Picket Line," began in our project to integrate a swimming pool in Chicago. It appeared in a *Time* magazine photo that week, and everyone said, "What is the country coming to? What is the Catholic Church coming to?"

Such anecdotes are small proof that the only good tradition is a living tradition. John Ryan took and built up this tradition. Its continuing influence on public welfare, political, and civic issues has helped to shape and reshape the United States. It is living still in the bishops' pastorals on the economy and on war and peace. In the USCC's office of Social Development and World Peace, in the works of George Higgins and Bryan Hehir and their successors Ron Krietemeier, John Carr, Sharon Daley, Nancy Wisdo, in the Campaign for Human Development, which just celebrated its twenty-fifth anniversary, and in all of you who think about and do the work of justice. In spite of all this effort, or maybe I should say in view of all of this effort, it is shocking that on the fiftieth anniversary of Ryan's death and the eighty-ninth anniversary of the publication of *A Living Wage*, many of the issues he wrote about are back with us. The rational, concise, and compassionate arguments that Ryan brought to the subject of wages in 1906 are grimly relevant today. John A. Ryan gave to what was largely a European, somewhat abstract, and relatively undeveloped body of social teaching a form and direction that made it accessible to American Catholics. He gave that tradition a sturdy and practicable intellectual grounding. By his writings and his own work he made a fundamental fact of this tradition explicit: Justice requires a connection between thinking and acting, including shaping public policy. It is easy to overlook how remarkable that achievement was. Ryan helped create a body of thought that escaped the realm of the abstract in the confines of the schoolroom. It also escaped becoming the program of a political party, which has in many places limited the influence of the Catholic social tradition.

In the United States the role of Catholic social teaching was critical as a primary mover in the union movement, Catholic support for the New Deal, the Civil Rights movement, and in the war on poverty. Today that tradition is a central player in the struggles over welfare, child care, housing, education, the death penalty, abortion, and euthanasia. The ability, the organization, and the imagination needed to keep such a set of ideas together to make them continually relevant to the political issues of the day is no small achievement. And at a time when bishops must often feel besieged from above and below, it is a tribute to Archbishop Roach and Bishop Lucker, and many of their fellow bishops that they remain such steadfast advocates in the struggle for justice and such articulate proponents of the tradition that John A. Ryan shaped to the needs of the American experience.

Much can be said of John Ryan's continuing influence by economists, philosophers, business people, ethicists, theologians, all people who are far more knowledgeable than I about his writings, about the economy, current business practices, and social ethics. So from my editor's perch at *Commonweal* I would like to do what editors do best: make some gross generalizations in a totally modest, objective, and nonpartisan fashion. And in keeping with our trinitarian religion I want to make three points. My first point is: doing justice requires real thought and real action. Ryan carried this off by bridging the world of academic and advocacy. *A Living Wage* opens with a foreword by Richard T. Ely. Ely was an economist and successively professor at Johns Hopkins, the University of Wisconsin, Northwestern University as well as the founder of the American Economics Association. He was among that band of Protestant reformers and social gospelers that played a critical role in the reforms of the progressive era, or if you hold to at least one of revisionist's view I read about last week, attempted to secure the Protestant hegemony over American culture. Ely's preface evinces a certain gingerly attitude toward Roman Catholicism itself, but he saw in Ryan's work a kindred spirit, a work bringing fact-filled and detailed analysis to an arena that was often filled with goodwill but vague preachments. As Ely wrote in that preface:

> We have had repeated efforts to stimulate the conscience of the Christian world to a keener appreciation of its duties to the men, women and children who toil for wages. A greater sensitiveness to right and wrong and economic affairs has undoubtedly been the result of this preaching of righteousness. Enlightenment has, however, not kept pace with good intention. On the contrary, nothing is more noticeable than the confusion of mind which very generally accompanies good intentions.

Sound familiar? Fortunately, neither Ryan nor Ely suffered from that confusion. They were two social scientists who felt no contradiction between their academic discipline and their moral and political engagement. What they wrote, taught, debated, and reviewed was at the service of justice, and not the minutia of narrow disciplinary or religious interests.

Today, in contrast, academic departments such as law, literature, and history seem beset by factions whose political or moral engagements are at the service of ideological interests. Some other academic fields, I think of economics and demography, pride themselves on the absence of political engagement but who nonetheless often seem to serve partial agendas. There are academic arenas where attention has turned from social issues to the commodification of social relationships. Thus, many social workers commit themselves to therapy and counseling often in private practice. Sociology attends to marketing and advertising as much as to housing, urban affairs, and the social conditions of the American people. It is, of course, no easy task to maintain the dual role of academician and advocate, but Ryan and Ely did. Their faith and their work were one. They held fast to both professional responsibilities and creedal commitments. They looked to the benefit of the whole society and not the interests or self-interests of a particular group. They worked as university teachers, as public intellectuals, as advocates, as people of faith.

My second point: doing justice is a social responsibility. The tradition Ryan helped to shape strikes a balance between the individual and the group, between the state and civil society. The dignity of the individual was paramount, yet as Ryan's public policy advocacy implies, finally the state is the guarantor of social justice. Government, markets, businesses, churches, voluntary associations, and private groups and individuals must create posture and maintain a just society, though their roles in doing so may shift over time. In the midst of the Great Depression the issues were jobs, wages, unions, and justice for working people. Business and government were responsible. In the postwar years attention shifted to segregation and interracial justice. First it was black churches and voluntary organizations, like the NAACP, that began the changes, and then it was government that pressed schools, voluntary groups, businesses, and individuals to provide remedies to do justice. A decade later our country turned to women's rights and equal opportunities for women. Individuals, groups, businesses, and government all bore responsibility for addressing the inequities.

Now we are in the midst of yet another shift. Today the role of government is under siege. Once again jobs, wages, unions, and workers are in a perilous state. Capitalism is bustling about the world and the United States has a reasonably strong economy, yet wages are flat and have actually declined in real buying power for most Americans over the last twenty years. The wage gap is steadily increasing between the highest and lowest paid workers, with the middle class moving steadily down the wage scale. Benefits like health care and pensions are being steadily eroded. Contract employees and temporary workers replace full-time workers. Some corporations, though making steady profits, are cutting back their work forces to impress Wall Street. The bargaining power of unions has been undermined by changes in the law, by the hiring of permanent replacement workers, as well as by the passivity of unions themselves in organizing new workers. The current Congress would like to get the government out of the regulatory business. Yet some considerable portion of that regulatory business is the foundation of the just society that the Progressive Era and the New Deal brought to American families and workers. I find it ironic that a movement calling itself conservative should be so eager for such rapid social change. It wants to dismiss and dismantle the procedures and processes of government, procedures and processes that often are the only balance to the limitless power of other institutions, particularly economic ones. Under this new regime it seems no one will be responsible for a just society. Not the government, not the market forces, not corporations or corporate leaders. Politicians who dare raise the obvious questions about taxes or the redistributive value of social programs are taken for fools. The spirit of the free market is loose in the land and a corollary of that seems to be that the only responsibility anyone has is to make as much as money as possible.

We want to do this and cut welfare too. It may be that our welfare system is dysfunctional and it may be that it encourages dependency. Critics are not wrong to argue that families and individuals have a responsibility to society. Ensuring justice cannot be only a top-down activity. But are we on the path back to a time when individuals and families bore the brunt of inequities in a changing economy? Today it is the poor, tomorrow it will be chunks of the middle class. Your students, our children and grandchildren, society—all of us have a right to expect that young women will not conceive children whom they have little prospect of raising and educating on their own. Young women, black and white, should be ready to marry the fathers of their children. Fathers and would-be fathers should be expected to marry. But as we urge moral reform and greater responsibility on the young, let us also look at the unemployment rate for young men. Look at the job market and look at the wages of those young men who are actually employed. Over 30 percent of 25-34 year olds earn less than what is needed to keep a family of four above the poverty line. If young women are to marry the fathers or would-be fathers of their children, those fathers and those mothers must have jobs—and have jobs that pay a living wage. Political, cultural, and some religious leaders want to pin the responsibility for repairing this situation on the poor and minorities, and I include among this group the so-called Christian Coalition. Such leaders preach moral reform, yet adopt a laissez faire attitude toward the behavior on rule-breaking of those who are better off, who are not, officially at least, on the public dole. They are content to overlook the moral turpitude of their own peers, while talking about the poor as if they were animals.

The Catholic social tradition says everyone needs to be responsible. Everyone is accountable for what they have been given and for what they do and don't do. And we all need an ethic and a theology of accountability. We need to look at how we are using the goods and resources we have at our command. We need to talk as John A. Ryan did about a living wage. In a more complex society, however, we need to talk about more than a living wage. The questions are knottier and more difficult than they were in 1906. What is the family wage today, especially when so many families are reconstituted? Where does child support fit in? And if child support is a child's right should divorce and remarriage be considered a luxury? Achieving a just wage and equal pay for women has been a critical and important battle that is still being waged. Yet what constitutes a family wage when we compare the combined wages of two corporate lawyers married to each other with the combined wages of a couple, each holding a minimum-wage job? We certainly need to reinvigorate the idea of a living wage. But perhaps it is also time to explore the idea of a maximum wage, wages beyond what families, men, and women need to live the good life. Ethicists, economists, sociologists, theologians ought to propose guidelines for establishing the upper limit of what families and individuals really need. And in the absence of a rectifying tax policy we ought to think about what responsibility this superfluous wealth might impose on each of us.

What is superfluous wealth? There is nobody in America with superfluous wealth. We know that. But the December 1994 cover of the *Atlantic Monthly* asks a question that lurks at the boundaries of our attention here in the United States: "Must It Be the Rest against the West?" Social justice questions are international. In an article on infertility *Newsweek* reports that in-vitro fertilization costs \$6,000-\$10,000 per cycle. In a world where children are hungry, abandoned, neglected, in our very own world right here in this country, there are social justice issues and allocation questions imbedded in that data. Indeed, last year's failed health care debate tried to ask some of them. Or what of the invisible wealth that many of us possess and over which we exercise so little control? Pension funds for example. The continuing influence of John A. Ryan and the Catholic social tradition are tools we should seize upon as we ask of ourselves and our society questions of fact, questions about morals, and questions about justice. For what are we responsible? To whom do we hold ourselves accountable?

Point three: justice is the work of everyone. That is the teaching of the Gospel and of Vatican II. In practice Catholics have tended toward a tidy division of labor. Clergy and religious do the work of justice and the rest of us admire them greatly. We admire John A. Ryan. We admire George Higgins, and we certainly admire the laypeople who work for the bishops. However, I'm addressing people who don't get a paycheck from the church. What is our responsibility for justice? One consequence of the declining number of nuns and priests is that unless laypeople do the work of justice, the work of justice will not be done. We do not need to be ordained to it. John Ryan did the work of justice. His writings reflect the seriousness and the sobriety with which he approached the injustices of his day. John Ryan did not dumb down his ideas or his prose. He was not sentimental. He did not shrink from the responsibilities that those ideas laid before him and laid before the church. If this is to remain a living tradition, if it is to have a continuing influence, then lay people must take up the work in a more serious and sustained way than we have. In the spirit of Ryan and Ely and others like them we must link the academic and the advocate. We must link thought and action. We must assume there is truly a connection between what we believe and how we live.

In the closing lines of *A Living Wage*, John Ryan's sparse words speak to us still. I paraphrase slightly:

> Men and women may be religious in the ordinary meaning of the term and yet remain so thoroughly dominated by the ethical code of unlimited competition that they are blind to the many forms of moral wrong which that code sanctions. There must be an appeal to the minds and hearts of individuals and the fullest utilization of the latent power of organizations and social institutions.

Nearly a century has passed since Ryan wrote those words, but they were echoed recently in a debate on family caps. The newspaper reports, "The Senator from Texas said, 'Those who are for the dramatic reform in welfare stand on the high moral ground in this debate.' And the Senator from Minnesota replied, 'Taking food out of the mouths of children—that's no moral ground.'" And so the voice of John A. Ryan lives on.

The Children of the Poor as Saving Remnant: John A. Ryan, Family Size, and the Common Good

JOHN BERKMAN

In this paper, I wish to look at John Ryan's considerable interest in questions of birth regulation. My thesis is twofold: first, that Ryan's views on the regulation of family size were integrally connected with his economic and political thought. Second, the right to enter the married state and the number of children one has is a moral question, and for Ryan it is also a social question.

In this paper I will not try to apply John Ryan's thought directly to contemporary questions of social policy—that is beyond my scope—but to show that Ryan's thought about marriage and birth regulation is integrally related to his better known work on 'economic' and 'political' questions. In doing so we bring together his Christian social thought, economic theory, and moral and social philosophy, which I take to be our goal for this conference.

I approach the subject of Ryan on birth control with more than a modicum of trepidation. I suppose it could be worse: I could be discussing abortion, homosexuality, or Ryan's views on women's equality.[1] But not much worse. So let me add that in this paper I come to the question of birth control in Catholicism almost like the cultural anthropologist. I did not grow up Catholic nor proximate to Catholic culture, and I have come of age in a firmly post-Vatican II era, or more relevantly, a post-*Humanae vitae* era. The issue of birth control has never been a publicly burning issue in my memory; whether Catholics should contracept was about as proximate to me as whether Amish should wear buttons on their clothing. I am aware that for a generation of Catholics earlier than myself, this is a harried and passion-provoking topic. Those listeners waiting to hear where I "come down" on the issue will be disappointed, because I do not plan to focus on the *means* of regulating fertility, which is, I take, to be the source of contemporary controversy. I do not intend to defend or critique Ryan's views on the means of regulating fertility, but to analyze his views about why people should have children, how many it is good to have, and why people must be allowed to freely choose *to have* children. In other words, my goal is to try to articulate the distinctively *social* reasons why the issue of birth control was so important to Ryan.[2]

A word as well about Ryan's mode of argumentation. He combines basic moral maxims (e.g. "justice," " the dignity of the human person") with a generous dose of pragmatism in pursuit of the goal of making incremental improvements in the economic conditions of the worker. Any reader of *The Living Wage* will be struck by his thoroughgoing concern for the practical, finding pragmatic and incremental solutions. In this, as in many things, John Ryan was a very unusual moral theologian for his day, especially if John Mahoney's characterization of traditional moral theologians as being overly legalistic, negativistic, and individualistic is at all accurate. Thus, for example, while the justification for the living wage itself is the moral principle of the dignity of the human person (Beckley, 120 n. 44), its attainment is subject to all kinds of contingent variables, including what Ryan calls social utility.[3] Similarly, while Ryan's views on birth regulation spring at least partially from his conviction about the right of the worker to enter the state of matrimony, we also find places in Ryan's work where his view of a morally superior family size is affected by—though not controlled by—issues of social utility.[4]

To adequately understand Ryan's attitudes toward birth control, we must begin with Ryan's defense of the living wage, or more specifically, the family living wage.[5] The family living wage is that wage necessary for the worker to support a family. Now, the next question is—how big a family? Since Ryan is not one to make the living wage any bigger than morally necessary, he is well aware that he must do two things: first, he must defend his view that a living wage ought to support a family rather than merely an individual, and second, he must come up with an actual number of children as the norm for setting the family living wage.

First, his justification of a living wage for a family.[6] Ryan argues that the right of the worker to freely choose to enter the state of marriage (and for Ryan, the concomitant right to have a family) is, along with personal freedom and the consumption goods of food and clothing, a right second only to the right to life (1916a, 57, 373-74; less strongly stated 1906, 117-18). Ryan believes the right to choose to enter the state of marriage is basic to human welfare for most people. Thus he says, "if the state were to abolish marriage, it would deprive the majority of an indispensable means of right and reasonable life"(1916a, 57). Here, Ryan is arguing for the legal right to freely choose to enter the state of marriage, as he has in mind certain social engineers who would like to see the state limit marriage and/or the number of children the poor may have toward the end of keeping the population down.

A further question: why does Ryan believe that he must defend the right of workers to enter the state of marriage and to have families?[7] A very simple reason: to ensure that the living wage is set at a level that supports a family. If the right to marriage is not understood as a basic right, then employers will not want to pay their married employees, much less their single employees, a family living wage. If the right to marriage is not seen as fundamental to all workers, then employers might try to pay single employees less, and this would make it much more difficult for married workers to find employment.

Certain industrialists described the situation differently. Ryan accused these industrialists, whom he called neo-Malthusians, of arguing that the poor should not have many or any children. Back in 1798, Malthus had argued that due to the exponential nature of human population growth, there would come a time when humans would want for food, unless human procreation was curbed. The neo-Malthusians of Ryan's day—generally voices representing the industrialists—claimed that not only were they *not* morally required to pay workers enough to support a family, but that further, it was morally wrong to do so, because to do so condoned irresponsible procreative proclivities among workers. The workers were"responsible for their own poverty." About the Malthusian view, first prominent in England in the mid-nineteenth century, Ryan says it "was a very comforting doctrine for the exploiters." Regarding the neo-Malthusians, Ryan says "The bourgeois advocates of birth control are preaching the same gospel to the toiling masses today"(1931, 272).[8]

One particularly malicious attack on the worker by these exploiters was, in Ryan's eyes, a charge against the "morals" of the poor, that they could not restrain their animal passions. This was the view of the economist W. I. King, who placed the ultimate blame for the poverty of the working classes not upon employers, but on the ancestors of the working class who brought

> into the world children whom they could afford neither to educate nor to train for some occupation the products of which were sufficiently in demand to make a living wage easily secured. Why indeed! Simply because these same parents were either incompetent, ignorant, or unwilling to restrain their animal passions." (1916b, 694)

King's eagerness to impugn the character of the ancestors of the poor raised the ire of Ryan, who considered the argument not only shallow and inhuman but also pharisaical. For whereas the ancestors of the poor made sacrifices "of all sorts" to give care to their children, "it is notorious that most of the [wealthy and their ancestors] employ devices that increase rather than restrict facilities for indulging the 'animal passions'" (1916b, 694).

In *The Living Wage*, the family living wage includes the support of four or five children. Ryan considers it reasonable to take as the basis for the living wage the average number of children found in the families of workers. This average is 4.3. Ryan discusses various difficulties with this as the basis for deciding how many children should be supported, concluding that despite its problems "it seems to be the best that is available" (1906, 120).[9] However, we should also note that Ryan's pragmatism also extended to what constituted a reasonable size family. Whereas he thought rural families could support on average six children, urban crowding made three or four a more reasonable number in the cities.[10]

Having presented his defense of the right of the worker to earn a living such as to be able to enter the state of marriage and support five children, we must note that Ryan's aim is not *merely to defend* the worker's *right* to have a goodly number of children. Ryan argues further, that, in general, large families are moral superior. The first important paper Ryan ever published, and the only one of importance prior to the defense of his dissertation *The Living Wage*, concerned precisely this issue, and was entitled "The Small Family and National Decadence" (1941, 80).[11] This piece blasted the "abnormal" decline in the birthrate of "native-born" parents.[12] Attributing this decline primarily to the practice of birth control, Ryan believed that the resulting "small family system" brought about "a decline not merely in the number but in the quality of our people." Ryan believed that small families were a principal cause of "enervating self-indulgence," and that large families demanded forms of discipline necessary for the successful life. As Ryan put it, the successful life is "accomplished only at the cost of continuous and considerable sacrifice, of compelling ourselves to do without the immediate and pleasant goods for the sake of the remote and permanent goods" (1916b, 691).

To better understand his defense of the large family, one could begin with his description of his own upbringing, in his quasiautobiography, *Social Doctrine in Action.*[13] In its opening pages, Ryan describes his parents, noting their key virtues of "religion, virtue, and a capacity for hard work." Ryan speaks extraordinarily highly of his mother, that she "performed all the housework (and many other tasks) and took care of her ten children, without assistance. . . ." He also confesses that he did not always cherish his parents' industriousness when he was a boy, but that in looking back he recognizes that it formed him very well, indeed, formed better than those formed in the "easier conditions that surround the present generation" (1941, 3). He continues in this biographical/hortatory way, saying that of the eleven children in his family, one died a few days after birth, and of the other ten, two became nuns, two priests, and six married. At this point he gets in a rebuttal to objectors to religious celibacy on the basis that it diminishes the birth rate,[14] proudly noting that the six married siblings produced 39 children, 99 grandchildren, and 36 great-grandchildren. He then says "The longevity of my mother in her not-too-easy economic conditions disproves another argument of birth-control advocates"[15] (1941, 3), continuing by saying that he is taking his eighty-four-year old mother on a trip to California the next week.

I want to again note that this question of the ideal number of children has occupied two of the first four pages of his autobiography. This question is certainly not a minor one in this man's heart, and it is an (or the) issue intimately connected with his description (and moral evaluation) of his mother, and most likely, of mothers in general.[16]

Ryan's argument for the moral superiority of the large family arose from a particular vision of the nurture of children; the large family was more likely to instill the virtues (e.g. industriousness) necessary for successful life. Ryan thought that the majority of people who would practice birth control would be doing it out of a "decadent" frame of mind, that it was usually an issue of convenience. For example, Ryan scolded bachelors, arguing that men who do not marry at a young age do not build the kind of character necessary to appropriately contribute to the common good of society. In other words, for the common good, most men ought to marry at a relatively young age. As Ryan says, "only in the family is it possible for the majority of men to develop those social feelings that are essential to the welfare of a democratic society" (1906, 284). Another element of Ryan's views about the danger of decadence likely arise from a belief that wealth—great wealth—is a snare.[17] In this, as an aside, Ryan has a degree of support from the gospels, though he would never, it seems, think to make that appeal. Rather, he is appealing to hard work, and building character, and that is best acheived for most people in the context of having a large family.

Ryan has a number of other "social" arguments against the regulation of births. At places in his work, Ryan claims to fear the possibility of a decline in population, and marshalls statistics about certain population declines in areas of the United States and Europe.[18] But elsewhere, he acknowledges that he is not so much afraid of the decline in population in general, but the decline in population of Catholics (1933, 34). In still other places, Ryan taunts the proponents of birth control, saying that while the line of the contraceptors will be dying out, the prolific and hardy Catholics will be controlling most industries and occupations of society (1931, 272-73).[19]

While it is clear that Ryan thought that for a generation not to reproduce itself was a bad thing (1933, 32), Ryan provides indications that his views on these matters were sufficiently pragmatic that he could envision a time when it would be possible for society to be *excessively* prolific.[20] At the end of an article published in 1916, Ryan showed his openness to the possibility that at some future time, if his nation found itself approaching a point where it was unable to feed itself, it might be incumbent upon his nation to seriously work to control its population. In thinking about the possibility of an inadequate food supply in the future, Ryan says

> Perhaps new methods of production will be discovered as far superior to those of the present as the latter are to the ones Malthus knew. On the other hand, perhaps large numbers of persons will some day be obliged to choose between temporary or permanent celibacy and long periods of abstinence within the marital union.[21] Here we are on uncertain ground. What we know is that for the present there is no occasion to worry . . . Sensible persons will not cross the bridge of overpopulation until they come to it. (1916b, 696, emphasis mine)

Here, we see that Ryan can foresee a time when Catholics might be morally obliged to have smaller families, and that issues of the common good of the race would trump other kinds of arguments for unlimited procreation. Having noticed that Ryan's pragmatism for the social good extends even to challenging his cherished vision of the large family, let us now turn more generally to comparing Ryan's work on birth regulation and the discussion as it has taken place in more recent decades.

Ryan believed that parental decisions about how many children to have in a family affected the character of the parents and the children, and thus was a question connected with serving the common good. These teleological arguments about birth control, while not exhaustive of his arguments against the practice, were central to Ryan's way of arguing about this issue. How does Ryan's approach compare with discussions in the last decades concerning contraception?

Whereas Ryan's arguments about ideal family size on grounds of over- or underpopulation were seen by him as fundamentally an economic issue, questions of economics are of relatively minor import in post-*Humanae vitae* discussions of the morality of birth control.[22]

My point is that contemporary arguments about contraception leave behind Ryan's concern for family size, of how the size of families affects children. Ryan's is a different question from that being asked by contemporary opponents of contraception, who ask a fundamentally negative question about what must not be done.

The most prominent contemporary Catholic opponent of contraception is Germain Grisez. For example, in discussing people who have no morally significant reason to contracept or not, Grisez says that

> In particular cases they might be inhibited by aesthetic, economic, or other considerations, including the Church's teaching against contraception. But such inhibitions are accidental to contraception as such [i.e. contraception considered from a moral point of view], and so we set them aside.[23]

For Grisez, issues of economics are allowed to play almost no part when considering contraception 'morally.'

Grisez has no objection to the regulation of fertility *per se*. It is not the *end* of regulating or preventing fertility that primarily concerns Grisez, but rather particular *means* of such regulation, or more precisely, particular possible intentions that may be present in the decision to regulate one's fertility. Having particular intentions, namely willing that a baby "not-come-to-be" is, according to Grisez, what makes one a contraceptor.[24] Further, Grisez argues that contraception "is wrong primarily and essentially because it is contralife."[25]

A strength of *Humanae vitae*, which locates the wrongs of contraception "in relation to other values, especially chastity, marital love and the sacred character of virtuous sexual activity in marriage,"[26] are those elements of it that push Christians to better understand the virtues to be pursued and the vices to be avoided, which will enable Christians as members of the body of Christ to graciously accept children from God and properly educate[27] children towards God.[28]

Although Ryan also included more "individualist" arguments, for example, about the regulation of conception as a perversion of nature, most of his arguments were with issues that he perceived to be selfishness in limiting or rejecting children. Thus, when Pope Pius XII gave an approving mention in 1954 of what comes to be called 'Natural Family Planning,' he is undermining—at least to some degree—a number of elements of Ryan's viewpoint. NFP may well be the central cause of the shift from "social" to "personal" forms of argumentation about the wrongness of birth control. Either way, we have entered a different debate than that in which Ryan was engaged. What is now central is not *the end* of having a certain number of children, of social questions about the ideal number of children, but in not acting in particular acts to prevent children. Righteousness in particular acts becomes far more closely associated with the rights and wrongs of fertility regulation than that of the more general disposition to graciously welcome children. Perhaps that is because this latter is not so easily discerned. But that perhaps is the true failure of the contemporary church, to be unable to recognize that the world does not place a high value on the welcoming of children, and to act as a counter-society to that.

Some final questions to consider:

1. Does family size have a bearing on the quality of the nurture of children? If so, what are "good," "better," and "ideal" family sizes?
2. If one is to enter the married state, is there an "ideal" age at which to enter?
3. What would Ryan say today about how many children should be included under a family living wage? Four or five children? Two or three children? One or two children?[29]

Now, my suspicion is that a lot of us do not merely not know how to answer these questions, we think it is inappropriate to try to answer them. But the problem with that is, if we do not want to answer these questions, can we come up with a family living wage for the 1990s?

BIBLIOGRAPHY

Anscombe, G. E. M. *Contraception and Chastity.* Bristol: Catholic Truth Society. 1980.

Beckley, Harlan. *Passion for Justice.* Louisville: Westminster/John Knox Press. 1992.

Curran, Charles E. *American Catholic Social Ethics.* Notre Dame, Ind.: University of Notre Dame Press. 1982.

Grisez, Germain. *Contraception and the Natural Law.* Milwaukee: Bruce Publishing. 1964.

Grisez, Germain et al. *The Teaching of* Humanae Vitae. San Francisco: Ignatius Press. 1987.

Noonan, John T. *Contraception.* New York: Mentor-Omega. 1965.

Ryan, John. *The Living Wage: Its Ethical and Economic Aspects.* New York: The MacMillan Company. 1906.

———. *Distributive Justice: The Right and Wrong of Our Present Distribution of Wealth.* New York: The MacMillan Company. 1916a.

———. "Family Limitation." *The Ecclesiastical Review* 54 (1916b): 684-96.

———. *Social Reconstruction.* New York: The MacMillan Company. 1920.

———. *Declining Liberty and Other Papers.* New York: The MacMillan Company. 1927.

———. *Questions of the Day.* Freeport, N.Y.: Books for Libraries Press, Inc. 1931.

———. "The Moral Aspects of Periodical Continence." *The Ecclesiastical Review* 89 (1933): 28-39.

———. *Social Doctrine in Action: A Personal History.* New York: Harper and Brothers Publishers. 1941.

Smith, Janet. *Humanae Vitae: A Generation Later.* Washington, D.C.: Catholic University of America Press. 1991.

Notes

1. Although I wish to be empathetic with Ryan in this paper, I do not wish to support his vision of gender roles. However, I believe Ryan's views on questions of birth regulation are instructive, even if I reject his views on the role of women.

2. In concentrating on the distinctly social reasons Ryan uses to attack contraception, I do not mean to imply that Ryan does not also give other reasons.

3. Ryan's views are that social utility never control what constitutes the just living wage, for ethical considerations ultimately trump economic considerations, but generally speaking, Ryan believed that in the long run, considerations of justice and social utility went hand in hand.

4. Thus, I see my task as somewhere between the vision of the first day—"the life and times of Ryan"—and that of the "social policy" of the third day.

5. Ryan does think in general that one should pay laborers the same if they do the same labor—even if one has other means besides their labor to survive (1906, 107), and that men and women have the right to the same living wage, even if the man is supporting a family (108) because "distributive justice requires that equally competent workers be rewarded equally." (108)

6. Ryan rejects the argument that wages ought to be tied strictly to work done, that is, tied strictly to market value. Since the issue is one of distributive justice, the resources of the earth must be distributed so that all may live in dignity. Human dignity requires that the employer pay a family living wage.

While Ryan does in places factor in issues of social utility in evaluating just wages (e.g. he believes people who have particularly unpleasant jobs—trash collectors and bootblacks—should get higher wages), the basis for the living wage is the dignity of the worker.

7. In places he asserts that it is hardly necessary for him to make this argument, "as very few would assert that the average man can live a normal and complete human life without marriage" (1916a, 374).

8. The view that workers should reduce their number of offspring was also supported by some who were genuinely sympathetic to the workers, thinking that if the workers had less children and thus created a smaller labor pool, then their labor would be in greater demand and wages would rise (1916b, 693; 1931, 271)

9. In this section Ryan makes no moral argument for the superiority of having certain numbers of children rather than others as he often does elsewhere.

10. Ryan states that married American Catholic women could, with safety and advantage, have on the average half a dozen each, even today. This is certainly true of our rural population. In our great cities, inadequate dwelling space and other deficiences and difficulties in the environment probably make this high average practically impossible. The obvious remedy is to provide all families with sufficient house room and facilities for recreation. This goal is entirely possible of achievement in a country as rich as ours (1941, 4-5).

Furthermore, Ryan is even willing to prescribe what, in postdepression terms, is a reasonably sized family—six in the country, and perhaps three or four in the cities. Of course, Ryan is talking about averages, and I expect would be as flexible on these estimates as he was with his estimates about what constituted a living wage. In 1906 he estimated a living wage at $700 a year, by 1910 he estimated $800, and $900 in New York, and in 1929 he considered the living wage ("the amount to enable a family of five, including three small children, to live at a minimum of health and decency in any of our large cities") to be between $1600 and $1800 dollars (1931, 201). Of course, in the same way that questions of how much constitutes a living wage may and do vary with inflation, they may and do vary with what our society considers "a minimum of health and decency." Considering Ryan's pragmatic assessment of what number of children a family may have on economic grounds, he certainly lays in place a basis for thinking about what would be stated by Pius XII in 1954 about limiting family size for "economic" reasons.

11. The paper was published in the *American Ecclesiastical Review* (February 1904).

12. There are issues of nationalism in Ryan's use of "native-born." See also 1906, 281-85.

13. In the preface he says the book is "an autobiography only in a restricted sense, for it is almost entirely concerned with my social and economic beliefs and activities" (vii). This, however, makes the few more anecdotal comments more significant, as they (intentionally or not) result in showing more trenchantly the key events and remembrances that shape his appropriation of his Catholic faith. I should also add that examining his biography is not meant to be reductive; I do not wish to state or imply that Ryan's argument for the superiority of the large family is simply a defense of his own upbringing, or merely an act of loyalty or gratitute to his mother!

14. I'm not sure who made that argument then, nor who would make it today!

15. Presumably, the argument that having many offspring shortens the lives of women.

16. One does not have to have a great imagination to know why this is an extraordinarily passionate question among Catholics!

17. Although I haven't been able to locate the quote, I recall reading that Ryan believed in a maximum wage, that paid to the President of the United States.

18. In places Ryan believes, as did some French bishops in the late nineteenth century, that birth control could result in the extinction of the human race, which would be a catastrophic failure of humans to fulfill what all other species manage to do—propagate themselves.

19. I should also add that at times Ryan's arguments belie more than a minor helping of nationalism. Two other arguments against birth control that I do not disuss: First, the against nature/perverted faculty argument (1916b, 687-

88). Second, refusing to procreate gives a lower form of marital life—refusing to be cocreators with God.

20. This is a complicated issue. In some places, Ryan emphasizes the large family quite independantly of population issues, but at other times this seems to be contradicted by the fact that population issues could negate such a good. Ryan would likely see this as the absolute justice issue that enabling existing people to have enough to eat could outweigh the subsidiary justice issue of being able to have large families.

21. One question is, what, in Ryan's view, will be the source of this obligation. To say that governments might oblige their citizens to choose between periods of celibacy or abstinence in marriage would be to deprive individuals of basic rights to marriage and the procreation of children that Ryan staunchly defends. In the Living Wage, Ryan sees marriage and the procreation of children as a right second only to that of preservation of life itself. He also argues that most individuals simply cannot be expected to live a life of celibacy. So it is hard to conceive of Ryan arguing that this could or should be a legal obligation

22. One might further show how privatized the issue of conception regulation has become by noting that whereas advocates of population control have no great difficulty advocating birth control in countries where they deem there to be overpopulation, one would scarcely expect such people to decry the limitation of families if there was a population shortage in their own country, or to begin to have more children out of a sense of societal duty. There seems to be no reason in principle why the church could not at some point in the future condemn both natural family planning as well as contraceptive methods, if there was a need for a greater population, either for the church or for society. Of course, I am not *advocating* this!

23. Grisez et al., "Every Marital Act," 48.

24. In his early *Contraception and the Natural Law*, Grisez did provide two reasons why procreation is a fundamental good: first, "having and raising children is practically universal phenomenon;" second, "from a biological point of view the work of reproduction is the fullest organic realization of the living substance." These are enumerated in Smith, *A Generation Later*, 348-49. But Grisez seems to leave these justifications behind in his later work. He may leave these behind because the former reason, based on universality, is also true of nutrition and defecation, but these are not goods one never acts against; as for the latter reason, it appears to be a form of a kind of argument that Grisez rejects as an is/ought fallacy. Instead, he focuses on the second way of showing the possibility that new life is a great good, by showing that preventing this end in particular ways is contralife.

25. Grisez et al., "Every Marital Act," 39. Oddly enough, Grisez claims in his introduction that "we also show how the Church's teaching on contraception

is tightly interwoven with her entire moral teaching concerning sex, marriage, and innocent life. Thus, the question of the morality of contraception cannot be treated in isolation."(Grisez, "General Introduction," 10) While Grisez does in fact link the issue of contraception with, for example, the taking of innocent life, he does so not by appealing to traditional church teaching, but to his moral principles. Grisez shows how his views on contraception are related with his other moral views, but not with church teaching on these subjects.

26. Grisez et al., "Every Marital Act," 38. Janet Smith, in her commentary on *Humanae vitae*, further locates a proper understanding of *Humanae vitae's* proscriptions on regulating births as inseparable from the Christian upbringing and education of children. Smith comments that §8 of *Humanae vitae* does not divorce conjugal love and the educating of children, and elsewhere notes that procreation and education (i.e. parenting), have always gone hand in hand in church teaching on the regulation of fertility. "Through [marital] communion, the spouses perfect each other so that they might share with God the task of procreating and educating new living beings." (*Humanae vitae* §8) Quoted in Smith, *A Generation Later*, 278.

27. For a fascinating discussion on the many meanings of 'education' in the medieval period and its importance in relation to the acceptance of children, see Noonan, *Contraception*, 337-41.

28. On this note, there should also be stressed a far greater responsibility for the church to support this welcoming of children, which includes displaying its commitment to properly care for the children it exhorts its members to produce. To counter the population-control people's motto of "every child a wanted child" should be the church's motto of "every child a well-fed and educated child." Properly understood by the church, this commitment would in no way constitute a supererogatory action to the less fortunate in its midst, but rather display its more basic and historical commitment in advocating the welcoming of children among its members. The church has not advocated the production of 'children' qua biological beings (whose nutrition and education are important but essentially separate issues), but has denied that these elements can or should be separated. The Thomistic argument against fornication has precisely been that the bringing of children into the world through a kind of relationship that will not tend to their proper upbringing and education is not to be pursued. As Noonan summarizes the view "It is better not to bear a child than to bear a child injured in his basic educational opportunities." (Noonan, *Contraception*, 338) To support conception without education and welfare is a failure not only of individual families, but of the whole body of the church.

29. Would he base it, as he did in 1906, on sociological data, or would he construct a moral argument in deciding this question? Ryan took the number of children for the standard to be 4 or 5 children—this in 1915. Ryan might well

say that today the modern family would include 2 or 3 children for a family living wage. (1906, 120, 122)

John A. Ryan and the Catholic Association for International Peace (CAIP)

PATRICIA McNEAL

On 5 April 1917, the day before the U.S. Congress declared war, James Cardinal Gibbons, speaking on behalf of the Catholic hierarchy and the American Catholic church, proclaimed that, "In the present emergency it behooves every American citizen to do his duty and uphold the hands of the President . . . in the solemn obligations that confront us. The primary duty of a citizen is loyalty to country. This loyalty is exhibited by an absolute and unreserved obedience to his country."[1] In pledging the loyalty of American Catholics to the nation Gibbons was reaffirming a tradition of Catholic "patriotism in wartime." This tradition, wrote one historian, "has been a hallmark of the American Catholic community," evident since the earliest days of the nation.[2] It was reinforced by a reaction to the anti-Catholicism prevalent in Protestant America and supported on a theological level by the just war doctrine.

The outbreak of this war provided the Catholic hierarchy with an opportunity to demonstrate its patriotic Americanism. In support of President Woodrow Wilson's crusade "to make the world safe for democracy," they formed the National Catholic War Council. Founded in August 1917, it functioned throughout the war "as a highly effective medium in almost every phase of Catholic participation in the war effort, from providing material assistance to chaplains serving with the troops to acting as an official agency designated by President Wilson to promote the war-loan drives."[3]

A few months after World War I ended in Europe, the American bishops issued their first pastoral statement since 1884. This document, titled *Lessons of War* and issued in September 1919, urged the United States to accept its unique role to "restore peace and order" according to "principles of reasonable liberty and of Christian civilization." In effect, the hierarchy condoned the war as a crusade and like many Americans they were now looking toward the reconstruction of American society.[4]

The success of the war council as a national coordinating agency for the church persuaded its supporters, principally, Bishop Peter J. Muldoon of the Diocese of Rockford, Illinois, to continue its operation after the war as a way for the church to maintain a national focus. The name was changed to the National Catholic Welfare Council (NCWC) and its headquarters was in the nation's capital. It became the primary agency to coordinate and promote Catholic interests and activities at a national level. Though there was initial opposition from some bishops who feared the council would limit their autonomy and authority, NCWC did succeed in providing the church with the type of national organization it needed and gave the bishops a national consciousness that taught them to think about issues that transcended local diocesan concerns.

The council originally had five departments: education, lay activities, press, missions, and social. But the one department "that has probably impinged more than any other on the national consciousness is the Social Action Department."[5] In 1920, the American Catholic hierarchy selected John A. Ryan to direct the new department, which was primarily concerned with social reform at home. However, under John A. Ryan's leadership, social justice was linked for the first time to the broader international interests of war and peace.

The genius of John A. Ryan was his ability to merge Catholic social thought with the American current of reform. The basis for this merger was natural law tradition.[6] Pope Leo XIII had positioned the natural law at the foundation of Catholic social ethics in his encyclical, *Rerum novarum*. Ryan took this aspect of papal social thought and applied it to the American economic and industrial environment. From this basic principle flowed Ryan's emphasis on a living wage, the importance of labor unions, and the need of the state to intervene and effect change in the social order. This positive role for the state in Catholic social theory did not mean an absolute trust in a particular government or administration that necessarily led to endorsing policy. Rather the natural law provided a language that allowed discussion of the morality of public policy in a pluralistic society.

After World War I the Catholic bishops wanted to present their own program for reconstruction of American society and set up their own committee to draft a document. The priest, John O'Grady, secretary of the Committee on Reconstruction, had the responsibility to produce such a plan. He turned to John A. Ryan, who at the time was writing his own program of reconstruction. O'Grady begged him for it and in February 1919 it appeared as the "Bishops' Program of Social Reconstruction." Without a doubt it was "the most forward-looking social document ever to have come from an official Catholic agency in the United States."[7]

Avid criticism of the 1919 statement did occur. Some segments of the Catholic community labeled it as "partisan, pro-labor union, or socialistic propaganda."[8] Nevertheless, it pointed the direction toward which many Catholics were moving in the years after World War I. One visible omission in this quest for social reform was the international issue of war and peace.

As was evidenced in World War I, Catholics were eager to prove their loyalty to the United States, and in seeking social reform they never challenged the place of the nation in the international community. Raised in an immigrant community, Catholic reformers were also not inclined to challenge the country's basic social system. They wanted reform, but only within the boundaries of the accepted American tradition. They looked to the government for help, not to criticize it. Thus, it was inevitable that one of the last issues Catholic reformers would confront was the responsibility of the United States in war and for peace. Moreover, the just war tradition worked against any consideration of this issue.

Ryan typified this acceptance in World War I when he wrote in his autobiography that "I acquiesced in the declaration of war because I assumed that the President and Congress were in a better position than I to make the right decision."[9] Like Ryan's system of social ethics, the just war had its basis in the natural law tradition. For Ryan the state was necessary, and its authority was both real and binding. This did not, however, mean that the state is above the law or that the state is the final arbiter of right and wrong. According to Ryan the state stands under the law and must be judged according to the principles of natural law.[10]

During World War I, however, Ryan was greatly influenced by the proposals of Pope Benedict XV (1914-1922) for ending World War I and reestablishing international order and peace. During his pontificate, Benedict XV was faced with the full impact of world war and its aftermath of hatred and destruction. A former papal diplomat, Benedict XV opposed war in any form and rejected the theory of the just war as historically outmoded and theologically inadequate. He earned the title Pontiff of Peace.

Pope Benedict XV was more in line with the humanist peace tradition within the church, which he expressed in his direct moral appeal to individual conscience, than to the internationalist tradition that emerged after the Council of Trent and was promulgated with qualification by Leo XIII. The internationalists placed their hopes for peace on the diplomatic efforts and military balances of Europe's governments. Benedict XV issued the encyclical, *Ad beatissimum,* at the outbreak of World War I. The encyclical outlined the causes of war and the methods for attaining peace. For Benedict XV the causes of war were lack of mutual love, disregard for authority, class war, and gross materialism; the path to peace embraced the Beatitudes and Christ's command that "you love one another as I have loved you." He called for a peace without victory and an end to hostilities, prophetically reminding the belligerents that true Christians must make the first offer of peace. "He was as close to a pacifist as any pope since Benedict XII during the Hundred Years War."[11]

Although the messages of Leo XIII and Benedict XV did not persuade the majority of Catholics nor Ryan to question the decisions of their government, Ryan was greatly influenced by the rejection of Benedict XV's proposal for ending World War I and reestablishing peace, which was sent to the belligerents on 14 August 1917. In responding to the international crisis Ryan established himself as the foremost advocate of the League of Nations. Ryan gave one of the first talks in support of the league at a meeting of the Knights of Columbus in Louisville in December 1918, five months before the covenant of the league was written into the Treaty of Versailles. In May 1919, he stated that the league was "the only means in sight to save the people of Europe from experiences perhaps worse than those of war."[12]

Ryan addressed his most urgent appeals for the league to Catholic bishops, whom he hoped would provide leadership on the issue; he also appealed to editors of the Catholic press because he believed that "the Catholic press was never more than 'spasmodic and half-hearted' in applying principles of Catholic political ethics to international questions."[13]

A closely related crusade to the League of Nations that attracted Ryan in the 1920s was international peace through disarmament. Not historically literate, Ryan was, nevertheless, well informed on matters within his own memory and he understood European problems, especially economic ones. He gave particular attention to the excessive burden the war debt placed on the German people; he believed this would be a source of continuing threat to world peace.[14] In 1928, Ryan appeared before the House Naval Affairs Committee as a representative of the Church Peace Union, an interdenominational group, to oppose the construction of new capital warships. The *Buffalo Catholic Union and Times* did not approve and demanded to know "How long, O! Lord! would Catholics have to put up with the intrusions of Father Burke and Dr. Ryan into political questions in the discussion of which they have no authority to speak except for their own ill-formed and ill-considered convictions?"[15] Ryan also applauded the Treaty of Locarno, the Kellogg Pact, and the World Court.

In 1922, while visiting England, Ryan met a British peace advocate, Joseph Keating, S.J., from whom he learned about England's Catholic Council for International Peace. After returning to the United States, Ryan discussed with some of his friends the idea of founding a similar Catholic peace organization. He received support from Robert McGowan and from Carlton J. H. Hayes of Columbia. Worth M. Tippy, Charles S. Macfarland, and especially Sidney L. Gulick, all of the Federal Council of Churches for Prevention of War, urged him to organize a peace movement among Catholics.[16] Frederick J. Libby, executive secretary of the National Council for the Prevention of War (NCPW) was also urging Ryan forward. Ryan at this time was serving on the board of the NCPW. These men propelled Ryan into a territory that Catholics had not entered. The popes had spoken vigorously for peace; the bishops had echoed them. But there it ended. Ryan did not exaggerate in 1925 when he said, "he could tell the whole story of American Catholic peace sentiment in a fraction of the sixteen hundred words that the *NCWC Bulletin* wanted him to write."[17]

The diversity of positions later evidenced in the 1930s by these individuals who had counseled Ryan in the formation of a Catholic peace movement reveal how loosely related peace societies were in the 1920s. In 1922, Ryan did not want to start an American Catholic peace movement, but he did want to form a group of Catholics who could serve as a pressure group to lobby for significant legislation on issues of war and peace in Congress.[18] Ryan's primary focus was the issue of social action, yet he did agree with the judgment of Bishop Peter J. Muldoon, episcopal chair of the Social Action Department, that "the department was not doing enough to educate Catholics on world affairs. It concentrated on domestic social justice alone."[19] Another priest, Joseph Burke, C.S.P., finally pushed Ryan in the direction of organizing a peace group among Catholics. He suggested that Ryan and his assistant, Raymond McGowan, also a priest, "get leading Catholics together at the 28th Annual Eucharistic Congress to be held in Chicago in 1925," and together they could begin to discuss the issue of international peace.[20]

The proposed meeting of fifty Catholic leaders took place following the close of the congress. The assembled group did not draw up any specific plans, but expressed a desire to meet again and established an organizing committee headed by Colonel P. H. Callahan of Louisville, Kentucky. The next conference took place in Cleveland on 6 October 1926; here a committee system was adopted to study, report upon, and help promote Catholic understanding and action on problems of world peace. An organizational meeting was then scheduled for April 1927, at the Catholic University of America in Washington, D.C.[21]

For this meeting Ryan was to chair the subcommittee on international ethics and prepare a working paper for discussion. His final product drew substantially from *The Church and War* by Franziskus Stratmann, O.P.; Stratmann believed no modern war could be just. Ryan's pamphlet became the principal manifesto of the new association when it was published in 1927 with the title *International Ethics.* This report rejected Stratmann's pacifist position, but attempted to limit the characterization of a just war and warned of the need for caution in invoking force. Ryan stated that "righteousness would surely not be protected if wicked men were permitted to have a monopoly on physical coercion."

With the problem of creating a Catholic group in mind, the subcommittee noted: "Justice requires a state to promote peace for the sake of its own members, while charity obliges it to pursue the same ends for the welfare of both itself and other nations. These duties rest not only upon governments, but upon peoples, particularly upon those persons and organizations which can exert influence upon public opinion and upon political rulers."[22] This 1927 meeting realized the goal of a Catholic peace organization: It adopted a constitution, elected officers, and chose a name, the Catholic Association for International Peace (CAIP). Its motto was that of Pope Pius XI's reign, "The Peace of Christ in the Kingdom of Christ." It was the first Catholic peace organization in American history.

> The Association did not look for mass support, but planned to seek to educate Catholics and non-Catholics on the Catholic point of view on international affairs, as drawn from what the Holy Fathers, the Bishops of the United States, and Catholic scholars had said on the principles of attaining world peace through justice and charity.[23]

Studies were to be made by experts and reports published on the principles of peace and their application to current issues. In addition, the association would promote annual conferences, lectures, and study circles to present Catholic opinion on subjects relating to international morality. CAIP was allotted office space in the NCWC headquarters in Washington as an independent branch of the Social Action Department and was given the use of NCWC facilities, including the news service.

During the 1930s it is impossible to separate the CAIP from the NCWC's Social Action Department because of the central roles of Ryan and McGowan in both organizations. Ryan's reputation as "American Catholicism's foremost social reformer" enabled him to link American Catholics and liberal, progressive groups.[24] McGowan, however, assumed primary responsibility for CAIP's organization and vision.[25] Both men believed that "highly trained laymen and laywomen would join priests in furnishing the material for the program of education for and the actual re-creation of the social order. Catholics should remake social institutions by gaining positions of power in business organizations and civil life.[26] Thus, the structure of CAIP was elitist from the beginning though it intended to reach the general population of the laity.

The CAIP urged its members to work within the framework of all existing organizations devoted to the cause of peace in the world, but it did little more than send pamphlet material upon request or provide a speaker for a peace rally. Some individual members did serve on national committees of various peace organizations. Ryan had served several years on NCPW's executive board. When the board in 1933, over Ryan's repeated protests, decided to intervene between the government in Mexico and the Catholic church, he resigned. President Roosevelt had instituted a "good neighbor" policy toward Latin America during the height of Mexico's anticlericalism, which resulted in antagonism between his administration and the Catholic church. Some American Catholics made Josephus Daniels, the newly appointed U.S. ambassador to Mexico, the scapegoat in their attempt to pressure the Roosevelt administration into meddling in the internal affairs of Mexico in support of the church. Between 1932 and 1936, "it was the most severe strain imposed on the generally harmonious relationship between Roosevelt and American Catholics."[27]

Thus it was the "Mexican question" and not pacifism that led to Ryan's resignation from NCPW. In his autobiography, Ryan admits that he was aware that many of the members of NCPW were pacifist, but it did not cause him any "unpleasant complications" in the years he was with them. Ryan goes on to say that it would have caused his resignation in 1939 when the council took a strong stand against President Roosevelt's recommendation to Congress to lift the embargo on the sale of arms in favor of Great Britain and France and again when they fought against the program for national defense adopted by Congress in 1940. Ryan's main criticism of NCPW was that they had become "hopelessly isolationist."[28] In his autobiography he writes, "Because I still have faith and hope in world peace through international action, and because I still believe that the precepts of the moral law bind nations as well as individuals, I reject and detest isolationism under any and every guise."[29]

CAIP's relations with peace organizations outside the United States were similar with those at home. To establish contact with Europe, Elizabeth Sweeney, as early as June 1929, wrote on behalf of CAIP to Franziskus Stratmann, head of the German Catholic Union for Peace, who in turn urged the need to prepare the way for an international peace conference. Stratmann held that no modern war could be a just war and also urged that war service and military service be declared an absolute contradiction of the teachings of Christ and of the Catholic church.[30] From this position he urged Sweeney to contact Joseph Clayton in England who had written on peace for the English Dominican periodical *Blackfriars,* the Polish Jesuit Graf Rostoworowski, Professor Ude of Graz University, Professor Keller of Freiburg University, and the War Resisters' International. CAIP, however, gave little cooperation beyond publishing a pamphlet called *Catholic Peace Organizations in Europe*. It also worked with the Carnegie Endowment for International Peace in publishing for American readers a five-hundred page work on internationalism and Catholicism. The work, *The Catholic Tradition of the Law of Nations,* was written by John Eppstein under the auspices of the Catholic Council for International Relations of Great Britain.

By 1937 CAIP's internationalism had resulted in opposition to neutrality legislation. CAIP contended that the Neutrality Act made no distinction between the aggressor nation and its victim.[31] In 1938, it reiterated its position by objecting to the "narrow conception of national interest upon which [the] Neutrality Act was based [an] attitude of washing our hands of responsibility in present crime [and it was] concerned primarily not with the prevention of war but with [the] avoidance of its consequences."[32] This paved the way for the CAIP to embrace wholeheartedly Roosevelt's move away from neutrality toward collective security.

The only stumbling block in this process for the CAIP was the Spanish Civil War and the ensuing debate between 1937 and 1939 over the Embargo Act. During this time President Roosevelt did not advocate a change in the Neutrality Act of 1937 and a lifting of the Embargo Act. Yet, in his "Quarantine Speech" at Chicago on 5 October 1937 he discarded the doctrine of neutrality for the United States and espoused the idea of collective security—the cardinal principle of internationalism. Despite this, he never lifted the embargo. Like Roosevelt CAIP was also ambiguous. It seemed logical by 1937 that CAIP was ready to reject strict neutrality but the American bishops and the "official" church statements from the NCWC came out in support of Franco in Spain and were against the repeal of the embargo, which would favor the Loyalists. Because of CAIP's close relationship with the NCWC, it chose to remain silent rather than confront the position of the "official" church.

Ryan, however, spoke out on the issue when he joined a group of 174 Catholic laymen and clergymen to defend the American church's support of the insurgents in the Spanish Civil War. The group issued a statement that insisted on the right of revolution against a government that made persecution of the church an integral part of its program. Ryan made no apologies about signing the statement. He had no affection for fascism and he believed the coming struggle in Europe would be between communism and democracy rather than between democracy and fascism. Even though this view set him off from most liberal opinion in America, he reminded himself that where religion was involved, liberals were likely to be "muddleheaded."[33]

After Franco's victory in Spain in 1939, such a conflict of loyalties would never again confront CAIP. Because the "official" church opposed Nazism, CAIP was able to speak out against strict neutrality when it touched on the German situation.

The shift of CAIP from support of neutrality legislation to endorsing collective security reflected the transformation taking place among other nonpacifist peace groups such as the Carnegie Endowment for International Peace, the Church Peace Union, the World Alliance for International Friendship through the Churches, and the League of Nations Association. All these organizations rallied around the concept of collective security and formed the Non-Partisan Committee for Peace Through the Revision of the Neutrality Law. Through this organization and others, the nonpacifist peace groups prepared the nation for war by emphasizing collective security rather than a position of neutrality. As a spokesperson for the committee in late 1939 Ryan expressed the consensus of the group when he stated in a radio broadcast that all Americans were "morally obliged to do all they reasonably can to defeat Hitler and Hitlerism."[34]

By 1940, Ryan was firmly convinced of his position on war and Hitler. In an article that appeared in *Commonweal* and was reprinted as a pamphlet *The Right and Wrong of War*, he wrote:

> The extreme pacifist position, that war as such is always wrong because it involves violence, does not deserve formal discussion. With the position of some recent Catholic authorities, that in our day war is practically never justified because of its awful consequences, I have considerable sympathy; but if Hitler and his government intend to substitute paganism for Christianity not only in Germany but in foreign territories which they have annexed in the last two years and if they are aiming at world domination, then I have no hesitation in saying that a successful war against this immoral Nazi program would be the lesser evil. In other words, such a war would be justified, despite the enormous ensuing destruction of life and property.[35]

When the United States declared its formal participation in World War II, CAIP unhesitatingly continued the Catholic tradition of patriotism in wartime.

When bombs came down on Pearl Harbor, Catholic debate of foreign policy ceased. The isolationism CAIP had tried to combat disappeared among American Catholics. The historian, George Q. Flynn, in his book *Roosevelt and Romanism,* contends that there was a moral clarity reflected in the American Catholic conscience on World War II, which had little to do with politics and everything to do with theology. A study of the statements of Catholic leaders concerning

World War II, according to Flynn, reveals that Catholics believed Hitler was a demonic force in history and the United States held a special place in God's plan of creation that placed God on their side during the war. These two religious assumptions, states Flynn, combined with the dominant teaching of the just war doctrine, turned the war effort into a moral crusade to promote a world of liberty and goodness. Catholics might have put some qualifications on their commitment, realizing that to identify God with any nation was a heresy in doctrine. Yet, Flynn contends that there were no such reservations voiced by Catholic spokespersons. Catholic leaders and their flocks had been trained to think in religious terms, thus it is understandable that they could "be lifted out of history and into a morality play.[36] By approaching the war as a moral crusade, Flynn concludes that Catholic leaders were left with an atrophy of their ethical feelings concerning the objects, tactics, and strategy of the conflict. They had become one with the Roosevelt administration in the attempt to win the just war.

Prior to World War II, CAIP never claimed a membership of more than five hundred.[37] However, because of the prestige of its members, especially John A. Ryan, the ideals of the association reached a wide audience. The internationalism of CAIP left the association with no alternative to war once it was declared. Ryan and his associates wished to achieve world peace through social justice, and the greatest strength of their approach to international problems was their economic interpretation and their clear recognition of the necessity of worldwide planning and control. In the absence of a strong international organization and with no ethic but the just war doctrine, CAIP ended up acknowledging the state as its final decision maker in matters of war. John A. Ryan and the CAIP accepted the decisions of its nation for international ends. In the face of Hitlerism the way to peace was through war.

Notes

1. John Tracy Ellis, "American Catholics and Peace: A Historical Sketch" (Washington, D.C.: United States Catholic Conference, 1970), 25, reprint from James S. Rausch, ed., *The Family of Nations* (Huntington, Ind.: Our Sunday Visitor, Inc., 1970).

2. Henry J. Browne, "Catholicism in the United States," in James Ward Smith and A. Leland Jamison, eds., *The Shaping of American Religion* (Princeton, N.J.: Princeton University Press, 1961), 77.

3. John Tracy Ellis, *American Catholicism,* 2d ed., rev. (Chicago: University of Chicago Press, 1969), 141.

4. Ronald G. Musto, *The Catholic Peace Tradition* (New York: Orbis Books, 1986), 240.

5. Ellis, American *Catholicism,* 144.

6. Jay P. Dolan, *The American Catholic Experience: A History from Colonial Time to the Present* (New York: Doubleday, 1985), 343.

7. Ibid., 346-69.

8. David J. O'Brien, *American Catholicism and Social Reform: The New Deal Years* (New York: Oxford University Press, 1968), 42.

9. John A. Ryan, *Social Doctrine in Action, a Personal History* (New York: Harper & Brothers, 1941), 137.

10. Joseph M. McShane, *Sufficiently Radical: Catholicism, Progressivism and the Bishops' Program of 1919* (Washington, D.C.: Catholic University of America Press, 1986), 41.

11. Musto, *Catholic Peace Tradition,* 171.

12. Harry W Flannery, "CAIP Fights for International Peace," U.S. Catholic (September 1963): 25 and 26. See also John A. Ryan's autobiography, *Social Doctrine*, 140, 141, 145.

13. Francis L. Broderick, *Right Reverend New Dealer John A. Ryan* (New York: Macmillan, 1963), 104.

14. Ibid., 135.

15. Ibid., 160.

16. Ibid., 136.

17. Ibid., 77.

18. Ibid., 138.

19. AMU, CAIP Collection, "Notes on CAIP" by Raymond McGowan, 4 August 1958.

20. Ibid.

21. Ibid.

22. Broderick, *Right Reverend New Dealer,* 138.

23. AMU, CAIP Collection, "CAIP Constitution," Section 2.

24. O'Brien, *American Catholicism and Social Reform,* 121.

25. AMU, CAIP Collection, letter dated 1 March 1963, Mrs. R. M. Patterson to Harry W. Flannery.

26. Dennis Robb, "Specialized Catholic Action in the United States, 1936-1949: Ideology, Leadership, and Organization," Ph.D. diss., University of Minnesota, 1972, 32.

27. George Q. Flynn, *American Catholics and the Roosevelt Presidency 1932-1936* (Lexington, Ky.: University of Kentucky Press, 1968), 150.

28. Ryan, *Social Doctrine*, 214, 215. Broderick in his biography of Ryan, *Right Reverend New Dealer,* states that Ryan resigned from NCPW because it was too pacifist.

29. Ryan, *Social Doctrine.*

30. AMU, CAIP Collection, letter dated 26 June 1929, Franziskus Stratmann, O.P., to Elizabeth Sweeney.

31. AMU, CAIP Collection, "Summary of CAIP Work 1927 to 1952," 7.

32. Ibid.

33. Broderick, *Right Reverend New Dealer,* 233, 234.

34. *New York Times,* 16 October 1939, cited in Charles J. Tull, *Father Coughlin and the New Deal* (Syracuse, N.Y.: Syracuse University Press, 1965), 217.

35. Ryan, *Social Doctrine in Action,* 216, 217.

36. George Q. Flynn, *Roosevelt and Romanism: Catholics and American Diplomacy* 1937-1945 (Westport, Conn.: Greenwood Press, 1976), 189.

37. AMU, CAIP Collection, "A History of the Catholic Association for International Peace 1927-1953," by Clarence L. Hohl, Jr., 55.

John A. Ryan and The Relationship between Spirituality and Work

Some scholars of John A. Ryan have mourned the fact that, in his voluminous writings, "the Right Reverend New Dealer" seems to have shared little about his spiritual life. He has, however, in his youth as well as in his waning years, offered some comments that allow us to reflect on his spirituality—his personal encounter with God, and the way that encounter affected his lived experience. We are fortunate to have the diaries that John A. Ryan kept as a seminarian and as a young priest. In these and in his autobiography we can catch a glimpse of his interior life—his goals, his thoughts, his prayers.

Ryan was ordained to the priesthood on June 4, 1898, a member of the first class to have spent four years in the new theologate, The Saint Paul Seminary. His archbishop, John Ireland, assigned him to begin graduate studies at the Catholic University of America in Washington, D.C., the following fall. In the interim, Ryan was appointed to be in charge of a small country parish for the summer—his one opportunity for exclusively parochial ministry. In his autobiography *Social Doctrine in Action* Ryan states: "These were among the happiest weeks that I have ever known, not only because they introduced me to the life and functions of the priesthood but because the people to whom I ministered were simple, genuine, unsophisticated, and unspoiled."[1]

By the following October, Ryan was in Washington, D.C.,—a student once again. He wrote the following in his diary:

> We are all called to be saints in the broad sense. That is, we can all participate in the spirit of Jesus Christ, "hide Him within our hearts," and show Him forth in our actions. But we cannot all, humanly speaking, accomplish this in a heroic degree; and in the strict sense, this alone is saintship.[2]

The next day he penned the following "correction," which seems to have been his editing process. In the second version he wrote:

> We are all called to be saints, and in the wider sense, we can all become saints. That is, we can all become imbued with the spirit of Jesus Christ, the model for saints, and show forth that spirit in our actions. The great majority, however, can practice saintliness only in a moderate degree, while the exceptional man who imitates and manifests Christ in a heroic degree is the real saint.[3]

It is interesting that the language of the "heart" falls by the wayside in the editing. What is clear in both passages, however, is that the spirit of Christ needs to "show forth in our actions." This was fundamental to Ryan's spirituality from his earliest days.

One of Ryan's intellectual heroes was Bishop John Lancaster Spalding of Peoria. When Ryan was chosen to give the valedictory address at his graduation from St. Thomas (Minor) Seminary in 1892, he later admitted that most of the ideas in it were drawn from Spalding's 1890 volume titled *Education and the Higher Life*. Ryan included a lengthy segment from Spalding's book in his autobiography. An excerpt from that quotation below may tell us as much about Ryan as it does about Spalding:

> Who will understand that to *be* is better than to *have*, and that in truth a man is worth only what he is? Who will believe that the kingdom of this world, not less than the kingdom of Heaven, lies within? Who, even in thinking of the worth of a pious and righteous life, is not swayed by some sort of honesty-best-policy principle? . . . Instead of giving your thoughts and desires to wealth and position, learn to know how little of such things a true and wise man needs; for the secret of a happy life does not lie in the means and opportunities of indulging our weaknesses, but in knowing how to be content with what is reasonable, that time and strength may remain for the cultivation of our nobler nature. Ask God to inspire you with some great thought, some abiding love of what is excellent, which may fill you with

> gladness and courage, and in the midst of the labors, the trials, and the disappointments of life, keep you strong and serene.[4]

Ryan credits Spalding for imbuing him with a solid foundation for his later work: "For many years he exercised a greater influence upon my general philosophy of life, my ideals, my sense of comparative values than any other contemporary writer."[5] Although the word "spirituality" was not in vogue in those days, (at that time it was categorized under "aesthetical and mystical theology"), Spalding's impact on Ryan—by his own admission—transcended that of the academic, and challenged him to explore the avenues of the spiritual life.

To what degree did Ryan's appreciation of his priesthood and his spirituality affect his commitment to social justice in both thought and action? At the testimonial dinner given in his honor on the occasion of his seventieth birthday, after receiving tributes from the high and mighty in Washington, D.C., he offered a response in which he specifically referred to the period about four years prior to his ordination, shortly after the promulgation of *Rerum novarum* (1891) by Leo XIII. He stated:

> I had already determined to devote as much as possible of my time and energy to the study of economic conditions, institutions and problems. I wanted to examine economic life in the light of Christian principles, with a view to making them operative in the realm of industry. It seemed to me that the salvation of millions of souls depended largely on the economic opportunity to live decently, to live as human beings made in the image and likeness of God. That this is the proper work for a priest, seemed clear to me from the teachings of ethics and moral theology; the moral law governs economic transactions, as well as every other sphere of conduct.[6]

The tributes to Ryan at the testimonial dinner were impressive, including addresses by Supreme Court Justice Felix Frankfurter, Secretary of Labor Frances Perkins, and the Right Reverend Joseph M. Corrigan, Rector of the Catholic University of America. President Roosevelt sent a message that was read at the dinner. It described Ryan well:

> The White House
>
> Washington, May 10, 1939
>
> My Dear Monsignor Ryan:

> Because of your perennially youthful spirit and your zest for service on behalf of your fellowmen—particularly the underprivileged—it is difficult to realize that you have attained the scriptural age of three score and ten.
>
> But your birthday gives your friends a welcome opportunity to break through the reserve which your modesty has built up and to tell you of their appreciation of the good works which you have wrought through all the years of your active career. With voice and pen, you have pleaded the cause of social justice and the right of the individual to happiness through economic security, a living wage, and an opportunity to share in the things that enrich and ennoble human life.
>
> Happily, at 70 you are unwearied in your labors. In extending congratulations, may I express the hope that for long years to come you may continue to labor for those causes of which you have been such an earnest advocate and unselfish champion.
>
> Very sincerely yours,
>
> Franklin D. Roosevelt[7]

Did Ryan's spirituality shine through his reserve? A personal letter at Christmas 1942 from Secretary of Labor Frances Perkins is evidence that Ryan's impact on the political world was deeply grounded in his spirituality. She wrote:

> I think of you often in these troubled days and always with gratitude that you forsaw and prepared the minds and hearts of so many of us in the U.S.A. for the conquest of poverty which it is so obvious is to be the concern of the world, for the next half century.
>
> I know it was your insight growing out of your love of God and understanding and acceptance of His Will that made this leadership possible for you.[8]

Ryan's spirituality and its relationship to his understanding of work—particularly providing work and fair wages for those in need—were grounded in his love for God and his commitment to priesthood as described above. The first essay in this section, by Herwig Arts, S.J., is a discussion of "The Spirituality of John A. Ryan." Arts explores Ryan's spirituality and finds it to be very compatible with that of Ignatius Loyola in his emphasis on "contemplation in the midst of action." Ryan, he contends, found God in a crowd of working-class people rather than in the solitude of a monastery. Ryan loved the concept of "human dignity" and believed that the relationship of human beings to God would develop only if they were allowed to have the basic necessities of life. He always asked the question—how can we help the innocent victim? According to Arts, "Ryan does not constantly rage against the rich but he cares about the poor."

The symposium that follows explores the relationship between spirituality and work emanating from three of the major religious orders in the Catholic Church. Gary Atkinson reflects on "Carmelite Spirituality and Work." He describes work in terms of purification and purgation. In the language of John of the Cross, it is a process of entering into a *night*—actually active and passive nights. However, "work is also a grace, a gift, by means of which we present ourselves and those we encounter" as expressions of the perfect person redeemed in Christ.

Thomas Bausch writes on "Jesuit Spirituality and Work: A Confluence with Catholic Social Thought and Servant Leadership." It complements Herwig Arts's description and analysis of Ryan's spirituality that he presented in Ignatian categories. Bausch reflects on a spirituality of work in the *Spiritual Exercises*, and describes how he believes it comes alive in Catholic social thought, particularly in the writings of Pope John Paul II. He further believes that the concept of *servant leader* as described by Robert Greenleaf in his book by that title allows people to be more specific in implementing Ignatian spirituality in daily work. Greenleaf, who comes out of the Quaker tradition, believes that "the successful manager is a person who knows how to listen, has empathy, works at healing, and is always working at being aware." A Jesuit spirituality of "finding God in all things," as well as the challenge in the *Spiritual Exercises* of "call" to build the Kingdom of God, lay the foundation for an understanding of work as participating in the creative and redemptive action of Christ.

Lastly, Richard Morton offers his synthesis of "Integrating a Franciscan Spirituality of Work into Leadership in the Workplace." He contends that the current challenge is to shatter the "stained glass window" that separates personal spirituality from its application in the work place. The Rule of the Secular Franciscan Order requires: "Let them esteem work as a gift and a sharing in creation, redemption, and service of the human community." The SFO Constitutions state: "For St. Francis, work was a gift and to work was a grace." Morton believes that the spirituality of Francis of Assisi can "help us transform our views of life, work, and vocation by God's grace from isolated categories of activity to integrated aspects of the truly Christian life."

John A. Ryan had a depth of spirituality that allowed him to be a servant leader. His words and work inspired others from various traditions to appreciate the gift of work, and live it in a productive and caring way, particularly with concern for those in need.

Notes

1. John A. Ryan, *Social Doctrine in Action: A Personal History* (New York and London: Harper and Brothers, 1941), 60.

2. John A. Ryan, Diary (October 12, 1898), Archives of the Catholic University of America, Washington, D.C. (Archives hereafter, ACUA.)

3. Ibid., October 13, 1898.

4. Social Doctrine in Action, 30. Emphasis mine.

5. Ibid., 29.

6. "Testimonial to Right Reverend John A. Ryan, D.D. on Occasion of His Seventieth Birthday Anniversary May 25, 1939," 16. ACUA.

7. Ibid., 13.

8. Frances Perkins to John A. Ryan, Christmas 1942. ACUA.

The Spirituality of John A. Ryan

HERWIG ARTS, S.J.

The famous American Benedictine monk and liturgist Virgil Michel once made the remark that Msgr. Ryan showed "too little insistence on the absolute need of the *spiritual* in social reform and on the need of a general spiritual revival.[1] In other words: he deplored a lack of truly priestly spirituality and of outspoken inner life in Ryan's writings. In the same way one of Ryan's former students, Fr. Russell Wilbur, once made the remark to his former teacher: "You are predominantly and almost exclusively an ethical personality." The implicit reproach here again was a lack of dogmatic theology and of spirituality. The question we want to try to answer here is therefore the following one: Was Msgr. Ryan primarily a professor and a moralist, concerned about social and political ethics, or was he above all a priest, whose social writings cannot be understood without an apostolic and religious background? Our answer would consist of two parts. First of all, we want to point to the really evangelical inspiration of all his moral ideas and ethical standpoints. And secondly, we will try to show that his genuine spirituality can be called "a theology of liberation avant la lettre."

In his remarkable book, *Tolstoy or Dostoevsky*, the Jewish scholar George Steiner quotes Berdiaev: "It would be possible to determine two types among men's souls, the one inclined towards the spirit of Tolstoy, the other towards that of Dostoevsky." And Steiner adds that if one wants to know better an intellectual person, one has only to ask that person if he or she prefers Tolstoy's or Dostoevsky's novels. "Press the reader closely and he will choose between them. If he tells you which he prefers and why, you will have penetrated into his true nature."[2] Two different and radically opposed Christian conceptions of human existence confront each other indeed. The first one is called by Steiner "the ethical type"; the second one "the mystical approach of religion." Well, Ryan was clearly much more in line with Tolstoy's spirituality.

The title of Tolstoy's very last book is also very typical for Ryan's attitude in spiritual matters: *"What do we have to do?"* For both Tolstoy and for Ryan, Christ was above all the inspiring example, whose style of life and preaching were in the first place a program of action in favor of the poor, the sick, and the expelled people. Ryan was not so much a missionary or a mystic as a man of action, inspired by Christ's teaching and by what he saw whenever he was in touch with "the least important of Christ's brothers and sisters." (Matt. 25:40)

In Ignatius of Loyola's terminology Ryan was a "contemplativus in action." It was *while* and *because* he was engaged in social and political activities that he felt he was living truly his priesthood. Spirituality was not for him a moment of relaxation or withdrawal toward solitude. But being concerned about the poor, he felt he was in touch with the Lord, who sent and called him to the poor.

"We act according to the way we see things. Our behaviour is a function of our experience," we read in R. Laing's *Politics of Experience*. Ryan was not a workaholic, but a man who saw and experienced something during his contacts with ordinary people. His activities and writings were the result of that inner experience. He found God rather *in* the crowd and *in* the multitude of the working class than in the silence of an inspiring monastery. And, as we know, these are different vocations in Christ's church.

In the journal he kept as a seminarian, studying theology, we read: "The social question is for us in a great part a religious question. . . . Where should the priest be, if not in the midst of this (social) movement, applying the Gospel everywhere? This is his paramount duty, to apply Christ's teaching to the practical aspects of the problems that confront us. . . . He must instill the Gospel doctrines of justice between man and man, of love for the poor and unfortunate. . . .[3]

In his private copy of J. Ireland's book *The Church and Modern Society*, Ryan marked very typically this passage: "It is deplorable that Catholics take refuge in sanctuary and cloister, and leave the bustling, throbbing world with its miseries and sins to the wills of false friends and cunning practitioners. These are days of action! Into the arena, priest and lay-man!"[4]

Ryan himself, as a seminarian, wrote in an article: "The masses will no longer be satisfied today with homilies on the emptiness of human life and the blessedness in store for the beyond the clouds. . . . The here and now have an importance not realized before."[5] For Ryan neither the natural and the supernatural nor the priestly and the moral should be separated. They always go together.

It is true that Ryan in his diaries and writings wrote very little on personal spiritual or inner experiences. We know, however, that he read Pascal, St. Augustine, St. Francis of Sales, and several books on the spirituality and theology of priesthood. Psychologically speaking, however, he was rather an introverted Irish character. Or to put it in the words of his biographer F. Broderick: he remained always "an Irish-American farmboy." In his autobiography Ryan notes: "From 1886 until 1892 I spent practically every day of my summer vacation in the fields—not contemplating nature but *wrestling* with it. But that labour was good for me, physically and spiritually."[6]

According to Ignatius of Loyola the aim of Christian spirituality is ultimately "to find God in all things" (i.e. not only in silence, retreats, ascetical practices, etc. but also in daily life, one's work, concerns, and human contacts). In that context one can say that Ryan found God above all in the problems of social and political morality and commitment. This brings us to a double question. Which sort of morality did Ryan propagate or defend, and in how far is there a real connection to be found between that moral concern and God?

A basic concept for Ryan was the idea of "natural law." A Thomistic idea of which he was very keen and which for centuries has been a fundamental principle in moral theology, even if that "human nature" until recently was mostly understood in a very static way. D. H. Lawrence once made the cynical remark: "If men were as much men as lizards are lizards, then they would be worth looking at." Well, Ryan considered it as his primal task to make it possible for human beings to lead a more human life. The question, however, whether phenomena as abortion, suicide, homosexuality, extramarital sexuality, etc. were to be considered as *normal* human practices or not, did mostly not even arise in the past. However, it is not so easy to define what is "human" and what not. To put it in Teilhand de Chardin's terminology: the process of hominization is not yet finished. Human life on the whole has to be made more human. Ryan in his neo-Thomistic perspection was convinced indeed that the "natural law" makes it perfectly clear for us what is to be called human and what not. In other words: what is in line with God's purpose when he created men in his image and what not.

In order to understand what "human nature" is, Ryan, however—and here he was very modern again—is convinced that one should not only know Thomistic philosophy, but one should also study human sciences, for example, economy, sociology, politics, and history. (It is a pity that Ryan seldom mentions psychology and anthropology in that context.) For Ryan any Christian moral theology remains worthless, unless it applies intelligently to the Christian principles the concepts of social, economic, and civil problems with which a modern person is confronted.

Ryan's main concern was to make it possible for everybody to live in economically and politically "human" conditions. He loved the concept of "human dignity." Provided that somebody lives in decent material conditions, he or she will be able also to live in a religious way. It would be cynical, according to Ryan, to preach about God's goodness or about the importance of the Eucharist, as long as the people concerned have to live in inhuman, "unnatural," or unjust conditions.

In fact Ryan is totally in line here with the theories of the famous American psychologist A. Maslow, who in his book *Motivation and Personality* makes the point that deeper spiritual needs cannot be felt unless the basic primal needs of man are somehow fuifilled. It would indeed be cynical to tell a hungry Jew in a Nazi concentration camp that though he will not get bread or soup today, he will be allowed to listen to a concerto of Beethoven, to visit an art collection, or to participate in a liturgical ceremony. First hunger and thirst have to be satisfied before more spiritual values can fascinate and attract us.

Ryan was convinced that the social and economic conditions in which not only Irish but also many American people had to live in his days were terrible, that is, inhuman or "unnatural." If that was the case in America, that was probably the case almost everywhere else as well. Injustice did cry to heaven. Therefore he advised not to preach about heaven unless you did protest against earthly injustice and above all unless you tried to remedy those unjust conditions.

The concept of "human dignity" was a basic one in Ryan's ethics. Ryan, who in his days was often considered as a revolutionary priest and even a socialist if not a Marxist, felt very relieved when he found the notion of "human dignity" back in the papal encyclical

Quadragesimo anno. He was an orthodox moralist, in line with the papal doctrine.

The reproach that he was a "socialist" was refuted by himself in the book he published together with M. Hillquit: *Socialism, Promise or Menace*. Ryan rejected socialism altogether for mainly three reasons. He was a defender of personalism (and therefore rejected any tendency towards collectivism, which he discovered in most Marxist writings). Secondly he was convinced that any form of Marxism was basically atheistic and often did persecute organized religion. And thirdly, Marxism, so he thought, did propagate sexual freedom and so did undermine marriage.

The second point we want to make in this short exposé is the fact that Ryan can be called a "theologian of liberation" avant la lettre. Moreover he avoided some one-sidednesses (if not errors) that in our days we sometimes encounter in some writings of the "theologians of liberation."

The Belgian theologian Adolphe Gesché, in his book on the problem of evil *Le Mal*, describes the most valuable insights and also some weaknesses of the contemporary theology of liberation. It is a striking fact that all the important insights he enumerates are already to be found in Ryan's works, and above all that the weaknesses Gesché discovered, were avoided by Ryan.

Gesché distinguishes two different traditions or tendencies in Christian theology and spirituality of evil. The first one, which he calls "Paulinian" or "Augustinian" is above all concerned about guilt, penitence, expiation, and confession. The main question here is: who is responsible and guilty? The focus is upon the perpetrator or sinner.

The second type of approach is the one of the books of Job and of the Synoptic Gospels. The accent is here upon the victim. The main question is not: who is to punished and how?, but how can we help the innocent victim? Ryan's theology belongs clearly to the second type. We need a world with more justice, and a world economically better balanced, so that new victims can be avoided. We have to search for the *roots* of evil, not only on the psychological level, but on the sociological, political, and economic level.

Like all theologians of liberation Ryan did not consider evil in the first place as punishment of God but as a challenge that obliges us to fight for a better world. The first moral issue is not: who is guilty?, but why are we obliged to fight against evil? The novelty of Ryan's spiritual approach was his constant care for the victim. Not only charity but first of all justice is required.

In his book *Death of Tragedy*, G. Steiner points out that in a Jewish and Christian perspective "tragedy" is no longer possible, since evil here has a spiritual meaning and the Providence is guiding everything, as opposed to a blind and fatal necessity. Ryan also "defatalized" history. Everything can be cured or at least changed for the better. Salvation is possible. Absolution is thinkable. But salvation for Ryan was not primarily an interior and spiritual reality. The fight against evil has also an economic and political dimension. The situation of the poor has undoubtedly a spiritual meaning: it is a find-spot of God. To paraphrase Bergson: "their existence (i.e. of the poor) is an appeal of God."

Unlike some contemporary theologians of liberation, Ryan does not relapse ultimately into a new theology of guilt, focusing this time not upon individual sexual sins but upon certain social and economic classes. Ryan does not constantly rage against the rich but he cares about the poor. He does not analyze so much the conscience of the rich but the situation of the poor.

And yet all this was done in a theological perspective. In his diary he notes: "I devoted an exceptional amount of time to the various theories and different opinions concerning the effects of original sin." Original sin for him meant: the fact that we find ourselves in a situation we did not want and we do not accept as such. That situation has to be humanized. It is the duty of every Christian to fight against the status quo of an economic and political world, which clearly goes on producing evil effects and unnecessary suffering.

His emphasis upon "original sin" meant among other things that he rejected Rousseau's main slogan: "L'homme est bon mais la société le corrompt."

As a convinced "personalist" Ryan knew that the human person is *not* just good and that it would be only society that has to be cured. Ryan rejected the Marxist determinism as though better social and economic conditions would produce automatically better human individuals. There is such a thing as a fundamental evil, not only in human society but also and above all inside the human soul or psychology.

Ryan rejected Rousseau's romantic idea of "le noble sauvage."

He was by no means a dogmatic theologian, who would have discovered new insights into the dogma of original sin. But, in the words of Fr. John Coleman, Ryan built a bridge between theological ideas and political praxis. That bridge was to be Christian ethics or ethical reflection upon Christian dogma. He was a "go between" from Christian eschatology to political praxis. For him it was evident that our fight against evil had to be more than a fight for better economic conditions and social structures, though he considered the latter as his special field. Not only because of a congenital preference or a spontaneous impulse, but because he strongly felt that the Catholic church had been absent too long in that important field.

In his book *A Testament of Devotion*, the Mormon theologian and spiritual writer Thomas Kelly writes: "Practice comes first in religion, not theory or dogma. And Christian practice is not exhausted in outward deeds. These are the fruits, not the roots. . . . A practicing Christian brings the Light into the world with all its turmoil and its fitfulness and re-creates it (after the pattern seen on the Mount)."[7] It seems to us that Ryan's roots must have been particularly deep—however silent he remained about them—because the fruits were so rich and so unforgettable.

Notes

1. Cf. P. Marx, *The Life and Work of Virgil Michel* (Washington, 1957), 216-17.

2. G. Steiner, *Tolstoy or Dostoevsky* (New York, 1959), 10-11.

3. Cfr., J. Fitzsimoni, "Msgr. J. Ryan, Prophet of Social Justice," *The Clergy Review* (Sept. 1954): 529-30.

4. Cfr., F. Broderick, *Right Reverend New Dealer: John A. Ryan* (New York: Macmillan, 1963), 15.

5. Cfr., *Ibid.*, 23.

6. J. Ryan, *Social Doctrine in Action* (New York: Harper and Brothers, 1941), 39.

7. Th. Kelly, *A Testament of Devotion* (San Francisco, 1992), 11-12.

SYMPOSIUM ON SPIRITUALITY AND WORK

CARMELITE SPIRITUALITY AND WORK

GARY M. ATKINSON

Human beings are creatures. Therefore they are finite, because no creature can be infinite. How obvious, you may say. Well it is, but it is important for the spirituality of work.

Finitude means that our human capacity to love is also finite. We have only a finite amount of human love within us, only so much love to go around. True, our ability to love can and should grow. As long as we are in this life, we are called to become more like God whose love is infinite. Still, at any given time, the amount of love I have for some object X must be subtracted from the amount of love I can give to some other object Y. When Christ says that no one can be a servant of two masters, he was expressing this simple truth.

Does this mean that to the degree I love God I am incapable of loving my neighbor? Well, no. I may love people or things *in* God. I may love some person or some thing because God wants me to love it, and to the degree and in the manner God wants me to love it.

Therefore, there are two kinds of love. There is love of God, persons, or things that is love in and for God. And there is love of God, persons, or things that is not. This latter sort of love is called *attachment*. Because we are finite creatures, the attachments we have at any given time preclude our loving God with our whole heart, soul, mind, and strength.

The doctrine of original sin means that we are conceived and born with attachments. We are born with loves that both are incompatible with love for God and incline us to act in ways contrary to God's loving commands. The task before us, always with the help of God's grace, is to destroy all attachments so that we might become perfect as our heavenly Father is perfect.

The task of destroying the attachments within us is called *detachment*, *purification,* or *purgation*, and it must be completed either in this life or in the next. Without total purgation, we will be incapable of entering God's presence. "Blessed are the pure of heart, for they (and only they) shall see God" (Matt. 5:8). The pure of heart are those of undivided heart, those whose loves have been purged of all attachments. Their loves are directed solely toward God. All else, if it is loved at all, is loved for God's sake and to the degree and in the manner in which God wishes it be loved. To become detached from persons or things, then, is not the same as ceasing to love them at all. It is to cease to love them in a manner contrary to God's will.

St. John of the Cross calls the process of detachment or purification the entering into a *night*. If your are in a room and night falls, the objects in the room do not cease to exist, but they cease to be visible. As long as you remain in darkness, they might as well not exist for all the effect they have on your senses.

The process of detachment has many facets, and John draws two distinctions among the several nights. He distinguishes between the nights of the senses and the nights of the spirit, but this distinction need not concern us. Our purpose is to attend to the contrast between the *active* and the *passive* nights.

The active night is a process that operates in a human manner. A soul in the active night uses its own natural powers, its understanding and will, to purge itself of the attachments that encumber it. Everything proceeds with the help of God's grace, but the manner of proceeding is human or *natural*. I *think* it would be good for me to do this or avoid that, and I *choose* accordingly.

In contrast, the passive nights proceed in a divine or *supernatural* manner. In the passive nights, God acts and we can only submit to his action. The passive nights are both more painful and more effective than the active nights. On the one hand, a soul in the passive nights may be unaware that God is acting on it. The soul may feel lost, even damned, alienated from God, whereas in truth God has never been closer. On the other hand, purifications that God produces in a superhuman mode of operation are more effective than any we could achieve by our human efforts, even those aided by God's grace.

The active nights typically are preliminaries to the passive ones. In the active nights we show God the sincerity of our love by our own efforts, feeble as they may be. When we have brought ourselves as far as we can using our human powers, God himself takes over and completes the process of purification, acting in a completely supernatural fashion in the passive nights. The total process of purification, though, is not linear. It occurs in phases of alternating and mixed activity and passivity in accordance with God's inscrutable providence.

You may well ask, what does all of this have to do with the spirituality of human work. The short answer is, everything. All we do, whether it be work, play, worship, family life, friendship, everything must be viewed ultimately in relation to the love of God and the process of our becoming perfect like him.

Thus, if I say that work must be understood in terms of purification and purgation, I hope I will not be taken to convey any negative attitude toward work. On the contrary, work is a grace, a gift, by means of which we present ourselves and those we encounter as expressions of the perfect person redeemed in Christ.

The Ascent of Mount Carmel is John of the Cross's magisterial treatment of the active nights. The book frightens many with its apparently extreme demands. It is an important text for anyone who would be perfect, but not everyone is ready for its full doctrine. We grow into it as the process of successive purifications begins to take effect on our mind and heart. For those who are ready I offer this quote from the concluding chapter of Part One.

Strive always to prefer,
not that which is easiest,
but that which is most difficult;
not that which is most delectable,
but that which is most unpleasing;
not that which gives most pleasure,
but that which gives least;
not that which is restful,
but that which is wearisome;

not that which is consolation,
but rather that which is disconsolateness;
not that which is greatest,
but that which is least;
not that which is loftiest and most precious,
but that which is lowest and most despised;
not that which is a desire for anything,
but that which is a desire for nothing.

Our daily work provides us with a rich mine of opportunities to practice the active night of the senses. We can consciously set ourselves to choose what is the most difficult, the most unpleasing, what gives least, what is wearisome, lowest, and most despised. In our workaday lives we constantly confront unreasonable people, unfair situations, demanding tasks. We have no choice about that, but we do have the choice of how we respond. We can, as I too often am wont to do, complain, refuse, get down on life, ask "Why me?" We can do this, but we don't have to, or at least not so much. We can, perhaps to our own astonishment, find ourselves slowly growing in holiness, growing in perfection, learning how to behave with that energetic generosity that is the mark of Christ and those closest to him.

Someone once was troubled by the thought that the cross he was obliged to carry as a Christian might be slipping through his fingers. The answer he received might or might not have brought consolation to him. But it is something that applies to every Christian: "When you can no longer hold on to the Cross, the Cross will hold on to you."

At the center of Christ's salvific act is the terrible and terrifying immobility of Christ's body fixed to the Cross. "Do you not know that all of us who have been baptized into Christ Jesus have been baptized into (submerged in) his death?" (Rom. 6:3) And that death was and is and must be a death by crucifixion. "I have been crucified with Christ" writes St. Paul (Gal. 2:20), and this process of crucifixion awaiting every Christian can at times be participated in only by a willing imitation of the immobility of the Crucified Lord.

Therefore, although our work provides us with numerous opportunities for energetic activity, it also presents us with occasions where precisely nothing can be done and our purification must proceed passively and not actively. Of course, acquiring the ability to distinguish the two sorts of situation is an all-important task calling for much thought, prayer, and counsel (spiritual and otherwise). And the stance of resignation and acceptance can too often serve as a cover for a selfish, lazy, or cowardly, refusal to undertake the duty assigned us. Nonetheless, occasions do arise where there just isn't anything to be done, and God's will is fulfilled in us by our patient endurance.

"Always be prepared to make a defense to any one who calls you to account for the hope that is in you" (1 Pet. 3:15), St. Peter instructs us. The fatigue, boredom, and unpleasantness commonly associated with our working lives are often inescapable realities, but they must also be seen as precious gifts. They are never to be repeated opportunities for growing in love for God and neighbor by progressively detaching ourselves from all that is not holy.

Jesuit Spirituality and Work: A Confluence with Catholic Social Thought and Servant Leadership

THOMAS A. BAUSCH

Introduction

The theme of this paper is that servant leadership as developed by that insightful Quaker, Robert K. Greenleaf, provides us with a philosophy of management that, combined with a deeply personal spirituality of work as drawn from Ignatian traditions, can bring Catholic social thought, so beloved by John Ryan, alive in the remainder of the twentieth-century and in the early twenty-first-century workplace. There is a powerful confluence of these three themes—Ignatian spirituality, Catholic social thought, and servant leadership—that provides us with the philosophy of management for today that is not only deeply moral and ethical, it is also deeply practical as we examine the issues of the day.

An Ignatian Spirituality of Work: Its Source

All that is Ignatian has its source in the *Spiritual Exercises*. The *Exercises* are by no means a book to be read, but rather a way, a road map, a set of exercises to help one find God in one's life and determine the direction one should take in response to the movements of the spirit.

They are based on Ignatius's own very personal experiences as he moved in his life from being a soldier/playboy to a person totally focused on Christ and doing the will of God. To quote a modern translation/interpretation, "The structure of the *Exercises* has the purpose of leading a person to a true spiritual freedom."[1] The purpose of this freedom, in the words of Ignatius, is to "enable each of us to become the fullness of the person we are and achieve our end of eternal happiness."[2] To quote Fleming's translation again: "God freely created us so that we might know, love, and serve Him in this life and be happy with Him forever."[3] God's purpose in creating us was "to draw forth from us a response of love and service here on earth, so that we may attain our goal of everlasting happiness with Him in heaven."[4]

The idea that we exist for God and others is the very foundational thought in these *Exercises*. The next key idea is that all that is created is good. The third idea is that we are indifferent to all that is less than God until we clearly understand the opportunity that will allow us to serve God best, including our work, and then we take it on with a passion.

In an age where we question meaning and purpose, in an age of rapid change and transition, it is necessary to grasp with Ignatius that God has created every person with desires that allow us to live a purposeful life, filled with meaning, based on love. It is through all that we do in marriage, study, religious life, recreation, and most certainly the work that we do, that we become truly ourselves with a deep sense of purpose, if we are always seeking to achieve the fullness of God's will for us—His love for us. This is not a selfish focus on "meeting all my needs and being all that I can be." This authentic growth of self is always based in serving others; it is always based on playing our particular role in the entire Paschal Mystery and the history of salvation.

This is the profound and purposeful nature of work—our own personal salvation, our serving of others, and the building of the Kingdom. We who are managers and leaders achieve our dignity and purpose through this work of management. Through the creation of vision it is the purpose of our work as managers and leaders to enable this sense of purposefulness to come alive in each person who works for us and with us. It is our obligation to all who have a stake in our organizations (the common goal) to ensure that this source of sustainable competitive advantage is created.

This deep meaningfulness comes alive in and through Catholic social thought and is captured by Pope John Paul II when he says that "we are the subject of our work."[5] It is through our work that we develop our personality, our full person, in community with and in service to others. This dignity and purpose that we achieve through our work, and the very necessity for us to be fully what God desires, is a forceful theme in all the Catholic social thought, in the documents on the church and on the laity in Vatican II and most especially, in terms of our era, in John Paul's work, especially *Centesimus annus*,[6] and in scores of presentations to many audiences.[7]

If work's purpose is to serve an individual's finality in dignity, each of us has a right to work. This purposefulness of work, and ultimate tie to our salvation, explains, among other things, why the human must have precedence over capital or any of the other factors of production.

Those called to the work of leadership and management will find that this Ignatian vision of work, which is also the depth of Catholic social thought, as articulated for the last hundred years (at least), especially in the work of John Paul, is given flesh by Greenleaf, who comes out of a Quaker tradition, in the concept of the *servant leader* as noted above. Spears, who probably has the best understanding of the complete body of work by Greenleaf, notes that one characteristic of the *servant leader* is a commitment to the growth of people.

> *Servant leaders* believe that people have an intrinsic value beyond their tangible contributions as workers. As such, *servant leaders* are deeply committed to the personal, professional, and spiritual growth of each and every individual within the institution. In practice, this can mean making available funds for personal and professional development, taking a personal interest in employees' ideas and suggestions, encouraging worker involvement in decision-making, actively assisting laid-off workers to find other employment, etc.[8]

The Concept of a Calling

The spiritual purposefulness of work in Ignatian spirituality is greatly deepened in his meditation on the call of Christ the King. The foundation of meaningfulness found in the Kingdom meditation is further developed in his reflection on the "The Two Standards" where the concept of call is further developed. The transcendent nature of our work comes through clearly in these two meditations. Flesh is given to the biblical idea of, "I have called you by name." That is, His call goes out to the whole of humankind, yet He specifically calls each person in a particular way. The dynamic of this quiet yet purposeful call to serve freely is very much a part of the imagery of the meditation on The Two

Standards. The battlefield imagery of Satan is conveyed with words like tempt, deceive, issue a summons, working for riches, honor, and pride. The imagery of Christ is developed using words like call, invite, share, sense of purpose, willingness to sacrifice for cause. Although the term is not used, the idea of "sharing of vision" clearly comes through both as a way to give meaning to personal work, but also as a function of true community in work.

It is this powerful acceptance of the call to the Kingdom that is the tie between the individual and community. The call is always very particular and special, "I called you by name," but it is done in community and to serve the community. This Kingdom begins in the here and now of our time, place, and circumstances.

In the logic of Catholic social thought the fulfillment of the call is not only the manifestation of the dignity of the human person, but the link to the promotion of the common good that "is the sum total of all those conditions of social living—economic, political, cultural—which would make it possible for women and men readily and fully to achieve the perfection of their humanity."[9]

Ignatian spirituality is a powerful foundation for combining these two constant themes of Catholic social thought—the dignity of the human person and the promotion of the common good. No one of us can fully respond to our call or fully be the subject of our work or develop as human persons except in and through serving the Kingdom, that is serving others through the promotion of the common good.

For a wonderful biblical reflection on all of these ideas, I urge a reading of the first six chapters of the Book of Nehemiah. This is also a powerful lead-in to help us to understand that what Greenleaf is saying is deeply spiritual. Nehemiah was a simple cupbearer for the King who felt the call to be a leader and who was willing to pay the cost of tremendous opposition that he was to face as a leader. Nehemiah's goal was to rebuild Jerusalem and fight the deplorable conditions that the Prophet Malachi describes (Mal. 1-2). However, as is shown as the story unfolds, this could not have been done without the concrete communal structures that Nehemiah provided. He, in the face of threats on his life, built a communal structure that allowed individuals to grow as persons of dignity as they contributed to the common good.

One should also note that Nehemiah did his work through use of the powerful Quaker technique of longterm teaching by persuasion. Greenleaf very clearly understood that part of the role of the *servant leader* in the building of community among those who work in business and other institutions. As a matter of fact, the desire to lead through institutions was a driving force early in his career. Understanding the tie between organization as community and the fulfillment of persons has powerful potential importance in today's world of total quality management, flatter organizations, and extensive delegation. It is the essence of the empowerment of the individual, essential to making the flat organization perform.

• • •

The whole dynamic of Ignatian spirituality is designed to help one make a decision and to focus on God's call. Once identified, this great privilege of playing our role in the Paschal Mystery places a huge obligation on each of us to select the means and to do the hard work necessary to achieve our ends with competence.

This is also a theme in Catholic social thought and one developed quite fully by Pope John Paul II. In an address to Spanish workers and businessmen in 1982 he said:

> The logical consequence (of work having a powerful meaning) is that we all have the duty to do our work well. If we wish to realize ourselves properly, we may not avoid the hard work necessary to become competent.[10]

The concept of *servant leadership* also has a reciprocal that I can only describe as conscientious and competent followership, and this is fully understood by Greenleaf, even if from a different tradition using a different vocabulary. But this is the power that *servant leadership* can release. It is the power released by the truly competent *servant leader* who is able to generate shared vision in an organization. The power of a shared vision in which there is ownership on the part of all parties can never be duplicated by any sort of motivation that is derived from self gain. It is the key to sustainable competitive advantage.

Reflection and The Spirituality of Work

The final aspect of the Ignatian spirituality of work on which I wish to focus is prayer and reflection. I believe that to develop this fully one must also relate leisure to both prayer and work, for the three are an integrated whole, but I leave this to another day and the work of Dr. Michael Naughton. For Ignatius, work flows out of one's prayer life. Work as vocation is truly the contemplative in action. Ignatius in no way saw prayer as an end in itself, he saw it as a means of communion with God. He was a man of balance after experiencing extremes in several directions. He insisted on a balance between prayer and the obligations of one's duties, rest, nutrition, etc. If he were alive today, he would insist on appropriate weight, cholesterol levels, blood pressure, and so on, without making these items little gods. He would simply ask, "all else being equal, how do I best serve God and neighbor?" But the key aspect of prayer life that he always insisted upon, no matter the circumstances, and vital if we are to relate prayer and work, is the examine of conscious or examine of consciousness, or to release the baggage of words, what John Haughey calls the "Backwards Looking Prayer."[11] If our work is to have meaning, as is true with the rest of our lives, it must be examined daily as well as periodically for long periods of time, as we set goals and directions. This is true be we managers, professionals, or blue-collar workers, no matter what our work. Daily we must ask, "Where did I find God and neighbor today and serve well? Where did I not find God and neighbor and not serve well?"

Pope John Paul's works on the integration of prayer and work are many and profound. The spirit of his thinking is captured in a homily he delivered on July 7, 1980 entitled "Action and Contemplation Support Each Other in our Daily Lives." He was reflecting on the Martha and Mary gospel story.

> And since this year is the Fifteenth Centenary of the birth of St. Benedict, let us recall his famous motto: "Pray and work," *Ora et labora!* These words contain a whole program, not of opposition but of synthesis, not of contradiction but of the fusion of two equally important elements.
>
> The result is a very concrete lesson for us which can be expressed as a question: to what extent are we able to see in contemplation and prayer a moment of real impact for our daily tasks? And, vice versa, to what extent are we able to strengthen our work to its very core with a leavening communion with the Lord? These questions can serve as an examination of conscience and become a stimulus for a renewal of our daily life, which will be at the same time more contemplative and more active.[12]

This talk was delivered to workers, not executives. Pope John Paul has spoken similarly to executives and professional workers. I note this for it is essential to provide all, including knowledge and professional workers, adequate time to balance their lives. The fusion of these two equally important elements must take place. The dependency of careerism including the symptoms of workaholism of eighty and more hours a week, are more destructive of the human person, since they grow out of pride, than the dependency of alcohol, drugs, sex, or tobacco. This dependency destroys both person and organization. Without judging the man, we see the end result in the tragedy of Peter Grace.

The need for reflection is absolutely essential to the concept of servant leadership and all of the ideas of Greenleaf. "Listening coupled with regular periods of reflection, are essential to the growth of the servant-leader."[13] This comes through in Greenleaf's concepts of awareness, persuasion, contemplation, and foresight, for all require reflection.

Notes

1. David L. Fleming, *Modern Spiritual Exercises: A Contemporary Reading of the Spiritual Exercises of Saint Ignatius* (Garden City, N.Y.: Image, 1983), 15.

2. Ibid., 20.

3. Ibid., 22.

4. Ibid., 33.

5. John Paul II, *On Human Work,* 19.

6. John Paul II, *Centesimus Annus* (Washington, D.C.: U.S. Catholic. Conf. 1991).

7. Robert Kennedy, Michael Naughton, and Gary Atkinson, *The Dignity of Work: John Paul II Speaks to Managers and Workers* (Lanhem, Md.: University Press of America, 1994).

8. Larry C. Spears, "Introduction: Servant Leadership and the Greenleaf Legacy," and Spears, Larry C., *Reflections on Leadership (*New York: John Wiley, 1995), 5.

9. Peter J. Henriott, Edward P. DeBerri, and Michael J. Schultheis, *Catholic Social Teaching* (Maryknoll, N.Y.: Orbis, 1992), 8.

10. Kennedy et.al., op. cit., 120.

11. John Haughey, S.J., presentation on "God at Work at Work," Peter Favre Forum, Milwaukee, College of Business Administration, Marquette University, May 1995.

12. Kennedy et. al., op. cit., 122.

13. Robert K. Greenleaf, *Servant Leadership* (New York: Paulist Press, 1977), 13.

INTEGRATING A FRANCISCAN SPIRITUALITY OF WORK INTO LEADERSHIP IN THE WORKPLACE

RICHARD MORTON, S.F.O.

I contend that St. Francis of Assisi was, in effect, a butterfly who spread his wings in the early 1200s and created currents of spirituality that continue to affect the world even to this very day.

Early in his conversion experience, while praying before an old icon of a crucifix in the abandoned and dilapidated Church of St. Damian, Francis had a most unusual experience. The painted image of the risen Christ crucified moved its lips and spoke. Calling him by name, Christ said: "Francis, go, repair my house, which, as you see, is falling completely to ruin."[1]

Francis, interpreting the command literally, began the arduous work of piling stone upon stone to repair the foundation and the walls of the building where he had been praying. It wasn't until later that the full understanding and impact of the words spoken from the cross began to penetrate and enliven his heart. The words, as he later realized, referred to the universal church that Christ "won for himself at the price of his own blood" (Acts 20, 28).[2] The real meaning of the message was, "Francis, go, rebuild my Church . . . "

The words spoken by Christ from the San Damiano cross, when understood in as broad a context as St. Francis grew to understand them, are a universal call to action to rebuild and to reinvigorate the church as a sign pointing toward the realization of the kingdom of God on earth.

After nearly eight centuries, this command to rebuild the church continues to resound around the globe.

I propose that it is through the leadership[3] activities of the laity in the workplace,[4] when done in collaboration with the sacred vocation of the ministers of the church, that the rebuilding of the church will most effectively be carried out. However, this cannot happen until the "stained-glass window," which presently separates personal spirituality from its application in the work place, is shattered.

Contained in a Franciscan spirituality of work are the seeds to begin the process of shattering the "stained-glass window" and rebuilding the church. The integration of a Franciscan spirituality of work into the workplace is most appropriate because of its heritage. It has always has been a basic tenet of Franciscan spirituality that the world is the cloister[5] and therefore there never have been any boundaries between the dimensions of a Franciscan's spirituality and any other aspect of their life. This concept gives permission and, we could say, demands that they carry their spirituality with them wherever they go, and yes, even into the workplace.

St. Francis is probably the world's best known, most recognized, and respected saint. Yet it is difficult to imagine that a spirituality of work could evolve from a saint immortalized all too frequently as a concrete yard ornament with a bird perched on his shoulder and several wild animals gazing at him admiringly. This over-romanticized caricature of the person of Francis could lead one to believe that Francis wasn't much of a man at all, but some lyric, almost mythic figure only in love with nature and the animals. Quite to the contrary however, Francis was a man of multiple spiritual insights who left a legacy that continues to impact the world in a profound and meaningful way.

Quite probably, Francis was not born with the best of work habits. His father was a prosperous cloth merchant who wanted nothing but the best for his favorite son and, as one might imagine, was very generous toward him. As a young man, Francis was more preoccupied with living the life of a troubadour and becoming a gallant knight than with working for his father. In fact, he never did apply himself to his father's business. After his conversion and the gathering of some early followers, Francis became serious about work, but it was now the work of his heavenly Father.

Francis quickly learned that work was holy and provided a pathway to achieving sanctity. In the midst of the hard-working townsfolk, Francis and the first friars devoted themselves to the task of sanctifying daily labor and bringing it back to the right relationship with God. The true meaning and value of work had been destroyed by love of gain and personal ambition.[6]

There were practically no limitations to where his brothers, the friars worked or the type of work they did. Every field of activity was open to them, including intellectual work.[7] The only prerequisites were that the work be directed toward the community rather than the individual, the work be carried out faithfully and with a sense of dedication as the Rule required, and that the work not destroy a spirit of prayer and devotion to God.[8]

A Franciscan Spirituality of Work

A Franciscan spirituality of work evolves from three fundamental concepts of an underlying Franciscan spirituality, namely, a focus on the humanity of Christ who is recognized especially in the poor; a sense of the mystery of God experienced in generous, creative love; and a distinctive familial understanding of the created world.[9] Franciscans recognize the world as good and as a gift from a loving creator.

The foundation for an articulation of a Franciscan spirituality of work for the layperson is contained in the Rule and Constitutions of the Secular Franciscan Order (SFO).[10]

The Rule states:

> Let them esteem work both as a gift and as a sharing in the creation, redemption, and service of the human community.[11]

The Constitutions further develop the concept of work.

> For St. Francis, work was a gift and to work was a grace. Daily work is not only the means of livelihood, but the opportunity to serve God and neighbor as well as a way to develop one's own personality. In the conviction that work is a right and a duty and that every form of occupation deserves respect, the brothers and sisters should commit themselves to collaborate so that all persons may have the possibility to work and so that working conditions may always be more humane.[12]

While these words were written for the members of the Secular Franciscan Order, their application is universal in nature. They provide the basis for a spirituality of work that can be followed by any layperson living in the secular world seeking to more effectively integrate their personal spirituality into the work place.

Beginning with the concept of human work as pure gift given to us by our creator, it is our unmerited opportunity to reflect the image of Jesus, who, by working as a humble carpenter and itinerant preacher, joined in the stream of work initiated by his Father at the beginning of time.

Work, as an unmerited gift, is effective for our growth and ongoing conversion as followers of Jesus and is therefore a grace contributing to our sanctification. In his Rule for the friars, Francis stated very emphatically, "Those brothers, to whom the Lord has given the grace of working, should do their work faithfully. . . ."[13]

The need for human work is imbedded into our very nature. Even before the fall of humanity as recorded in the poetry of the story of creation, "The Lord God took the man and settled him in the garden of Eden, to cultivate and care for it" (Gen. 2:15). The invitation to cultivate and care for the garden, this work, was part of God's mystery of generous, creative love.

The garden is replete with a treasury of all that is necessary for the further creative development of our home on this planet. Everything has been provided: Brother Sun, Sister Moon and the stars, Brother Wind, Sister Water, Brother Fire, and Sister Mother Earth.[14] We, as Sisters and Brothers of Creation, have been endowed with the capacity to use our skills and abilities to combine, modify, and adapt these resources through the gift of work. It is through this work that God provides us the opportunity to become cocreators.

The cocreative capacity with which we have been endowed is also evident in the arts, music, literature, the sciences, the various structures of society that regulate the relationships between human beings, and other arenas of human consciousness. These all serve to enliven the human spirit and add meaning to our existence.

Our human work not only provides an opportunity for us to be cocreators but also to be "co-redeemers." Christ came to ". . . make all things new" (Rev. 21:5). During his ministry on earth, he accomplished the redemption of humankind. However, there continue to be areas that need to be made new, to be set free, and, in essence, to be redeemed. We, as the Mystical Body of Christ, continue his presence in the world and his ministry of ongoing redemption.

Franciscan spirituality recognizes the face of the crucified Christ in the poor and the marginalized, the suffering, and the lonely. This realization provides the motivation to apply our creative energies and resources to relieve the distress and deprivation of the all too many people who are in need. As stated in the Constitution on the Church in the Modern World, "Indeed, we hold that through labor [work] offered to God, man is associated with the redemptive work of Jesus Christ."[15]

With this in mind, the Christian is challenged to be of service to others. We are to be of the same spirit as Christ, who Matthew defines as ". . . the son of Man who has come, not to be served by others, but to serve. . ." (Matt. 20, 28). In the spirit of universal kinship, we serve others by our work. Work unites us with our brothers and sisters around the world. Our collaborative efforts to be of service to one another by our work provides the goods and services needed by the world community to sustain and enhance its existence as the creative expression of God.

The fathers of the Second Vatican Council stated in the Constitution on the Church in the Modern World that, "[Jesus Christ] conferred an eminent dignity on labor when at Nazareth He worked with his own hands. From this there follows for every person the duty of working faithfully and also the right to work."[16] Francis knew that all should work. Those that could work but chose not to, were, in effect, stealing from those that did work. The following story deals with the brother who never worked.

> . . . and yet [he] ate more than several at table. When the saint [Francis] observed that he was a friend of the belly, one who shared the fruits without sharing the labor, he once said to him: "Go your way, brother fly, for you want to eat the sweat of your brothers and to do nothing in God's work. You are like brother drone who wants to be first to eat the honey, though he does not do the work of the bees."[17]

If work is a duty then to work is a right. For there must be opportunities for a person to work so the duty to work can be fulfilled. When there is a scarcity of work, we are to be concerned enough about the welfare of our brothers and sisters to do whatever is necessary to provide meaningful employment. For without work, it is not possible to confront a primary reality of living in the secular world, namely, that work is the means to provide the basic human necessities such as food, shelter, clothing, health care, and education, to name a few. In addition, there are other needs that, while not necessities in the strictest sense, are still desirable and humanizing.

In providing for our own livelihood, however, consideration must be given to the needs of the common good. Work is not meant to be a means by which we maximize our wealth and possessions at the expense of others. It is an opportunity to practice the virtue of moderation out of a concern for the poor in whose face we find Christ.

Integral to providing a means of livelihood is the concept of a just remuneration for the work accomplished. The parallel concern is for the remuneration to be earned by a contribution of the appropriate amount of work effort. Both are a matter of justice.

There is another sense to the meaning of the word livelihood and that is the sense of liveliness, to be more fully alive, to be more fully human. From this alternate meaning, we can recognize that livelihood is not only measured in terms of possessions and dollars. It is also measured in terms of personal identity, self-esteem, self-worth, and personal growth. These qualities are of critical importance to the overall well-being of the individual. Work should contribute to whatever makes a person more human and not be demeaning.

In the distinctive familial understanding of the world of creation, it is an injustice to our sisters and brothers to show disrespect to an individual just because of the type of work she/he does. This is especially true when disrespect is shown to the poor and the marginalized of our society who, too often, have the least desirable of jobs. James R. Jennings, Associate Director, Campaign for Human Development, comments on Pope John Paul II's encyclical on work, *Laborem exercens*, as follows:

> The ancient world put people into classes according to their work. Manual work, considered unworthy of free men, was given to slaves. Christians changed all of this by taking the Gospel as their point of departure. The one who, while being God, became like everyone else in all things, did manual work at a carpenter's bench. This is the eloquent expression of the "Gospel of work": the value of work is not measured by the kind of work, but by the fact that the one who does it is a person.[18]

Out of respect for the person of Christ reflected in all workers, our places of work should be places of safety, comfort, and convenience appropriate to the type of work being done. It is the responsibility of all to work together in an effort to obtain the best working conditions possible.

In summary, St. Francis esteemed work as a gift from a benevolent and loving creator. A centerpiece of a Franciscan spirituality of work is the humanity of Christ as reflected in the worker. In essence, workers are in collaboration with their coworker and brother, Jesus Christ, in continuing the creative-redemptive process.

Personal Reflections

It is appropriate that I share with you some of the personal experiences of my life as a secular Franciscan who has attempted to integrate a Franciscan spirituality of work into his work environment.

Presently retired, I was formerly an electrical engineer by profession and spent my entire career with one large, multinational corporation. During the last fifteen years of my career, I served as an engineering manager/middle-manager. Although my position was not at a level to sway corporate policy to any significant extent, there were always opportunities to affect decisions and activities within my area of influence and responsibility. Each of us has a circle of influence at any particular time. This is the area in our life where our actions, beliefs, and credibility have the most influence and to which the Lord calls us to stewardship. From the Franciscan perspective, this is the concrete reality where we can go "from gospel to life and life to the gospel."[19]

While employed, I always looked on my tenure with the company as that of one being self-employed. As a manager, I behaved as though I owned the business of the group I managed. This gave me a mind-set of interdependence. I told those working with me that we could do anything we needed to do to be successful as long as it was moral, ethical, and legal. Within these parameters, we were able to assemble a world-class organization while finding opportunities to support policies and programs reflecting the gospel way of life. I had no qualms about seeking out and hiring persons of ethnic or racial minority groups or who had some type of disability. Some of the best employees I ever hired were in these categories.

I found that many corporate policies were based on the best of Christian principles. As a Christian-Franciscan manager, I felt it was my duty to sensitize my coworkers to their value. Several years ago a program to promote the appreciation of diverse cultures and a diverse workforce made its way through the organization. I thought the initiative was excellent and volunteered to become one of the primary instructors for the program. The effort to promote high ethical standards in all phases of the business as well as the exercise of proper stewardship for nature through recycling efforts are two other programs that I was able to promote. There were also opportunities to encourage the support of worthwhile charitable fund drives such as United Way and the Food Share program. Three or four times our group raised the most money even though we were one of the smaller groups in the building.

Perhaps the greatest challenge I faced as a manager was honoring and enforcing the union contract. As far as I was concerned, the union contract with all of its arbitration decisions was morally and legally binding. Most of my peer managers did not hold similar feelings. There were many times when it was to our department's disadvantage to keep all the agreements. Nevertheless, nearly all the grievances served on our department were resolved within the department without the need to proceed to the next step of an arbitration hearing. Very few disputes ended up in arbitration. My goal was to set an example for the more strident, anti-union managers.

Fortunately, there was never a situation in my career when I was expected to violate any of my own personal standards or values. However, this does not mean that I agreed with every company policy statement or decision. There were times and circumstances where the practice of benign neglect of some directives was appropriate and necessary if I was to conduct my work life according to gospel values.

Conclusion

It is impossible to fully develop a Franciscan spirituality of work and especially its application to leadership in the workplace in this short a paper. However, I have attempted to summarize my understanding of the Franciscan vision of the topic and provide a few examples from my own life where my work was touched by their influence. The spirituality of Francis as passed down through the centuries contains the wisdom and the power to help us transform our views of life, work, and vocation by God's grace from isolated categories of activity into integrated aspects of the truly Christian life. The realization of a loving, creating Father gifting each of us with our brother and sister creatures as helpers and signposts to the suffering and risen Christ can redeem and enliven the world around us. But we must embrace Francis's message and put it into practice. Let me refer to the admonition of St. Francis to his followers in regard to working for the kingdom of God. "My brothers, we must begin to serve our Lord and God. Until now we have done very little."[20]

Notes

1. "Il Celano, 10," *St. Francis of Assisi, Writings and Early Biographies: English Omnibus of the Sources for the Life of St. Francis,* Marion A. Habig ed. (Chicago: Franciscan Herald Press, 1973), 370.

2. Ibid., 371

3. Ibid., 1.

4. *Lumen Gentium*, 36, *The Documents of Vatican II*, (New York: Guild Press, 1966), 63.

5. From *Sacrum Commercium*, written circa 1227:

Taking her [Lady Poverty] to a certain hill, they [the brothers] showed her the whole world, as far as she could see, and said: "This, Lady, is our cloister." "Sacrum Commercium, 63," *Omnibus*, 1593.

6. A. Gemelli, *The Franciscan Message to the World* (London, 1934), 44.

7. "To Brother Anthony, my bishop, Brother Francis gives greeting: It is agreeable to me to have you read sacred Theology to the brothers, so long as over this study they do not extinguish the spirit of prayer and devotion, as is contained in the rule" Chronicle of the 24 Generals, #55, *The Words of St. Francis*, James Meyer, O.F.M. (Chicago: Franciscan Herald Press, 1952), 62.

8. Cajetan Esser, O.F.M. and Englebert Grace, O.F.M., *Loves Reply*, Ignatius Brady, O.F.M., trans. (Chicago: Franciscan Herald Press, 1963), 219-20.

9. Zachary Hayes, O.F.M., Keynote Presentation, First Joint Conference of the Franciscan Federation and Franciscan Friars Conference, Anaheim, California, August 22, 1995.

10. Laypeople, deacons, and diocesan priests are members of this portion of the Franciscan family.

11. Article XVI, *Rule of the Secular Franciscan Order* (National Fraternity of the Secular Franciscan Order (SFO), 1615 Vine Street, Cincinnati, OH, 45210), 21.

12. Article 21, *Constitutions* (National Fraternity of the Secular Franciscan Order (SFO), 1615 Vine Street, Cincinnati, OH, 45210), 7.

13. Rule of the Order of Friars Minor, Chapter 5. *The Rule and the General Constitutions of the Order of Friars Minor* (The Franciscan OFM Conference of North America, 1988), 6.

14. See THE CANTICLE OF BROTHER SUN above.

15. *Constitution on the Church in the Modern World*, 67. (Washington, D.C.: National Catholic Welfare Conference, 1965), 71.

16. Ibid.

17. "II Celano, 75," *Omnibus*, 426.

18. "An Outline of *On Human Work*, II, 6," James R. Jennings, Associate Director, Campaign for Human Development.

19. Article IV, *SFO Rule*, 9.

20. “Bonaventure, Major Life, XIV, 1,” *Omnibus*, 737.

Bibliography of Works by and about John Augustine Ryan

COMPILED BY BETTY BIGELBACH

Books

A Living Wage: Its Ethical and Economic Aspects. New York: Macmillan Co., 1906, 1920.

Francisco Ferrer, Criminal Conspirator. St. Louis: B. Herder Book Co., 1911.

Alleged Socialism of the Church Fathers. St. Louis: B. Herder Book Co., 1913.

Socialism: Promise or Menace? Morris Hillquit, coauthor. New York: Macmillan Co., 1914.

Distributive Justice: The Right and Wrong of Our Present Distribution of Wealth. New York: Macmillan Co., 1916; revised 1927, 1942.

The Church and Socialism and Other Essays. Washington: The University Press, 1919.

Social Reconstruction. New York: Macmillan Co., 1920.

The Church and Labor. Joseph Husslein, coauthor. New York: Macmillan Co., 1920.

The State and the Church. Moorhouse F. X. Miller, coauthor. New York: Macmillan Co., 1922.

Declining Liberty and Other Papers. New York: Macmillan Co., 1927.

The Catholic Church and the Citizen. New York: Macmillan Co., 1928.

Questions of the Day. Boston: Stratford Co., 1931.

A Better Economic Order. New York: Harper and Brothers., 1935.

Seven Troubled Years, 1930-1936: A Collection of Papers on the Depression and on Problems of Recovery and Reform. Ann Arbor: Edward Bros., Inc., 1937.

Catholic Principles of Politics. Francis J. Bohland, coauthor. (Revised edition of *The State and the Church*.) New York: Macmillan Co., 1940, 1952.

Social Doctrine in Action: A Personal History. New York: Harper and Bros., 1941.

Pamphlets

Henry George and Private Property. New York: Columbus Press., 1910.

The Church and Interest-Taking. St. Louis : B. Herder Book Co., 1910.

Minimum Wage by Legislation. St. Louis, Mo.: Central Bureau of the German Catholic Verein, 1911.

Social Reform on Catholic Lines. New York: Columbus Press, 1913.

Family Limitation, and The Church and Birth Control. New York: Paulist Press, 1916, 1921.

Catholic Church vs Socialism. New York: New York Evening Mail, 1918.

Bishop's Program of Social Reconstruction : A General Review of the Problems and Survey of Remedies. Washington, D.C.: National Catholic Welfare Conference, 1919.

Catholic Doctrine on the Right of Self-government. New York: Paulist Press, 1919.

Capital and Labor. Washington, D.C.: National Catholic Welfare Council, 1920.

Denver Tramway Strike. Denver Commission of Religious Forces, 1921.

A Catechism of the Social Question. New York: Paulist Press, 1921.

The Christian Doctrine of Property. New York: Paulist Press, 1923.

Supreme Court and the Minimum Wage. New York: Paulist Press, 1923.

The Proposed Child Labor Amendment. New York: National Child Labor Committee, c.1924.

Industrial Democracy from a Catholic Viewpoint. Washington, D.C.: Rossi-Bryn Co., 1925.

Human Sterilization. Washington, D.C.: National Catholic Welfare Conference, 1927.

International Ethics. Ethics Committee, co-author. Washington, D.C.: Catholic Association for International Peace, 1928, 1942.

The Ethics of Public Utility Valuation. Washington, D.C.: National Popular Government League, 1928.

Foreign Policy Association. The Vatican-Italian Accord, discussed by Count Carlo Sforza, Charles Marshall, John A. Ryan. 116th New York Luncheon Discussion, March 16, 1929. New York: Foreign Policy Association, 1929 (Pamphlet #56).

Unemployment. What Can Be Done About It? Washington, D.C.: Social Action Department, National Catholic Welfare Conference, 1929.

Equal Rights Amendment in Relation to Protective Legislation for Women. Washington, D.C.: National Catholic Welfare Conference, 1930.

Moral Aspects of Sterilization. Washington, D.C. : National Catholic Welfare Conference, 1930.

Catholic Principles and the Present Crisis. Washington, D.C.: Catholic Conference on Industrial Problems, 1932.

The Catholic Teaching on Our Industrial System. Washington, D.C.: National Council of Catholic Men. 1930, 1934, 1939.

Shall the NRA Be Scrapped? Washington, D.C.: Catholic Conference on Industrial Problems, 1934.

Roosevelt Safeguards America. New York: National Democratic Committee, 1936.

The Relation of Religion to Communism, Fascism, and Democracy/ Catholicism. New York: American Sociological Society, 1937.

The Constitution and Catholic Industrial Teaching, New York: Published for the Social Action Dept, National Catholic Welfare Conference by the Paulist Press, 1937.

Relation of Catholicism to Fascism, Communism, and Democracy. Washington, D.C.: National Catholic Welfare Conference, 1938.

Can Unemployment Be Ended? Washington, D.C.: American Association for Economic Freedom, 1940.

The Obligation of Catholics to Promote Peace, Washington, D.C.: 1940.

The Citizen, the Church and the State. New York: Paulist Press 1941.

American Democracy vs Racism, Communism. New York: Paulist Press, 1941.

Original Sin and Human Misery. New York: Paulist Press, 1942.

International Post-War Reconstruction. Washington, D.C.: Social Action Dept., National Catholic Welfare Conference, 1942.

The Norm of Morality. Washington, D.C.: National Catholic Welfare Conference, 1944, 1949.

Articles

"The Ethics of Speculation." *International Journal of Ethics* 12 (April 1902): 335-47.

"Unpaid Laborers of America." *Catholic World* 81 (May 1905): 143-56.

"The Method of Teleology in Ethics." *New York Review* 2 (July-August 1906): 409-29.

"Is the Modern Spirit Anti-Religious?" *Catholic World* 85 (May 1907): 183-93.

"Fallacy of Bettering One's Position." *Catholic World* 86 (November 1907): 145-56.

"Is Stock Watering Immoral?" *International Journal of Ethics* 18 (January 1908): 151-67.

"The Wage Contract and Strict Justice." *Catholic University Bulletin* 14 (January 1908): 50-56.

"Cost of Christian Living." *Catholic World* 86 (February 1908): 575-88.

"The Study of Social Problems in the Seminary." *Catholic Education Association Bulletin* 5 (November 1908): 444-52.

"May a Catholic Be a Socialist?" *Catholic Fortnightly Review* 16 (February 1, 1909): 70-73.

"Does the Church Condemn Moderate Economic Socialism?" *Catholic Fortnightly Review* 16 (July 1, 1909): 391-94.

"A Programme of Social Reform by Legislation." *Catholic World* 89 (July & August 1909): 433-44 and 608-14.

"The Church and the Teaching of Her Theologians Concerning Interest on Loans." *Catholic Fortnightly Review* 16 (August 1, 1909): 441-44.

"The Church and the Workingman." *Catholic World* 89 (September 1909): 776-82.

"Minimum Wages and Minimum Wage Boards." *Survey* 24 (September 3, 1910): 810-20.

"Henry George and Private Property." *Catholic World* 93 (June 1911): 289-300.

"Ethical Arguments of Henry George Against Private Ownership of Land." *Catholic World* 93 (July 1911): 483-92.

"Private Ownership and Socialism." *Catholic World* 94 (January 1912): 497-504.

"Minimum Wage Boards." *Survey* 27 (January 20, 1912): 1623-24.

"Why Private Landownership Is a Natural Right." *Catholic University Bulletin* 18 (March 1912): 228-36.

"British Miners and the Minimum Wage." *Survey* 28 (April 6, 1912):10-11.

"Abuses of Private Landownership." *Catholic World* 95 (September 1912): 789-801.

"Methods of Reforming Our Land System." *Catholic World* 96 (October-November 1912): 1-18, 156-69.

"Minimum Wage Legislation." *Catholic World* 96 (February 1913): 577-86.

"Socialism: Problem or Menace?" Morris Hillquit, coauthor. A debate in seven monthly installments. *Everybody's Magazine* (October, 1913-April 1914).

"Personnel of the Industrial Relations Commission." *Catholic World* 98 (November 1913): 221-24.

"Industrial Paganism in the Black Hills." *Survey* 31 (November 1, 1913): 140-41.

"Good and Bad Labor Unions." *Survey* 31 (January 10, 1914): 451.

"Social Legislation and a Constitutional Crisis." *Survey* 31 (February 14, 1914): 626-27.

"The Morality of Interest on Capital." *Catholic University Bulletin* 20 (April 1914): 263-77.

"The Social Justification of Interest on Capital." *Catholic University Press* 20 (May 1914): 337-51.

"Unemployed and the Churches; a reply." *Survey* 32 (June 27, 1914): 342-43.

"Task of Minimum Wage Boards in Minnesota." *Survey* 33 (November 14, 1914): 171-72.

"Minimum Wage Laws to Date." *Catholic World* 100 (January 1915): 433-42.

"Rome Brown and the Minimum Wage." *Survey* 33 (March 13, 1915): 660-61.

"Minimum Wage and the Predicament of the Employer." *Survey 34* (May 1, 1915): 122.
"Minnesota's Social Legislation Halted by Liquor Debates." *Survey* 34 (May 8, 1915): 145.
"Fears of the Minimum Wage." *Survey* 34 (May 22, 1915): 184.
"Cooperation a Partial Solvent of Capitalism." *Catholic World* 101 (May-June 1915): 157-65, 343-51.
"Catholic Church and Birth Control." *Harper's Weekly* 61 (August 7, 1915): 144.
"Earning the Minimum Wage." *Survey* 35 (November 6, 1915): 150.
"Catholic Church and Birth Restriction." *Survey* 35 (March 4, 1916): 671-72.
"Problem of Complete Wage Justice." *Catholic World* 103 (August 1916): 623-37.
"New Theory of Political Sovereignty." *Catholic World* 106 (November 1917): 237-43.
"Freedom of Speech in War Time." *Catholic World* 106 (February 1918): 577-88.
"Social Aspects in America of the War." *Studies* 7 (March 1918): 80-93.
"Supreme Court and Child Labor." *Catholic World* 108 (November 1918): 212-23.
"Labor's Program of Reconstruction." *America* 2 (February 15&22, 1919): 466-68 and 493-95.
"Some Principles of Social Reconstruction." *Everybody's Magazine* 40 (May 1919): 72.
"Annual Meeting of the Bishops." *Catholic World* 109 (July 1919): 433-49.
"Vocational Education in a Democratic Society." *Catholic World* 109 (August 1919): 613-21.
"Catholic Doctrine on the Right of Self Government." *Catholic World* 108 (December 1918-January 1919): 314-30, 441-54.
"Present Wages and Prices." *Catholic World* 110 (January 1920): 433-43.
"Americanism in Industry." *The Annuals* (American Academy of Political and Social Science) 90 (June 1920): 126-30.
"Land Without Ruins; A Poem." *American Federalist* 27 (December 1920): 1111.
"Some Questionable Trade Union Practices." *National Conference of Catholic Charities Proceedings* 7 (1921): 31-38.
"Purpose of the State." *Catholic World* 112 (March 1921): 803-14.

"Erroneous Theories Concerning the Functions of the State." *Catholic World* 113 (April 1921): 50-61.

"Proper Functions of the State." *Catholic World* 113 (May 1921): 169-80.

"Lusk Reports Brazen Industrial Feudalism." *Nation* 113 (July 27, 1921): 99-100.

"Need of Legal Standards of Protection for Labor." *American Labor Legislative Review* 11 (September 1921): 221-26.

"Moral Obligation of Civil Law." *Catholic World* 114 (October 1921): 73-86.

"Duties of the Citizen." *Catholic World* 114 (January 1922): 459-73.

"Rights of the Citizen." *Catholic World* 114 (March 1922): 781-86.

"The Case Against the Industrial Court Idea: An Argument for Arbitration Plus an Industrial Code." *Dearborn Independent* 22 (April 29, 1922): 10.

"Teaching of the Catholic Church." *Annals of American Academy of Political and Social Science* 103 (September 1922): 76-80.

"Relation of Recent Supreme Court Decisions to Labor Unions and Industrial Legislation." *National Conference of Social Work Proceedings.* (1922): 284-87.

"Legalized Despotism in Virginia." *Catholic World* 117 (April 1923): 67-73.

"U.S. Supreme Court Decision." *Catholic World* 117 (May 1923): 200-204.

"Our Self-amending Constitution." *Survey* 50 (August 1, 1923): 480-81.

"Wage, Hours, Sanitation, Safety." *National Conference of Social Work Proceedings* (1923): 103-9.

"Charity Among Nations." *Catholic World* 118 (January 1924): 433-42.

"Workmen's Compensation in the District of Columbia." *American Labor Legislation Review* 14 (March 1924): 17-19.

"The State and Industry" *Salesianum* 19 (April 1924): 17-24.

"Hilaire Belloc as Prophet of Woe." *Catholic World* 119 (June 1924): 321-25.

"Proposed Child Labor Amendment." *Catholic World* 120 (November 1924): 166-74.

"Proposed Child Labor Amendment." *National Educational Association Journal* 14 (March 1925): 87-88.

"Prohibition, Pro and Con." *Catholic World* 121 (April 1925): 31-35.

"Do the Prohibition Laws Bind in Conscience?" *Catholic World* 121 (May 1925): 145-57.

"Cancel War Debts and Reparations." *Annals of American Academy of Political and Social Science.* 120 (July 1925): 62-64.

"Anthracite and Ethics." *Catholic World* 122 (December 1925): 297-306.

"Liberty and the Roman Catholic Church." *Nation* 122 (June 16, 1926): 660-61.

"Religious Persecution in Mexico." *Outlook* 143 (August 18, 1926): 534-35.

"Church and Labor." *American Federationist* 33 (November 1926): 1311-14.

"Christian Principles of War and Peace." *Catholic World* 124 (November 1926): 209-15.

"Spiritual Element in Social Work." *National Conference of Social Work Proceedings.* (1926): 62-70.

"Church, State and Constitution." *Commonweal* 5 (April 27, 1927): 680-82.

"Is Birth Control Right?" *Forum* 78 (July 1927): 15-19.

"Institute of Pacific Relations." *Catholic World* 126 (October 1927): 1-11.

"The Pope and the Presidency: The Catholic Reply to the Opposition." *Current History* 27 (March 1928): 778-85.

"A Catholic View of the Election." *Current History* 29 (December 1928): 377-81.

"Unemployment: Causes and Remedies." *Catholic World* 128 (February 1929): 535-42.

"Pope and the Presidency." *Current History* 27 (March 1928): 778-85.

"Labor Injunction in the Light of Justice." *American Federationist* 35 (March 1928): 290-93.

"Anti-Saloon League." *Catholic World* 128 (November 1928): 129-39.

"Civil Law Binds the Conscience." *Catholic World* 124 (November 1928): 224-25.

"Assaults Upon Democracy." *Catholic World* 128 (March 1929): 641-47.

"Basic Economic Facts in the Condition of the Indians." *Catholic Charities Review* 13 (March 1929): 85-88.

"Enduring Anti-Catholic Tradition." *Commonweal* 9 (April 24, 1929): 719.

"Social Objectives of Catholics." *Catholic Charities Review* 13 (April 1929): 114-16.

"Who Shall Obey the Law?" *Commonweal* 9 (April 3, 1929): 616-18.

"Senate Bill for the Regulation of the Soft Coal Industry." *Catholic Charities Review* 13 (June 1929): 184-86.

"Evolution of an Anti." *Commonweal* 10 (June 26, 1929): 211-13.

"Birth Control: the Perverted Faculty Argument; Discussion." *Ecclesiastical Review* 81 (July 1929): 70-72.

"Rejoinder to a Moderate Prohibitionist." *Catholic Charities Review* 13 (September 1929): 225-27.

"Puritanism, Prohibition, Catholicism." *New Republic* 60 (September 11, 1929): 101-2.

"The Senate Looks at Unemployment: I. Important Facts Which It Clearly Saw" *Commonweal* 10 (October 2, 1929): 550-52.

"The Senate Looks at Unemployment: II. Important Facts Which It Failed to See." *Commonweal* 10 (October 9, 1929): 578-80.

"The Experts Look at Unemployment: I. Higher Wages for the Masses." *Commonweal* 10 (October 16, 1929): 612-13.

"The Experts Look at Unemployment: II. A Shorter Work Period." Commonweal 10 (October 23, 1929): 636-38.

"Civic Loyalty of Catholic Officials." *Catholic Charities Review* 13 (November 1929): 285-88.

"Protective Legislation for Women." *National Catholic Welfare Conference Bulletin* 11 (November 1929): 23-24.

"Economic and Social Topics in the President's Message." *Catholic Charities Review* 14 (January 1930): 9-11.

"Place of the Family in Christian Society." *National Catholic Welfare Conference Review* 12 (January 1930): 6-7.

"Commoner." *Commonweal* 11 (January 15, 1930): 302-5.

"Is Prohibition a Catholic Principle?" *New Republic* 61 (January 22, 1930): 254.

"Patriotism versus Conscience." *Catholic Charities Review* 14 (February 1930): 33-34.

"London Conference." *International Relations News Letter* 1 (March 1930): 1-2.

"Pope's Encyclical on Education." *Current History* 31 (March 1930): 1087-88.

"Poverty in the United States." *Studies* 19 (March 1930): 73-85.

"Questions of Prohibition." *Catholic Charities Review* 14 (April 1930): 97-101.

"New Morality and Its Illusions" *Catholic World* 131 (May 1930): 129-36.
"Catholicism and Liberalism." *Nation* 131 (August 6, 1930): 150-52.
"Mr. Hoover and the Depression." *Commonweal* 12 (September 3, 1930): 436-38.
"Mr. Hoover and National Welfare." *Commonweal* 12 (September 10, 1930): 457-59.
"Unemployment: the Coming Winter." *Catholic Charities Review* 14 (November 1930): 223-25.
"Unemployment: A Failure in Leadership." *Catholic World* 131 (July 1930): 385-93.
"Our Obligation to the Dependent Aged." *Catholic Charities Review* 15 (January 1931): 3-4.
"High Wages and Unemployment." *Commonweal* 13 (January 7, 1931): 259-61.
"High Wages vs. Excessive Capital." *Commonweal* 13 (February 25, 1931): 460-61.
"Moral Teaching of the Encyclical on Christian Marriage." *Ecclesiastical Review* 84 (March 1931): 264-71.
"Wickersham Report." *Catholic Charities Review* 15 (March 1931): 67-71.
"Just Wages and Rerum Novarum." *America* 45 (May 9, 1931): 105-6.
"Some Effects of Rerum Novarum." *America* 45 (April 25, 1931): 58-60.
"Encyclical and Labor Organization." *America* (May 16, 1931): 128-29.
"Priests Concern with Unemployment." *Ecclesiastical Review* 84 (May 1931): 464-75.
"Encyclical on Labor." *Catholic Charities Review* 15 (June 1931): 167-70.
"Pope Leo XIII's Magna Charta of Labor." *National Catholic Welfare Conference Review* 13 (June 1931): 10-11+.
"Cardinal Mermillod and the Union of Fribourg." *America* 45 (June 6, 1991): 200-201.
"Papal Encyclical on Labor." *Survey* 66 (June 15, 1931): 307.
"Encyclicals of Leo XIII and Pius XI." *Current History* 34 (July 1931): 486-87.
"The New Things in the Encyclical." *American Ecclesiastical Review* 75 (July 1931): 1-14.
"Unemployment and the State; Excerpts." *American Labor Legislation Review* 21 (September 1931): 309-10.

"Should America Cancel Her Foreign War Debts?" *Congressional Digest* 10 (October 1931): 248+.
"International Aspects of Unemployment." *Catholic World* 134 (November 1931): 129-36.
"Necessity of Federal Relief for the Unemployed." *Catholic Charities Review* 15 (November 1931): 287-90.
"Greed Is the Witch; Reply." *Commonweal* 15 (December 23, 1931): 215-16.
"International Aspects of Unemployment." *National Conference of Social Work Proceedings* (1931): 239-51.
"Golden Mean in re Prohibition." *Commonweal* 15 (March 9, 1932): 522.
"Pope Pius XI: 1922-1932." *Catholic Action* 14 (March 1932): 4.
"Relief for the Unemployed-Whose Responsibility?" *Catholic Charities Review* 16 (March 1932): 67-70.
"Behind the Balanced Budget." *Commonweal* 15 (April 27, 1932): 721-22.
"Indictment of the Present System." *Catholic Action* 14 (May 1932): 18-19.
"Family and the Wages Policy." *Catholic Charities Review* 16 (September 1932): 199-202.
"Irish Land Annuities." *Commonweal* 16 (September 28-October 5, 1932): 502-5, 530-32.
"National Responsibility in the Present Crisis: Catholic Doctrine." *Catholic World* 136 (November 1932): 169-74.
"After the Depression." *Ecclesiastical Review* 87 (December 1932): 5-6+.
"Responsibility of Congress Toward Unemployment." *Catholic Charities Review* 16 (December 1932): 306-8.
"Views on Jobless Relief: Excerpts from Address." *Catholic Action* 14 (December 1932): 18.
"A New Social Order." *Catholic Action* 14 (October 1932): 15, 18, 31.
"American Catholics and American Socialism." *American Ecclesiastical Review* 87 (December 1932): 584-92.
"Prohibition and Tolerance." *Commonweal* 17 (December 14, 1932 and February 1, 1933): 186, 382-83.
"Catholic Church and Social Questions." *Annals of American Academy of Political and Social Science* 165 (January 1933): 48-56.
"Must Unemployment Continue?" *Commonweal* 17 (January 4, 1933): 264-65.

"Ethical Aspects of Some International Problems: I. The Tariff." *America* 49 (May 6, 1933): 103-7.

"Ethical Aspects of Some International Problems: II. The International Debts." *America* 49 (May 13, 1933): 131-32.

"Public Works." *Catholic Action* 15 (May 1933): 15.

"Revival of Minimum Wage Legislation." *Catholic Charities Review* 17 (May 1933): 133-135. Erratum 17 (June 1933): 165.

"President Roosevelt's Economic Program." *Studies* 22 (June 1933): 194-204.

"Moral Aspects of Periodical Continence." *Ecclesiastical Review* 89 (July 1933): 28-39.

"Greed in Economic Life." *Catholic Action* 15 (August 1933): 11+.

"Making the Anglo-Irish Treaty; Reply to E.O. Boyle." *Commonweal* 18 (August 25, 1933): 408-9.

"Civic and Political Morality." *Catholic Action* 15 (September 1933): 9+.

"Catholic Conference on Industrial Problems." *Catholic Action* 15 (October 1933): 9+.

"NRA and the Constitution." *Commonweal* 18 (October 20, 1933): 577-79.

"Philosophy of Capitalism." *American Catholic Philosophical Association Proceedings* (1933): 35-46.

"Labor Organization Today." *Catholic Charities* 17 (November 1933): 291-93.

"Economics and Ethics." *National Conference of Catholic Charities Proceedings* 19 (1933): 65-72.

"Shall the NRA Be Scrapped?" *National Conference of Catholic Charities Proceedings* 20 (1934): 50-62.

"Decision of the Supreme Court on the Minnesota Moratorium Law." *Catholic Charities Review* 18 (February 1934): 36-40.

"Large Catholic Families; Reply." *Commonweal* 19 (February 2, 1934): 384.

"New Deal and Social Justice." *Commonweal* 19 (April 13, 1934): 657-59.

"Fallacious Arguments of the Birth Controllers." *Catholic Action* 16 (April 1934): 9-11.

"Aims of the New Deal Explained." *Catholic Action* 16 (May 1934): 14.

"Roosevelt Recovery Program." *Studies* 23 (June 1934): 218-30.

"Pope Pius XI and a New Social Order." *Catholic Action* 16 (June 1934): 14-15+.

"Are We On the Right Road." *Commonweal* 20 (October 12, 1934): 547-49.

"Concept of Social Justice." *Catholic Charities Review* 18 (December 1934): 313-15.

"What About Industrial Recovery?" *Catholic Action* 17 (March 1935): 7-8+.

"The Concept of Social Justice." *Catholic Charities Review* 18 (December 1934): 313-15.

"Quack Remedies for the Depression Malady." *Catholic Charities Review* 19 (April 1935): 104-7.

"Work Relief and Industrial Recovery." *Catholic Charities Review* 19 (May 1935): 132-34.

"Sterilization, Futile Immorality." *Forum* 94 (July 1935): 29-31.

"Substitute for NRA Needed." *Catholic Action* 17 (July 1935): 4-5.

" Social Justice in the 1935 Congress." *Catholic Action* 17 (September 1935): 7-9.

"Economic Internationalism." *Commonweal* 21 (January 25 and February 1, 1935): 359-61 and 396-98.

"Trend of Recovery." *Commonweal* 23 (January 3, 1936): 273.

"Economic Progress and Distribution." *Sign* 15 (March 1936): 490-91.

"Open Letter to the Editor (Roosevelt's Address on the State of the Union; with Editorial Reply.)" *Catholic World* 143 (April 1936): 1-9, 22-36.

"Moral Obligation of the Federal Government to Provide Low-Rent Housing." *Catholic Charities Review* 20 (May 1936): 137-38.

"Significance of Encyclicals' Commemoration." *Catholic Action* 18 (May 1936): 4.

"Addresses of Archbishop Mitty and Monsignor Ryan Feature San Francisco Meeting of C.C.I.P." *Catholic Action* 18 (July 1936): 11+.

"American Presidential Campaign." *Studies* 25 (September 1936): 379-89.

"Monsignor Kerby; Progressive Leader." *Catholic Charities Review* 20 (September 1936): 228-30.

"Condemnation of 'L'Avenir'; Commentary of the Mirari Vos of Pope Gregory XVI." *Catholic Historical Review* 23 (April 1937): 31-39.

"Economists on the Depression." *The Sign* 15 (January 1936): 335-37.

"Teaching of Encyclicals on Interest." *Catholic Action* 18 (April 1936): 7-8.

"The Catholic Church and Capitalism." Part VII of series "Religion and Radicalism." *Common Sense* 5 (September 1936): 12-13.

"The Need for an Amendment." *Christian Front* 5 (October 1936): 153-55.

"Organized Social Justice." *Commonweal* 23 (December 13, 1936): 175-76.

"The Sit-Down' Strike." *American Ecclesiastical Review* 96 (April 1937): 419-21.

"Court Reform and Minorities." *Commonweal* 25 (April 16, 1937): 683-85.

"Third Labor Encyclical; Atheistic Communism." *Commonweal* 26 (May 14, 1937): 61-63.

"The Supreme Court Debate: I. Court Reform and Minorities." *Commonweal* 25 (April 16, 1937): 383-85.

"March Study Topic: Fascism, Communism and Democracy." *Catholic Action* 20 (February 1938): 19-21.

"Looking Forward." *Christian Front* 3 (February-April 1938): 26-28, 58-61.

"Georgian Plan." *Commonweal* 27 (March 11, 1938): 549.

"What Democracy Means to Me." *Scholastic* 32 (March 19, 1938): 29.

"Business Recession." *Catholic Digest* 2 (April 1938): 48-52.

"Program of the Milwaukee Catholic Social Action Conference." *Catholic Action* 20 (April 1938): 9-10.

"Monsignor Ryan's Economic Program." *Catholic Action* 20 (June 1938): 20.

"Political Causes of International Disorder." *Commonweal* 28 (October 21, 1938): 667-69.

"Anti-Semitism in the Air." *Commonweal* 29 (December 30, 1938): 260-62.

"Pope Pius XI and the Social Order." *Catholic Action* 21 (March 1939): 19-20.

"Economic Reorganization in the U.S. ; excerpts." *Catholic Action* 21 (June 1939): 15.

"Monsignor Ryan at Seventy." *Catholic Charities Review* 23 (June 1939): 163-64.

"Social Justice and the State." *Commonweal* 30 (June 16, 1939): 205-6.

"Legislation and a Christian Social Order; excerpt." *Catholic Action* 21 (July 1939): 7.

"Belief in God and Religion Fundamental Element of Democracy; excerpts." *Catholic Action* 21 (August 1939): 4.

"Religion, the Indispensable Basis of Democracy." *Vital Speeches* 5 (August 15, 1939): 667-70.

"Confusions About the War." *Commonweal* 31 (March 22, 1940): 464-67.

"Recent Episcopal Statement: Church and Social Order." *Catholic Charities Review* 24 (March 1940): 68-69.

" Due Process and Mr. Justice Black." *Catholic World* 151 (April 1940): 36-39.

"Anti-Alien Dempsey Bill." *Catholic Worker* 7 (May 1940): 3.

"At the Catholic University of America, 1898-1902: Autobiography." *Commonweal* 32 (Aug 9-16, 1940): 321-23, 344-46.

"Present Day Evils: excerpts." *Catholic Action* 22(October 1940): 6.

"Growth of Interest in Catholic Social Teaching: Summary." *Catholic Action* 23 (January 1941): 5-6.

"Program of Aid to Destitute Migrants; Summary." *Catholic Action* 23 (January 1941): 5.

"Ethics and Political Intervention in the Field of Social Action." *Review of Politics* 3 (July 1941): 300-305.

"On the Anniversary of the Encyclicals." *American Catholic Sociological Review* 2 (June 1941): 83-89.

"International Post-War Reconstruction." *National Catholic Educational Association Bulletin* 38 (November 1941): 14-29.

"The Common Good." *Survey Graphics* 30 (November 1941): 633.

"How Must the Confessor Deal with an Onanist? Reply to Reverend Francis J. Connell." *Ecclesiastical Review* 107 (October 1942): 283-86.

"Right of Private Property Is No Exemption from Ethics." *America* 68 (October 24, 1942): 62-64.

"Two Objectives for Catholic Economists." *Report of the First Annual Convention of the Catholic Economic Association* (December 28-30, 1942): 45-48.

"Labor after the War." *American Federationist* 50 (February 1943): 21-22+.

"Labor and Economic Construction after the War." *Vital Speeches* 9 (February 15, 1943): 266-69.

"Monsignor John A. Ryan Commends Negro Progress." *Interracial Review* 16 (March 1943): 40.

"Labor After the War; Abridged." *Catholic Digest* 7 (April 1943): 22-24.

"Catholic Position on Labor Legislation for Women." *Congressional Digest* 22 (April 1943): 120.
"Is There a Catholic Issue?" *New Republic* 108 (April 12, 1943): 477-78.
"Thunder on the Left: Postwar Storm Brewing." *America* 69 (May 8 + June 12, 1943): 117-19, 278.
"Labor and Reconstruction after the War." *American Catholic Sociological Review* 4 (June 1943): 65-75.
"Post War Depression?" *Commonweal* 38 (June 18, 1943): 226-27.
"Place of the Negro in American Society." *Catholic Mind* 41 (July 1943): 13-22.
"Beveridge Plan." *Catholic Action* 25 (September 1943): 6-7.
"Catholics and Liberals." *New Republic* 109 (September 20, 1943): 395-97.
"Bishop's Program of Social Reconstruction." *American Catholic Sociological Review* 5 (March 1944): 25-33.
"Labor's Role After Victory." *Catholic Mind* 42 (March 1944): 156-59.
"Catholics and Birth Control." *American Mercury* 58 (April 1944): 504-5.
"Noble Priest, Great Prelate." *Catholic Action* 26 (July 1944): 13.
"Assault upon Democracy." *Commonweal* 40 (October 13, 1944): 608-11; Discussion 41 (October 27, 1944): 36-37.
"Some Economic Aspect of European Relief and Rehabilitation." *Review of Social Economy* 3 (December 1944): 1-8.
"Speech Before the Catholic Economic Association, Chicago, excerpts." *Catholic Worker* 12 (February 1945): 1+.
"Question of Punishment of War Criminals." *Catholic Action* 27 (March 1945): 3-4.
"America and the Rehabilitation of Europe." *Current Religious Thought* 5 (March 1945): 12-16.
"FDR: In Memoriam; excerpts." *Catholic Action* 27 (May 1945): 19.
"Roosevelt and Social Justice." *Review of Politics* 7 (July 1945): 297-305.
"Ethical Aspects of the Tariff." *Catholic Mind* 43 (September 1945): 528-33.
"Liberalism and the Mexican Crisis of 1927: A Debate Between Norman Thomas and John A. Ryan." *Catholic Historical Review* 45 (October 1959): 309-26.

Essays

"Democratizing Industry." *Book of Modern Catholic Prose.* Comp. Theodore Maynard. New York: H. Holt and Company, 1928.

"Catholicism and Democracy." *Religion Today; A Challenging Enigma.* Ed. Arthur Swift, Jr. New York: McGraw, 1933.

"Unchanging Ethics in a Changing World." *Religion and the Modern World.* University of Pennsylvania. Bicentennial Conference. Philadelphia: University of Pennsylvania Press, 1941.

"Economic Philosophy of St. Thomas." *Essays in Thomism.* Ed. Robert E. Brennan. New York: Sheed and Ward, 1942.

"Dignity of Personality." *Democracy, Should It Survive?* William J. Kerby Foundation, Washington, D.C. Milwaukee: Bruce, 1943.

"Religious Foundations for an Enduring Peace." *Conference on Science, Philosophy and Religion. 4th Symposium.* New York: The Conference, Distributed by Harper Brothers, 1944.

"Social Service and Social Reform." *Best Sermons* Ed. G. Paul Butler. New York: Harper Brothers, 1944.

"Living Wage; Excerpt." *People Shall Judge.* University of Chicago. Chicago: University of Chicago Press, 1949.

"Opposition to Contraception." *Social Problems in America.* Ed. Alfred Lee and Elizabeth Lee. New York: H. Holt, 1949.

"Social Justice and the State." *Commonweal Reader.* Commonweal (Periodical). New York: Harper, 1949.

Unclassified Publications

"A Country Without Strikes." *Catholic World* 72 (November 1900): 145-57.

"Labour and Labour Legislation." *Catholic Encyclopedia.* New York: Robert Appleton Co., 1907-1912. Vol. 8, 719-24.

"Labour Unions, Moral Aspects of." *Catholic Encyclopedia.* New York: Robert Appleton Co., 1907-1912. Vol. 8, 724-28.

"Private Ownership and Socialism." A Review of John Kelleher, *Private Ownership: Its Basis and Equitable Conditions* (Dublin: M.H. Gill & Son, 1911) In *Catholic World* 94 (January 1912): 497-504.

"Letter to "Dear Mr.-," *Public Ownership* 14 (January 1932): Inside Cover.

"Farm Relief Levies Not Taxes." Letter to the Editor of the *New York Times,* April 9, 1933.

"The Supreme Court Debate: I. Court Reform and Minorities." *U.S. Congressional Record-Appendix,* Vol. 71, Part 9 (May 19, 1937): 1194-95.

"Address on the Occasion of His Seventieth Birthday Anniversary." *U.S. Congressional Record-Appendix* Vol. 84, Part 13 (May 26, 1939): 2254-56.

"Neutrality." Radio Address on October 15, 1939. *U.S. Congressional Record-Appendix,* Vol. 85, Part 2 (October 16, 1939): 313-14.

"Shall the Embargo Be Lifted?" Radio Address on October 24, 1939. *U.S. Congressional Records-Appendix,* Vol. 85, Part 2 (October 26, 1939): 513-14.

"The Unemployment Problem" ("Can Unemployment Be Ended?") Address Delivered at the Catholic Conference on Industrial Problems, New Orleans, May 8, 1940. *U.S. Congressional Record-Appendix,* Vol. 86, Part 15 (May 16, 1940): 3003-6.

"Letter to the Honorable William H. King, Chairman, Committee on Immigration, United States Senate, July 6, 1940." *U.S. Congressional Record-Appendix,* Vol. 87, Part 16 (July 31, 1940): 4730.

"The Enemy is Hitler." *U.S. Congressional Record-Senate,* Vol. 87, Part 7 (September 29, 1941): 7565-66.

"Religion as the Foundation of Freedom." Radio Address on September 29, 1941. *U.S. Congressional Record-Appendix,* Vol. 87, Part 14 (October 13, 1941): A4627-28.

"The Economic Philosophy of St. Thomas." in Robert E. Brennan (ed.), *Essays in Thomism.* New York: Sheed & Ward, 1942, 239-60.

"Unchanging Ethics in a Changing World." in University of Pennsylvania Bicentennial Conference (ed.) *Religion and the Modern World* Philadelphia: University of Pennsylvania Press, 1942, 41-61.

"Labor and Economic Reconstruction after the War." Address at Catholic Sociological Convention, Cleveland, December 29, 1942. *U.S. Congressional Record-Appendix,* Vol. 89, Part 9 (January 16, 1943): A154-55.

"The Dignity of Personality." in the William Kerby Foundation (ed.), *Democracy: Should It Survive?* Milwaukee: Bruce Publishing Co., 1943, 15-18.

UNPUBLISHED MATERIAL

"Some Ethical Aspects of Speculation." Unpublished licentiate dissertation, No. 184. School of Sacred Theology, Catholic University of America, Washington, 1900. Typewritten.

John A. Ryan Papers. Department of Archives and Manuscripts, Catholic University of America, Washington, D.C.

Journal. September 29, 1892-October 24, 1898.

Class Lecture Notebooks, St. Paul Seminary.

"De Legibus." For course in moral theology. [1902-1904?]. Notebook 2.

"De Jure." For course in moral theology[1902-1904?] Notebook 4.

Class Lecture Notebooks, Catholic University of America.

"De Jure et Justitia in Genere." For course in moral theology [1916-1920?]. Notebook 10.

"De Justitia et Jure (2)." For course in moral theology [1916-1920?] Notebook 11.

"De Contractibus." For course in moral theology [1916-1920?] Notebook 12.

"Rerum Novarum." For course in industrial ethics [1916-1920?].

"Catholic Doctrine on Industrial Relations." Notes on *Rerum Novarum and Quadragesimo Anno*, for course in industrial ethics [after 1931].

Correspondence.

Franklin D. Roosevelt to John A. Ryan, Albany, September 1, 1932.

Franklin D. Roosevelt to John A. Ryan, Washington, September 24, 1935.

John A. Ryan to Franklin D. Roosevelt, [Washington], September 24, 1935. Copy. Franklin D. Roosevelt to John A. Ryan, Washington, November 16, 1936.

John A. Ryan to Franklin D. Roosevelt, [Washington], March 22, 1939. Copy.

Franklin D. Roosevelt to John A. Ryan, Washington, December 30, 1942.

Frances Perkins to John A. Ryan, [Washington], Christmas, 1942.

Addresses.

"Better Health Care." Radio Address on the program "For This We Fight," November 13, 1943.

"Statement on Behalf of F.E.P.C. at Interview with President Truman." [Spring 1945.]

Obituary Scrapbook, September 16, 1945-

John A. Ryan Scrapbooks. In the Archives of the Archdiocese of St. Paul/Minneapolis, St. Paul, Minnesota.

"A Living Wage." Reviews and comments, 1906-

Review of Ryan's books, 1913-1923.

Reviews and news clippings, April, 1929-May, 1935.

"Promotion to Monsignor." Vol. IV, 1933.

Reviews and news clippings, May 1935-December, 1937.

Reviews and news clippings, May 1938-February, 1943.

"Social Doctrine." Reviews and comments, 1941.

Reviews and news clippings, February, 1943-April, 1945.

CORRESPONDENCE

John A. Ryan to Frederick Kenkel. In: Kenkel, Frederick. *Papers, 1871-1952.* University of Notre Dame Archives.

John A. Ryan to Patrick Henry Callahan. In: Callahan, Patrick Henry. *Papers, 1908-1939.* University of Notre Dame Archives.

John A. Ryan to Vilhjalmur: Stefansson. In: Stefansson, Vilhjalmur. *Papers and Correspondence Concerning the Straits of Anian and Maldonado, 1931-1941.* (Location Unknown.)